POPULUS

POPULUS

Living and Dying in the Wealth,
Smoke, and Din of Ancient Rome

GUY DE LA BÉDOYÈRE

abacus
books

ABACUS

First published in Great Britain in 2024 by Abacus

3 5 7 9 10 8 6 4 2

A CIP catalogue record for this book is available from the British Library.

Hardback ISBN 978-1-4087-1515-4
Trade Paperback ISBN 978-4087-1559-8

Typeset in Spectrum by M Rules
Printed and bound in Great Britain by Clays Ltd, Elcograf S.p.A.

Papers used by Abacus are from well-managed forests
and other responsible sources.

Abacus
An imprint of
Little, Brown Book Group
Carmelite House
50 Victoria Embankment
London EC4Y 0DZ

An Hachette UK Company
www.hachette.co.uk

www.littlebrown.co.uk

Rosemariae
coniugi carissimae ob memoriam iuventutis
quam laeti simul perigimus,
et vera incessu patuit dea.

CONTENTS

Appendices

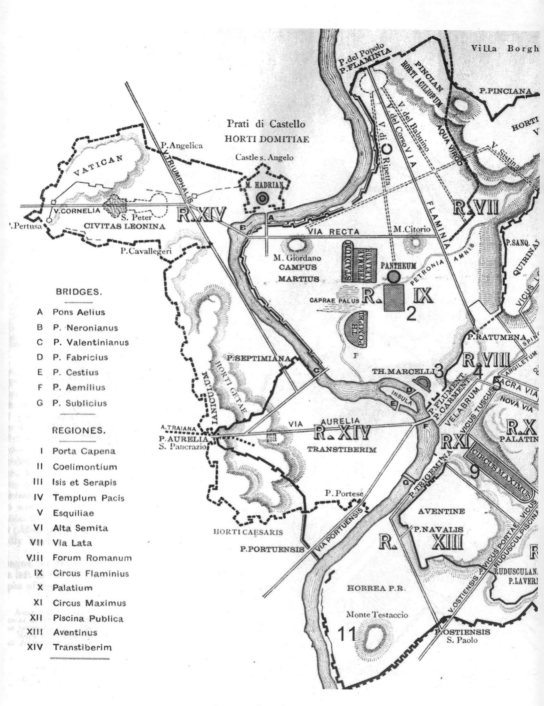

Figure 1: Plan of ancient Rome
1 – Baths of Diocletian; 2 – Pantheon, basilica of Neptune, and Baths of Nero
(Field of Mars), with the Theatre of Pompey to the left; 3 – Theatre of Marcellus;
4 – Capitoline Hill; 5 – imperial forums across this valley; 6 – Colosseum;

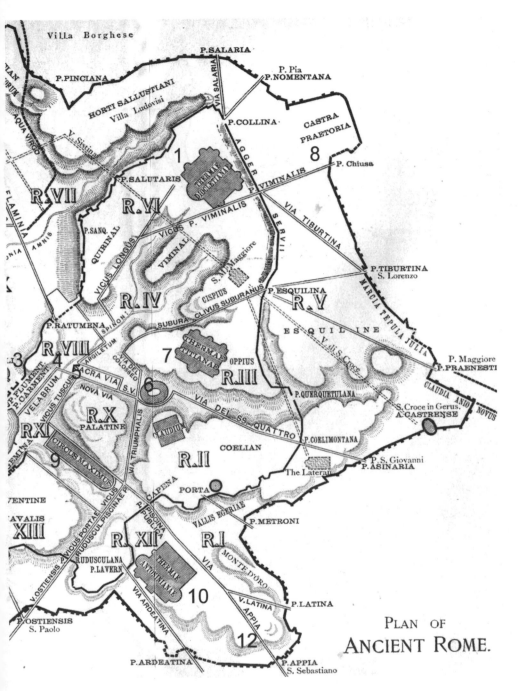

7 – Baths of Titus (on the site of the Golden House of Nero), and later Baths of
Trajan; 8 – Castra Praetoria (Praetorian Camp); 9 – Circus Maximus, overlooked
by the Palatine Hill; 10 – Baths of Caracalla; 11 – Monte di Testaccio; 12 – Via
Appia (Antica). From W. Ramsay's *Manual of Roman Antiquities*, 18th edition 1894.

FOREWORD AND INTRODUCTION

In my opinion, nothing is more satisfying than that people should always want to know what sort of a person a man had been.

Pliny the Elder[1]

J ust outside the Porta Maggiore in Rome is an incongruous sight. A prominent Roman tomb made in the shape of a stack of bins for kneading dough stands surrounded by modern streets and overhead cables, silent amid the racket from the traffic that churns around it endlessly. This was the burial place of the ashes of a successful freedman (*libertus*) called Eurysaces who lived in the first century BC. He had a sense of humour. 'It is *obvious* this is the tomb of Marcus Vergilius Eurysaces, baker, contractor', proclaims the inscription.[2] The tomb is thus an elaborate joke, hence the text and the substitution of dough bins for the usual cremation urns. Apparently not in the least despondent at the thought of his death, Eurysaces had made a small fortune from his nearby bakery business on a state contract for supplying the dole and was keen for everyone to know it for all eternity. The tomb was wedged into what was originally a narrow road junction. It

1

towered over the endless cavalcade of carts, animals and pedestrians that entered and exited the ancient city on either side.

Without his tomb we would know nothing about Eurysaces and his wife Atistia because, not surprisingly, he appears nowhere in any surviving written source from the period. The monument only survived because three centuries later it was built into the tower of a gate on the new walls of Rome raised by the emperor Aurelian (270–5). Eurysaces and Atistia serve as the perfect example of the random record available to us for life for the ordinary people (*populus*) of ancient Rome. The tomb is a reminder that Rome was once their home, where they worked and lived as man and wife, just as it was for the unknown millions who have left no trace of their lives apart from the wear on coins that passed through their hands and the countless potsherds in the ancient city's rubbish that underpins modern Rome.

My first visit to Rome was one evening at Easter in 1975. It is impossible to forget turning a corner and seeing for the first time the three surviving columns of the Temple of Castor and Pollux in the Forum dimly lit in the crepuscular gloom of a Roman night, and behind them the huge silhouette of the imperial palaces of the Palatine Hill.

From those halls and vaulted chambers, emperors had ruled, some wisely, others with unspeakable barbarity, some for decades and some for only days or weeks. Few lived to die in their beds. Most were murdered, whether in Rome or in some far-off province, or died in battle. Beyond and all around were other vast edifices from antiquity: among them the Arch of Titus, just beyond it the remains of Vespasian's Colosseum, and nearby the colossal remnants of Augustus' Temple of Mars Ultor (the Avenger), built to commemorate his defeat of the tyrannicides who had murdered Julius Caesar.

The most compelling thought was of the Roman people themselves who crowded into the Circus Maximus to cheer for their favourite charioteers, jeered at the defeated gladiators in the Colosseum, jostled, argued, or 'idled at the forum' (as Catullus put it), worshipped at the temples, rioted, fought and feuded during elections, and watched as great military triumphs brandished Rome's spoils, admiring the fruits of Rome's vicious wars of conquest.[3] They had once lived in any one of the innumerable houses and tenement blocks, packed the narrow backstreets and alleys dodging the litters carrying the high and mighty, and gathered in the markets to buy food and other necessities. The real stories of their lives subsist in the written sources, whether the words of the Roman historians and writers or the inscriptions. Although the record is incomplete in so many ways there is no other ancient civilization which has left such a dramatic and vivid written record of the people who lived then.

In our own troubled times, there is something reassuring about discovering how much of the human experience is common to other ages. With the Romans we have an exceptional record that includes not just the deeds and carryings-on of emperors but also the lives of ordinary people. It takes a moment to realize just how unusual this is. There is no comparable archive for the entire medieval period. It is not until early modern times that the survival of tombstones and ephemera in the form of letters and diaries makes it possible once more to become aware of the existence of modest individuals whose lives made no impact on the grand backdrop of history.

There was much about the Roman world that on the face of it seems alien or even horrible to us, especially the extreme brutality of Rome's wars and mass entertainment, but in so many other ways the Romans were just like us. They had ambitions, families, beliefs, hopes, fears, frustrations, and joy. More than anything else, though, they had an acute sense not only of self but also of their mortality. This is what led so many of them to leave a record of their lives, usually in the form of tombstones or religious dedications and which makes it possible to write a book like this about them.

Some of those whose lives were centred on Rome, especially some of the emperors and the elite, ranged freely around Italy and the Roman Empire. Besides having homes and political or other essential interests in Rome, they often owned country houses and estates, in Campania and the Bay of Naples with its islands like Ischia and Capri. The epicentre of their existences, though, was always in Rome itself, even if

3

they cherished the chance to hide themselves away in what they liked to depict as rural boltholes.

That, of course, begs the question: what did being Roman mean? For those who could trace their ancestry, whether real or imagined, back to the city's earliest days the answer was obvious. Being 'Roman' was also a state of mind that could be acquired to a greater or lesser degree by moving to the city or its orbit. This was especially for those who could claim to be Roman citizens while also proudly clinging on to their regional or provincial identities. There were millions of people who might – and many did – perceive themselves to be 'Roman', yet never set foot in Rome or even Italy.

Rome was packed with people from all over the Empire and beyond. They made for a constant procession of visitors, soldiers, chancers, commuters, and rogues frequenting the congested streets, forums, shops, tenements, and townhouses. They even briefly included Cleopatra VII of Egypt, flaunted in Rome by her lover Caesar who bestowed on her 'high honours and rich gifts'.[4] For many of these people, living in Rome may only ever have been a fleeting or occasional experience, albeit a powerful and memorable one, while others eked out their entire existence within the city. The focus of this book is what it was like to be Roman in the city of Rome, but this necessarily involves being flexible about where some of the information comes from.

There is a good reason for this. Although the records for life in ancient Rome are remarkably extensive, they are far from comprehensive. This means that we must necessarily draw on evidence from other places in the Roman world to provide us with analogies and supplementary information. The most obvious sources are the Campanian cities of Pompeii and Herculaneum, destroyed by Vesuvius in 79. The recovery from both cities of extraordinary quantities of material relating to everyday life in the late first century means they are fundamental to our understanding of the experience of being Roman. It is reasonable to make this assumption, even with the proviso that these places were Italian country towns with different histories from that of Rome, and with their own local traditions. The records of individuals, as well as

4

the physical remains of public buildings, commercial premises, and shops amply demonstrate that life in Pompeii and Herculaneum had become indisputably Roman. There was after all a great deal of traffic of all sorts between both places and Rome. Pompeii and Herculaneum show above all else how being 'Roman' often involved the conflation of regional or provincial identities with identifying oneself also as being part of the Roman world.

For the most part this book is concerned with the individual, whatever their station in life. All these people were also affected by ideas and concepts that defined the experience of being Roman and it is essential to look at these as well. Among these was, for example, the nature of how the Romans were ruled. Under the Republic, the Romans were expected to accept that they were being governed by what passed for a form of democracy, with male freeborn Roman citizens voting in their magistrates and being presided over by an elected assembly of elders known as the Senate. There were huge tensions in a system that was riven with corruption and vested interests. The Senate was controlled by a self-serving and wealthy elite. Voting in the late Republic was manipulated by money and violence. Slaves and freedmen had no electoral rights, and women were excluded from the process also. The collapse of the Republic was born out of a catastrophic series of events and degeneration that involved Rome being at the mercy of a succession of generals (known as the *imperatores*) drawn from the elite who embarked on a series of alliances and feuds that led to the civil wars of the 40s and 30s BC.

The result was the effective end of the Republic and the emergence of Augustus as the first emperor. The Romans now found themselves being ruled by what amounted to a hereditary monarchy but in a system designed to mask that with a pretence that a single man with supreme authority had restored the Republic under his protection (see below, this chapter). The Roman world was characterized by numerous contradictions and twists that at least most people were prepared to accept and live with, rather than endure any more of the violence that had torn the Republic apart.

Therefore, the reader will find, where appropriate, some consideration of these more abstract ideas. Such incongruities, which one might just call 'fudges', formed an important part of the Roman mindset because they created the framework in which the Romans lived and affected how they thought and behaved. Our own lives might differ in detail from those of the Romans, but we too live in a ramshackle haze of contradictions and fuzzy detail which define the present time.

The Romans were certainly consumed with a sense of their magnificent success and entitlement. This did not bring any peace of mind, a paradox that was another defining characteristic of their civilization, especially under the emperors. The phenomenal wealth Rome enjoyed caused a moral crisis as the descent into luxury and indulgence seemed to be destroying the qualities that had made Rome great in the first place. A common belief among Rome's elite, especially the historians drawn from the upper classes, was that Rome's success had destroyed the idyll of early Roman society, when men of fortitude, modesty and restraint who worked on the land and fought to defend their homes had made Rome great. Some of the elite now looked around at the city and saw an increasingly febrile mob accustomed to extravagant public facilities and state handouts, and an aristocracy ever more interested in unrestrained extravagance and self-indulgence.

The Augustan historian Livy was enslaved to the reactionary notion that the Romans had once been a higher and better people. Rome had become 'burdened by its magnitude', he said.[5] Catullus envied a friend of his called Furius for being too poor to own a slave, a money box, or even a fire because it meant he had nothing to be afraid of or worry about.[6] A century later the poet Juvenal wrote that 'profligate Rome sets no end to its extravagance' and that everything in Rome came at a price.[7] Even this plaintive Roman navel-gazing has its echoes in our time, an era increasingly hag-ridden by a sense of guilt at our profligacy and wanton waste of resources and privilege.

SOURCES AND HISTORY

This book depends mainly on ancient sources and inscriptions drawn from the last two centuries of the Roman Republic and the first two or three centuries of the emperors. This reflects the material available. It was a period that charted Rome's emergence as the supreme international power in the Mediterranean world with the defeat of Carthage in the Second Punic War, its acquisition of a vast Empire that reached its greatest extent under Trajan over three centuries later, and then its gradual decline into the chronic instability of the third century AD which followed the death of Commodus in 192 and lasted at least until the accession of Diocletian in 284.

The reader will soon see that this book is by no means limited to that epoch. Other stories and evidence have been drawn from Rome's earliest days and on into the fourth century AD, a period of around a thousand years. The earlier material was important to the Romans, even if much was imagined and idealized. They constantly looked back to the city's earliest days for inspiration, admiring Rome's mythologized heroes and what they imagined was a time when the Roman people maintained higher standards of morality, self-sacrifice, hard work, and self-discipline.

Much historical literature has survived from the latter days of the Republic and from the reign of Augustus to that of Severus Alexander in the early third century. With a few exceptions, later Roman historians leave a great deal to be desired and are lacking in both detail and reliability. Surviving inscriptions belong predominantly to the last century of the Republic and then from Augustus into the first half of the third century AD. Some key sources are far more important than others. Cicero is, for example, the dominant source of information about political events in late Republican Rome, Tacitus for the reigns of Tiberius and parts of the reigns of Claudius and Nero.

No attempt has been made to tackle the material in consistent chronological order. The sources are distributed far too randomly across time to make that sensible or even desirable. The question of dates is discussed below. Livy's history of Rome, compiled during the reign of Augustus, is a key source for the rise of Rome right up to and through the fall of the Republic but much is lost or only known to us in later summaries. The further back Livy trawled, the more his efforts were compromised by the absence of proper annals and records, and he was aware of this. To make good some of the gaps in Livy, historians have to turn to the works of others such as the Greek historians Polybius and Diodorus Siculus, which are also affected by missing sections.

Tacitus, who wrote around the beginning of the second century, is a superb source for much of the period AD 14–69 but whole sections have been lost, for example his account of the reign of Caligula (37–41). He is unmatched by any other ancient Roman historian but was mainly concerned with great matters of state, the army, and the imperial family. Tacitus knew only too well how unpredictable events impacted on human history. This was what helped provoke his interest in the way his world had been shaped. *Eventusque rerum, qui plerumque fortuiti sunt*, 'fate and circumstance are generally due to chance', he said.[8] His interest in the emperors and the activities of the elite meant all the rest were largely dismissed as background noise, the *vulgus*, 'common people'.[9] He tells us relatively little about the day-to-day experiences of ordinary life in Rome. Yet it is so often the evidence for their lives that brings us that sense of the common experience of being human.

Tacitus rarely mentions his prime sources, which are not available to us anyway. Suetonius, who wrote only a little later, produced a colourful account of the same period but by using a different device. He composed individual biographies of the dictator Julius Caesar and then the emperors from Augustus to Domitian. They contain gossip alongside important factual accounts of events and help flesh out some of the gaps in Tacitus. Like so much of Roman history they focused on events and personalities in Rome, much from before Tacitus and Suetonius themselves were born. Cassius Dio was in a similar position, apart from the latter sections of his work in which he describes events in the late second and early third centuries that he had often witnessed

8

personally. A contemporary historian for this period, Herodian, often differs in significant detail, thereby calling both into doubt and therefore by implication Tacitus and Suetonius.

For historians like Tacitus and Suetonius, the Empire was the setting in which the emperors and the senatorial class played out their power games, making for a grand drama. Conversely, their contemporaries, the poets Martial and Juvenal, provide us with entertaining and picaresque glimpses of Rome in the late first and early second centuries. They have no equals at any other time. Valerius Maximus, who lived in Tiberius' reign (14–37), compiled and published numerous 'memorable deeds and sayings' of individual Romans and others drawn from other writers, many of whose works are otherwise lost. He arranged them into nine thematic sections, specifically to save readers the time and trouble of tracking them down. The text has survived in full, and it provides us with invaluable information about what the Romans admired, such as valour and moderation. Pliny (Gaius Plinius Secundus) the Elder recorded countless anecdotes and theories in his magisterial *Natural History* but he died during the eruption of Vesuvius in August 79. No other Roman ever filled his sandals. Third-century and later written sources (apart from Dio, Herodian, and Ammianus Marcellinus) are generally poor and unreliable. This is a particular problem with certain 'biographies' of some of the third-century emperors.

We are also fortunate to have some collections of correspondence, most notably the letters of Cicero and then later those of Seneca, and Pliny the Younger, nephew of the Elder. Inevitably, these exceptional windows into life in Rome, Italy, and the provinces feature extensively in this and other books. They illustrate an imbalance in our sources that we can do nothing about, but it is better to celebrate that we have these ones at all. Nonetheless, we cannot be certain that the texts are those of the actual letters sent since in general our texts must derive from retained copies. They may well have been modified for publication, either by the writers or later editors. This is known to have happened, for example, with the letters of Samuel Pepys (1633–1703) when a selection was first published by Richard, Lord Braybrooke, in 1825. Braybrooke silently telescoped or rewrote the texts wherever he thought fit. Comparison with extant original manuscripts makes it possible to prove what he had done; we obviously cannot do this with Roman correspondence.[10] The letter format was also a literary device. When the author retained a copy, its text might have been suitably altered and 'improved'. In some cases, the letter may never have been sent and instead had been composed purely for the purposes of embellishing the archive.

The inscriptions and graffiti which supply us with the names and careers of ordinary Romans turn up in various places. Some survive in their original location, such as a cemetery, while others are to be found on altars, religious dedications, or in the remains of buildings. Many have been moved from their original locations, perhaps reused as a step in a house, or converted into a drain cover. Often these are the only reasons they have survived. Unless they bear a reference to the consuls of the year, or an emperor, they can usually only be dated by style. This is an unavoidable weakness of the evidence. It means that when looking at life in ancient Rome it means sometimes associating several pieces of information from different sources separated by periods of time equivalent to that separating us from the reign of George III (1760–1820) or more.

Evaluating the reliability of any of our sources is a great challenge, especially when ancient historians report events involving speech. James Boswell (1740–95) was well-known, even notorious, in his lifetime for his journal and records which he kept on a regular basis. He set down in writing numerous episodes and events, his principal focus being the experience of his friendship with Dr Samuel Johnson (1709–84). Boswell was exceptional in his practices and highly skilled at recreating a vivid and dynamic sense of conversations taking place before his eyes and in which he was a participant. He claimed to write down these occasions as soon as possible after they had taken place. His archives acted as the basis of his *Life of Johnson*, the most celebrated biography in the English language.

Nonetheless, it has always been a matter of debate just how authentic Boswell's accounts of Johnson's pronouncements and interactions with others truly are. There is a good case to be made that Boswell recreated these scenes (and they were 'scenes', often with stage direction notes) in Johnson's style, which Boswell was so familiar with that he could do this plausibly. It is impossible to know to what extent the results were more to do with his skills as a writer rather than mere transcriptions. This is despite many of Boswell's papers and notes being extant, and the biography going through several editions in his lifetime, with numerous revisions.[11]

When we are dealing with a Roman source recounting an interaction between an ordinary person and an emperor there are no means of knowing whether the tale is fabricated and hearsay, possibly even confusing the emperor involved with another. It may thus be only a pastiche of a real encounter, an authentic anecdote, or often pure invention. None of the necessary records like Boswell's exists to substantiate such episodes and he, at least, knew his subject personally.

The Romans had an acute sense of what they called their history, though it was a version of events that suited their self-belief, as all national histories usually are. It was by our standards frustratingly lacking in precise detail, especially for the earliest periods, but peoples are defined as much by their foundation myths as by the authentic sequence of events. The absolute 'truth' of exactly what happened is therefore impossible to find, but that is no less true of what happened yesterday in London or Washington DC. There is nothing to be gained by complaining about it. The claims and counter claims erupt the moment after the events they purport to describe took place. In a Radio 4 bulletin the BBC's political editor Chris Mason reported on a meeting that had taken place a short time earlier between the serving British prime minister Rishi Sunak and the former incumbent Boris Johnson. Mason mischievously observed that 'accounts of the meeting differ considerably'.[12] What chance then of unravelling the truth twenty centuries later? Most of the variant accounts will probably disappear over time leaving at best one, if any, which is then treated

11

as if it is the whole truth and nothing but the truth because the only alternative is to ignore the whole occasion.

The only truth is that it turns out there is and never was an absolute truth on which everyone could have agreed even while whatever-it-was was happening. All one can do, said C.S. Lewis, is ask 'who influenced the ancient writer, and how far the statement is consistent with what he said in other books, and what phase in the writer's development, or in the general history of thought, it illustrates, and how it affected later writers, and how often it has been misunderstood', all the while unable to acknowledge the knotty question of whether any of it was true in the first place.[13]

Those myths therefore tell us at least as much about the culture they belong to as any other source of information, just as the Battle of Britain and the American Revolutionary War now exist in a blur of fact and myth. The Romans, both collectively and individually, perceived and defined themselves as participants in their drama, depicting and describing themselves accordingly.

The same applies to the stories about the early emperors provided by, for example, Suetonius. He told them because they were current in his time and had become familiar tropes in Roman cultural identity. He knew his readers and while he played up to their expectations, he was also preserving for a distant future how rulers like Caligula and Nero were already perceived, rightly or wrongly.

Both these emperors were inextricably linked by Roman historians to scurrilous tales of incest and sexual deviancy, as well as barbarity and cruelty. We cannot now unravel whether there was any truth in these stories. We have no more evidence to support the tales than is available to us to demolish them. It is therefore more useful to us now to understand that the allegations and rumours were important components in Roman popular culture, especially if they emerged many years after the event. They formed essential ingredients in depicting Caligula and Nero as stock tyrants, later joined by others such as Commodus and Elagabalus. Accepting that there is likely to have been some basis in truth in the stories written about them, however little, is not the same as credulously accepting them at face value. Rumours only usually have currency because existing perceptions give them some degree of plausibility. The challenge for us, and it is usually an insurmountable one, is to wrest the truth from the puff. Endlessly nit-picking to question their credibility, however, only makes for a tiresome and tendentious read. It also ultimately negates their value since the only effect is to suggest they are all unreliable, which is neither interesting nor helpful. Of course, the sources still need to be read with a critical eye. I have noted where I think this is of special relevance.

In his celebrated *The Innocents Abroad*, Mark Twain recounted how in the late 1860s he was shown in the Church of the Holy Tabernacle in Jerusalem what purported to be the grave of Adam. He wryly observed that 'there is no question that he is actually buried in the tomb which is pointed out as his – there can be none – because it has never yet been proven that the grave is not the grave in which he is buried'.[14] Twain could not have better described the problem that faces all historians, and especially ancient historians. The evidence usually does not exist to resolve beyond doubt many questions, and the result is an endless parade of hypotheses, ranging from the preposterous to the reasonable. They hang on largely because there is usually no conclusive evidence either to substantiate or to refute them. This is no less true of many questions about the Roman Empire and especially those about the true nature of some of the emperors. As ever, the issues usually come down to what people want to believe. In that context the beliefs the Romans held about their leaders are as relevant to our understanding of what it meant to be Roman as any scholarly theory, and perhaps more so.

Roman culture was filled with the idea of stereotypes, just as ours is, though unlike us the Romans had no qualms about pigeonholing people. Nor had they any inhibitions about bigotry and prejudice, especially about foreigners. Bars and taverns, for example, were thus routinely seen as places where all kinds of ne'er-do-wells gathered to get up to mischief. If that evokes a memory in the modern mind of, for example, the famous tavern scene in the movie *Star Wars* populated by intergalactic freaks and outlaws, then that only brings our own world closer to that of the Romans. Their streetside cookshops and cheap apartment blocks were filled with the flotsam and jetsam of a vast empire.

EMPERORS

The reality about the status of an emperor was submerged beneath a curious collection of Republican magistracies and other honours which were maintained in a remarkable and durable charade (this is discussed in detail in Chapter 2). Rome and its people reigned supreme across much of Europe, North Africa, and the Middle East. This empire had been won by predatory conquest. In the first century AD Roman civilization was advancing remorselessly towards the zenith of its power.

It seems not to have mattered who the emperor was, at least to most of the Roman people, whether they were senators or slaves or anywhere in between, and regardless of where they lived in the Roman Empire. The face of the current incumbent stared out from the coins in their hands, but so did the faces of his predecessors whose money might circulate alongside new issues for generations. Each symbolized the notion of imperial authority vested in a single ruler over whom the average Roman had no power whatsoever unless he or she joined a rabid mob bent on dragging the emperor out of the palace and killing him.

Ordinarily, the machinations and intrigues in the imperial palace made little or no difference to the way most ordinary people lived on a day-to-day basis. The drama of civil wars when rival emperors battled it out could, and did, devastate the communities unfortunate enough to be in the vicinity. To almost everyone else such catastrophes were distant curiosities manifested only on the sudden appearance of new coins bearing the name and face of a new emperor. There is some evidence that ordinary Romans took the misbehaviour of their rulers seriously. Taking to the streets was one option but those coins also occasionally served as targets for resentment when, for example, a chisel was taken to a coin portrait of Nero as a means of symbolically killing him.

Nevertheless, ordinary people could and did write to the emperor or addressed him in person at an imperial audience to importune him for some service or concession, such as citizenship for the child of a serving soldier who had formed a relationship with a provincial.

The Roman emperor was thus by comparison with our own time surprisingly accessible. Sometimes ordinary people came across the emperor by chance and took the opportunity to make a request. Hadrian was on a journey once — we do not know where and given his travelling habits it could have been in Italy or anywhere else in the Empire — when a woman spotted him and tried her luck. She had barely started speaking when Hadrian dismissed her with 'I haven't time'. He had miscalculated. She fired back with 'cease, then, being emperor'. A chastened Hadrian dismounted and listened to her, though we do not know what her grievance was.[15] The story is in Cassius Dio, recorded by him at least sixty years after the event. No one has the slightest idea how it was transmitted down through time and whether it was embellished or modified. Many decades earlier, and to his annoyance, Cicero had discovered that certain jokes were being attributed to him that he knew he had never cracked.[16] This is another phenomenon which might be coined as prestige attribution, a process by which an action, comment, or saying is given false authority by attributing it to someone whose reputation enhances its credibility and significance.

DATING ROME

The Romans counted their dates 'from the foundation of the city', *ab urbe condita*, or 'from the birth of the city', which corresponds to what we call 753 BC, though they scarcely ever enumerated these dates on coins or monuments.[17] Years were normally distinguished instead in official records by the names of the two consuls elected at the start of each year, the lists of which survive. Emperors listed their titles on coins and inscriptions but did not distinguish them from those that they had held prior to becoming emperor. For example, Domitian held the consulship seven times prior to his accession in 81. Thus, as emperor in the year 84 his coins and inscriptions recorded his tenth consulship (given as COS X), for example. It is the consul lists that have played the largest part in compiling a continuous sequence of years, calibrated in modern times to absolute calendar years by various other factors, such as eclipses recorded by Roman historians. Rome's second millennium began in what we call the year 248 and was the subject of massive celebrations by Philip I (244–9).

There is thus no doubt that the Romans had calculated a chronology for their history, leaving them with a clear idea of when Rome had come into being, even if the earlier sections were largely fiction with a nominal basis in fact. Rome's origins were famously modest, beginning as a collection of farming villages on a few low hills on the banks of the River Tiber. At the time the settlements would have seemed unexceptional and insignificant, as indeed they were. A series of unique factors and chance saw them coalesce into a single force that spent generations pursuing territorial and economic feuds against neighbouring communities. This gradually developed over centuries into dominance of Italy and then, most importantly of all, by the end of the third century BC Rome had also defeated Carthage, its greatest rival, in the First and Second Punic Wars. This opened the way to dominance of the whole Mediterranean world.

Roman history stretches from that mythical foundation of Rome in 753 BC right through to the collapse of the Western Empire in the late fifth century AD. The Eastern Empire lasted till the fall of Constantinople in 1453. This was the extraordinary story of how a group of villages by a river in Italy grew into Rome, the most powerful city in the ancient world.

*

This book is not a history of ancient Rome. Many excellent books serve that purpose already. It is instead about some of the experiences that were to be had in Rome and of being Roman, from seeing the bodies of criminals and public enemies hurled down from the Capitoline Hill to enjoying the peaceful empty streets of Rome during a few days when it seemed that almost the whole population had taken itself off to watch the chariot races in the Circus Maximus.

Rome was both glamorous and ghastly, a place where phenomenal extravagance was on display alongside the rotting bodies of crucified criminals, where the wealthy loafed on ivory couches at dinner while outside the streets ran with offal and excrement. Samuel Johnson said (or allegedly said) in 1775: 'I think the full tide of human existence is at Charing Cross.'[18] He was talking about London, of course, but he might as well have been describing the imperial forums in Rome, the Baths of Caracalla, the cookshops and food markets, or the endless stream of traffic that arrived daily up the Via Appia or along the road and river from the port at Ostia.

The satirist Juvenal thought little of historians whom he dismissed as 'lazy' or 'slothful', disparaging the amount of oil for lamps and time wasted on thousands of pages to no purpose apart from the ruin of historians.[19] Ironic, then, that he and others like him have played such an important role in handing down everyday vignettes of life in the Rome of his time, providing us with the words and colour to populate the empty ruins of a temple in Rome, a street in Pompeii, and a tenement block in Ostia.

The chapters have been compiled on a largely thematic basis. Inevitably there are frequent instances of overlap. Although freedmen are, for example, covered in their own chapter, they pop up in numerous other instances throughout the book, as do the guilds to which so many of them belonged. I make no pretence that the topics and examples in this book could possibly represent a definitive selection and nor could they serve as a comprehensive guide to life in ancient Rome. The quantity of available material, just as with the Roman army in the companion volume *Gladius*, would make

17

anything more a practical impossibility and sheer folly to attempt it. The choice is personal. For every story, anecdote, or inscription included, many others had to be passed over. The intention is to provide variety and something of the sheer visceral intensity of life in ancient Rome, including what still seems familiar to us as well as the outlandish.

While some records are comprehensive, many others are incidental. Our knowledge of a temple or cult may come only from a single aside in a passage concerned with another topic. Full references are provided for every story, anecdote, and inscription. These are often not considered necessary nowadays for an ancient history book aimed at a wider readership. In such books it seems the reader is expected to accept the modern writer's authority and reputation as the sole validation of the points made. This creates an unnecessary degree of separation between a modern readership and the Romans. That is a pity. Everyone is entitled to have the opportunity to know where the material in a book such as this has come from and to pursue it if they wish, rather than to be expected to take something for granted, or to have to engage in an interminable search to find it. Moreover, today it is easier than ever before for anyone to consult these sources for themselves online, and every reader interested in pursuing the subject further should do so. Details of how to do so are contained within the Further Reading section.

If I had anything in mind as an inspiration while writing this book, it was the writings of Valerius Maximus and Pliny the Elder (hereafter Pliny). Both men created idiosyncratic anthologies of the Roman world in the first century AD and both texts have come down to us. Valerius Maximus preserved some remarkable stories that would otherwise have been lost. Pliny's work was called a natural history but was so far-ranging that it amounts more to a vast and almost unlimited literary cabinet of curiosities. Both men drew freely on records available to them across time and space and were unconcerned with chronology or other technical niceties. They had evidently taken enormous delight in their work, enjoying the liberty to allow their curiosity to range freely, and were unencumbered by our modern obsessions with specialisms. Anyone stimulated by this book, or any other book on the subject, to read further about the experience of living in Roman times could do no better than to start with them.

Exploring the Roman world through its sources is also to throw open a window on a complex urban civilization that operated without electricity or true mechanization of any kind. Countless inventions that we use without thinking, from reading glasses to air conditioning and washing machines to pneumatic suspension, were unknown to them. In our own digitized environment, where electricity and machines are ubiquitous and life without either is unthinkable for most of us, it can be sobering to realize how recent and precarious our way of life is. Yet the self-reliant Romans managed to live, work, and play without so much of what we take for granted that it can be almost impossible for us to imagine how they achieved what they did.

History is, if nothing else, a voyage of discovery through the human experience and our own small part in it, 'figuring the nature of the times deceas'd'.[20] The Romans more than any other ancient civilization have influenced and affected our lives indelibly. We use their letters and many of their words, celebrate their greatest achievements while condemning their failings, and look on in awe at the physical remains of their era. Their voices echo through our everyday lives.

Guy de la Bédoyère
Augusta, Western Australia, where apart from final revisions this book was completed in March 2023

NB Dates throughout this book are AD (sometimes given as CE by others) unless otherwise specified as BC (sometimes given as BCE by others). Where appropriate, AD is supplied to avoid doubt.

1

CITYSCAPE

The smoke, the wealth, and the din of Rome.

Horace[1]

R ome at its height was the biggest city in the western ancient
world. It had a population of around a million at its peak
though no records survive to substantiate that claim. The
estimate is based on its physical extent when compared to medieval
and early modern European cities whose population sizes are known,
at least approximately. The true figure may on occasion have been
greater, though it is certain that the total fluctuated continuously,
depending on circumstances. Ancient Rome was also large compared
to cities of the Middle Ages. It was bigger than its own medieval counterpart by a considerable margin. London did not reach a similar size
until the eighteenth century, a time when the tumult in its streets
and markets gives us something of an idea of how similarly congested,
noisy, and vibrant life in Rome must have been. At its greatest extent
imperial Rome ranged from 1.8 to 3 miles (3–5 km) across. Today there
are still large open areas within that part of the modern city, beneath
which lie buried vast tracts of urban archaeology.

This heaving setting included magnificent public buildings like the
baths and temples, palatial houses of the rich, festering slums made
up of congested apartment blocks, and everything and anything in

between. The River Tiber snaked its way through the middle. Up the river came an endless succession of barges bringing in goods from around the Roman world. Down the river floated the sewage that poured in night and day along with the bloated bodies of dead animals and the victims of execution and murder.

For the most part the lives of the Romans, whatever their class, were short and harsh. The mood was always on a knife edge, which was hardly surprising given how many people lived in Rome. There was no sophisticated crowd management or disciplined and organized policing. In a society where fights to the death formed a core part of public entertainment, brutal muggings were endemic, and where masters could beat their slaves to a pulp on a whim, it was hardly surprising that the state authorities used violence to maintain control. The only additional ingredient needed was an arbitrary and unstable emperor who had learned that with a single word anyone who crossed him could be executed, and a moment later be killed himself.

A flashpoint could erupt at the chariot races, a sport that was wildly popular. The crowds who gathered in the Circus Maximus, or another of the stadiums, were already whipped up into a frenzy before they arrived. Tertullian thought the circus the place 'where frenzy reigns supreme'.[2] Buoyed up and emboldened, it was common for the spectators to start shrieking at the attending emperors to hand out favours and benefits. On one occasion, the dangerously volatile Caligula (37–41) was confronted by a circus mob screaming at him for taxes to be reduced, he allegedly having taxed everything possible. Caligula grew angry. The crowd shouted louder, and his fury increased. He ordered 'agents' (probably members of the Praetorian Guard) to infiltrate the protestors and arrest any suspects, to be executed on the spot. The large number of deaths, and presumably the sight of people being summarily killed, had the desired effect. The crowd calmed down because 'they could see with their own eyes that the request for fiscal concessions resulted quickly in their own death'.[3]

The inhabitants of Rome, perpetually on the move in and out through the gates and packing the streets and public facilities as well as their own homes, were dwarfed by the buildings. The sun was barely able to creep down the narrowest alleys beside which most Romans lived, only briefly illuminating the dirt, peeling plaster and filthy streets while casting fleeting shafts of light into tenement apartments and shops and onto streetside shrines. Only a short distance away that same sun burnished the glittering temples of the Forum with their garishly painted statues of the gods, the emperors, and other greats, as well as the spoils of war and other decorations. The air was fouled by countless furnaces, sacrificial fires, and lamps (see Chapter 10), and the senses ravaged by the commotion and noise.

Walking among the Romans, or being carried, were visitors who had made the arduous journey to the city in search of fortunes, work, libraries, safety, or simply to gawp. The Romans themselves found their way across the Empire in a host of different capacities, among them governors, administrators, soldiers, traders, and tourists (though precise information on individual origins can be elusive – see Chapter 15). Those who returned to the city brought with them their experiences, souvenirs, new words, and habits as well as exotic cults. Cicero memorably described Rome as a 'city made up from a collection of nations, in which there are many traps, many tricks, all kinds of vice going the rounds, and the arrogance, insolence, evil, pride, hatred and troubles of many people to be endured'.[4] He was discussing the challenges faced by a man seeking election to office, but his comments paint a familiar picture to this day of life in almost any city.

Some of Rome's people had been born and had grown up in the city. Others came from across Italy or almost anywhere across the Roman world or beyond, including soldiers, civilians, traders, chariot racers and gladiators, priests, and slaves. Taking account of its physical spread, including vertical building, Pliny said it was clear no city had ever matched Rome for magnitude.[5] Juvenal described the financial pressure of living in the city. 'Everything in Rome comes at a price', he said, with everyone dressing beyond their means to show off their status and having to rent dungeons at a cost that would pay for an elegant country house anywhere else. 'We all live in pretentious poverty', he wailed.[6]

The Romans created divine personifications of all sorts of ideas and places, following a well-established tradition in antiquity. Roma was among of the most conspicuous, Macrobius observing that 'it is well known that all cities are under the protection of a god'.[7] The city was visualized as a female warrior with helmet, shield, spear, and trophies. Roma epitomized the Roman sense that their city was a living entity, an impression easy to understand given the place's scale and endless change.

Rome's origins as a settlement went back to when it was supposedly founded in 753 BC by Romulus, a descendant of the mythological Trojan hero Aeneas, and who became its first king. Aeneas had brought his followers from the burning ruins of Troy to find a new homeland. In Italy he found the right place, marrying into the Latins, and creating a new race that would become the Romans. The archaeology, naturally enough, tells us nothing about Aeneas and Romulus but it does show that during the eighth century BC various rural settlements had grown up in the region.

Their peoples spoke different languages that pointed to their distinct original development. Latin was, for example, about as different from Etruscan as it is possible to be and in time acquired numerous foreign words, mainly of Greek origin. Although Latin inherited many Etruscan words, Etruscan is still barely understood. But over time contacts between the various communities became more and more common. Etruscans even temporarily ruled in Rome. These peoples of central Italy also had wider contacts, mainly among the Greeks whose traders and settlers had spread throughout the western Mediterranean and especially into Sicily and southern Italy. By late Republican and imperial times educated Romans were normally competent in Greek and the better off included Greek books in their libraries.[8] There were also the Phoenicians from further east who brought links to North Africa and the Middle East as well as the decaying power of Egypt.

Typically for a time when the Bronze Age was giving way to the Iron Age, these settlements were ruled by chieftains who represented the apex of societies dominated by local aristocracies. Their individual prestige was based on the ability to control territory. They devoted much of their time and energy to fomenting territorial disputes. Among these communities, Rome, for reasons that were not immediately apparent, became more important than the others but its influence and power were still restricted to a small area. Under these early chieftains, whom the Romans knew as kings, the city evolved into the most significant power in the region. It had also already moved beyond being a simple rural settlement. By the sixth century BC Rome already had its first sewer system, which had made it possible to start draining the valley where the Forum would develop. The elite were investing in large and well-appointed stone houses. A mark of the tensions that existed were the early city walls that surrounded a lozenge-shaped area around 1 x 1.2 miles (1.5–2 km). Rome's great fortune was to oversee the road crossing the Tiber on the land route up the west coast of Italy. The Tiber served as a corridor to maritime trade from across the known world. Rome was also close enough to the coast to control the port which grew up at Ostia.

In 509 BC the Romans expelled their king, the Etruscan Tarquinius Superbus, and founded the Republic. Rome was now ruled by a pair of annually elected magistrates, the consuls, who presided over a hierarchy of lesser magistracies. They were originally drawn from the Senate, a council of aristocrats (patricians) based on a property qualification. The wealthy conducted business in one of Rome's forums, temples and other public buildings, or in their extravagant private houses. The Republic remained the system of government until Augustus became the first emperor in all but name. Even then, he maintained the fiction that he had restored the Republic, a tradition followed by his successors. Republican offices and institutions continued.

We know little about early Republican Rome until its latter days, from which some monuments survive. Evidence for life in the city predominantly belongs to the first century BC, when the Republic was in its death throes, and under the emperors who followed. By the reign of Augustus, Rome had gone from controlling an area little more than a radius of 60 miles (100 km) away to vast tracts of territory across

Italy, Spain, Gaul (France), the Balkans, Greece, Asia (Turkey, Syria), and North Africa (from 30 BC including Egypt). The impact on the city had been colossal but it was only from the reign of Augustus on and the stability that it brought that it became possible for investment in infrastructure and private opulence on an astronomical scale.

ROME OF THE EMPERORS

By the reign of Vespasian (69–79) Rome had fourteen regions in which there were allegedly 265 street crossings, each with its own guardian spirits called the *Lares*. The road junctions were a way of defining long-established individual neighbourhoods.[9] Known as *vici*, a word for a settlement, they were overseen from Augustus' time by their own magistrates, the *vicomagistri*, with the cult of the Lares playing a key part in the management and identity of each. Only in the ruins of Ostia and Pompeii can the physical evidence of similar localities still be seen. A three-way junction was known as a *trivium*. The word trivium has led to our own 'trivial' because a trivium road junction was regarded as being of unmatched ordinariness and insignificance; the goddess Trivia was the divine personification of such locations.[10]

The people in each neighbourhood, numbering perhaps 3,000–4,000 on average based on the estimated population of Rome at up to a million, are likely to have been broadly familiar with each other, living and working cheek by jowl. The men were often involved in the local *collegia* (guilds), generally based on a common profession or participation in a cult (and often both) and mainly dominated by freedmen. This way they made up for their lack of political rights by becoming prominent in their guilds.

These organizations had constitutions, calendars, officials, and internal elections, and had interests and influence that involved them with religion and mainstream politics. Belonging to a guild was a matter of pride, and the members looked after their own. The guilds acted as factions, their more important members using their roles as patrons to enforce the participation of their clients in their commercial interests and to act as muscle not only on their behalf but also for their own patrons, who included senators. As a result, the guilds became powerful agents in Roman politics and commerce. By being associated with one side or another the rivalry easily spilled over into violence. Their rituals and nature associated them with cults and the overall effect was to make them far more akin to modern Masonic lodges than just trade organizations.

The traffic and the constant activity passing through those 265 crossways meant that Rome suffered from chaos and a perpetual din. Pedestrians were deafened by the clatter of iron-rimmed cartwheels on the lumpen volcanic boulders of road surfaces and were scattered on all sides to make way for the rich. 'Only the wealthy get to sleep in Rome', complained Juvenal about the row in Rome's streets.[11] Martial wrote an epigram explaining why he escaped to his villa at Nomentum (now Mentana), a small town about 18 miles (29 km) from Rome, so often. Martial moaned about noisy schoolmasters, the row from bakers and coppersmiths, the clinking of coins on the moneychanger's table, and even the racket when pots and pans were bashed together at night during a lunar eclipse to ward off evil spirits.[12]

There were the wealthy and their wives, borne through the streets in litters, like Afer who was ostentatiously carried aloft by 'six Cappadocian slaves', scattering the throng of pedestrians while they loafed inside, blocking out the rabble by hiding behind curtains, and 'a gaggle of well-groomed clients' scuttled along in attendance.[13] Even in death the elite took precedence. Their seated cadavers were carried first to the rostra in the Forum for a relative to declaim to the crowd the deceased's magnificent achievements. Next, the propped-up corpses were carried through the streets to be cremated and interred beside the roads outside the city boundaries.

The people forced to make way for the glorious dead included the ordinary citizenry and the huge numbers of slaves and freedmen trying to go about their business. Some were on their way to the baths, others perhaps to promenade in one of the great elegant free gardens and leisure complexes such as the Porticus of Livia. They were also liable to be roughly pushed aside by soldiers who beat them up if they protested.

The Romans were unabashed about seeing foreigners and immigrants as stereotypes. Of Commodus' chamberlain Eclectus, Herodian said, 'As an Egyptian he was characteristically given to act upon his impulses and be controlled by his emotions.'[14] Pliny referred to the 'falsehoods of Greeks', while Cicero said 'a great many are deceitful and unreliable', advising his brother Quintus to be on his guard against them while serving as propraetor in Asia.[15] Some of the most memorable accounts and descriptions conversely come from those who visited Rome from afar. The Greek orator Aelius Aristides was one who was staggered by what he saw in Rome during Hadrian's reign, seeing the city as a place into which everything made in the world could be obtained.

Some Romans, mainly as administrators, soldiers, or traders, ventured far and wide across the Roman world and beyond. They included those who brought back looted works of art and trophies, such as from Corinth in Greece after it fell to Rome in 146 BC. Possession and display of such items in Rome became a matter of prestige for some of the more acquisitive and ostentatious elite.

In 139 BC a Roman diplomatic mission led by Scipio Aemilianus, victor of the Third Punic War, arrived in Alexandria to eye up Egypt. He and his colleagues were greatly impressed by Egypt's cities and wealth but were mystified by its rulers' failure to make the most of the country's potential.[16] Egypt was fading fast under the last Ptolemaic pharaohs who had become dependent on the Romans to stay in power. Three or four Roman traders turned up in 116 BC and left an inscription recording their names on the island of Philae (near Aswan) with its shrine of Isis.[17] There must have been many other such opportunists. In 112 BC, a senator called Lucius Memmius made the journey too. Little is known about Memmius' career but a papyrus recording his visit has survived. He arrived at Alexandria and was planning to sail up the Nile to visit the main attractions. He was treated with obsequious glee by his fixers who organized how he was to be greeted with 'magnificence' at every location.[18] Memmius was even to be provided with treats to be thrown to a sacred crocodile. The papyrus' survival is, of course a matter of chance; the mere fact of the visit proves that there was an easy way of finding passage to Egypt and taking advantage of a well-established tourist industry. These visitors brought back tales of their experiences. They contributed to a growing Roman interest in Egyptian art and religion though it was not until 30 BC that Egypt became a Roman province. Genuine Egyptian antiquities were brought to Rome and Italy while a domestic artistic industry sprang up in which Egyptian themes and imagery ('Nilotica') were created for Roman homes and public places.

THE GARRISON OF ROME

Roman government was dependent on the army to enforce its measures and act as the state's presence, but in the Republic a general was supposedly banned from marching his men into Rome. Sulla did just that and went down in infamy. Sulla had also had to punish soldiers for looting. To prevent any further misdemeanours, he posted guards around the city.[19] In 43 BC, during the fall of the Republic, the triumvirs Octavian, Antony and Lepidus brought their armies into Rome and even brazenly displayed standards throughout the city.[20] It was only under the emperors that soldiers became a permanent feature of Rome in the form of the elite Praetorian Guard and the lesser urban cohorts, serving as an integral part of how the Roman state enforced its power and control over a huge and potentially volatile population.

Praetorian soldiers had been in existence since the late Republic when the various generals appointed elite cohorts of troops to act as their personal guards. The name was derived from *praetorium*, the word for the commanding officer's campaign tent or residence in a fort. Augustus formalized this type of ad-hoc arrangement into a permanent force. His new Praetorian Guard was placed under the command of two prefects. This was a smart move that neatly circumvented the possibility of a senatorial commander, whose rank might have made him a potential rival emperor. It also divided control of a force that could in theory have been used by a single commander to mount a coup. That nearly happened under Tiberius when his praetorian prefect, Lucius Aelius Sejanus, not only engineered his sole command of the force but also then tried to topple the emperor. Even more dangerously, Sejanus had brought the Guard into Rome and based them in the Castra Praetoria on the north-east side of Rome where two sides of the compound still stand today. There they remained until the reign of Constantine the Great (307–37) when the Guard was disbanded for backing Constantine's enemy Maxentius.

Under Augustus there seem to have been nine praetorian cohorts with a nominal strength of 500 each (known as quingenary cohorts). The total fluctuated, especially during the civil war of 68–9, but by the end of the second century there were ten cohorts with a nominal strength of 1,000 each (milliary cohorts).[21] Scattered evidence from around the Roman Empire shows that praetorians were detached individually and in units on various tasks almost anywhere and everywhere as required. These frequently included retired praetorians, who so long as they had had an honourable discharge signed up again for further service. They were known as *evocati Augusti* ('men recalled [to arms] by the emperor').

Praetorian soldiers were an ever-present sight in Rome, including their mounted contingent, the *equites singulares* who had their own barracks and stables. Praetorians escorted the emperor, guarded the palace, and spied on the public. Depending on who was emperor at the time, they were all too likely to take on second jobs as they pleased. Most notoriously of all they were sometimes responsible for deposing and making emperors, usually in return for exorbitant demands of donatives and other benefits even though they were already the most highly paid and privileged soldiers in the entire Roman army.

The urban cohorts (*cohortes urbanae*) were created by Augustus to act as a city police force but were placed under the leadership of the prefect of Rome. In the year 23 there were three urban cohorts, perhaps the original number. The urban cohorts were increased in number to four cohorts in 69, by which time they were milliary (900 men each), if not already.[22] They acted as a useful counterfoil to the Praetorian Guard.

Fires were endemic in Rome and extremely dangerous in a congested ancient city with many buildings made of wood. A fire in 7 BC resulted in Rome being divided into fourteen administrative wards. At that stage Rome relied on 6,000 watchmen in four cohorts. Another fire in AD 6 was the catalyst for creating the 3,500-strong *cohortes vigilum*, raised mainly from freedmen. The *vigiles* were dispersed around Rome in designated bases (*stationes*) so that they could be on hand to deal with fires and help prevent structural collapse.[23] The vigiles could also serve as a check on the power of the Praetorian Guard. It was the vigiles under the command of their then commander Sertorius Macro who helped bring about the downfall of the over-ambitious praetorian prefect Sejanus in 31.

The men of the Praetorian Guard were notorious for roughing up citizens, whether on official business or just because they felt like it, shoving them out of the way on the city streets. In the aftermath of his assassination, Caligula's uncle Claudius was made emperor by the Praetorian Guard. They escorted him to the Palatine Hill to meet the Senate, the soldiers treating the crowd 'very harshly' as they pushed their way through.[24]

Ordinary citizens dared not get into a fight with a soldier in Rome. It was impossible to make a complaint or go to a magistrate to seek redress for injuries received. Cases against soldiers could only be heard in a military court in the praetorian camp, guaranteeing the presiding judge would be a centurion, and the jury made up of their compatriots, passing sentence on the complainant to be knocked about by the other men.[25] Conversely, a soldier pursuing a court case could be sure to have it heard immediately, unlike everyone else.[26]

Under Commodus' exceptionally lax rule (180–92), the Guard's behaviour deteriorated further. After Commodus was murdered at the end of 192, the stickler for discipline Pertinax was made emperor. 'Orders were issued to the soldiers to stop their insulting behaviour to the populace, and they were forbidden to carry axes or to strike any passer-by.'[27] This creates an astonishing image of armed soldiers habitually assaulting innocent civilians in the streets of Rome. At the end of March 193 they killed Pertinax. For this they were cashiered and sent packing by Septimius Severus (see p. 164) as he took control at the end of that phase of the civil war of 193–7, being replaced by loyal troops seconded from his regular legionaries. The reformed Praetorian Guard continued to play an important and unpredictable role in Roman history but was finally disbanded by Constantine I in 312.

INEQUALITY

Rome's swarming cosmopolitan population epitomized the inequality of the era. Apart from the imperial family, the richest were men like the Quintilii brothers who built a vast, sprawling villa beside the Via Appia in the late second century AD. Today its colossal ruins still match those of public buildings and dominate the western skyline on the way into Rome from Ciampino Airport. The poorest were the lowliest slaves, usually captives from Rome's wars of conquests. Nevertheless, there was still opportunity. A slave could be freed, and as a freedman make his way in business to see his sons rise to high office. Urbanus and Clarus were slaves freed by their master Aulus Memmius on the same day and took his name, as was the custom. After Clarus died Urbanus commissioned a tombstone for him on the Via Appia, commemorating their lifelong friendship.[28] Euhodus was another freedman, but he commissioned his own memorial. Euhodus had risen to sell pearls on the Via Sacra in Rome, affluent enough to buy his own slaves and free them too, reserving places for them in his tomb but — he was keen to add — absolutely no one else.[29] Some slaves accumulated enough money to buy their own freedom and do well (see Chapter 7).

SUCH IS ROME

The acute sense of time and place these records have handed down to us makes for an unparalleled picture of life in the Roman Empire, and especially Rome itself. In the reign of Domitian (81–96) Martial told his friend Lupercus to head down to a part of the city known as the Field of Potters ('Argiletum'). There he would find a shop belonging to Atrectus opposite the Forum of Caesar, and on its doorposts the advertisements posted by poets of their works for sale, including Martial's.[30] His anecdote is a trifling one, but like the graves on the Via Appia it is just another of the countless windows flung open on life in Rome.

Aelius Aristides was gushing in his admiration for the extraordinary quantity of goods that arrived every day from across the Empire and beyond, even as far as India. The flow was 'constant', the result therefore was 'abundance', and thus Rome was a 'common market for the world'.[31] The description was a rhetorical exercise, but it also had some truth in it. The ingress of so much merchandise was facilitated by what was by then a sophisticated harbour at Portus, close to Ostia at the mouth of the Tiber.[32] Even today, a vast mound of amphorae sherds in Rome called Monte di Testaccio bears witness to the astronomical quantity of olive oil alone that arrived to fuel the city's lamps and fill cooking pans. Publius Sulpicius Menophilus, a freedman of Greek origin, buried his wife in the mid-first century AD and tells us that he was a *doctor de portu oleario* ('instructor at the oil port') in the Vicus Victoria.[33] The location is unknown, as is his expertise, but one possibility is on the banks of the Tiber near the Forum Boarium (cattle market), with this oil port being probably among several in the city.

The geographer Strabo described Rome in the days of Augustus. Strabo came from the city of Amasia in the Roman province of Pontus (in northern Turkey). He was suitably impressed, though when he wrote many of Rome's most famous features were yet to be built. He said that Rome was a place built out of necessity rather than choice, that it lacked natural defences, and even the hinterland to support a city.[34] A key factor turned out to be that 'the fertile and extensive country' around Rome was taken over by the Romans using their 'valour and toil'. Those two virtues were certainly familiar themes in the Roman self-image, though it caused them no end of anxiety when they looked at the effete, complacent, and indolent attitudes that success had led to.

The resources available to Rome, said Strabo, which included wood and stone as well as the availability of food, were the key reasons for its success. He was staggered at how the city was in a constant state of flux. Houses were being built all the time, and just as quickly demolished or burned down in accidental fires to make way for new and better ones. Horace, writing around the same time, used his experience of life in Rome to come up with the metaphor 'demolishing, building, changing square to round' to describe the experience of leading a life out of kilter with any sense of order.[35]

Strabo might have been Greek, but he admired the Romans. He pointed out that while the Greeks had chosen superb locations for their cities, the Romans had shown far greater foresight by providing roads, aqueducts, and sewers. In an era without power-driven machinery, Roman engineering skills took on even greater significance. Using cuttings and embankments to level out roads, the Romans made it possible for their horse- and oxen-drawn carts to haul much greater loads in and out of the city than might otherwise have been possible, supplementing what was brought upriver from the port at Ostia in barges. The roads were, of course, packed with all kinds of traffic from the litters and carriages of the rich and their entourages to slaves dispatched on foot to carry out business on behalf of their owners. Migrants, vagabonds, and itinerant tinkers joined them, along with the *tabellarii* ('letter carriers') who bustled along with packages of letters that might have been travelling across the Empire for weeks or months.[36]

Strabo was amazed by the impact of competitive munificence that had driven major public building projects in the late Republic and under Augustus. The focus was in and around the Field of Mars (Campus Martius) in the northern part of Rome. This vast grassy, open space, decorated with works of art, was home to sports and chariot racing 'where that multitude of people exercise themselves' against a backdrop of hills leading down to the Tiber. No wonder, then, that Strabo described it as a stage-painting. Close by was the Field of Agrippa, different in tone because of its complex of temples, theatres, and amphitheatre, and embellished tombs of the great among which was the Mausoleum of Augustus. This huge drum-shaped structure held the cremated remains of Augustus' family and towered above its surroundings with a central hill-like mound planted with poplar trees. To the south of this zone was the Capitoline Hill (Capitolium), home to the Temple of Jupiter Capitolinus, 'first in honour among their [the Romans] temples'.[37] This small craggy stronghold over-looked the valley in which the ancient Forum lay nestling between the Palatine and Esquiline Hills, now steadily growing into 'one forum after another'. Yet more works of art were displayed there and in the Porticus of Livia, such as the statues of Aesculapius and Diana in the Temple of Juno which stood within the porticus, a building they shared with several other statues including work by the celebrated sculptor Praxiteles.[38]

Strabo had conveniently forgotten, or deliberately overlooked, the Rome of the backstreets where the political gangs of the late Republic had gathered to wreak murderous havoc on their rivals. The slums where most of the people lived were just a noisy and dangerous back-drop. The Forum of Augustus' central feature was the Temple of Mars Ultor ('Mars the Avenger'), built to commemorate the war against Caesar's assassins, Brutus and Cassius. Behind it was a vast stone fire-wall (which still stands), built to block out not only the ever-present danger from fires that ripped through the buildings and leapt the narrow streets, but also the sight of the congested tenements beyond.

PLINY'S ROME

The Rome that Strabo visited might have been impressive enough to overwhelm him, but it would have paled compared to what was to come. The natural historian Pliny wrote his own description around half a century later of the 'wonders of our own city'.[39] As far as he was concerned, the buildings of Rome had 'vanquished the world', not, of course, that he was really in any position to make such a judgement. By Pliny's time Rome had been embellished further, most notably by Vespasian's Temple of Peace, but he remained greatly impressed by what Agrippa had achieved during Augustus' reign. Agrippa had repaired the sewers, adding '700 basins, not to speak of 500 fountains and 130 *castella*'. The latter were the *castella divisiorum*, reservoirs that received water from the aqueducts and then divided it among different channels to public fountains, private houses, and public facilities including baths. Their purpose was functional, but Agrippa had still made provision to decorate the facilities with '300 bronze or marble statues and 400 marble pillars'. The whole project allegedly took a year.[40]

Pliny was particularly struck by the contrast between the modest houses 'of those who made this Empire great, who went straight from plough or hearth to conquer nations and win triumphs, whose lands occupied less space than the sitting rooms' of Caligula and Nero.[41] Their palaces 'surrounded the whole city'.

As a man of scientific leanings (at least by the standards of his day), Pliny was most fascinated by the extraordinary achievement of the sewer network fed by seven rivers that had been made to combine into one as they tumbled downhill. The force of their currents drove all of Rome's effluent out, but sometimes met the huge back pressure of floodwater in the Tiber. Even then the sewers did not collapse. They resisted earthquakes, and the pressure from above caused by collapsing buildings falling down or disintegrating when compromised by fire.

AQUEDUCTS

Rome was served by aqueducts that channelled a constant flow of fresh water 'in such quantities that veritable rivers flow through the city and the sewers'.[42] These fed countless street corner fountains of the type still to be seen at Pompeii and Herculaneum.

The Aqua Virgo began flowing in 19 BC after having been built by the energetic and ever-resourceful Agrippa, tapping springs 8 Roman miles out of the city that rose on the estate of a man called Lucullus. The story behind its name was that soldiers hunting for water were directed by a young girl to the marshy spot where the springs emerged. They followed her directions and discovered that not only was she correct but there was also a 'vast quantity of water'. To commemorate this, a small temple was built there and embellished with a painting of the occasion. Roman hydraulic engineering made tapping the water possible by using concrete to build an enclosure wall around the swamp. This contained the waters, allowing them to rise to a point from which they could be taken off and sent flowing down the aqueduct to Rome, joined along the way by other streams to maximize the flow.

Although aqueducts are always pictured today as stately arcades of arches supporting the channel, they were often carried in part underground, depending on the lie of the land. In the Aqua Virgo's case just over 90 per cent of its length was subterranean, and only 5 per cent was carried on arches.[43] Nonetheless, the remains of Rome's above-ground aqueducts bear witness to the colossal engineering feats involved in making Rome's growth possible. No wonder, then, that Sextus Julius Frontinus, who was placed in charge of Rome's aqueducts by Nerva (96–8), contrasted them with the 'idle pyramids, or the useless (but famous) works of the Greeks'.[44]

There were teams of imperial slaves known as *aquarii* (watermen) allocated to maintaining the aqueducts outside Rome and other teams who looked after the installations within the city as they brought the water down into private houses of the rich, public fountains, and the baths. One gang which was inherited from the Republic numbered 240 slaves, the other had 460 and was created under Claudius, both made up of specialist trades. Until reforms were brought in under Nerva they were being constantly diverted to private work for profit. Their costs were covered by rentals of water rights, which included their wages (*commoda*), showing that although they were slaves, they did receive an income.[45]

The aqueducts required not only constant maintenance, but also measurement of flow rates and quantities. The Aqua Claudia produced the strongest flow but that, of course, made it also the most susceptible to wear and tear. There were other problems. The flow was reduced by water being taken off through legitimate grants for private use. When Frontinus ordered an inspection, he found that around 28 per cent was being siphoned off illegally with other inconsistencies caused by fraud in the way the flow was measured. Frontinus found theft going on from other aqueducts.[46]

This magnificent resource was being systematically ripped off almost all the way along its length by those who lived in its vicinity. They were helped by the aqueduct workers obligingly tapping into the main watercourses for private use in return for backhanders. Their rackets included installing a new supply when a legal right to draw water was transferred to someone else. The watermen kept the old supply open and sold the water off for themselves. It also turned out that many landowners were also diverting the flow 'to water their gardens' to such an extent that the depredations were slowing the supply to public fountains and facilities to almost nil.

To his dismay, Frontinus discovered that 'irrigated fields, inns, garret accommodation, and even brothels' were helping themselves, usually with permanent fixtures to make sure they never ran dry, the fraud being concealed in some cases by using false names. These fixtures were installed by puncturers, *punctis*, men who were responsible for networks of secret pipes running under the pavements to all the various businesses.[47] In the event, though, it seems there were no prosecutions. It would, after all, have been extremely difficult either to pursue legal action, or to institute the level of monitoring and security to prevent the thefts carrying on. Nerva (96–8) adopted a lateral solution: he legitimized the illegal drawings by simply declaring them to be a state benefit, though it was necessary for anyone wanting to take water to apply for a grant from the emperor, such grants being not transferable to subsequent owners of the property. Nevertheless, the old abuses were stamped out, with the bonus being the great deal of lead that was recovered from illegal branch pipes.[48]

THE DAY THE EMPEROR CAME

A remarkable description of Rome survives from just after the middle of the fourth century AD. By then ancient Rome's greatest monuments dominated the skyline, the city now a vast accretion of ceaseless building, demolition, fire, and rebuilding. It is the wreckage of this Rome that exists today, still dominating the centre of the modern city and forever popping up in modern construction projects like the extension of the metro system.

Among the visitors to Rome in the year 357 was Constantius II. He had already been emperor for two decades. His name and likeness were known across the Empire from Britain to Egypt, mainly from a ubiquitous bronze coin issue jubilantly announcing 'the restoration of happy times'.[49] This was his first visit to the greatest city in his world. Luckily for us, the historian Ammianus Marcellinus was on hand to document this momentous event. Constantius might have been the most powerful individual in the Roman Empire but for one day at least he might as well have been almost anyone who had arrived by sea at the port near Ostia and travelled up the road, or the Tiber, to enter Rome.

Constantius steeled himself with a fixed and motionless gaze as befitted an absolute monarch.[50] Once within the city's walls he could contain himself no longer and dropped his guard. He had turned into a tourist like any ordinary mortal for he was, according to Ammianus, 'dazzled by the array of marvellous sights'. Constantius passed vast baths, the Colosseum, and the imperial forums where he reached the

Forum of Trajan and 'stood fast with amazement' at an achievement so staggering Ammianus thought it unsurpassable. Constantius was left with the challenge of how he could possibly add to what he had seen. He resolved that all he could do was erect in the Circus Maximus the largest Egyptian obelisk known, adding to Rome's suite of imperial trophies (see Chapter 12).

Constantius saw the city at its greatest height when most of the major public buildings and monuments were in place. He was acutely aware that they had all played a part in Rome's great story, just as every ordinary Roman knew. Who had built them, and when, and why was of enormous significance, and so was what had happened there. The ghosts of the Roman past were everywhere. There were the Gemonian Stairs down which the executed body of Sejanus, Tiberius' over-ambitious praetorian prefect, was hurled in 31, and the Colosseum in which Commodus had competed as a gladiator, to the eternal shame of his office. Julius Caesar was assassinated in the porticus beside the Theatre of Pompey. Caligula had set himself up in the Temple of Castor and Pollux for passers-by to worship as a god. Nero threw vast and extravagant parties replete with unprecedented debauchery. Vespasian and his son Titus staged the great triumph through the streets to celebrate their victory of the Jewish War, and demolished Nero's Golden House palace to build the Colosseum. At the Praetorian Camp the imperial bodyguard auctioned off the Empire on a day in 193 that would go down in infamy.

MONEY AND ITS ODDITIES

After pottery, Roman coinage forms the largest body of surviving portable physical evidence for the era. Although Rome was using coins by the third century BC, it was not until the Second Punic War (218–201 BC) that the system became regularized. The new coinage introduced the silver denarius and the silver sestertius, worth a quarter of a denarius, along with a wider system of smaller denominations. The denarius was similar in size and weight to an Attic (Athenian) drachma; some Roman writers used the term interchangeably.[51]

The exigencies of intensive and sustained warfare had made a reliable and regular coinage system essential. The money was needed to pay soldiers and for supplies and war contracts. Warfare, and thus the army, therefore played the first and permanent long-term role in monetizing the Roman world. Originally made from available stocks of bullion, personal contributions of silver items and spoil, the silver coins were later manufactured in astronomical quantities from mined silver in the territories Rome had seized.

The everyday monetization of Roman society is well illustrated with examples from Pompeii and the surrounding area. The Pompeian freedman banker Lucius Caecilius Iucundus handed over the sum of 1,652 sesterces on 14 July 58 during the reign of Nero for the second year's rental of a fullery (laundry) in a five-year period. The money was paid to a slave of the colony of Pompeii called Privatus and equates to approximately 4.5 sesterces per day.[52] Since 5 sesterces per day would have worked out at 1,825 over the year, 1,652 sesterces (about 90 per cent) probably represented a discount. That is as far as we can take the example since we have no idea what the daily turnover of a fullery was, or any other costs incurred in the rental agreement.

Pompeii also offers us the chance to see the coinage in use frozen in time. Or, rather, it would, had more of the thousands of coins recovered been recorded in precise contexts. Nevertheless, enough is known to paint a picture of a town where base-metal coinage was used on an everyday basis to facilitate countless small transactions, for example in a streetside bar. Gold and silver were far more likely to be used for portable wealth storage. These were the coins chosen when people tried to escape the eruption, assuming, of course, that they possessed gold and silver coins in the first place. One escapee who had taken refuge at Oplontis, close to Pompeii, had taken two bags of coins. The first had eighty-one brand new gold *aurei* (a considerable sum equal at the time to the annual pay of sixteen legionaries or enough to buy three slaves with change) of Vespasian, while the other was made up of Republican silver coins. These were by then a century old but were made of a higher level of silver purity than the coins issued under the early emperors. Apart from bags and pouches, the Romans (who did not have pockets) used a variety of small boxes, some with sliding lids, to carry coins around with them, or wore bronze armbands with an integral coin container.

A bar in one of Pompeii's main commercial streets had been abandoned along with 1,485 base-metal coins which were clearly made up of takings and the till float.[53] Since some of those who lived in Pompeii or in the area and were wealthy enough to have gold and silver were unfortunately killed, it has been possible to recover some of the caches of gold and silver coins that they were desperate to rescue. Under more normal archaeological conditions these bullion coins are scarce discoveries (for obvious reasons) and usually only found either in unrecovered hoards or as single losses, with gold being particularly rare. Within a household, especially the better-off ones, high-value coins might be stored in a sturdy chest in the *tablinum*, the room between the *atrium* and the peristyle, or concealed in jars or pots and buried somewhere. Hoarding was a habitual activity, as the only reasonably secure way of concealing liquid wealth. Hoards were added to, or coins removed from, according to needs. Roman coin hoards found today are those left behind because their owners were prevented by circumstance, forgetfulness, or death from recovering them.

Basic arithmetic was an essential part of education, given the coinage and weights and measures systems. The main currency unit of exchange was the sestertius, and for the most part transactions were recorded in *sestertii* (English: sesterces). During the Republic the sestertius was only briefly issued as a small silver coin (between c. 211 and 208 BC), tariffed at 2½ copper asses and as ¼ of a silver denarius (there being 10 asses to the denarius, the origin of the name *deni aeris*, 'ten asses of copper').[54] There were 25 denarii to the gold *aureus* but in practice both silver and gold circulated at a premium, with commission charged by moneychangers to convert base metal denominations into bullion.

By the reign of Augustus, the sestertius and as had been re-tariffed. There were now 4 sesterces to the denarius and therefore 16 asses to the denarius, but the names remained unchanged. The sestertius was equal to 2 *dupondii* or 4 asses, and even the as had its own half (*semis*) and quarter (*quadrans*). The terminology was archaic. In the days of the emperors a denarius might have been worth 16 asses, but its name still referred to its old value of 10 asses. Dupondius meant 'two weights', referring obliquely to the fact that an as was short for *assipondium*, which meant a 'copper unit by weight' (as came from *aes*, 'copper') and had once been represented by a pound of bronze. Dupondius thus meant 'two pounds (of bronze)', even though by imperial times it was an ordinary sized coin weighing about 13 g.

The name of the sestertius was even more obtusely outdated. The word translates as 'the third part being a ½ [semis]', belonging to the time when a sestertius had been worth 2½ asses.[55] The only possible equivalent way of understanding this is if the old British half-crown (worth 2½ shillings) had been re-tariffed at 4 shillings but remained called a half-crown. A sum in sesterces was abbreviated to two vertical strokes II followed by an S, thus creating a representation of its original meaning. The two vertical strokes were usually joined with a central horizontal line that ran on to the S and to us looks like HS. None of these peculiarities was likely to confuse or trouble the Romans at all since the words were just part of everyday parlance and were used without thought.

The use of the sestertius as an accounting term was an established convention. Although sesterces were ubiquitous as circulating coins, under the emperors they were large and cumbersome (typically 30–33 mm in diameter and weighing around 27 g, whereas a denarius was around 18 mm and weighed about 3.1 g but was worth four times as much). Caecilius Iucundus' fullery rental bill of 1,652 sesterces mentioned above was equivalent to exactly 413 silver denarii. He is far more likely to have paid it in silver or gold (or both), which was probably routine for large sums. In his case the choice was between around 44 kg in brass coins or just 1.3 kg in silver. Even more weight could be saved by gold for which just 16 gold *aurei* (c. 120 g, struck at ⅟₆₀ lb) plus the balance in 13 denarii would have been sufficient.

Forging was endemic, making it even more essential that the average Roman was familiar with the weight and appearance of coins. Silver coins were a favourite target because they were more profitable to fake. One method was to create moulds from a genuine denarius and then cast copies in base metal which were plated with silver obtained by melting down other genuine coins. Another technique was to place a thin leaf of silver foil over a coin and press it into soft lead, creating a facsimile of that side of the coin in silver. The technique was repeated with the other side, providing a forger with two pieces of silver foil which were joined with solder, the void being filled with base metal. In a world with cheap, and usually, servile labour forging can make economic sense, especially with the vast difference in intrinsic value between base metal and bullion coins. The Romans were canny, though. It is clear from archaeological site finds that they took care to spend the fakes that came their way since these are far more common as singleton finds in marketplaces and similar locations, than in hoards for which they were usually spurned in favour of good coins. Pliny said that fake coins had become a popular subject for study, to the extent that forgeries could cost a collector more than the genuine article.[56]

The end of conquering new territory came in the early second century. In an economy where growth and wealth depended on seizing resources from elsewhere, this created inevitable problems. A shortage of bullion and an increasingly greedy and volatile soldiery led to the state debasing the currency. In the third century the denarius was gradually replaced by a double-denarius coin (the so-called *antoninianus*) with less silver than two denarii in it. In a few decades the silver content even of this had been dropped to virtually zero as inflation gradually drifted out of control. Gold coinage became elusive. The process of decline was slow enough that most people would not have noticed on a weekly or monthly basis. But by the fourth century the average Roman was being confronted with a litany of failed attempts at reforming the coinage, sometimes involving the overnight discovery that an issue had been abruptly devalued.[57] Gold had been successfully reformed with the new standard *solidus* ($\frac{1}{72}$ lb) but silver had almost disappeared. By then small change consisted of vast numbers of individually almost worthless bronze coins that probably circulated by weight in bags.

For all its peculiarities and incongruities, Roman coinage represents a rare way in which we can feel and hold something from the Roman world that has usually changed little in appearance. A brass sestertius dropped on a table today sounds as it would have done in Rome, and in the hand creates the same sensation of weight. Most coins of all denominations from the reign of Caligula on bear a portrait of the reigning emperor, and sometimes members of his family, communicating their likenesses to everyone. For those who could read, the coins bore abbreviated imperial titles, slogans, and sometimes records of events together with representations of gods, personifications, symbols, buildings, records of military victories, and other important cultural imagery.

Monetization therefore affected almost everyone and meant almost everyone had access to the marketplace, and the ability to accumulate through saving, at however modest a level. The Roman world was scarcely an egalitarian place but when it came to the availability of coinage and a universally recognized system open to all it came closest.

Throughout this book are dozens of examples of what it was like to live in Rome, Ostia, Pompeii, and Herculaneum. It is easy to build up a picture in Rome's case of an ancient version of Gotham City riven with problems like dangerous housing, political corruption, riots, public executions and murders, the cruelty and oppression meted out on slaves, streets filled with footpads and other threats. Those were all part of life in ancient Rome.

There was another side, and it goes a long way to explaining why people lived in Rome. The city offered work, places to live, and security. There was the prospect of the grain dole, free public entertainment on an unprecedented scale, and other handouts. While that entertainment included the gore of the gladiator fights and the mass killing of prisoners and animals, it also included the exhilaration of the chariot races, the comfort of the baths, and the elegant peace of the public porticus with their gardens and other facilities. Rome also offered relatively clean water and sanitation of a standard not to be seen again in European cities until the 1800s. There was also the sense of excitement and pride to be had from living in the most glamorous and successful place in the known world. Above all, living in Rome and being Roman had become a state of mind.

2

THE ROMAN MINDSET

For the Roman people I have set neither boundaries nor time
limits; I have given them empire without end.

Jupiter's promise to Aeneas[1]

S
allust, writing in the mid-first century BC, was intrigued by how
the Romans had achieved their success. 'As I read and heard of
the many illustrious deeds of the Roman people at home and
abroad, on land and sea, it chanced that I was seized by a strong desire
to find out what quality in particular had been the foundation of such
great exploits.' His conclusion was that it all came down to the 'emi-
nent merit of a few citizens', only for the state subsequently to have
'become demoralized by extravagance and sloth'.[2]

In every direction, down every street and alley, marketplace and
porticus, the people of Rome were confronted by layers of time. It
was impossible for them to imagine when Rome did not exist and nor
did they try to. For them the past and present stood side by side and
encased them in a robust but illusory sense of permanence, self-belief,
and destiny.

Livy began his history of Rome with the observation that, unless he
was deceiving himself, 'no state was ever greater, none more righteous
or richer in good examples, none ever was where greed and luxury
came into the social order so late, or where poverty and frugality

47

were so greatly and for so long held in honour'.[3] Such sentiments had become a familiar trope. The Roman sense of self was thus founded on a feeling of unassailable probity and moral superiority, couched in terms of a chauvinistic patriotism found in many other times and places. A consequence of this culture was the admiration felt by the Romans for their heroic ancestors and a romanticization of their rural origins. This was unlike our own time when wallowing in guilt for wrongs, real or imagined, committed by our predecessors is a dominant theme.

Understanding how the Romans thought and what they believed about themselves helps explain why they behaved as they did. Predestination and entitlement were enshrined in a mythologized history and religious dogma. The city lay at the heart of that identity. Theirs was a strictly hierarchical society founded on a presumption of pre-eminence, but it was also based on a notion of the purity of Roman origins. Florus said that 'the Roman people during the seven hundred years from the time of King Romulus down to that of Caesar Augustus, achieved so much in peace and war, that if a man were to compare the greatness of their empire with its years, he would consider its size out of all proportion to its age'. With a straight face, he went on to describe the 150 years before the reign of Augustus as the time when Rome 'pacified the whole world', ignoring the endless wars of conquest and civil wars of what had been probably Rome's most bloody era.[4] He was, of course, making a rhetorical declamation, or in our terms spouting the official line.

SONS OF THE SOIL

Roman writers loved to celebrate the great men of the Roman past who spurned luxury and indulgence and bemoaned the decadence of their own times when wealth and consumption had become the only measures of success. They exulted in a fantasy of the good old days, a paradise when Rome's farmers, their hands encrusted with grime, dropped their ploughs to pick up swords and fight a war for freedom and security and then returned to the fields.

'It is from the farming class that the bravest men and the sturdiest soldiers come, their calling is most highly respected', so said Marcius Porcius Cato (Cato the Elder). Cato lived from 234 to 149 BC, witnessing the privations of the Second Punic War in his youth and the explosion in wealth that followed Rome's victory. By the second half of his life Rome's momentum had become unstoppable. This venerable old statesman was esteemed in Roman culture for his strict adherence to the old virtues of modesty and restraint, and his rejection of any degenerate habits, particularly anything that smacked of being 'Greek'.[5] Appropriately enough, among his many published works was a treatise on farming. It was practical in structure and dedicated to the idea that agriculture was the most respectable way to make money. More than 250 years later Martial said of a scythe, 'the settled peace of our Emperor has bent me to unwarlike uses. Now I belong to the husbandman, formerly I belonged to the soldier.'[6]

Those rural values were inextricably linked in the Roman mindset. It was precisely because their forebears had worked hard and done so persistently in the face of adversity while remaining honourable that had made them so admired, not least because this culture had produced Rome's great military leaders. Their heroic exploits had not only protected the city from its enemies but also led on directly to the conquest of Italy and beyond.

Honourable Roman women were chaste and modest (a quality known as *pudicitia*). Women's position in society was firmly fixed below that of men. According to Cicero the principle had been established by the ancestors that, thanks to their 'feebleness of judgement', women should always be under the power of guardians.[7] They were expected to commit suicide, or their families to kill them, if their honour was questioned. If they escaped that fate, their duty was to churn out children. Women were simultaneously regarded as potentially weak and susceptible, easily falling prey to the temptations of luxuries, widely believed in Roman male society to be a uniquely feminine failing – a man inclined that way was damned for being effeminate. This moral anxiety plagued elite Roman society.

As the city grew, many among the elite embarked on a self-indulgent yearning for the 'good old days' and country life. This became a common trope in their writings but many of the elite in the late Republic presided over large slave-run country estates, often amassed by evicting peasant farmers. The latter had been especially susceptible to losing their land when they were called up to fight in Rome's wars during the third to first centuries BC and were away for months or years. Although this was illegal, rampant corruption and greed among the elite had made sure they got away with it. Reformers, like the tribune Tiberius Gracchus in 133 BC, were liable to be murdered by those with vested interests.

Several generations later, Cicero's (see pp. 136 ff) career in law and politics tied him for extended periods in the city during some of the most decisive events in Roman history. He idolized farming 'in which I find incredible delight', looking back with admiration at the self-discipline of senators who had lived on their farms and believing it to be a way of life best suited for a wise man. These senators had to be summoned to Rome by messengers to attend the Senate. Such were the distances involved that the messengers were called *viatores*, 'travellers'. Cicero recalled the time when the senator Cincinnatus was ploughing fields when he was told he had been elected to the dictatorship, and how other senators were back in those days summoned *a villa*, 'from the farmhouse'.[8]

Cicero was hardly likely to have engaged in much of the farming himself. He was wealthy and had a large complement of slaves. The scene was set for satire, and the poet Horace weighed in appropriately. He mocked a moneylender who escaped into his rural bolthole to prune plants, shear sheep, store honey, and pick pears and grapes, but no sooner had extolled the virtues of his agricultural bliss than he called in his loans and then set out to find more people to lend the funds to.[9] On another occasion, though, Horace said 'what you seek is here at Ulubrae, if a balanced state of mind doesn't escape you', perhaps more colloquially in English 'everything you need is at Ulubrae if you can keep a sense of proportion'.[10] Ulubrae, a rural town about 30 miles or 50 km from Rome, had become a synonym for an escape to the country, a bolthole that was capable of providing all the important things in life. Horace's point was that those bent on escaping Rome by travelling to exotic places overseas had no need to go so far – real pleasure and fulfilment was to be had only down the road. A century later Martial sneered at Sparsus, a man so wealthy that he could afford a palatial establishment in Rome containing all the pleasures of the countryside, by coining the famous phrase *rus in urbe*, 'countryside in the city'.[11]

As far as Cicero was concerned, by the 60s BC Rome had become a place only interested in the prospect of fleecing 'rich and flourishing cities' by coming up with spurious pretexts for declaring war against 'foreign nations'.[12] When he wrote Rome had enjoyed almost two centuries of practice in harvesting the wealth and resources of the lands seized in war or bequeathed by rulers who believed Roman rule was the least damaging prospect for their nations' futures. In practice this meant acquiring agricultural produce, human labour, minerals, and stone. The acquisitive habit was engrained and was even applied to places that were not, on the face of it, lucrative prospects. The stability and security created by peace, enforced by the Roman army along with popular acquiescence and the mechanisms of provincial government, made it possible for provinces to be harvested more profitably. In these circumstances the necessary physical and administrative infrastructure could be developed. That included an extensive roadwork and the Mediterranean Sea which were essential to the movement of goods. The Roman state's demands for tribute and taxation also played an important role in encouraging the growth of markets and exchange.

Rome's acquisitiveness accelerated after the Second Punic War (218–201 BC). 'The more you take, the more it grows', said Cato the Elder.[13] He was only referring to a mountain of salt which lay close to the 'finest iron and silver mines' of Spain, captured by Rome during the war, but he might as well have been writing about almost any other aspect of the Roman economy over the next few centuries. The monumental scale on which the silver and lead mines of Roman Spain operated, witnessed, and described in astonishing detail by Polybius in the mid-second century BC, set the tone for other provinces.[14] The silver was needed by the Roman state to pay the army and the army conquered the provinces that provided more resources, including more silver.

PAST HEROES

In the well-known epic film *Spartacus*, the consul Marcus Licinius Crassus is shown in one scene at his house in Rome musing out loud to his slave Antoninus. The setting and the occasion were fictional, as was Antoninus, but the screenplay captured vividly the notion of Rome as a being, a living force above and beyond the insignificance of human beings. Crassus describes how Rome cannot be withstood by any man – the city must be served, and everyone must abase themselves and grovel before Rome, 'you must – love her.'

Although that scene is fanciful it encapsulates the sense that self-sacrifice for the sake of Rome was an integral part of Roman identity. The sentiment was authentically Roman and resonates with a speech composed by Dio, supposedly addressed to Pompey during the Cilician pirate crisis to encourage him to accept command of a force to clear the seas (see Chapter 9).

The tradition of past heroes and others whose qualities made them pre-eminent role models was well-established in Roman lore. In or around 508 BC in historical tradition, an Etruscan army had marched towards Rome, then protected by an early circuit of walls and the Tiber. The farmers, then engaged in tilling soil on the city's hinterland, downed their tools to transform themselves into soldiers and made their way to take up arms to defend Rome. There was a potentially disastrous weak point in the defences: the Sublician Bridge over the Tiber.

The Etruscans under Lars Porsena arrived at the Janiculum Hill on the west bank of the Tiber which they seized and prepared to make their assault across the bridge and into the city. A Roman farmer-soldier, Horatius Cocles, had been posted on the bridge as a sentry. Horatius yelled out orders to destroy the bridge while he held it. He advanced to the western end of the bridge to hold it singlehandedly, but two of his compatriots, shamed by his heroism, joined him. They were forced back as the onslaught began and Horatius told them to leave. Horatius provoked the Etruscans into a rage by insulting them as the slaves of kings. As one they hurled their spears at him which he caught with his shield. The Etruscans charged but at that moment the demolition work was finished, and the bridge collapsed. Horatius prayed to Father Tiber, the god of the river, to receive him and dived in and swam to safety. 'The immortal gods in admiration of his bravery kept him safe and sound.' Appropriately enough for such heroism Horatius, and his 'love for all the fatherland', was awarded all the land he could farm.[15]

A statue of Horatius was erected on the old bridge to commemorate this event and remind every Roman who crossed what had happened there. The figure was still standing in Vespasian's time: Pliny recorded it in a list of statues of past heroes who had been similarly honoured.[16] A century after that Florus described Horatius as one of the prodigies and miracles of that war, who included Cloelia, a woman handed to Porsena as a hostage but who escaped and made her way back to Rome by swimming over the Tiber on horseback. 'Today', he said, 'were it not for the fact that they are recorded in our annals, they would be regarded as fantastic', by which he seems to mean they would have seemed like implausibly fabulous characters out of a heroic myth.[17]

Another favourite story was that of Gaius Mucius Cordus. He was the first of 300 Roman nobles prepared to be sent to assassinate Lars Porsena. He mistook Porsena's scribe for the king because they were similarly dressed and killed him instead. He was captured and brought before Porsena. Mucius Cordus next placed his right hand in a sacrificial fire, showing no sign of pain, and assured Porsena that men like himself had no concern for their own bodies when pursuing glory – he would die as resolutely as he would kill, and that the other 299 would follow until Porsena was dead. Appalled, Porsena sent Mucius Cordus back to the Romans and then sued for peace. Mucius Cordus was subsequently awarded the cognomen Scaevola ('left-handed'), because his right hand had been destroyed, which was passed down through his family.[18]

Rome had female heroes too, but they were measured by different standards. In the well-established legend Lucretia, wife of Lucius Tarquinius Collatinus, was raped by Sextus Tarquinius, son of Tarquinius Superbus, the last king of Rome, in c. 510 BC. Lucretia was then confronted by a family council but had brought along a concealed sword. She was so consumed by shame that she committed suicide on the spot. The fallout resulted in Superbus being forced off the throne and the Roman Republic established. Collatinus then served as one of the first consuls. Lucretia was described by Valerius Maximus as 'the leader of Roman chastity'. He considered her death to be so courageous that he could only explain it, typically for a Roman man, by claiming that a 'male soul' had been mistakenly planted in a woman's body.[19]

During the war with the Gauls which led to the humiliating sack of Rome in 390 BC, a Roman army was routed. The Gauls headed towards a city which now had no garrison. Nonetheless, in typically Roman fashion the debacle was turned into a story of heroism. 'It was then, as upon no other occasion, that the true Roman valour showed itself', Florus proudly recounted. Rome's elders met in the Forum, consecrated themselves and returned to their homes dressed in their robes of office and waited. There they would then die 'with proper dignity'. When the Gauls entered they found the elders in their senatorial robes and for a moment thought they were faced by gods and spirits. The elders sat there motionless and refused to say anything. Eventually the Gauls realized that they were confronted with ordinary human beings. They ran them through and burned their houses down before settling down to occupy Rome.[20]

Horatius and Lucretia, and the stoical senators, were seen by later Romans as the benchmark and as defining characteristics of what had made the city great. By the same token, dishonour could not only condemn an individual but also besmirch his whole family. 'The disgrace is not the same for a single man to receive the stigma of ignominy, as is the disgrace for a house full of children and grandchildren to be stained with infamy, for this bespattering with infamy defiles and disgraces many simultaneously', said the senator Marcus Cornelius Fronto to the emperor Marcus Aurelius.[21]

Publius Cornelius Scipio Africanus (236–183 BC) led Rome to victory in the decisive Second Punic War. By the mid-first century AD Scipio's career was as remote to us as the American War of Independence, but he was still held in the highest esteem. Seneca the Younger, Nero's tutor, paid a visit one day to Scipio's villa at Liternum in Campania. Seneca was transfixed by the tiny windowless bath chamber in which Scipio had used to wash himself in dirty water. He admired how an exhausted Scipio had cleaned off the sweat of farm work, including ploughing. Just in case his correspondent was horrified by the grubbiness and dinginess of the facility, Seneca reminded him that Scipio smelled of the 'army, farm work, and manliness'.[22]

DESTINY

By the late Republic, the city was the visible proof of Roman success. When a successful general was voted a triumph and paraded his success through the streets of Rome for several days on the trot, ordinary people might be the lucky beneficiaries of a free handout of goodies.[23] It was an easy step from such tangible evidence of success for the Romans to believe that their success was preordained. No wonder, then, that Vergil had Jupiter say in his epic poem the *Aeneid* that he promised an empire without limits in time or space.[24] At the time such a thought must have seemed plausible and even reasonable, at least to the Romans.

Not long after Vergil wrote those words about Rome's divinely sponsored entitlement to an unlimited empire, a physical monument of the fact was created for public display. The Porticus of Octavia in Rome boasted a map of the known world. The building had been begun by

Augustus' sister Octavia, using a design made by Agrippa. Augustus finished off the work.[25] The porticus was a major public facility and consisted of a large open rectangular space surrounded by colonnades behind which were rooms and buildings available for public use. There were several in Rome. Typically, the porticus featured among other facilities gardens, colonnades, libraries, dining rooms, and temples, and served as a venue for public leisure and entertainment. Pliny, who tells us about the map, went on to explain that Italy's role was 'to unite scattered empires' by bringing together all sorts of nations and people through a common language.[26] This sort of comment is important. It shows how Rome and the Romans wanted to depict themselves as not only favoured by the gods but also as a people who were doing everyone else a favour by amassing an empire.

FAKE HISTORY

The Roman world had a propensity for what is now called 'fake news', or at any rate 'fake history'. The earliest Roman historians were untroubled by this, and so it seems was everyone else, especially the elite. The result was historical fact buried and obscured by a suffocating weight of fanciful notions of family grandeur, personal and national achievements, allegorical events serving as metaphors for later times, anachronisms, and invention.

Later Roman historians were more sophisticated, but only up to a point. They recognized the problem but did little to overturn it. When Livy was writing his history of the Roman people in the late first century BC, he found it was a struggle to work out which (if any) of the accounts or authorities he had available to him for Rome's earlier history could be relied on. He concluded that none of them were trustworthy. In his research he was inconvenienced by the way families had manufactured traditions of the heroic deeds and high office held by their forebears.[27] Cicero had similar concerns, explaining that funeral orations were an important reason for Roman history becoming so distorted. These speeches were utilized by families to create all sorts of false claims to elite status and descent from celebrated ancestors, sometimes predicated on nothing more than the coincidence of a name.[28] The Fabii family even claimed descent from Hercules, but since Augustus and Julius Caesar posed as the descendants of Venus this sort of spurious lineage had become commonplace.

Those with the means and influence installed shield portraits of their ancestors in public places like temples, so that anyone passing by would be made aware of the family's great status. These curious images consisted of a three-dimensional sculpture of an ancestor's head and upper body projecting from a round or oval shield-shaped frame. The shield was a traditional motif that was supposed to symbolize the valour of the man depicted in the portrait. According to Pliny, the first to commission such pieces was the consul Appius Claudius Sabinus in 495 BC.[29]

Juvenal found this celebration of lineage ridiculous. 'What do pedigrees do?' he asked, and poked fun at those who tried to base their own worth on the achievements of their ancestors and displayed their painted portraits or battered busts with chipped features. 'What fruit will boasting a Corvinus [a famous general of the civil war of 68–9] on your ample family tree do, thereafter to trace through multiple branches grimy dictators and cavalry commanders?' he sneered, pointing out that a man could pack his hall with the wax images of his ancestors, but that virtue was the only true mark of nobility.[30]

THE PURSUIT OF PLEASURE

Rome had become 'burdened by its magnitude', said Livy.[31] The central dogma was the belief that the acquisition of an empire had come about because of the great and special qualities of the Romans under the auspices of divine providence which favoured the Romans because they were so special. Conquered nations, if they acquiesced, could share in this bounty, and were expected to be grateful. The paradox in this mindset was that their success had led the Romans not only to enormous wealth and unmatched power, but also to the contamination of the qualities that had made the Romans powerful (see Chapter 5 for Verres).

Livy was clear about when this sort of problem had begun. He looked back to the early second century BC when the Roman army first campaigned in Asia Minor (Turkey). That was when 'the first beginnings of foreign luxury were introduced into the city'. Incoming extravagances included costly fabrics, couches and other specialised furniture such as one-legged tables. Banqueting descended into decadence with haute couture cooks, a profession once derided as suitable only to the 'most worthless of slaves', and female musicians. These were, Livy warned darkly, trifling compared to what was to come, and proceeded to itemize the loot paraded through Rome by Gnaeus Manlius in his triumph of 187 BC.[32]

Marcus Acilius Glabrio, a plebeian and former tribune of the plebs (201 BC), had led the Roman forces to their victory at Thermopylae against the Seleukid king Antiochus III 'the Great' in 191 BC. He collected booty which was variously sold or divided between his men. His triumph included a display of 3,000 lb of uncoined silver, hundreds of thousands of Greek coins, and other bullion.[33] From there it was but a short leap to political corruption. In 189 BC Glabrio used his funds as handouts to potential voters when he stood for censor, placing 'a considerable number of men under obligation to him', outraging some of the patricians who regarded him as a plebeian upstart and not worthy of such an office.

An attempt to prosecute Glabrio followed. Cato accused Glabrio of keeping a considerable amount of the booty for himself and not placing it in the triumph. As Livy acidly observed, since Cato was a rival candidate for the censorship his argument was undermined. Glabrio pulled out of the election, evading a hefty fine because no one would then vote on it. Just before the battle at Thermopylae (191 BC), Glabrio had also vowed to build a Temple of Pietas in the Forum Holitorium (vegetable market). He proceeded to do this by arrangement with the Senate and included a gilded statue of his father, 'the first to be set up in Italy'.[34]

A notorious episode came with the fall of Corinth in 146 BC to the general Lucius Mummius following his defeat of the Achaean League. What followed was a classic example of Roman despoliation of a city, but in this instance it went a stage beyond destroying Corinth and selling the population into slavery by engaging in the wholesale theft of works of art.[35] Mummius 'now took possession of their arms, all the offerings that were consecrated in the temples, the statues, paintings, and whatever other ornaments they had … he sold the inhabitants, confiscated the land, and demolished all the walls and buildings'.[36]

The purpose was punitive and precautionary to prevent a recurrence of Corinth leading another federation of cities, but the removal of artworks smacked of an arrogant and greedy need to acquire 'instant' culture. In any case a large number were destroyed on the spot, some even being used to throw dice on by soldiers. A painting of Dionysus by the artist Aristides survived, subsequently displayed in the Temple of Ceres in Rome until that building was accidentally burned down. Some of what Mummius took must have been placed in the Temple of Hercules he dedicated in Rome. Other works were freely given away by him, since he cared little for art himself, to locations in Rome and in the country beyond, Strabo commenting that 'the most and best of the other dedicatory offerings' in Rome came from the sack of Corinth by Mummius.[37] A legend grew up that the fires in Corinth were so intense they accidentally created a new form of bronze made out of copper alloyed with gold and silver. 'Corinthian bronze' as it was known became highly desirable in Rome, with both the corrupt governor Verres and his prosecutor Cicero allegedly being particularly susceptible.[38]

Sulla laid on magnificent public banquets, but the ostentatious over-catering reached absurd proportions with vast quantities of meat being wasted and having to be thrown into the Tiber.[39] The profligate became addicted to an array of collecting and fads. Rock crystal became a particular favourite, one woman who was not especially wealthy paying out 150,000 sesterces for a single ladle made from it. The value was vested in rock crystal being irreparable if broken. Another highly sought-after material was the mysterious substance myrrhine, its nature now unknown, used to make expensive tableware.[40]

Josephus said that Caligula 'left none [of the Greek temples] unpillaged'. He demanded that paintings, sculptures, and any other statues and offerings be seized from the temples, justifying his actions by saying it was 'not right that beautiful objects should stand anywhere but in the most beautiful place, and that was the city of Rome'. Caligula had to draw a line at the statue of Zeus at Olympia, created by Phidias. The engineers who had been told to remove it reported that it would disintegrate if moved. Caligula was informed by letter but before he could erupt in murderous rage he had been assassinated.[41] The statue no longer exists, having been destroyed in antiquity. Lollia Paulina, who was married to Caligula for six months in 38, all but outdid her husband. Pliny said she turned up to an ordinary betrothal banquet wearing jewellery worth 40 million sesterces, apparently acquired by her grandfather through bribes and gifts in the East.[42]

Trophy hunting had become a way of life for the Romans. Rome was embellished with works of art and valuables ransacked from one defeated enemy after another. Had the Romans ever been barracked by their victims to return the booty to its rightful cultural owners, as happens more and more in our own time, Rome would have faced being emptied out.

The elite in early Rome, or at any rate a vocal part of it, were traumatized by how their mighty city and its people had descended into self-indulgence. Velleius Paterculus, writing during the reign of Tiberius (14–37), was convinced that while Rome had feared the rival power of Carthage the city and its people had been vigilant and dedicated to military readiness. With Carthage defeated at the end of the Second Punic War, Rome gave way to idleness and pleasure. Investment in public magnificence was followed by private luxury. 'The old discipline had been abandoned in favour of the new order', he moaned.[43]

Paterculus would have frothed at the sight of the tomb of a freedman *purpurarius* called Gaius Pupius Amicus, a member of a profession devoted to the expensive and exclusive practice of dying clothes purple, the ultimate expression of high status.[44] The tomb of Pupius Amicus was found at Parma in northern Italy. This suggests he was servicing a wider popular market among those who, despite the law restricting its use to those of senatorial status, had decided to adopt the trappings of a social class to which they did not belong. More to the point, they could evidently afford to, and the tomb's proud epitaph was its owner's way of flaunting his aspirant market. Petronius' *Satyricon* depicts the freedman Trimalchio also flaunting his five gold rings which only those of senatorial and equestrian (Rome's secondary aristocratic tier, based on a lower property qualification, originally based on the ability to provide a horse when fulfilling military service) status were allowed to wear, as well as the 'broad purple stripe'. Cato would have turned in his grave.[45]

The orator Quintilian was appalled by the obsession with grooming and cosmetics, instead of being satisfied with a natural appearance:

> There are even some who are captivated by the shams of artifice and think that there is more beauty in those who pluck out superfluous hair or use depilatories, who dress their locks by scorching them with the curling iron and glow with a complexion that is not their own, than can ever be conferred by nature pure and simple, so that it really seems as if physical beauty depended entirely on moral hideousness.[46]

By the late first century Tacitus had come up with a new twist. Rome's barbarian enemies were to be admired for staying true to the principles Rome had once so proudly espoused. He created a speech which he put into the mouth of a fictitious Caledonian chieftain in Britain called Calgacus, when describing the war in Britain during the period 78–84:

> Robbers of the World — now they search the sea after all their ravaging has exhausted the land. If the enemy is rich, they are greedy.

If he is poor, they are ambitious. Neither East nor West has satisfied them. Alone among men they covet wealth and poverty with equal passion. To plunder, slaughter, and steal they falsely call ordered rule, and where they make desolation, they call it peace.

This verdict on the Roman world was irremediably bleak, but it was deliberately so.[47] The setting was the preamble to the final battle in the campaign into the far north of Britain led by Agricola, the general and governor of Britain who was also Tacitus' father-in-law. The year was 84, three years after the accession of Domitian, forty-one years since the Roman conquest of Britain had begun, and more than three centuries since Rome had burst out of the Italian peninsula to seize Sicily and become the principal predatory international power of the ancient world. The speech was a rhetorical device Tacitus had utilized to give his readers a moral lesson in how Rome had lost its core values, but it also depicts how Roman ambition came at a huge price for its victims.

Well over a century later, Cassius Dio stuck to the same theme. He described the Romans as being taken over by the faults and weaknesses of the people they had conquered, tainted by exposure to 'Asiatic luxury . . . thus, this terrible influence, starting in that quarter, invaded the city as well'.[48]

None of this elitist navel-gazing is likely to have troubled most of the ordinary population of Rome. As far as they were concerned, they lived in the epicentre of international power and wealth, enjoying the unlimited benefits of Empire. If that meant handouts of booty, money, food, and other trinkets that was fine. It was left to poets like Tibullus to ruminate on how 'it is not love but booty that this age of iron praises'.[49]

THE MAKING OF AN EMPEROR

A popular misconception about the Roman world is that it was run with ruthless efficiency, characterized especially by images of the army with its serried ranks of legionaries. Countless other incongruities and inconsistencies existed throughout Roman society and they began right at the top. The real genius was in making such a system work and this is another important aspect of understanding the Roman mindset.

In 57 BC one family's self-interest overturned an important tradition by twisting the law. On this occasion it involved a priesthood. Dio recorded the incident, commenting on the damage done. 'Although the law expressly forbade any two persons of the same clan to hold the same priesthood at the same time, Spinther, the consul, was anxious to place his son Cornelius Spinther among the *augures*, and since Faustus, the son of Sulla, of the Cornelian gens, had been enrolled before him, he transferred his son to the gens of Manlius Torquatus. Thus, though the letter of the law was observed, its spirit was broken.'[50] There are many other recorded instances, running all the way from country towns to how Rome was ruled.

There was not even any such thing as a 'Roman emperor', in the sense of there being a formal title to that effect. The position did not exist, at least not in any constitutional sense. The closest was *imperator*, which gives us the word emperor, but that meant 'commander-in-chief' or 'general'. It was a military acclamation and originally had no connotations of supreme executive and monarchical power. Imperator was related to *imperium*, the temporary power of military command granted by the Senate to a consul.

When Octavian's fleet defeated Antony and Cleopatra at the Battle of Actium in 31 BC, he became the most powerful man in the most powerful state in the ancient world. He took the wreckage of the Republican constitution and created one of the most ambiguous political systems in world history. He adapted what he found, and had indeed already been part of himself, rather than creating a radical new system. Octavian said he was appealing to tradition, and the customs of the Roman people's ancestors (the *mos maiorum*, 'the ways of the greats'). That went hand in hand with his claim to be restoring the rule of law.

The Roman people, including the Senate, willingly accepted his rule. Octavian 'enticed everyone with the pleasantness of peace', said

Tacitus.[51] Octavian's position was, in a constitutional sense contradictory. Since he claimed to be restoring tradition, he could not openly declare himself to be a monarch. Nor could he obliterate the power of the senators since along with the Roman people they formed the body politic of the Roman state, the *res publica*. Had he done so, he would have faced conspiracies to topple him and indeed he did not eliminate this threat entirely. Octavian had to find a way in which the Senate could appear to be in possession of all its traditional powers and prerogatives, while simultaneously ensuring that his authority over the state was unchallenged.

Octavian's solution was to be granted powers by the Senate on an individual and temporary basis. These, of course, were renewable. By fragmenting his monarchical power that way, Octavian disguised its collective totality in a novel manifestation of the Republic. In 27 BC the name Augustus was proposed for him by the Senate. This elevated him to a level above all others, his personal *auctoritas* (authority) outclassing that of all other men. Augustus meant 'the revered one' and it defined his unique status with its vague allusion to a quasi-religious identity. The term *princeps* neatly contained this paradox by labelling him as a 'first among equals'. Augustus had become to all intents and purposes what we called an emperor, though he took care never to describe himself as such. The pretence fooled no one, and everyone was content to be fooled.

For the historian Cassius Dio, writing two centuries later, the situation was easy to understand. Augustus had complete power over the administration of the Roman Empire for the simple reason that he was in control of state revenues and the army. The point was a subtle one. The state revenues were just that – they were in public ownership but in practice they were spent as Augustus wanted.[52] Augustus himself explained how this was so. His personal rank and standing exceeded everyone else's even though he had no legal powers that exceeded his colleagues in any of the individual Republican magistracies.[53]

The force of Augustus' personality, position and the power he wielded through his control of the army and the public finances meant that 'the power both of the people and of the Senate passed entirely into the hands of Augustus, and from his time there was, strictly speaking, a monarchy . . . in order to preserve the appearance of having this power by virtue of the laws and not because of their own domination, the emperors have taken to themselves all the functions, including the titles, of the offices' of the Republic, said Dio.[54] Although all the features of the old Republican system carried on, including elections, 'nothing was done', he added, ' that did not meet with Augustus' approval'. Ironically, the only office omitted was that of dictator yet that was the one which an emperor's complete power in practice resembled. As Dio went on to note, the title *imperator* had come by his time two centuries after Augustus to indicate the independent authority of the emperors, regardless of whether they had ever fought in a war.

For some senators it was all too much. They wanted to go back to the good old days of 'liberty' and 'democracy', but even under Augustus there were none left who could remember far enough back to know whether any of that was true or had ever been. The myth proved to have long legs. After the assassination of Caligula in 41, his co-consul for that year, Gnaeus Sentius Saturninus, spotted his chance to make a stand. On the spur of the moment, he leaped to his feet to tell the Senate of his joy that liberty had been restored, even if for only a moment. 'One hour is enough to those that are exercised in virtue, wherein we may live with a mind accountable only to ourselves, in our own country, now free, and governed by such laws as this nation once flourished under.'[55]

Sentius Saturninus and his ilk did not see Augustus, Tiberius, and Caligula as members of a new order of ruler. They were, in his eyes, merely the latest manifestation in a sequence of ruling imperators who had gradually 'dissolved' the Roman version of democracy. One by one, he believed, they had subverted the law to rule at their own pleasure and thus create tyranny, with Caligula being the latest and worst example of the phenomenon. People were too scared, he said, to contradict the emperor and in the interests of living in peace had been willing to live 'like slaves'. Sentius Saturninus wanted Caligula's assassins celebrated and rewarded. All this was predicated on the Republican idyll of his imagination, though he conceded that the greatest days were long in the past and therefore impossible for him to remember.

In the heat of the moment, and clearly overcome by the occasion and his chance to shine as an idealist of the old school, Sentius Saturninus had forgotten that he had already sold out. While he romanced the Republic, he was wearing a ring with a gemstone bearing the image of Caligula. Another senator darted up to pull it off his finger and the image was promptly smashed on the spot, an interesting literary record of Roman *damnatio memoriae*. With all his dewy-eyed sentimentality, Sentius Saturninus was simply another manifestation of the elitist Roman buoyed up in the myth of the great Roman fantasy of its earlier days. In any case, the Republican ship had long sailed, and he could bleat all he liked. Within a few hours Claudius had been made emperor and the new order continued unabated.

The unique basis of Roman imperial rule was unlike the concept of monarchy which is more familiar to us from the medieval world. A Roman emperor occupied no such unassailable constitutional, inherited, and divinely sponsored position, at least not in any formal sense. This was precisely why someone like Sentius Saturninus saw the first three emperors as a succession of generals who had arbitrarily assumed supreme power. One story at least was put about that Augustus had been fathered by Apollo, and Augustus always took care to remind everyone he was the son of the deified Julius Caesar who had claimed descent himself from Venus via her son Aeneas.[56] Such claims aside, until well into the third century, 250 years after Augustus came to power, every emperor maintained the public impression that he was merely in possession of an unprecedented portfolio of magistracies and other honours which he held on a temporary basis from the Senate, and was serving as a guardian of the Republic. The Senate remained on paper the supreme authority, even if in practice this was a pretence.

During Augustus' reign the word imperator, abbreviated to IMP, began to gravitate on coins and inscriptions from being a subsidiary acclamation to the beginning of the titles. He referred to himself as 'Imperator, son of the deified Caesar' (IMP CAESAR DIVI F). This did not become routine until the reigns of Vespasian (69–79) and Titus (79–81). The result was that an emperor could be referred to with both the generic term imperator and the enumerated acclamation equivalent. The word imperator at the beginning of the legend had become part of the emperor's name. Since the word was in practice synonymous with Augustus' power to rule, it became the origin of our word emperor where the meaning of that power is enshrined solely within that label.

There was no historical work or manual which might have explained to Augustus or any of his successors how to operate as a supreme monarchical ruler within the Roman world, especially while avoiding any suggestion of trying to be a king. That was what had cost Caesar his life in 44 BC when he was assassinated soon after he accepted the title *dictator perpetuus* ('dictator for life'). The Republican constitution allowed for a temporary dictatorship during a national emergency but becoming one permanently was still unthinkable at the time and smacked of kingship.

The title imperator did not confer constitutional political authority on an emperor. That instead was managed in a strange permutation of the Republican constitution. During the Republic, tribunes of the plebs were elected annually. The position was created in 493 BC to placate the plebs and provide them with legal protection against the ruling patrician class in the form of two annually elected consuls (until 367 BC the consulship could only be held by patricians; thereafter it was also opened to the wealthiest plebs who fulfilled the property qualification). The tribunes defended the interests of the plebeians and had the power to propose legislation and veto the Senate's legislation. A tribune could also veto another tribune. In practice, tribunes were drawn from among those of senatorial rank (but only those of plebeian status). This meant that it was easy to pack the tribunate with senatorial stooges who could veto any tribune who set out to introduce reforms. Tribunes served for a year and during their term of office they were inviolate.

As an emperor Augustus did not serve as a tribune, and nor did any of his successors. Instead, from 23 BC onwards (at least) Augustus was granted the powers and privileges of a tribune and had them renewed annually. This was a device he dreamed up as part of his pretence that all he had done was restore the Republic. Now he could pose as the defender of the people's interests while simultaneously keeping the Senate in check. Thereafter, every emperor held the annually granted tribunician power and could always claim he was only in receipt of that power on a temporary basis – he had not seized it.

The historian Appian explained that Augustus had effectively assumed the same sort of powers as his adoptive father and great-uncle Caesar had done as dictator. This overcame the need for any form of election or other authorization for his position, largely because his 'government proved both lasting and masterful', thanks to his success and the fact that everyone feared him.[57]

If the word 'tribune' sounds as if it ought to have something to do with three then that is correct, but as with so many Roman terms the original significance had been long lost. In remoter times each of the three original Roman tribes had sent three tribunes to the army. It was from these military tribunes that the tribunes of the plebs were later first chosen. Although the two consuls were the closest the Republic had had to officials with monarchical-type powers, the word came from *consulere* and meant someone who was supposed to consult the people and the Senate.[58] Since repeated election as a consul was prohibited under the Republic, Augustus only held it twice after 23 BC. Most emperors only held the consulship intermittently.

Most, if not all, of these technical details were of little or no interest to the average Roman. From the reign of Augustus on, the vast majority accepted his monarchical rule and that of his successors. Republican sympathizers engaged in a few plots to restore the Republic but none, including the assassination of Caligula in 41, succeeded. Augustus' system would last for the rest of Roman history but with the Senate's role increasingly marginalized.

*

The Romans lived in a curious world characterized by an intense sense of self and destiny but were troubled that the standards which had made them great were being destroyed by their success. One aspect of the Roman world that was far less subject to change was the idea of family and the home.

3

DOMUS ET FAMILIA

Certain Roman citizens are fathers of families, others are sons of families, some are mothers of families, others again are daughters of families. Those are fathers of families who are their own masters, whether they have arrived at puberty or not; in the same manner those who are under the control of others are either the mothers of families, or the sons or daughters of families. For any child who is born of me and my wife is under my control; also a child born of my son and his wife, that is to say my grandson and granddaughter, are also under my control, as well as my great-grandson and great-granddaughter, and so on with reference to other descendants.

Digest of Justinian[1]

The senior man, sometimes known as the *paterfamilias*, had powers of life and death over the members of his family, including errant wives or daughters whose honour had in any way been called into question. His title *dominus* referred to the sovereignty of his power within the family domain and over his home and household (*domus*). Respect for age traditionally outclassed all other considerations. Older men were greatly esteemed, and their authority would not normally be questioned. They took priority, even enjoying escorts of young men to take them home after dinner parties.[2]

Nonetheless, women normally controlled the day-to-day management of the household (as the *materfamilias*).

The *paterfamilias* had comprehensive legal rights that included control of the family finances, the marriages of his children and other descendants. These could, and often did, include adoptive members of the family. Under the emperors, the imperial family operated by the same principles. Augustus regarded the Roman Empire essentially as a Julio-Claudian family patrimony. He tried every route possible to ensure transmission of his power over the Empire down through his descendants. In this he was only partially successful. To begin with, he had to leave the Empire to his adoptive stepson Tiberius. Of the four emperors who followed Augustus only two, Caligula and Nero, were directly descended from Augustus, though all were descended from his wife Livia. With Nero's death, the dynasty came to an end. It was a fate that plagued every Roman family head.

For the wealthiest Romans the 'family' meant a complex network of relationships involving far more than the nuclear unit. The critical factor in all cases was the common descent from one man. This descent could also be created legally through adoption. Adoptive children, especially sons, were in every respect legally indistinguishable from blood descendants. A man's sons and their families all came into his orbit, as did the freedmen of the household, and the slaves. A Latin word for a slave, *famulus*, is the origin of both the Latin and our word for a family. Families were also held together by intense emotional bonds. Evidence for these is most apparent in funerary monuments, usually in the expressions of grief at the loss of a spouse or child (see Chapter 15).

Marriages were arranged for political and financial reasons, with dynastic descent and transmission of property the greatest priorities. This was demonstrated by how the same word, *sponsa*, was used to refer to both the girl and the money promised as part of the arrangement between two families. Sponsa was derived from *spondere*, which meant 'to promise solemnly', and is the origin of our word 'spouse'. A father who had promised his daughter in marriage had 'promised her away' (*despondisse*), passing the girl from his jurisdiction to another man's; the latter being known as *sponsus*, the 'betrothed'.[3] There does seem to have been a legal principle at one time that a woman who managed to spend three consecutive full nights away from her husband in a year would have broken her husband's authority over her.[4]

Average lifespans were far shorter than today, thanks to the risks inherent from disease, accidents and violence, and from war, placing a family's fortunes in potentially great jeopardy should the male line fail. Therefore, the loss of a fertile young wife would normally be followed by seeking a replacement. Women could do nothing without the permission of the men of their families and were expected to marry and produce children in rapid succession from their early teens, while facing all the risks of childbirth, and at the same time – if they were poor – to work long and endless hours in a variety of occupations.

According to the censor Metellus Numidicus at the end of the second century BC, marriage was a necessary evil. 'If we could get on without a wife', he told the Romans, 'we would all avoid that annoyance', conceding that since Nature had made it impossible to live without women they were essential for 'lasting well-being'.[5] One wonders whether the woman called Aelia Tryphera would have been pleased to know she was described on her tombstone by her husband Aelius Proximus as *ultra modum*, 'above average' for a wife when it came to her purity and chastity.[6] Presumably, Proximus had not found her too annoying.

An odd aside is that marriages traditionally did not take place in May, June being the preferred option. Plutarch was uncertain exactly why and provided several possible explanations. One was that April was sacred to Venus, and June to Juno, both of whom were goddesses associated with marriage. Perhaps, he wondered, it was to do with Mercury being worshipped in May, or because June was better associated with youth through the word *iunior*.[7] Clearly, he had no idea and nor, presumably, did anyone else.

After the marriage ceremony, a Roman bride said to her husband upon arrival at her new home, 'where you are Gaius, there am I Gaia'.

As with so many Roman traditions, the reason was lost in time. One possibility was that the names served as male and female synonyms for, respectively, the lord and master and the lady and mistress. But there was also Gaia Caecilia (also known as Tanaquil), wife of Rome's early kings and mother of Tarquinius Superbus, the last king. She was 'a fair and virtuous woman, whose statue in bronze stands in the Temple of Sanctus. And both her sandals and her spindle were, in ancient days, dedicated there as tokens of her love of home and of her industry respectively', said Plutarch.[8]

THE LOYAL AND BRAVE WIFE

A damaged inscription from Rome, dating to the late first century BC, records a husband's eulogy for his wife. Their names are lost but the text records the devotion of the couple. He praised her for her virtues and how she had offered him a divorce because she could not bear him children. Her greatest virtue seems to have been that she had devoted herself to avenging her parents' murder and defending her husband with exceptional bravery. She predeceased her husband after forty years of marriage.[9] Ever since the exceptionally long text's discovery on various broken fragments, it has been assumed the couple concerned were Quintus Lucretius Vespillo, who had been proscribed by the triumvirs (Octavian, Mark Antony, and Lepidus) during the 30s BC, and his wife Turia. She had hidden her husband above the ceiling in their house.[10] The text fits Turia's story well (see p. 105 for more detail).

The murder of Turia's parents took place in the countryside, which cannot have been far from Rome. We do not know why they were killed. Turia, assuming it was her, assiduously pursued the culprits until they were brought to justice. This brave woman also beat off a gang of heavies sent over to attack her husband by the corrupt and murderous senator Titus Annius Milo (see 'Arson and Anarchy' in Chapter 10, pp. 142–3, for Milo's thuggery).

Not all wives lived up to such high standards. During the same proscriptions the wife of a man called Septimius was having an affair with a friend of Antony's. She was keen to marry her lover but obviously her husband presented an inconvenient obstacle. She went to see Antony and persuaded him to put Septimius on the wanted list. Unaware of her duplicity, Septimius fled home. She feigned horror on his behalf, let him in and shut the doors to keep him inside until Antony's murderous thugs turned up to kill him. They duly eliminated him, and the faithless wife married her lover the same day.[11]

UNDERSTANDING AND UPRIGHT WIVES

Women were expected to conform to a different set of standards from men. Tertia Aemilia was the wife of the mighty hero of the Second Punic War, Scipio Africanus. His brilliant victory against the Carthaginians at the Battle of Zama in North Africa in 202 BC, hence the name by which he was known, had ended Carthage's ambitions and made Rome the supreme military and trading power in the Mediterranean. Scipio was inevitably highly esteemed as the model of Roman manhood. His wife was also admired for a reputation that was based on how she had been prepared to overlook her husband sleeping with a slave girl. Tertia Aemilia's reasoning was simple: had she acknowledged her husband's infidelity, she would have been implicitly questioning his self-control and thus his credibility as a great Roman hero, husband, and father. Undermining him was unthinkable, given Scipio's reputation, so Tertia kept her mouth shut and concealed his hypocrisy. When Scipio died, she freed the girl and permitted her to marry a family freedman.[12]

Cicero's brother Quintus looked back on their mother Helvia admiringly. Writing to Cicero's slave Tiro one day, he recounted a tale about her thriftiness, another virtue Roman wives and matrons were supposed to aspire to. In her case it seems that she kept an eagle eye out for anyone in her household, which must mean her slaves, from stealing the wine. 'It was her custom to put a seal on wine-jars even

when empty to prevent any being labelled empty that had been sur-
reptitiously drained.'[13]

Pliny the Younger was invited by his friend Junius Mauricus to
recommend a suitable husband for Mauricus' niece. He was delighted
to recommend a young man, making special comment on his looks
and the bonus of his descent from a grandmother called Serrana
Procula noted for her exemplary strict moral sense (*severitatis exemplum*).[14]
Mauricus' niece, probably only in her early to mid-teens, would have
had no choice in the matter. Had the girl lived up to conventional
expectations, she might one day have earned herself a similar epitaph to that composed for Amymone, wife of a man called Marcus.
Amymone was said to be, as well as the best and beautiful, a woman
who had worked wool, together with all the other suitable virtues of
modesty, thrift, and *domiseda* ('content to remain at home').[15] Augustus
would have approved. He had made sure his daughter and granddaugh-
ters 'were taught spinning and weaving'.[16]

The way Amymone was commemorated had a rhetorical tone.
This was bound to happen to some extent because of the formulaic
way tombstone inscriptions were composed, some certainly having
been bought 'off the shelf' with the name of the deceased being added
later. There was another reason. Amymone's husband Marcus was also
talking about himself, even if he did not realize it. Had Amymone been
anything other than he had described her as, that would have reflected
badly on him. Her qualities were thus really a testament to his own
qualities as a Roman man. A husband whose wife did not live up to
Roman society's expectations would be considered weak, vulnerable,
and effeminate. It was therefore important also that if she died then
she was permanently memorialized in a way that would enhance the
standing of her family and her husband.

Some funerary texts also have a tone of sincerity about them. In
such cases there is no good reason why we should doubt the sentiments
expressed. Urbana died and was buried in Rome by a husband who made
a point of saying that he had added words to the text 'so that those who
read them may understand how much we held each other dear'.[17]

Pliny the Younger was also greatly impressed by Calpurnia, his third and much younger wife, whom he married after being widowed twice, an occupational hazard for any man who was fortunate to live a moderately long life. Calpurnia attended her husband's public readings to enjoy the praise he was given but remained behind a curtain (*discreta velo*). He described her as being thrifty and of high intelligence and missed her when his work kept them apart. More to the point, her virtues honoured her family. Later she became pregnant by Pliny but was too young to realize and had a miscarriage. He believed she had inadvertently endangered her life, saying she had not 'taken the proper precautions' without specifying what those were. Calpurnia was seriously ill, but Pliny was greatly relieved to be able to report her recovery. We have no idea whether any other children followed.[18] A freedman called Publius Julius Lysiponus lived to seventy-one. His tombstone commemorated his two wives, Donata and Rhodine, with whom he said there had been 'no discord' and they had been 'obedient', bearing him three sons, one of whom had died aged not far short of his sixteenth birthday. The marriage to Donata had lasted eighteen years, probably ending with her death, and that with Rhodine twenty-eight years.[19]

Pliny and Lysiponus' experiences were all too common, but not every man bothered with a second marriage. A freedman called Publius Quinctius was widowed in the late first century BC when his freedwoman wife Quinctia died. They had both been slaves of a man called Titus. Quinctius next took up with a freedwoman of his, Quinctia Agate, but never married her. On the tombstone that records the two women, she was simply *concubina*, 'his concubine', a word that means she with whom he shared his bedroom.[20]

AN IDEAL FATHER

The poet Horace was conscious of the fact that his father had been a freedman, and thus before that a slave. He was grateful that Augustus' friend Maecenas was not such a snob that he looked down on persons of obscure origin. Horace described how under the early kings of Rome there had been plenty of men of low birth who had served in high office and been of the highest probity. Horace was greatly appreciative of Maecenas for recognizing his personal qualities, but he was keen to stress his belief that his own success was down to his father. It was his father who had spurned an ordinary education and instead taken the young Horace to Rome to study as if he was of senatorial or equestrian status. He had even ensured that his son went about in the company of slaves so that it appeared he came from a family of esteemed inherited aristocratic wealth. His father watched over him, 'he kept me chaste', preserving his son from shame and scandal. Horace's point was a snipe at Roman snobbery that prioritised wealth and birth over qualities of character – he could, he said, never be ashamed of a father like his and would never consider apologizing for his birth as so many others were inclined to.[21]

CARING PARENTS

On the road that lay between Ostia and the new Trajanic harbour town at Portus still lie the remarkable remains of a cemetery on the Isola Sacra, wonderfully preserved after being buried in wind-blown sand dunes. Some of the tombs are mausolea, once containing the remains of entire families and others. Many are individual memorials. They include one dedicated to Petronia Stolida, the most dutiful daughter, by her parents Caius Petronius Andronicus and his wife Petronia Maritima. Petronia Stolida had lived twenty years, twenty-two days, and four hours during the second century AD.[22] The parents, we can assume, were the freedman and freedwoman of a man called Caius Petronius though they did not say so. Andronicus probably worked at the port, servicing Rome's insatiable needs. Their daughter's name has real poignancy about it. *Stolida* means 'dull-witted' or 'stupid'. In our more sensitive era this probably seems shocking but at the time it was used as a statement of fact by the parents. Their daughter's condition had clearly not affected their love for her. They had paid for a well-carved, but small, marble memorial stone which had been carefully affixed to Petronia's brick and tile tomb.

THE PROUD GRANDFATHER

Marcus Cornelius Fronto wrote to his son-in-law Aufidius Victorinus in around the year 164 in a determined effort to describe Aufidius' son, Fronto's grandson, as a chip off the old block. The child was constantly barking *da* ('give it!') at his indulgent grandfather who then passed over paper and writing tablets, 'things which I should wish him to want'. Fronto took equal pleasure, perhaps more, in noticing that the little boy shared his love of grapes and fascination in birds: 'I had from my earliest infancy a passion for such things.'[23]

POOR CHILDREN

There was no Roman welfare state, no government department of social security, in a form that we would recognize. There was a concept of philanthropy in which the state and men of means might provide public facilities or endowments. As one might have expected, for all the wealth of the Roman world children were far more likely to be orphaned by disease and war than today. That was an easy route through which a child might slide into slavery but for some there were initiatives that could transform their prospects.

Pliny the Younger wanted to provide 500,000 sesterces to be used to help maintain poor freeborn Italian children in his hometown of Comum (Como). Concerned that the capital sum would be squandered by the town, he instead handed over land of that value to an agent in Comum and then rented it back. This way he paid back an annual rent of 30,000 sesterces (or 6 per cent) to Comum to use his own land. The technique preserved the capital sum and would survive his death since the rent was far less than the market value of the land.[24] The gift of the capital sum was recorded on an inscription installed on Comum's public baths, which also recorded the baths Pliny had given the city. His precautions are an interesting comment on how funds might be misused, or even misappropriated, by civic authorities. (For Pliny the Younger's initiative to educate poor children, see Chapter 5.)

Trajan commemorated the *alimenta* system on some of his coins, though it began under his predecessor Nerva.[25] An inscription from Veleia in northern Italy in his name and dated to 109–112 set aside over 1 million sesterces to make provision for 245 legitimate boys and 34 girls, with more money set aside for an unknown number of illegitimate children. The arrangements lasted until the reign of Aurelian (270–5) at least but were paid for from the spoils of Trajan's mid-reign Dacian war. Loans were made to landowners as mortgages who then paid an annual sum to the *alimenta* fund. According to Pliny the Elder its purpose was to increase the numbers of young men who would later join the army and vote; the effect then would be to bolster the dominance of Italians and thus reinforce the idea that the Roman world was presided over by Rome and Italy.[26]

DYSFUNCTIONAL FAMILIES

Roman families were vulnerable to the distress and damage caused by unexpected sickness and death, and in that respect far more so than today. The Romans were just as capable of making problems for themselves. Tuditanus lived in the early first century BC and had no son. He left his estate to his daughter (who was the mother of the remarkable Fulvia, wife of Mark Antony), much to the outrage of male relatives. One, Titus Longus, who was most closely related, went to court to have the will changed on the basis that Tuditanus was given to behaving in peculiar ways. Tuditanus was also reputed to have visions, which probably means he hallucinated. The court rejected the suit, arguing that what was written in the will was more important than who wrote it.[27]

Aebutia was the widow (apparently) of a man called Lucius Menenius Agrippa. Her will was *plenae furoris*, 'full of madness', according to Valerius Maximus. Her two daughters, Pletonia and Afronia, were girls of equal virtue. For some entirely mercurial personal reason, and not based on anything either of the young women had done for good or ill, Aebutia decided to leave the whole of her substantial estate to Pletonia, setting aside only 20,000 sesterces (a small sum compared to the estate) for Afronia's children. Afronia decided not to dispute the will, deciding instead that she should honour her mother's wishes which, of course, served largely to illustrate how little she deserved her treatment by her mother.[28]

Pompeius Reginus discovered that he had been omitted from his brother's will in favour of beneficiaries who were not even family members. Reginus decided to unseal his own will and read it out in public, revealing that his brother was one of his principal heirs and had also been left an additional 15 million sesterces. Reginus complained bitterly to his friends about how he had been treated but did not challenge his brother's will in court, even though his brother's decision had clearly been designed to be deliberately insulting.[29]

Attia Viriola was a woman of a senatorial family whose husband was a praetor. Her aged and widowed father was in his eighties and evidently a sprightly fellow who took up with a second wife and brought her home. Clearly enamoured of his new bride, Attia's father decided to cut his daughter out of his will just eleven days after the wedding. This had all emerged when he died, perhaps worn out by the duties of his new marriage, much to Attia's fury. She went to court to claim the old man's estate, which turned out to be a major occasion with 180 jurors in four panels, speeches, supporters, and members of the public. In the event, the stepmother lost her share (⅙) of the estate, though the panels were divided.[30]

Some families were more considerate. Murdia lived and died in the first century BC. She was married twice but, according to one of her sons who commemorated her, she 'made all her sons heirs in equal share', and left legacies for her daughter and surviving husband. In her lifetime she had enjoyed an income from part of her first husband's estate which had come out of patrimony due to the son who memorialized her. This was restored to him by her will. The son praised her impartiality and righteousness, as well as all her other virtues.[31]

Married couples, of course, fell out too. Sometimes, divorce was arranged for pragmatic reasons. Where for whatever reason a marriage had broken down or turned into an inconvenience, then divorce had become a relatively simple matter. Livia divorced her husband Tiberius Claudius Nero to marry Octavian (afterwards Augustus), because that was what she and Octavian wanted for both political and personal reasons. Her husband acquiesced. This reflected a trend towards the idea by the mid-first century BC that marriage ought to be more of a matter of mutual consent. That was theoretically as easily withdrawn as it was granted. For those marriages that had hit a rocky patch there was the opportunity to visit the shrine of the goddess Viriplaca on the Palatine. It functioned as a primeval form of marriage counselling. There a husband and wife could rattle off their grievances about each other and then head home 'in harmony'.[32] Viriplaca's name meant 'placater of man', which Valerius Maximus, who is our only source, understood as meaning that men's rank took primacy over women, but which was contained within a union of mutual affection.

Divorce was a better outcome than doing away with one's spouse. In around 151 BC, two senatorial wives called Publilia and Licinia were found guilty of poisoning their husbands. They were put to death by being strangled.[33]

THE SERVANT GIRL'S STORY

According to one story, almost two hundred aristocratic women embarked on an astonishing bout of murdering their husbands. In 331 BC dreadful weather was followed by many deaths in Rome. They were caused by a mysterious disease that killed many of the senators; almost every one of them who fell sick later died. Not surprisingly, this caused great disquiet. Then a servant girl emerged from total obscurity and went to Quintus Fabius Maximus, the curule aedile, and asked for immunity from prosecution if she told him what had been going on. She made the extraordinary claim that the senators' wives were poisoning their husbands and invited a senatorial delegation to follow her. They allegedly found twenty Roman matrons preparing poisons to add to existing stocks they had already accumulated. The women denied the charges and were invited to drink the poison themselves. They did so and expired. Their own household staff made accusations against many more such women and eventually 170 were prosecuted, but the phenomenon was put down to madness rather than any conscious and deliberate attempt to kill. Livy, our only source for the story, was unsure it was true, observing that not all his sources reported it.[34] Whatever the truth (which is probably very little, if any), the mere existence of the story clearly played into the Roman perception of women, their emotional unreliability and weakness, how they could threaten the state, and their susceptibility to 'hysteria'.

EXPECTATIONS

Moral transgressions cast a stain on the whole family. Women were especially liable to be punished for them, even if they were the victims of abuse or unwanted attention. Their moral and sexual virtue (pudicitia) was a fragile commodity, easily shattered by the slightest hint that their probity was tainted. Pliny was appalled at how an especially fine Chinese cloth had become popular just 'so that Roman matrons can go see-through in public'. This compounded an existing problem with women using depilatories and thereby exposing their genitals. This added to the sense of female decadence and degeneration which was perceived as having a corrosive effect on wider public morals.[35]

By the fifth century BC a cult of the goddess Pudicitia had grown up, separated into one for patrician women believed in later Roman times to have been in the Forum Boarium and one for plebeian women, probably on the Quirinal Hill. Only matrons of impeccable virtue were supposed to be allowed to sacrifice to Pudicitia. The plebeian version of the cult fell out of use because, the historian Livy said, 'it was degraded by polluted worshippers, not matrons only but also women of every class'.[36] The point, of course, was that claiming to have impeccable moral virtue was, for a woman, a literal matter of life and death.

A freedman called Pudens made much of his wife Gratia Alexandria who died aged twenty-four years, three months, and sixteen days, probably in the second or third century. Doubtless enjoying the link to his own name (the word *pudens* means modesty), he said on her tombstone that Gratia was a remarkable example of pudicitia. He added a spot of virtue-signalling with the observation that she 'reared her children with her own milk-filled breasts'.[37] The word for reared, *educavit*, meant more than the simple process of nourishment. It had connotations of imbuing children with all her personal qualities and suggested that this was a matter of personal choice. In other words, Pudens was suggesting that Gratia had specifically turned her back on what any other woman of means might have done by not hiring a wet-nurse. Pudens thus positioned his late wife as someone more in touch with Rome's traditional values.[38]

A shocking aspect of Roman society was that women were more at risk from being killed by their families than by strangers, or so it seems. They were expected to live within their homes, but they remained under the close watch of the men of the family (which in Roman terms meant the wider extended family and household), ever vigilant for any possible misdemeanours. The slightest question of a woman's integrity could not only destroy her, but also her husband or father for failing to keep her in check. There were many possible instances in which she might legally be killed, even if the true guilty party was another man.

This idea went back to the earliest days of Roman society and the story of Lucretia. Men who killed their 'errant' daughters were also admired. Stories of 'honour' killings were handed down through the days of the Republic, some through sources that no longer survive, to be recounted by later authors. In 449 BC a senator called Appius Claudius took a fancy to the daughter of a centurion called Verginius and proceed to pester the young woman, Verginia, including the offer of money and promises. Verginius was regarded as a plebeian of unimpeachable moral rectitude. Appius was unconcerned that Verginia was betrothed to a man called Icilius, or that she came from a lower social class.

Frustrated by Verginia's rejection and taking advantage of her father being stationed away at Algidus, Appius engaged one of his clients called Marcus Claudius to accost Verginia in the Forum and claim that she was his slave. Despite protests from the crowd, the hapless woman was dragged to a court presided over by none other than Appius. The hearing was a farce but erupted into a protest by Icilius and a demand that Verginius be recalled. Appius conceded but then sent a letter to the fort at Algidus demanding to have Verginius forcibly detained. His letter arrived too late. Verginius was already on his way and arrived in the Forum with his daughter the next morning to solicit support. Appius ignored all the pleas, mounted the tribunal and pronounced Verginia to be Marcus Claudius' slave. Confronted with an intractable situation and one which he could not overturn, Verginius grabbed a butcher's knife and stabbed his daughter to death on the spot, saying to her 'in the only way I can, I assert your freedom'. He then fled the city. A furore ensued with Verginius now symbolizing the rising tension between the plebeians and patricians. Verginia's ghastly fate went down in Roman tradition as an honourable event – Verginius had done 'the right thing'. Indeed, he was esteemed as a plebeian who had acted in the proper way that a patrician should have. He had protected his house from being 'contaminated by disgrace'.[39]

During the late Republic an equestrian called Aufidianus learned 'that his daughter's virginity had been betrayed to Fannius Saturninus by her tutor'. He had both his daughter and the tutor put to death. It was not only women who suffered from such desperate attempts to maintain family honour. Publius Maenius had a favourite freedman, who of course therefore formed part of his former master's wider household. The freedman had kissed Maenius' daughter, even though this was put down to some sort of accident, presumably an ill-timed spontaneous gesture. Either way, the freedman was put to death on Maenius' orders. His rationale was, in his terms, simple. His daughter needed to understand the fragile nature of chastity and that if she was ever going to be married, she would have to be a virgin, and one who also had not kissed another.[40]

LEGALIZED BRUTALITY TOWARDS WOMEN

From the time of Romulus, during Rome's mythologized early history, comes the story of Egnatius Maetennus. In those days women were prohibited by law from drinking wine. When he discovered his wife had been drinking, he beat her to death. Far from being vilified for this monstrous act, Romulus acquitted him, and Egnatius went down in Roman lore as some sort of dystopian role model. Another wife was said to have been starved to death by her family after she was caught having broken open the box which held the keys to the wine store. Both stories are at the least part-myth, but they had survived because they were considered exemplary ways of keeping control of women. In 186 BC a senatorial consular commission had investigated allegations that women had been making 'impure use' of Bacchanalian rites. A large proportion were found guilty. Instead of the state legal system dealing with them, they were taken home to be executed by their own families on whom they had brought disgrace.[41] Today they serve as salutary tales of the inequality in Roman society and the legalized brutality heaped on women for their transgressions.

Valerius Maximus said that however bad the Bacchanalian abuses had been, the 'severity of the retribution' had set things right. He continued with the tales of Publicia and Licinia, both guilty of strangling their husbands.[42] He had no interest in their motives or mitigating circumstances and was only concerned to report that for their crimes they too were killed by their families who had passed sentence themselves. Apparently, the idea was to speed up justice rather than wait for a public trial.

Some of these long-established customs and attitudes were enshrined in law under Augustus as part of his concern about the prevalent immorality at the time of his rule. They fell under the authority of the Republican magistracy of the censor whose authority covered public morals.

There were at least some sanctions against men who assaulted or raped women though in this case it amounted to little more than superstition. There were many temples to Diana in Rome, but wise men stayed away from the one in the Vicus Patricius. A man had once attempted to rape a woman who was worshipping there but was attacked by the dogs that lived at the temple. They tore him to pieces.[43]

THE PRIVATE HOUSES OF ROME

Roman houses, especially for those of means, were inevitably important expressions of status and directly reflected the owners' means. Houses had to accommodate the core family and relatives, including adopted members, and the slave staff who cleaned, cooked, and maintained the house and its garden, as well as attending to the family's personal needs and admitting visitors. It is difficult today when exploring a surviving example to appreciate the bustle and noise that might have been going on, as well as the inescapable fumes emanating from the kitchen, oil lamps, burned offerings in the household shrine, and even light industrial activity.

Armies of builders and artisans were engaged in ceaseless building, rebuilding, repairs, renovation, and the clearance of ruins after one of Rome's endemic fires. Decorative features, such as wall-paintings, were installed according to the owners' means and pretensions. Most, however, lived in homes or apartments that were basic in the extreme, if they had a home at all.

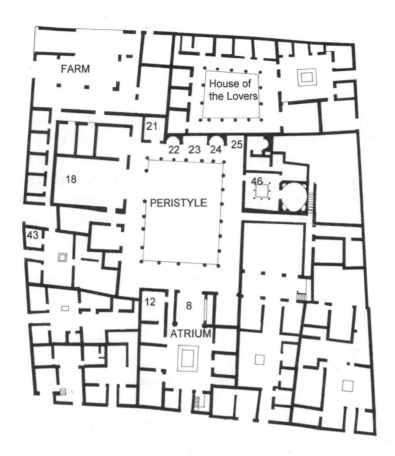

Figure 2: House of the Menander, Pompeii
This plan shows the Insula of the Menander at Pompeii (north is at the bottom). The
House of the Menander (Region I, Insula 10, building 4) did not occupy the whole block.
A visitor entered (centre, bottom) through the *fauces* corridor to the *atrium* (8) to see the
peristyle garden beyond with a series of decorated exedrae (21–25) on a main line of axis
that created an illusion of symmetry, despite the asymmetric plan. Room 12 and its
counterpart on the other side of room 8 faced subsidiary lines of axis, as did the transverse
view from the *triclinium* (18) through deliberately displaced columns. Room 46 was part
of the baths, an unusual domestic feature in an urban setting. A narrow corridor led to
rooms set aside for farm equipment and accommodation for slaves leading up to where
room 43 was. Other, self-contained, houses can be seen filling up the rest of the block,
including the eccentric quadrilateral layout of the House of the Lovers.

The family lives of Romans were reflected in and defined by their
homes. The importance of Pompeii, Herculaneum and Ostia lies

principally in their major private houses since nowhere else do so many survive together with enough evidence to help us understand how they functioned. Little in the way of domestic architecture survives in Rome apart from some on the Palatine Hill such as the so-called House of Augustus, and traces of a few others such as the substructure of the home of Marcus Aemilius Scaurus, the curule aedile of 58 BC, and the fifty cubicles or so of his slaves (see Chapter 7).

The atrium house mirrored Roman society in its design and reinforced it by defining public and private space, as well as zones for the different levels in the domestic hierarchy. No two are exactly alike, though most conform to a basic pattern. The differences are in scale and duplication. Extant examples are remarkably unprepossessing from the street, apart from in some cases an imposing doorway which led into a house characterized above all by the way it looked inwards. Windows on the outside walls, if they existed at all, were tiny and had iron grilles to prevent intruders. There was rarely any attempt to create an imposing, or indeed any, façade. The exterior walls were usually plastered and painted in plain colours and in Pompeii's case at least were liable to be sprawled with electoral slogans promoting candidates and insulting rivals.

A visitor passed through the main door through a deceptively unceremonious passage (*fauces*, 'jaws'). On either side of the entrance there were often rented shops fronting the street. The visitor then reached the atrium, a large entrance hall which was lit by a rectangular opening in the roof called a *compluvium*. The roof pitched down on all four sides to the central compluvium, maximizing the amount of light let in, especially in the earlier and later part of the day. Large *atria* needed columns to support the roof at each corner of the compluvium. Rainwater was collected in a small rectangular recess in the floor immediately below called an *impluvium*. It was in the atrium that the household shrine (*lararium*) for the household spirits (Lares) was usually situated. This hall was a public space, but around it were gathered the bedrooms (*cubicula*) for the members of the owning family.

To the northern European the atrium seems dark and cavernous, but it offered shade and relief from the heat of the Mediterranean summer sun. This was where the owner of the house conducted the morning *salutatio*, which was when he accepted calls from his clients, exchanged news with them, received updates about the businesses they operated for him, heard their complaints and woes, told them what he could do to help them and what he expected from them in return. It was also here that he presided over the daily household religious ceremonies, honouring the Lares. In the most elaborate atria, architectural features and frescoes were designed to emulate something of the civic architecture in and among which the owner conducted his public business and to impress his guests.

Beyond the atrium lay the *tablinum*, which lay between the atrium and the *peristylium* (peristyle garden) beyond. This room acted as the nerve centre of the owner's estate and business. Here he worked with his slaves and freedmen to deal with paperwork recording transactions, leases, contracts and so on. These were all stored in the tablinum, secured in a strong box. Structurally, the tablinum was open to both the atrium and peristyle but in practice wooden shutters were often available to be pulled across to make it private.

The peristyle was an internal garden surrounded by a covered ambulatory. It offered a peaceful open-air refuge from the chaos of the streets. The gardens were carefully laid out and so long as a public water supply was available fountains and pools often formed part of the decorations. The function of individual rooms around the peristyle is not always clear. A dining room (*triclinium*) was frequently located next to the tablinum while others probably included further bedrooms and private chambers for family members. Service rooms occupied and used by slaves were concealed behind hidden corridors, tucked away on the periphery of the house.

The architect Vitruvius described the basic atrium house design.[44] He was keen on emphasizing symmetry and proportion. The reality was usually different. No two houses at Pompeii, Herculaneum, and Ostia are like. The defining factor was the location of the plot in the first place and next the idiosyncratic evolution of each block which determined the size and shape of the space available for each house (see Fig. 2). Needless to say, there was no guarantee the architect and builders were up to the job. Cicero oversaw the building work at his brother Quintus' house in the countryside but was frustrated to discover the architect was doing his best to go as slowly as possible. Even worse, Diphylus had installed columns that were neither vertical nor correctly placed. They needed to be replaced. 'One day he will learn to use a plumbline and string', moaned Cicero.[45]

Some houses in Pompeii and Herculaneum show how skilfully eccentricities in the ground could be disguised with the positioning of columns and lines of sight to create pleasing architectural axes and an illusion of symmetry. The idea was to impress a visitor by drawing attention to features such as paintings and maximizing views of and across the peristyle. The House of the Menander, among Pompeii's largest houses, shows this to particularly good effect (Fig. 2).

Such houses were decorated with plastered and painted walls in a series of styles best observed and understood at Pompeii. By the time of Pompeii's destruction, the so-called 'Fourth Style' was in full sway. This included elaborate architectural frames containing panels depicting various mythological or figured scenes in florid colour. These served to display the artistic pretensions of the owner and emulated the vast quantities of paintings to be seen in public spaces (for example, Vespasian's Temple of Peace, see Chapter 12). Extravagance and ostentation became ever more important. An equestrian called Mamurra, who was a military engineer of Caesar's in Gaul in the mid-first century BC, was allegedly the first to install marble veneers across whole walls in his house in Rome, as well as solid marble columns.[46] For most owners, a similar effect was created with paint and moulded plaster for the walls and brick and plaster for the columns. Mosaics were first seen in Rome during Sulla's time between 82 and 79 BC but for the most part these were simpler geometric designs until well into the imperial period when elaborate colour motifs and figured panels became more common. Such embellishments were, of course, the preserve of the affluent or the pretentious (or both). For most Roman people ordinary cement floors, sometimes strengthened with broken-up fragments of brick and tile, were the norm along with simple plastered walls painted in plain colours.

The arrangements in Pompeii, where the largest number of these houses survive, varied considerably from house to house and this must have been reflected throughout Rome. Some of Pompeii's *insulae* each had several atrium houses, all packed in together and almost invariably involving considerable alterations over time. Times were changing and so was the pressure on living space.

TRANSITION

The earthquake of 62, seventeen years before the eruption of Vesuvius, destroyed a small atrium house on one plot in Herculaneum, among others. The remains were cleared away and a cheap new house was built using a wooden framework, with wattle-and-daub and plaster (*opus craticium*). By abandoning the old atrium design, the builder of the new house could create more living accommodation. Two apartments (one upstairs, one down) and a shop were built. By using an overhanging balcony, the upper-storey space could be increased further. The risk was that the construction technique was more prone to collapse and susceptible to fire. The result was a cramped, dark and poorly ventilated living space.

APARTMENT BLOCKS

Had Herculaneum and Pompeii escaped destruction in 79 it is a certainty that many of the atrium houses known from both towns would have been significantly altered or cleared away to make room for the apartment blocks which became commonplace at Ostia and in Rome.

The backstreets of ancient Rome have almost entirely disappeared, giving us little idea of how ordinary Romans lived, especially in the tenement or apartment blocks that proliferated after the great fire of 64 during Nero's reign. New laws had been passed about height and spacing. Remarkably though, part of one such structure can still be seen right in the heart of modern Rome at the base of the Capitoline Hill, just beside the steps to the church of Santa Maria Aracoeli. It was built of brick during the reign of Trajan and in many ways bears comparison with modern city blocks in Rome. The ancient street frontage consists of individual shops, open now but once closed with pull-down wooden shutters or doors. Further shops were above on the next two levels, and only on the fourth surviving level does there seem to have been basic accommodation, probably used by those who lived and worked in the shops. The set-up was matched on a much larger scale by the Trajan's Markets complex not far away of which much still stands. The ruins of Rome's port at Ostia where substantial remains of similar blocks still survive give us by far and away the most vivid flavour of the ordinary neighbourhoods in which most Romans eked out their lives. There it is still possible to stroll along the sidewalks past the ruins along ancient streets, shop entrances, junctions, and local shrines.

Ostia's so-called 'House of Diana' is a well-preserved apartment block, located on the south-west corner of a block, surviving to the first floor. The original height is unknown, but such buildings were limited by law to 60 Roman feet (17.8 m) to reduce the risk of fatalities in fires. Roman fire equipment lacked the necessary pressure to pump water any higher. The height limit was sufficient for at least four levels (average height of a storey is 3.5 m), and possibly a smaller fifth, but even with such controls the risks to those in the upper floors were high. Juvenal described how a fire on the lower floors could leave a resident on the top floor slumbering away obliviously.[47] The House of Diana was built in the mid-second century AD but was modified and strengthened a century later.

Internal staircases entered from the street provided access to the upper floors. The rooms were generally lit from outside, rather than the atrium house's internal courtyards, making another crucial difference from traditional townhouse building. This was not necessarily a good thing, especially in winter. Martial complained that the window in his flat did not close properly, making the place an ice box.[48] In the House of Diana's case, the architect had light available only round the south and west sides (it backs onto others on the north and east sides). He incorporated a small open inner court to provide light for the east and north wings. This is as small as it could be without being useless, showing that he had to provide the largest possible amount of living space.

A terracotta relief of Diana on the courtyard wall names the house. No attempt was made to cover the brickwork with decoration. A number of the internal rooms have mosaic floors and wall-paintings dating to the time of construction and also to the early third century. Water could not be easily supplied to the upper floors, so tenants made do with street fountains, though the House of Diana had its own in the central courtyard. A latrine was provided in the south-east corner. Two rooms were later converted to a mithraeum by the late second century or possibly later in the third century.

One possibility is that the ground floor of the House of Diana was used as a cult headquarters for a crossroads shrine immediately across the road on the evidence of inscriptions mentioning a guild, but this is unproven. In any case this will not have affected the prime function of the building, which was to accommodate a large number of people, though the presence of a local guild was probably far from unusual.

Apartment blocks did not have to be cramped and downmarket. In the early second century AD a part of Ostia away from the busy commercial centre, but close to the sea, was the scene of a remarkable piece of prestige property development that showed how the market for housing was changing. The development, now known as 'the Garden Houses', involved apartment blocks and shops built during Hadrian's reign. They were built to a higher standard, stood in a secluded courtyard, and were fitted with a water supply.

Roman family relationships, at least for the elite, were defined to a large extent by dynastic, political, and financial interests. For the aristocracy what mattered was the preservation of honour, the maximization of influence and property, and ensuring a line of descent. Sex and passion existed in abundance alongside, creating the potential for all sorts of disruptions and upheavals. While the Romans engaged enthusiastically in sex and lacked many of the inhibitions more commonplace in recent centuries, tensions resulted from traditional moral standards that they struggled to keep in place when confronted with reckless abandon and indulgence.

4

SEX AND PASSION

To the Spirits of the Departed, Tiberius Claudius Secundus.
He has everything here with him. Baths, wine, and sex destroy
our bodies. But only baths, wine and sex make life worth living!
Good health to you and yours. He made this for his wife Merope
Caesonia himself, his family and his descendants.

A tombstone found in Rome[1]

R oman historians were always interested in recounting in lascivious detail the decadence and dissolute behaviour of the emperors and the elite. This formed a crucial part of the well-established rhetorical denigration of a villain. Stories about Nero's orgies and bizarre sexual practices at his dinner parties, and Elagabalus' wide-ranging tastes and indulgences, have been a source of fascination since antiquity. It is harder to unravel ordinary people's tastes and interests though the colourful depictions of sexual activity in Pompeii make it clear the Romans were in general relaxed about sex.

One set of public baths by the Marine Gate (Porta Marina) at Pompeii, the main entrance used by visitors today, used images of sexual positions to identify individual clothes lockers. The designs were probably a joke rather than a sign the place was packed with copulating couples night and day. Pompeii's streets and streetside facilities provide an idea of what Rome must have been like. Brothels have been discovered, and even small rooms round the outer edges of well-appointed houses seem to have been rented out for the use of prostitutes. Trinkets decorated with or made in the shape of erotic imagery, the erect phallus being the most popular, were everywhere but not in official or state art. They were personal items with a purpose not necessarily obvious to us. The phallus was an apotropaic device that warded off evil. They were often placed above doorways, as can still be seen at Pompeii, protecting the interior from the ingress of bad spirits through the door.

One day in the earlier part of the first century BC, the dictator Sulla was at the theatre. In those days men and women sat together. A woman called Valeria, who came from an esteemed family and had been recently divorced, visited the show. She walked past Sulla and grabbed a little tuft of wool from his clothing. A startled Sulla swung round to be told by Valeria not to be surprised: 'I only want a little piece of your good luck for myself.' Sulla was excited by this and took it for a pass though Valeria was allegedly fairly innocent. He tracked her down and married her. As far as Plutarch was concerned, this was a good example of how a man had acted like a boy and been carried off 'by a good-looking face and a saucy manner through which the most disgraceful and shameless passions are naturally excited'. The story thus served as a sign of weakness, and a lack of self-control, useful for the purposes of a Roman historian seeking to moralize and condemn his subject.[2]

Pliny recorded how the Greek philosopher Democritus had criticized those who used sexual intercourse merely as a means of procreation. 'By Hercules', Pliny said, 'the less one treats it like that, the better', and went on to point out how it 'cures pain in the loins, dullness of vision, unsoundness of mind and melancholy'.[3] Easy, then, to see how in our time the pandemic lockdown rules that separated couples caused so much profound unhappiness.

It was taken for granted that a wealthy older man would have favourite boys as sexual partners. Slaves of either gender were often forced into having sex with their owners. The distinctions we make today about sex between people of the same or different genders did not exist. It was thus commonplace for a man to be in a long and fruitful marriage with a woman, have casual sex with young female slaves or prostitutes and also to have male partners. Same-sex marriage did not exist and would not have been countenanced since Roman marriages, especially among the elite, were usually arranged for the purposes of property and procreation. Sometimes a male owner's interest in a female slave evolved naturally into happy marriage; indeed, he may have purchased her and freed her for that purpose.

For all the relaxed attitudes to sex, Roman culture was clear that falling prey to sexual temptation was a weakness, a crucial loss of control. Female attributes were identified as demeaning characteristics of certain men, especially those who succumbed to luxury and vice. Such individuals were damned for being 'effeminate' because they were threats to the Roman male sense of identity. Accusations of effeminacy or allusions to men having the defects of fallen women were also part of the wider cut and thrust of Republican politics. A political enemy of Caesar's called Curio said he was 'every woman's man and every man's woman'.[4] The criticism here, though, was not that Caesar might have had bisexual tastes, but that when he slept with men he took on the subordinate and thus the effeminate role. That was the damaging allegation.

Although effeminacy meant 'tender' or 'delicate', its real power was in being used to suggest that a man was weak and womanly. The word when applied to a man was also synonymous with suggesting degeneracy, tied up with a love of luxury, another vice widely believed to be a female weakness. Sallust identified the growth of *avaritia* (avarice), especially for money, and how 'virtue began to lose its lustre'. In his description avaritia is a miasma, a poisonous substance in the atmosphere that pervaded a man's body and soul and 'effeminated' him.[5] The praetorian tribune Cassius Chaerea, one of Caligula's assassins, was outraged by the emperor's behaviour and treatment of him. One barb that really hurt was when Chaerea was placed in charge of enforcing tax payments, but exercised his duty with compassion for the difficulties pursuing payment placed some people in. Caligula accused him of 'womanly weakness' and took other opportunities to mock Chaerea by choosing female words with obscene allusions.[6] These allegations were to lead directly to Chaerea killing him.

Sex therefore was about more than the physical act. There were more complex associations which depended to a large extent on one's social class. Men were able generally to act as they pleased and were especially free to impose themselves on partners of lower status who were in no position to resist. Even women of their own rank were, apparently, fair game. Augustus allegedly slept with the wives of men whose political ambitions and plotting he wished to know about, or at least that was the pretext he conveniently came up with to explain what an unkind person might have criticized as rank hypocrisy. We have no idea whether the women concerned were coerced or were willing to be seduced. As an elderly man Augustus was alleged to have developed a taste for virgins, sometimes even provided for him by Livia (allegedly).[7]

SEX OBSESSION

Pliny's *Natural History* explored every topic possible. Sex was a particular source of curiosity for him, mainly because human beings seemed to him to be obsessed with it to the extent that they indulge in it whenever possible but never find true satisfaction. What struck Pliny as especially peculiar was that human beings appear to be disgusted by themselves immediately after sex, an activity that uniquely among the creatures of the Earth, he said, is engaged in 'at any time of day or night'.

Messalina, third wife of the emperor Claudius, never became an Augusta (the term applied to an empress), Claudius apparently holding back her rise to prominence which was perhaps just as well given that she fell spectacularly from his favour when her bigamy and other nefarious activities were exposed.[8] She was notorious for her recreational activities behind her husband's back. On one occasion she was alleged to have competed with a famous prostitute and beat her record by having sex with twenty-five men in a single day. Pliny went on, 'among human beings, men have thought up every perverse variation on sexual gratification, which are crimes against nature, but women have come up with abortion. Compared to wild animals, how much more culpable are we? Hesiod said that men have more libido in winter and women during the summer.'[9]

Juvenal thought that decadence of all sorts had become part of everyday life. His explanation was that in the past poverty kept women at home at their chores, while the men had distractions like fighting off Rome's enemies such as Hannibal. The arrival of luxury had led, he wailed, to criminality and alcohol-fuelled lust. 'What decency does Venus see to when she is drunk? When she cannot distinguish head from tail, eats giant oysters at midnight, pours bubbling narcotics into her unmixed Falerian wine, and swigs from perfume-flasks, while the ceiling spins dizzily around, the table dances, and every light is seen double!'[10]

The perfume and unguent trade symbolized imperial Rome's love of luxurious products, inextricably linked with sexual indulgence and excess. Novius Successus was the *quaestor* (administrator) of a guild of *thurarii* (perfume dealers) and *unguentaria* (unguent and incense dealers) in the second century AD, at which time the market was well-established and primarily servicing the upper classes.[11] The guild concerned made a dedication to Salus ('Health') of the imperial house. This was a routine loyalist dedication for a commercial guild, and it also reflected a suitable level of deference to their monied customers.

ADULTERY

A father who discovered that his married daughter had committed adultery and had caught the adulterer, whether in his own home or his son-in-law's, was legally entitled to kill the man and his daughter and would not be punished. As for the cuckolded husband, he was legally entitled to kill the man who had seduced his wife if the culprit fell into one of several professions, which included actors, gladiators, criminals, freedmen, and slaves. He was also supposed to divorce his wife on the spot. There was an incentive for such drastic action. Failing to punish the adulterous intruder could lead to prosecution for running his wife as a prostitute.[12]

Cato the Elder, who served as censor himself in 184 BC, delivered an oration on the subject in the second century BC called *On the Dowry* and explained that 'a husband . . . judges the woman as a censor would, because it is thought proper he has supreme authority, if anything wrong or repulsive has been committed by the woman'. Cato went on to add that if the woman had been adulterous then her husband was entitled to kill her without fear of any action being taken against him. The law made no such reciprocal provision: a woman was prohibited from taking any action against her husband for being adulterous.[13]

Augustus managed to avoid ordering the killing of members of his family under the laws he had passed himself, but he came close. His wayward daughter Julia, mother of his grandsons Gaius and Lucius whom he had hoped might succeed him, presented him with an almost impossible challenge. Her licentious behaviour was finally exposed in 2 BC. She was said to have engaged in every possible form of vice, including drunken parties in the Forum. Her behaviour was embarrassing and humiliating especially as it appeared everyone else had known except him. When he finally discovered what had been going on, Augustus considered having her executed. Since Julia was his only child, he was unable to bring himself to punish her with death. Instead, he had her exiled, initially to the island of Pandateria but after five years she was permitted to return to Italy and live out her days in Rhegium (Reggio Calabria).

During Nero's reign in 58, Pontia was a married woman seduced into adultery by Octavius Sagitta, a tribune of the plebs who was infatuated with her. Sagitta successfully persuaded Pontia to leave her husband and agree to marry him, but his plans fell to pieces when Pontia decided she had the chance of a richer husband and turned Sagitta down. He conned her into accepting a final night together, which he claimed would help him learn self-control. The pair duly turned up, Pontia with a maid and Sagitta with a freedman in tow. The couple argued and Sagitta stabbed Pontia to death, as well as wounding the maid, who fled. Although Sagitta's guilt was not in doubt when the crime was uncovered, his freedman claimed to be the culprit and that he had acted to settle the wrong Pontia had done Sagitta. This initially impressed some people, but the maid told the truth. Sagitta was executed after a case brought before the Senate by Pontia's father.[14]

A few years later Domitian (81–96) came close to executing his wife Domitia for adultery. Persuaded to exercise restraint instead, he murdered her lover, an actor called Paris and his pupil, just because he looked like Paris. Some of the people punished for adultery in his reign had been his partners. The victims included one guilty only of taking her clothes off in front of a statue of Domitian. For this she was executed.[15]

Adultery could be a topic for humour. Rome had its own version of frustrated housewife and milkman story. Juvenal lurched into a scurrilous diatribe about women being roused to a frenzied passion by the mysteries of the fertility deity *Bona Dea* (Good Goddess), whose rites were exclusive to women. Clearly titillated by stories of the festivals in which women worked themselves up into a state of passion, at which point they pounced on men, he decided that if none was immediately available, the women would go first for the slaves and then as a last resort for a partner the *aquarius* (the man who delivered water to private homes). Juvenal went on to make a famous, but usually misquoted and misunderstood, comment. Today this is almost invariably wheeled out as a warning to leaders whose guards might turn against them. In fact, Juvenal was talking about women. He reminded his readers of the old adage, 'put on a lock and keep your wife indoors', and then asked, 'who will guard the guardians'. What he meant was that it was all too likely the wife would turn to her guards for sex since women could not be trusted to control themselves. 'High or low, their passions are all the same. She who wears out the black cobblestones with her bare feet is no better than she who rides upon the necks of eight stout Syrians.'[16]

VESTAL VIRGINS

The Vestal Virgin priestesses, whose purity was central to their sanctity, were naturally subject to more strident conditions than other women. They guarded Rome's sacred hearth and were chosen by the chief priest (*pontifex maximus*) when they were between six and ten years old. They lived in in a special house known as Vesta's Atrium in the Forum and were supposed to serve at least 30 years. Many stayed in post until their deaths. Vestal Virgins who failed to observe their strict code of chastity were liable to drastic punishments ordered by the *pontifex maximus*. These included being buried alive in a small chamber and slowly starved to death, as Sextilia was for infidelity.[17] In 216 BC, during the Second Punic War when Rome was at its most vulnerable both physically and psychologically, two Vestal Virgins, Opimia and Floronia, were convicted. It had been discovered they were having affairs. One was buried alive near the Colline Gate, the traditional location for the punishment, and the other committed suicide. Floronia's lover was called Lucius Cantilius, a scribe who served the priests. The chief priest sentenced him to a beating so fierce that he died.

Livy explained that the Vestals' 'wickedness' had come in the 'middle of so many misfortunes' (it came shortly after the catastrophic defeat by Hannibal's army at Cannae that year). It was deemed to be an omen requiring oracular advice. The Sibylline oracular books were treated by the Romans as the most valuable of their possessions.[18] The texts were consulted, and a senatorial envoy sent to Delphi in Greece to ask for advice from the oracle of Apollo on what prayers and other gestures would be needed to propitiate the gods. This led to the human sacrifice of a Greek man and woman in the Forum Boarium, something Livy said was 'alien' to humanity.[19]

A century later another massive scandal broke in 114 BC when it emerged that three Vestal Virgins called Marcia, Aemilia, and Licinia had been conducting clandestine affairs. Marcia had taken a single equestrian as her lover, but the other two had 'a multitude of lovers and carried on their wanton behaviour with each other's help'.[20] The trysts seem to have started when Aemilia had an affair but had inveigled the other two into having sex with her lover's friends. They allegedly drew more men into the web, trapping them into silence by having sex with each of them.

The women managed to keep their activities secret until one of their slaves, a malicious and manipulative fellow called Manius, informed on them out of revenge. The Vestals had relied on him to help keep their activities under wraps and had promised him his freedom. When they failed to deliver on their side of the arrangement, he broke the story. It would cost them their lives. In a first trial Aemilia was found guilty and sentenced to death, Marcia and Licinia being acquitted to general outrage at the idea that certain members of Rome's elite were actively participating in such an outrage, as Manius had claimed. In 113 BC Marcia and Licinia were re-tried and condemned to death by live burial, a punishment also inflicted on four of their lovers.

The episode had been a traumatic one for the Romans so once more they turned to oracular inspiration for a solution, as Plutarch explained: 'since the deed was plainly atrocious, it was resolved that the priests should consult the Sibylline books. They say that oracles were found foretelling that these events would come to pass for the bane of the Romans, and enjoining on them that, to avert the impending disaster, they should offer as a sacrifice to certain strange and alien spirits two Greeks and two Gauls, buried alive on the spot' in the Forum Boarium. 'In memory of these victims, they still to this day, in the month of November, perform mysterious and secret ceremonies.'[21]

THE MEN WHO LOVED THEIR WIVES

For a man to love his wife would normally be considered a virtue. Not in Rome where such emotional indulgence was dismissed as effeminacy. Even public displays of affection were frowned upon. Cato saw to it that a senator called Manilius was expelled from the Senate. The punishment cost Manilius the consulship. The man's crime had been to kiss his wife openly in front of their daughter. Cato claimed he only showed his own wife any similar affection when it was thundering outside, and thus looked forward to such occasions.[22]

Plautius Numida was a senator who lived probably in the late second century BC. Numida's wife died, for reasons now unknown, but when he heard the news, he was plunged into a despair of total grief and stabbed himself. His suicide attempt failed because his slaves intervened and saved him, bandaging him up. The moment he could, he tore off the dressings to expose the wound and expired, so 'great a conjugal flame was hidden in his breast'.[23]

When the general and senator Pompey married Caesar's daughter Julia as his fourth wife in 59 BC, she was only sixteen. Pompey was in his late forties. The union was purely political from the outset. It cemented an alliance between two of the three most powerful men in Rome (the third was Crassus). Pompey did something remarkable: he fell in love with his new young wife. Indeed, he seems to have become infatuated with her.

The relationship became famous, but not out of admiration. Instead, Pompey's idolization of Julia was sneered at as an example of his weakness. Plutarch described the way this great man had dropped his guard. Pompey had become vulnerable and exposed himself to his enemies, among them the leading degenerate of the era, Publius Clodius Pulcher (about whom more later). According to Plutarch: 'Pompey himself also soon gave way weakly to his passion for his young wife, devoted himself for the most part to her, spent his time with her in villas and gardens, and neglected what was going on in the Forum, so that even Clodius, who was then a tribune of the plebs, despised him and engaged in the most daring measures.'[24]

A few years earlier Octavia had proved herself not only a woman of moral courage but also of guile and with a willingness to challenge her brother Octavian (later Augustus). The triumvirs, Octavian, Antony, and Lepidus, had ordered Titus Vinius to be executed as part of a cycle of vicious proscriptions of their enemies. Vinius' wife, Tanusia, hid him in a chest at a house owned by one of their freedmen. As a result it was believed that Vinius had been killed. Tanusia bided her time and asked Octavia to help. It was arranged that during a festival Octavia would make sure that only Octavian would come into the theatre, instead of all three triumvirs. This went according to plan and Tanusia was able to confront Octavian with the chest and her living husband. Octavian was so astonished that he let husband and wife, and the freedman Philopoemen, off.[25] It is obvious that Octavian could simply have ordered Vinius' immediate execution; the involvement of his sister in the ruse was almost certainly the decisive factor in staying his hand.

Another woman, whose name is uncertain but was possibly Turia, was commemorated on a touching and extended epitaph at Rome around the same time (see p. 73). Roman epitaphs, especially of women, were usually terse and perfunctory records that did little more than confirm her age and the men to whom she had belonged, whether her husband or father. There were exceptions and several appear in this book. Turia was granted an unusually long inscription by her bereft husband that extolled her virtues over a marriage that had lasted forty-one years. She was probably therefore in her mid- to late sixties. He was older by some margin and distressed that fate had left him to outlive her.

Turia's husband, Quintus Lucretius Vespillo, was another man proscribed by Octavian who had been granted a pardon. Lepidus opposed the pardon and Turia had prostrated herself before him to plead for her husband. Lepidus had picked her up and dragged her along as if she was a slave. Under normal circumstances this was would have earned her opprobrium for daring to intervene in public affairs, but in this instance she had acted as she did in order to show up Lepidus for what he was. Evidently her actions worked. Vespillo survived and the couple eked out what was left of their childless marriage on their own. The only thing that had angered Vespillo was Turia's suggestion that they divorce so he could try for children with another woman.[26]

OUTRAGEOUS BEHAVIOUR

Two of the most notorious figures of the late Republic were Fulvia
(83–40 BC) and her first husband, Publius Clodius Pulcher (92–52 BC).
His dissolute behaviour destroyed any chance she might have had of
an upstanding reputation. Among other exploits and a reputation for
being an agitator, Clodius Pulcher was notorious for allegedly dressing
as a woman in 62 BC so that he could trick his way into the women-
only rites of the Bona Dea. His plan was to seduce Caesar's second wife
Pompeia who presided over the cult. He was also accused of incest with
his sister Clodia.[27] Clodius Pulcher was caught and sent for trial, but
Caesar's reaction is particularly interesting. Caesar declined to give
evidence because he knew Clodius Pulcher's friends would ensure his
acquittal. Consequently, he was asked why instead he had divorced his
wife. 'Because', Caesar replied, 'I thought my wife ought not even to be
under suspicion.'[28] Like any man of substance he knew any doubt about
his wife's sexual virtues could damage him. A memorable aspect of the
story is that Caesar's mother, Aurelia Cotta, a woman of impeccable
virtue, presided over the household with an eagle eye. According to
Plutarch, Pompeia was in fact not 'unwilling' when it came to Pulcher's
advances, but Aurelia Cotta effectively made it impossible for her to
get together with one of 'the most notorious evil livers of his time'.[29]

The lax morals of Clodius Pulcher allegedly ran in the family. His
sister Clodia's unhappy marriage to Quintus Caecilius Metellus Celer
led to her having a number of affairs, including possibly one with the
poet Catullus.[30] Her liaison with Marcus Caelius Rufus became the
most well-known because Clodia accused her lover of an attempted
poisoning. Cicero defended Caelius Rufus and used Clodia's infidelity
as a stick with which to beat her, as well as referring to the rumours
that she had committed incest with Clodius. 'Why had the vices of
your brother more weight with you than the virtues of your father,
your grandfather, and others in regular descent ever since my own
time?' His purpose in criticizing Clodia was just as much to damage
Clodius further.[31] An honourable woman could enhance a man, and

by the same measure one accused of sexual impropriety could destroy him. Cicero castigated Clodia to save Caelius and did so by showing how she had damaged her own family (see Chapter 3 for more on this theme). It was also possible for a man to bring disgrace on his family, but, as we have seen, men were usually judged by different standards.

Fulvia married Mark Antony next. Their respective falls were treated as evidence of her defective and malign personality, exerting her destructive capacity to effeminate him. Antony's career after her death in which he married Octavian's sister Octavia but abandoned her and Rome for the attractions of Cleopatra and Egypt was regarded as proof of Fulvia's depravity and her influence on him. It was typical of Roman society that a man's fall was based on a woman, rather than his own failings. These included suggestions that he was subservient to a woman and even sexually passive.[32]

Fulvia's career was treated as being so incongruous for a Roman woman that the criticisms hurled at her tell us a great deal about how women were expected to behave. Fulvia played a proactive role in supporting Antony after he and Octavian had first fallen out. She backed him politically, and even militarily when she led the defence of Praeneste against Octavian's forces. Octavian broke into the city in February 40 BC and let Fulvia go. She escaped to Greece, but died there, allegedly being distressed by Antony criticizing her for involvement in the war.[33] Thereafter she was condemned by Roman historians for failing to be the respectful, compliant, and appreciative woman a proper Roman wife should be. Velleius Paterculus said Fulvia had 'nothing of the woman in her except her gender', blaming her for *tumultus* ('disorder', 'agitation') thanks to her actions.[34] According to Plutarch, she had incomprehensibly shown no interest in spinning or weaving and spurned ordinary men, preferring to seek the domination of a man who ruled or commanded.[35] She was thus an outstanding example of the Roman idea of a female aberration who refused to be contained within the rational and organized framework defined by men.

CONTRACEPTION

Infidelity was conveniently concealed if no pregnancies resulted from a liaison or, if they did, they happened to women who were safely married. Augustus' daughter Julia was famously alleged to have been habitually unfaithful and promiscuous during her marriage to his friend and military compatriot Marcus Vipsanius Agrippa. She was said to have snapped at anyone who commented on her infamous conduct with the tart response, 'I carry a passenger only when the ship is full.'[36] In other words, she took the simple precaution of only having affairs when she was already pregnant. This suggests that she took care to confine her many affairs to before Agrippa died in 12 BC, though allegations about her activities continued thereafter and led to her being exiled, as mentioned earlier.

Such precautions, of course, prevented conception, but there were other techniques if, to extend the metaphor, the ship had already left port. Claudius' wife Messalina, also alleged to have engaged in numerous affairs, appears not to have become pregnant again after 41, following the birth of Britannicus. It is impossible now to know whether their sexual relationship had ended (though Suetonius implies Claudius' interest in her did not cool until later), if they used such methods of contraception as were available, or whether either of them had become infertile.[37]

Preventing pregnancy for a sexually active woman was not easy, though coitus interruptus was an obvious means. One recommended technique involved attempting to obstruct the ingress of sperm by applying to the vagina a compound of white lead mixed with olive oil, honey, or cedar or balsam sap. Another even more eccentric procedure was to tie onto a woman with a strip of deer hide a couple of worms found inside a 'hairy spider' with a notoriously large head.[38] Julia's solution of only sleeping with lovers while pregnant was not open to Messalina. The affairs she was said to have had did not apparently result in any other pregnancies but there is no evidence to suggest she used contraceptive techniques or anything else to achieve that.

One remaining possibility is that for medical reasons she had become unable to bear more children.

SEMPRONIA

Lucius Sergius Catilina (known as Catiline today), of a Republican senatorial family, was an ambitious young man who thought nothing of using murder and other crimes to forge his career path, helped along his way with the support of Crassus. This was not particularly unusual during the 60s BC but in 64 and 63 he lost elections in his bid to become a consul and was abandoned by Crassus. The defeats turned his mind and he embarked on a suicidal conspiracy to overthrow the state. He found support from unusual quarters, including ageing prostitutes and the remarkable Sempronia.

The story was that around this time Catiline acquired a motley collection of supporters. These included several women who, when younger, had enjoyed a lavish lifestyle funded by working as prostitutes. As they grew older, their incomes fell but they made no change in their lifestyles and fell headfirst into debt. Catiline thought that these women would be handy for stirring up trouble among city slaves and arranging arson attacks, and that either their husbands would be persuaded to join as well or they could be murdered.

Sallust described one of these women, Sempronia, as a woman who had the boldness and daring of a man. She was the wife of a consul, but her family origins are uncertain. He was puzzled by the contrast with her sound family origins, looks, successful and fruitful marriage, as well as her education and other accomplishments. These included her ability to write poetry, her wit, charm, and her amusing but modest conversation. Despite all those assets, 'she also had other abilities of the type which encourage decadence. She held honour and decency in lower esteem than anything else. She took no more care of her reputation than she did of her money. She was so lustful that she more often approached men than vice versa. She had already broken numerous solemn promises, used perjury to default on debts and had been an accessory to murder. Her extravagant living plunged her into debt.' Sempronia was therefore regarded as an enigma, but for all her fame her ultimate fate is unknown.[39]

PROSTITUTION

Records known as the Regionary Catalogues, dating to the fourth century AD, list forty-five or forty-six brothels in Rome, broken down into the fourteen Augustan regions they operated in. In Juvenal's time two centuries earlier one notorious spot was 'near the chapel of the wanton Isis', as was part of the complex attached to the Theatre of Pompey.[40]

Prostitutes touted for business in the Forum and myriad other places, including one said to have been a virtuous and respectable matron who cost more than others but was noted for her unusual cleanliness.[41] Catullus referred to the women whose patch was the ambulatory by Pompey's theatre, including one who bared her breasts at him when he was looking for a friend.[42] According to Martial, there were also the *bustuarias moechas*, best translated as 'prostitutes of where the funeral pyres are'. In other words, they touted for business among the tombs.[43]

Manilia was a prostitute with a reputation for keeping a rowdy apartment in Rome. Aulus Hostilius Mancinus, who served as a curule aedile at an unknown date (but the implication of the source is that it was some time back in the earlier Republic), brought a lawsuit against Manilia, alleging that one night he had been hit by a stone thrown from the apartment. To prove his point, he demonstrated the wound he had received. Manilia was no pushover. She appealed to the tribunes of the plebs, declaring that Mancinus had turned up with a garland on his head (which meant party dress) and that therefore it would have been foolish to let him in. Mancinus had refused to back off, demanding to be let in and using force, so he had had to be driven off by throwing stones at him. The tribunes' verdict was that it was unseemly for Mancinus to be seen out dressed like that and forbade him from bringing his legal action.[44] The story was thus about a great deal more than prostitution. Men like Mancinus expected not only to be able to do as they pleased, but also to exploit their privileged positions to twist the law. Luckily for Manilia, the tribunes of the plebs found in her favour and his suit was thrown out.

DINNER WITH HERCULES

In remoter times a prostitute called Larentia did well. The keeper of a temple of Hercules loved gambling but one day could find no one to throw dice with him. He challenged Hercules to play, throwing the dice once for himself and once for the god. The temple-keeper lost and his forfeit, which he had promised, was to provide dinner for Hercules and a female companion for the night. Larentia was summoned and locked in overnight. While there she was visited by the god who told her to pay special attention to the first man she saw in the Forum and befriend him. She did just that when she met a wealthy but unmarried man called Tarrutius. He took her in, allowed her to run his estate and left it all to her when he died. She in turn left the property to Rome in her own will and was honoured accordingly thereafter.[45]

HIGH-CLASS PROSTITUTES

Not surprisingly, prostitution catered for all levels of society. While some sought punters in among the tombs there were also the high-class courtesans. The young Pompey Magnus was familiar with the celebrated beauty Flora, or so she claimed. Her story was that she went around with his bitemarks on her after he had slept with her. Pompey's friend Geminius fell in love with her. This annoyed Flora who told Geminius she must reject him because of Pompey. Geminius went to Pompey who told him he could have Flora and thereafter refused to have anything to do with her, much to her grief and distress.[46] Pompey was later noted for his faithfulness to his wives.

In the year 19 during the reign of Tiberius a scandal broke about how Roman women of status were working as prostitutes in order to evade the legal sanctions imposed on 'normal' women for sexual misconduct. The traditional view, at least in Roman lore, was that a prostitute was sufficiently punished merely by admitting to her vices, even though prostitution was a routine part of Roman city life. This time, after a woman called Vistilia had advertised her availability, the Senate introduced measures to make sure 'the lust of females was curbed'. Women whose fathers, grandfathers, or husbands were equestrians were prohibited from profiting by selling their bodies. Vistilia was banished to the island of Seriphos (in the Aegean).[47] Tiberius also tried to prohibit anyone attending a brothel with a coin or a ring bearing Augustus' name.[48]

Some practitioners claimed a higher standard of service and respectability. There was a prostitute in the imperial period called Vibia Calybenis, a *lena*, or 'madam', defensively commemorated on a family tombstone for earning her living 'without cheating others'. One word for a prostitute, *meretrix*, meant 'female wage earner'.[49] Another probable prostitute, Allia Potestas, was memorialized on an epitaph also of indeterminate imperial date. It recorded her respectable virtues as a matron before moving on to some ambiguous compliments that appear to record how much more she cost than other prostitutes and her cleanliness in the Forum.[50]

During Nero's reign, he and his thoroughly dissolute praetorian prefect Tigellinus were said to 'enter the brothels and without let or hindrance have intercourse with any of the women who were seated there, among whom were the most beautiful and distinguished in the city, both slaves and free, courtesans and virgins and married women; and these were not merely of the common people but also of the noblest families, both girls and grown women'.[51] This picaresque description was clearly designed to invoke a more general sense of moral degeneracy in Rome under Nero and how he had infected even those of old and esteemed families. Whether it was true is another matter altogether.

ADVERTISING FOR BUSINESS

At Isernia in central Italy between Rome and Naples one innkeeper and his wife set up a monument to their business which they operated under what were evidently trade names. He was called Lucius Calidius Eroticus and she was Fannia Voluptuas. The names do not need translating. The stone's text continued with an exemplar vignette of a discussion with a customer of his bill which included the cost of bread, wine, relish, hay for a mule, and a girl. The girl had cost 8 asses, which at the time the inscription was made in the second century was equivalent to a little under half a day's pay for a legionary.[52]

At Pompeii hints on where to pick up prostitutes were everywhere. More references to prostitution have been found in Pompeian graffiti than any other profession by a considerable margin. One was inscribed at the rear entrance of the House of the Menander, one of the town's most extravagant houses. In this case the advertisement was for Novellia Primigenia, a prostitute who worked in a nearby town called Nuceria 'in the prostitutes' quarter'. Her name was probably also another trade name because Novellia means 'fresh' or 'new'. These wealthier houses always faced inwards, accessed through a main street door, but otherwise nowhere looking out onto the street. Instead, rooms or suites around the outer perimeter of the block were let out separately to serve as taverns or other businesses, and often apparently for the use of prostitutes. Whether they were being run with the direct involvement of the affluent family who owned the house is unknown, but the prostitutes were clearly operating with their connivance.

Anyone strolling into Pompeii up through the Marine Gate and who took a seat en route to catch their breath on the steep slope could read about Attice. At two sesterces (8 asses) she charged about the same as the girl at Isernia. Those who had availed themselves of the services on offer in Pompeii were inclined to record their experiences on the walls in the brothels, thus 'Facilis fucked here', or 'Scordopordonicus fucked well whomsoever he wanted'. A *scortator* was a fornicator and was linked to the neuter term *scortum* which could be applied to a male or female prostitute. Scordopordonicus was a distasteful pseudonym, presumably adopted by someone who prided himself on frequenting the brothels. In one curious instance a single word was used, *conticuere* ('fell silent'), as it happens the first word of Book 2 of Vergil's *Aeneid* which starts 'All fell silent' (*conticuere omnes*).[53] There can be no doubt that the dozens of brothels in Rome were embellished with similar comments. At the Ostian private baths of Trinacria ('the three corners', a Latin name for Sicily, thus 'the Sicilian Baths') was a mosaic inscription in one of the warm or hot baths that read *statio cunnulingiorun*, a misspelling of *statio cunnilingiorum*, 'the place of the fanny-lickers'.[54]

Martial was familiar with such establishments. He described visits to labelled cubicles, enticed in by a 'boy or a girl', protected only by a curtain and a bolt to secure it. He dismissed the need for anyone who 'either sodomizes or fucks' to be so modest as to insist on any gaps being blocked up with plaster.[55]

Prostitutes were fortunate during the reign of Elagabalus (218–22) to find in the emperor, notorious for his sexual excesses, a friend. 'He gave an order that an amount of public grain equal to one year's tribute should be given to all the harlots, procurers, and catamites who were within the walls, and promised an equal amount to those without, for, thanks to the foresight of Severus and Trajan, there was in Rome at that time a store of grain equal to seven years' tribute.'[56] One should always be wary of such accounts. The source concerned wrote about a century later and is both anonymous and unreliable. It was presenting a stereotypical picture of a tyrannical emperor and his stock suite of perversions.

SEDUCTION

Ovid was no less conscious of the ideals of womanhood while avidly enjoying the pursuit of married women into adulterous affairs, prostitutes, and casual liaisons. One route he recommended was to inveigle oneself with a woman's maid for all sorts of insider information on her mistress's timing and habits.[57] Among other opportunities he famously cited the circus as a perfect meeting place where one could be ignored by everyone else and enjoy the titillating possibilities the tight-packed seating afforded. Ovid had all sorts of hints on how to seduce a woman, starting with finding out which horses were running, which was her favourite and then cheering the same one on. From that it was a short hop to brushing dirt off that had chanced to fall on her breasts or pretending that some had. He even explained how such gestures, which included telling other spectators not to bash into her, were an easy way of winning over the simple minds of women.[58]

Today, Ovid's habits would be seen as abusive behaviour but even at the time his antics were a dangerous way to carry on. He would be exiled by Augustus for his blatant flouting of traditional morality, even though his conduct was probably far from unusual.[59] His recommendations on how to pursue an affair involved hints to women on posing as a loyal wife at dinner while at the same time making signs and gestures to her lover. Yet elsewhere he also condemned the mythical Tarpeia for her greedy betrayal of Rome to the Sabines.[60] Ovid's comments show how important it was for a wife to go about in public at least as a woman of unassailable virtue, while at the same time exposing another side to Roman life. Of course, part of his purpose was to create vaguely erotic literature, but he also illustrated the enduringly complex ambivalence about women in Roman society.

WISHFUL THINKING

Martial reserved some of his most vicious verbal cruelty for a woman called Vetustilla. Her name was almost certainly a pseudonym since it meant something like 'the Young Hag', an ageing woman for whom hope was struggling against reality. Almost bald and nearly toothless, Vetustilla had a 'grasshopper's chest and the legs of an ant', a deeply furrowed brow, and a bust like 'a spider's web', a huge mouth, and she smelled like a goat among other defects. According to Martial, she was still hoping to remarry 'even after two centuries of widowhood'. The bath attendant was so horrified by Vetustilla's appearance that he let her in only after he had extinguished his light, and then only in the company of the prostitutes who touted for business among the tombs.[61]

Juvenal was intrigued by Ogulnia (a conventional Roman name with no hidden meaning), a woman in reduced circumstances who squandered what little remaining wealth she had on young men:

> Ogulnia, in order that she may go in due state to the games, hires a dress, and attendants, and a sedan, and pillow, and female friends; and a nurse, and blonde girl to whom she may issue her commands. Yet all that remains of her family plate, and even the last remnants of it, she gives to well-oiled athletes. Many women are in straitened circumstances at home; yet none of them has the modest self-restraint that should accompany poverty or limits herself within that measure which her poverty has allotted and assigned to her.[62]

For all these anecdotes and stories, the survival of many tombstones recording long and happy marriages bears witness to the fact that the Roman world was as varied as our own when it came to relationships. Nonetheless, the inequality in Roman society between male and female was entrenched and institutionalized. That became most obvious in the world of work and professional careers, especially among the upper classes.

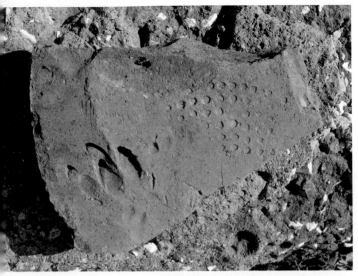

Tile from Ostia, bearing the pawprint of a dog and the footprint from a sandal with characteristic nails. The circular tile was probably destined to serve as a segment in a composite column used extensively in Roman domestic architecture but captures a moment in the hustle and bustle of a tilery in the city when a new tile was trodden on before being fired. The business was probably owned by a freedman, and the footprint was probably made by a slave.

Tomb of the baker Eurysaces, Porta Maggiore, Rome. A freedman who became wealthy in the mid-first century BC supplying bread for the dole. His tomb was made in the form of a bread oven. It survived by being built into a city gate (now demolished) 300 years later. c. 30–20 BC.

A selection of Roman coins. Top row: brass sestertii of Nero, Vespasian, Trajan, and Marcus Aurelius. Note that Nero's face has been cut in as a casual gesture of *damnatio memoriae*. Middle row: Republican silver *denarius* (110–109 BC), copper *quadrans* of Caligula, gold aureus of Nero, copper *as* of Domitian, brass *dupondius* of Domitian, silver denarius of Trajan. Bottom row: double-denarii (antoninianii) of Caracalla, Gordian III, and Probus showing gradual debasement, silvered bronze follis of Maximianus I, gold solidus of Constantius II. All struck at Rome except the last two (Cyzicus and Antioch respectively). To the left and right: US quarter dollar and UK 10p for scale.

The Thermopolium of Asellina, Pompeii. A painting of the *Lares* (household gods) overlooks the tavern' food-serving bar with the tops of large ceramic jars which contained the food. Pompeii had around ninety or more known such establishments in the excavated area. First century AD before 79.

Herculaneum, the entrance hall (*atrium*) to the Suburban Baths, among the best-preserved Roman baths buildings. The herm sculpture doubled as a fountain for patrons. Probably built by a member of the senatorial family, the Nonii, c. AD 40. The structure provides an unmatched experience of wandering around the dark vaulted chambers of a small urban bathing establishment.

Herculaneum, so-called House in Opus Craticium. As the population rose, one response to demand for accommodation was to replace the traditional atrium house with cheaper buildings made of a timber frame with rubble walls. These made it possible to create self-contained apartments upstairs and downstairs, expanding the space by building out over the sidewalk. The design was flimsy and susceptible to fire. This example was built c. 62–79. By the late first century the design was giving way to better built apartment blocks.

Pompeii, House of the Menander. Skilful use of lines of sight, adjusted column spacing and placement of rooms allowed the creation of visual axes to maximize the effect on a visitor. This is the view from the entrance corridor through the public spaces of the atrium hall and across the peristyle garden to decorated exedrae beyond. Examination of the plan (see text, Chapter 3) shows how this was achieved.

Ostia, the House of Diana. Ostia preserves parts of many brick and concrete four- to five-storey apartment buildings of the type that proliferated throughout Rome from the late first century AD on, designed to reduce the risk of fire. Accommodation was basic, but walls were usually plastered and painted. The ground-floor street frontages were occupied by shops. The street leads to the Capitol temple, visible at the end and dedicated to the Capitoline Triad of Jupiter, Juno, and Minerva. Built c. 150.

Pons Aemilius, Rome. Several bridges joined the main part of Rome on the east bank of the Tiber to the western region, now known as Trastevere, and were filled with foot and wheeled traffic constantly. The Pons Aemilius dated back to the third century BC but was rebuilt in travertine by Augustus. It was damaged several times in antiquity and the Middle Ages. Now only a small section survives.

Ostia, entrance to the warehouse and commercial headquarters of the freedmen Epagathus and Epaphroditus whose names suggest they were of Greek origin. Businessmen like them were the bedrock of Rome's commercial activities throughout the imperial period, some doing extremely well out of the opportunities afforded by supplying and feeding cities across the Empire but none more so than Rome. Built c. 150.

Tombstone of the freedmen Demetrius and Philonicus, from Tusculum, near Rome. Their former master, one Publius Licinius, would have set them up in businesses and in return expected their loyal service. The stone carries depictions of the tools of their trades. Demetrius appears to have been a carpenter (right-hand side), while Philonicus seems to have worked in the mint striking coins (top). It is unclear why they were buried together, unless it was a simple matter of friendship, economy and convenience though it is likely they died at different times. c. 30–10 BC.

In the traditional Roman *atrium* house rainwater that fell through the *compluvium* roof opening collected in the *impluvium* pool beneath. From here it drained into a subterranean tank. Next to the *impluvium* was usually a stone cylinder through which buckets were lowered by rope to draw up water for the household's use. The wear from countless such operations caused the prominent grooves visible here, and bear witness to the endless drudgery household slaves were forced to endure. House of the Black Salon, Herculaneum, destroyed in 79.

Ostia, Piazza of the Corporations. Around a large open piazza shipping companies had offices where merchants and customers could negotiate contracts. Outside each one, mosaic panels indicated the individual companies' businesses. This company displayed an image of a lighthouse, probably Ostia's (but modelled on the Pharos at Alexandria). It was likely involved in shipping grain from Egypt and Sicily. Once offloaded, the grain was transported up the Tiber on barges to be stored in massive warehouses for sale or distribution as part of the grain dole.

Pompeii, an electoral slogan. Pompeii's street walls were liberally painted with inscriptions (programmata) from the annual election campaigns. This one is in support of Lollius, a candidate for the aedileship. In highly abbreviated Latin (*Lollium d(ignum) v(iis) a(edibus) s(acris) p(ublicis) o(ro) v(os) f(aciatis)*), it read, '*I beg you to elect Lollius, suitable for roads and public and sacred buildings*'.

Ostia, tombstone of Petronia Stolida, the most dutiful daughter, by her parents Caius Petronius Andronicus and his wife Petronia Maritima. Petronia Stolida had lived twenty years, twenty-two days and four hours during the second century AD. *Stolida* means 'dull-witted' or 'stupid'. Their daughter's condition had clearly not affected her parents' love for her. They had paid for a well-carved, but small, marble memorial stone which had been carefully affixed to Petronia's brick and tile tomb.

Ostia, tomb of Gaius Annaeus Atticus in the form of a diminutive brick pyramid to hold his cremated remains in the cemetery on the Isola Sacra between Ostia and Portus. The tomb's inscription says he came from Aquitania in Gaul and that he was a painter. He died aged thirty-seven but there is no mention of a wife or family. The monument was probably inspired by the pyramid of Cestius, a member of the senatorial order, whose impressive tomb still stands, now incorporated into the Aurelian Walls of Rome by the Ostian Gate.

5

CURSUS HONORUM

Dishonest behaviour, bribery, and a quick profit were everywhere.
Although everything I saw going on was new to me — and I
looked down on them with disdain — ambition led me astray and
I, having all the weakness of youth, could not resist. Regardless
of my efforts to dissociate myself from the corruption that was
everywhere, my own greed to get on meant that I was hated and
slandered as much as my rivals.

Sallust[1]

Sallust forged his political career in the 50s BC, the time of
Julius Caesar and the other imperators in the latter days of the
Roman Republic when political corruption and competition
was at its height and ambition its most ruthless. Rome had become
used to factions and feuding, often spilling over into violence on the
streets. Few could match Caesar for his ruthless pursuit of his interests.
Once he had reached the top and become dictator, he was alleged to
have said 'it would be harder to push him down from first to second
place than from second to last place'. While on campaign in the Alps,
Caesar came across a remote barbarian village. His companions joked,
wondering whether such a wretched and sparsely populated place had
candidates competing for office and vying to become the first man in
the settlement. Caesar said he would rather be top man in the village
than second in Rome.[2]

Accusations of corruption tainted Sallust's career. He was even expelled once from the Senate for immoral behaviour. His most famous work is his account of the war against Lucius Sergius Catilina (108–62 BC) who in 63 BC organized a conspiracy to overthrow the Roman Republic. In his introductory passages Sallust described his path into politics and how he started as young and idealistic before he descended into the dark side, explaining why he was a wealthy man when he retired. To begin with, Sallust said, he was dedicated to politics only but found himself confronted by the discovery that, in Rome's fetid public arena, restraint, integrity and virtue had no currency at all. He was trying to impress on his readers (and himself) that however he had ended up he was fundamentally a decent man.

For successful men of high status – and it largely was for men – the prospects of power and wealth were considerable. This really took off after the Second Punic War at the end of the second century BC when the Roman dominance of the Mediterranean world had become unstoppable. For men of senatorial status, an education was essential if they were to make their way through the hierarchy of magistracies, military positions and administrative appointments to the consulship – the *cursus honorum*, or 'career of honours'. Indeed, our word 'ambition' comes from the Latin *ambitio* which meant 'walking (or going) around' in the context of seeking votes, in our terms 'canvassing'.[3] A well-equipped candidate took with him around the streets a slave called a *nomenclator* who fed his master the names of anyone they bumped into who was eligible to offer his vote or support.[4]

In 146 BC Lucius Hostilius Mancinus stood for the consulship after leading the entry to Carthage that year in the Third Punic War, during which he had commanded the fleet. Well aware that his achievements ought to help his chances, he arranged for a picture of the Carthage assault to be displayed in the Forum to serve as a visual aid while he could explain what he had done to anyone walking by. This novel method of soliciting votes was so successful that Hostilius Mancinus was elected to the consulship for 145 BC.[5]

Sallust was one of many Roman politicians who learned that money mattered most when it came to acquiring power and holding onto it. Cicero observed that men needed money in the first instance to pay for necessities, but that for the most ambitious their love of money was all about power and having the means to stump up for favours or bribes, or even bankroll a private army. 'For example', he pointed out, 'Marcus Crassus said not long ago that there was no amount of wealth sufficient for the man who wished to be premier citizen in the nation, unless he could finance an army with the income.'[6]

Marcus Licinius Crassus (115–53 BC) was a hugely important Roman statesman and general of the mid-first century BC as the Republic degenerated into a lethal free-for-all. By the late 70s BC he had already played an important part in crushing the slave revolt led by Spartacus, which gave him unmatched prestige. He amassed the wealth so essential to giving himself the necessary military backing through several different routes. His most imaginative and celebrated practice was organizing his own construction team consisting of over 500 slaves. He had seen how frequently houses in Rome's packed quarters burned down. Crassus then waited like a spider for fires to break out. His scouts would turn up and offer to buy a burning house for a knockdown price. This ingenious tactic presented the hapless homeowner with a choice between a paltry price or a pile of ashes worth nothing. Most caved on the spot and accepted the money. It was, after all, generally an offer they couldn't refuse. Crassus' men would move in and develop the bargain piece of real estate he had just bought, and then put it out for rent. That way 'most of Rome ended up belonging to Crassus'. Those who turned down the offer of cash on the spot ended up with a ruin and had to bear the cost of repairs or rebuilding themselves.[7]

During the late Republic, political ambitions and high stakes led to violent factionalism in Rome. Even senators could coalesce into murderous gangs. For those of lesser birth, life was far more hand to mouth eking out a precarious existence on the streets of Rome. For a man born into a senatorial family, the expectation was that he would rise through a series of elected magistracies climaxing in the consulship to military commands, and lucrative provincial administrative posts such as governorships. During the Republic, achieving such a high office and a military command could bring a man close to supreme power over the Roman world. With so much at stake the explosive level of rivalry is unsurprising. The potential for corruption was enormous, and so were the possibilities, but it all began at school.

SCHOOLING AND EDUCATION

Education was a rare commodity in ancient Rome. Most ordinary Roman children had little chance of anything more than the rudiments, if even that. Girls were rarely educated but a few lucky wealthy ones were, and some gained considerable reputations. Boys were trained in literacy and arithmetic to begin with, the wealthier ones proceeding to a more sophisticated curriculum in which other subjects like philosophy and astronomy were studied, but always with the emphasis on literature and the art of public speaking. Greek was part of the curriculum, but the future general and statesman Gaius Marius (c. 157–86 BC), who came from a poor Italian background, was believed to have refused to be taught Greek. 'It was ridiculous', he said, 'to have to be taught a language by members of a subject people.'[8] Conversely, the young Cicero had stunned his classmates with his learning. They dashed home to tell their parents about this prodigy. Some of their fathers came to the school to see the boy wonder in action.[9]

Seneca said that children should be soundly trained from the start, but it was essential to avoid the opposite extremes of unlimited freedom or crushing the child's spirit. He also noticed that the richer people are, the quicker they are to become angry especially when egged on by flatterers telling a person they are not being accorded a respect appropriate to their station.[10]

The wealthier the family, the more likely it was that care of the young would be farmed out to female slaves and freedwomen in the first instance. These women were liable to be retained in the family for many years and were remembered fondly by their former charges long into adulthood. Pliny the Younger gave his nurse a farm to provide her with an income and took steps to make sure it was properly managed in order to maximize profits for her benefit.[11]

Children, after infancy, might pass under the care of a male slave called a *paedagogus* whose responsibilities included escorting the child to school. Naturally, there was always the risk that a child would regard his nurse or pedagogue with more affection than anyone else, or vice versa. The nurse also had to be carefully chosen in case the child learned sloppy speaking habits.[12] Martial had to deal with his freed-man pedagogue Charidemus who could not let go. Charidemus took his responsibilities seriously and to such an extent that he drove the adult Martial half mad with frustration, as well as terrorizing Martial's household staff. Martial described Charidemus as another Cato the Elder since his objections included a Cato-like revulsion for the grown Martial's degenerate tastes for purple robes and anointing his hair.[13]

Pedagogues served the imperial family too. Philetaerus was an imperial freedman pedagogue 'of the boys [i.e. sons] of Caesar' in the late first century or early second century, dated by the style of the tombstone of a female slave in his household on which he tells us about himself.[14] Girls from affluent families also benefited from being educated this way. Livia Medullina was betrothed to the future emperor Claudius and had her own pedagogue, a freedman called Acratus who loyally made a dedication to her. Tragically, she fell ill and died on the day set aside for the marriage.[15]

The richest might have had private tutors, but otherwise those lucky enough to have an education were sent to a school to receive it. Most acquired only a basic knowledge of literacy and arithmetic. That meant they could at least manage everyday life in the market and running a business, as well as being able to read public announcements and other news.[16] A boy educated to that level might well then gravitate to an apprenticeship in a profession that would bring him an income, for example a training as a woodworker or sculptor.

There was no system of state education or curriculum (though in fact most schools offered much the same curriculum, albeit with varying success). As a result, every school was a one-off, its success or lack of determined by the teacher and resources available to him. There was no formal training or professional qualification. The quality of schooling boiled down to how much the family could afford and the personal reputation and ability of individual teachers. Among the most celebrated was Lucius Orbilius Pupillus, an orphan from Beneventum who enlisted in the army and became a teacher in his hometown when he was demobbed. He moved to Rome after fifteen years and became famous for his punishments and refusal to show any deference to men of the highest rank.[17] In 56 BC Cicero had his brother's son, Quintus junior, taught in his own house by the grammarian Tyrannion of Amisus, whom he greatly esteemed, while the boy's father was in Sardinia. Tyrannion had been brought to Rome as a prisoner of war in 72 BC.[18]

Schools added to the everyday noise pollution the average Roman had to put up with. Martial was infuriated by being wakened before dawn by the sound of a teacher yelling at his students and preparing to beat them, claiming the row drowned out the shrieks from the crowd in the Colosseum. He did not mind being woken occasionally, but what really grated was being kept awake, and wondered whether it might be possible to offer the teacher the same salary in return for being silent. Martial was not being especially generous. Teachers were poorly paid, and the job was often thankless.[19]

Pliny the Younger planned to use some of his wealth to help endow a school in his hometown of Comum after discovering there were no available teachers there. He had no children of his own at the time and indeed, as far as we know, never had any despite his hopes (and several wives) but was prepared to put up one-third of the necessary funds to source and hire teachers. Worried about the prospect of corruption, if the civic authorities had become involved in recruiting staff, which he had seen elsewhere, Pliny wanted the balance contributed by parents who would thus have a vested interest in making sure the best teachers were found. The idea, he hoped, would ultimately lead to the school having an excellent reputation and thus attract students from further afield. He did not address the problem similar schools have today of sustaining ongoing investment when the original students have grown up and they and their parents have moved on.[20]

The emphasis for higher status boys was always on literacy and the ability to write and speak in public. This meant for the younger boy a great deal of time spent on texts that filled his head with poetry, and literary and legal texts. Girls were much more likely to be trained in skills of household management. This was underpinned by the expectation that they would be married, perhaps as young as twelve or thirteen, and then embark on childbearing for as long as they were physically able. Tragically, death in childbirth was all too common (see Chapter 15).

Boys might move on at the age of fourteen, if their families had the resources, to a more advanced level of education under a *rhetor*. This stage, the closest equivalent to our university education, was designed to prepare a boy of senatorial or high equestrian status for a career in public life, serving in high office and in the law. He was taught in Latin and Greek. The priority was rhetoric, which with constant training and practice prepared him in public speaking and poetry interpretation, the latter being considered an essential prerequisite for being able to read with full understanding, expanding the vocabulary, and thus learning how to write. Knowledge of poetry together with music also gave the boy access to philosophical works, like Lucretius' *On the Nature of Things*, which were written as poetry. Most of all, though, recommended the oratorical instructor Quintilian, a boy's education should result in *voluntatem bonam*, 'the will to do well'.[21]

For a boy of senatorial rank, the future might mean a period as a tribune in a legion before advancing to the cursus honorum of magistracies and major administrative posts. Until at least the end of the second century BC at least ten years' military service was considered essential for a man in pursuit of political office.[22] Practical instruction followed school by accompanying his father or a relative to follow a well-known orator and see him in action in the Senate or in the courts. That way the young man would learn how to put his education into practice.[23] Under the emperors a high-ranking equestrian could aim himself at some of the most important and powerful offices in the Roman world, such as prefect of Egypt, prefect of Rome, prefect of the Praetorian Guard, or even promotion to the senatorial order.

Excelling in education was not the only way to reach the top. Trajan (98–117) was a brilliant soldier and was chosen by Nerva to succeed him as emperor. But, said Dio, 'Trajan was not educated in the formal sense of the word with respect to speaking but he knew what it consisted of and could apply it. He possessed all qualities to a considerable level.'[24] Conversely, the childless Trajan took steps to educate his relative Hadrian to ensure he had the necessary background and experience to serve as his heir. By the third century low-born soldier emperors had become increasingly common, many rising through the ranks entirely based on merit and luck to seize power. For the ordinary ranker, to become the supreme ruler of the Roman world had become a possibility, even for those of provincial or barbarian origins. Few of these emperors died in their beds. Having usually toppled their predecessor by murdering him, most were killed after short reigns in turn by assassins, army mutineers, or on the battlefield.

EDUCATED WOMEN

Girls of low or modest birth had limited prospects. The expectation that they would grow up to be wives and mothers first and foremost was well-established. There are many examples of girls who had been put out to work as artisans and other professions such as hairdressing well before the age of ten, though many of these must have been slaves. Children's fingers and hands were small enough to make them suitable for close and fine work, assisted by their keener eyesight. Those who grew up free, or were freed, were likely to be involved in family businesses, especially if they were married to a freedman running a commercial operation supported by his former master. Indeed, in many cases the husband and wife had probably been freed together from the same household.

By the early first century BC it was becoming more common for Roman women of upper-class origins to benefit from the type of education once limited to males. Even so, a girl was only likely to benefit from a more sophisticated education if a personal tutor was found for her. Some fortunate women gained considerable reputations for themselves. Quintus Caecilius Epirota, a celebrated freedman tutor, was hired for Caecilia Attica by her father, Cicero's friend Titus Pomponius Atticus. He was sacked after being accused of improper conduct towards his pupil.[25] Caecilia Attica was already the wife of Marcus Agrippa (from around 37 BC when she was fourteen), a union that brought her directly into the future Augustus' circle, but she seems not to have lived long because by 28 BC Agrippa had married Octavian's niece Claudia Marcella Major (the Elder) as part of Octavian's efforts to build up and perpetuate the Julio-Claudian dynasty.

Hortensia, daughter of the lawyer and orator Quintus Hortensius, was an unusual instance of a woman whose education and abilities had enabled her to participate in public life – within limits. She defended in court the rights of women whose husbands had been penalized by excessive taxation imposed on them by the triumvirs Octavian, Antony and Lepidus. Hortensia's speech was written down and was admired on its merits, and not because it was the work of a woman, though the fact that it had been was a matter of note. She was not unique. Gaia Afrania who died in about 48 BC successfully defended her own interests in court, acting in this capacity before any of her male relatives could do so on her behalf. In another case, Maesia of Sentinas defended herself so effectively that she was acquitted, and even enjoyed the privilege of being identified by her town (Sentinum, near modern Sassoferrato, north of Rome) rather than by her father or husband.[26]

Educated women could easily be seen as a threat to Roman male dominance. Valerius Maximus revelled in his revulsion for Afrania's conduct. He accused her of shamelessness and compared her speaking to the sound of a dog. Likening her speeches to animal noise was a crude and lazy way of demeaning a woman. In Roman public life it was bad enough if a physically feeble man allowed himself to sound shrill like a woman. In the early third century the jurist Ulpian said that Afrania was the reason an edict was passed prohibiting a woman from representing anyone else in court and 'performing the functions of men'. Maesia earned the nickname *androgyne*, which can be translated as a 'masculine, heroic woman'. The label in her case might have been a compliment, but it could also have been insinuating that she was intruding on male territory. Hortensia was forgiven by Valerius Maximus because she was only speaking up for women's interests.[27]

ELECTIONEERING

The theory of education was all very well, as was the conscientious rearing of a boy for public life. The reality often turned out to be different once the young man concerned was confronted with the cut and thrust of public life. Cicero said there was 'no pleasure to be had now from politics anywhere', but that did not stop politics from being an enduring pastime in Roman city life.[28] Being elected into the hierarchy of magistracies was crucial to a successful career and gaining influence and wealth. The word for election, *petitio*, had various meanings which included 'thrust' and 'attack' as well as standing for office.

The day of an election could involve huge numbers of people from across Italy gathering in Rome, many struggling to find anywhere to stay, as happened in 123 BC. They came together in the Field of Mars but even that was not large enough and some had to climb up to the rooftops to shout support for their candidate.[29] With so many people participating, it is unsurprising that elections had the potential to turn into explosive occasions.

Gaius Marius came from a country town not far from Rome which firmly placed him outside the traditional aristocracy in the city. His family had means and connections which was just as well because he was desperate for office. He managed to become a tribune of the plebs with the help of Caecilius Metellus, a member of a family who acted as patrons for Marius' family.

Next, Marius stood for the aedileship, and aimed immediately for a senior position. It soon became apparent that he was going to lose so he changed horses and stood for a lesser aedileship instead. That did not impress the electorate who promptly passed him over for being immodest. Although Marius had uniquely lost two elections in one day, this did nothing to dent his high opinion of himself. He finally managed to squeeze his way into a praetorship but was prosecuted for bribery.[30] It was only the beginning of Marius' career, but his antics showed what was necessary for an ambitious young man without scruples if he was to forge a career in Rome's political system.

One day in the mid-50s BC the general Pompey was standing near to where the elections for the aedileships were taking place. With so much at stake, and amid the jealous factionalism that Rome was riven with at the time, an explosive fight broke out, resulting in fatalities. Pompey was showered with blood so members of his staff quickly provided him with clean clothing (this must have been a normal part of the baggage of a man of substance out on business in Rome) and rushed the soiled garments back to his house. His horrified and pregnant young wife Julia (Caesar's daughter) collapsed, believing he had been murdered, and had a miscarriage (for this marriage, see Chapter 4).[31] The story, though, is more important for what it says about voting for office in Rome in the perilous days of the late Republic and how dangerous it could be for ordinary people attending an election.

In 54 BC Cicero was outraged at the way bribery and corruption had taken off yet again, and how a large sum of money had been lined up to bribe the voters who were entitled to cast the first votes in the *comitia centuriata*. 'The whole matter was an inferno of ill-will', he said.[32] This assembly was made up of Roman citizens divided into blocks of one hundred (centuries) in a hierarchy based on wealth. In the Roman voting system, the tribes voted in order of precedence. Once enough votes had been cast in favour of a candidate to give them a majority, the votes of the remaining tribes became redundant and rendered them electorally impotent. The process of voting in order was carefully recorded and continued to be so for centuries afterwards.[33]

Nowhere else in the Roman world has produced as much evidence for electioneering as Pompeii. Most belongs to the last few years of the city's history before it was destroyed in August 79. The electioneering was part of the rapacious competition for civic office which came with huge obligations but also the potential to increase a family's status, influence over local commerce, and thus the chance to become richer. Pompeii's raucous and corrupt local politics of early imperial times preserved much of what had characterized late Republican Rome.

Freeborn citizens of Pompeii were eligible to vote, so long as they fulfilled a property qualification, and this was organized by dividing a town into voting districts, in Pompeii's case five. Within the districts support for candidates came from individuals (often associates of the candidate) or special interest groups, such as the commercial guilds. An important accomplishment, especially for a 'new man' (*novus homo*) trying to make his mark as a new entrant to the nobility by being the first of his family to be elected a consul, was to have fame as a speaker. In Rome it was also essential to drum up as much support as possible among, for example, legal clients, the guilds, fans of the candidate's oratory who followed him around to applaud his declamations, and to seek support from the traditional nobility, the Optimates ('the Best'). Gratitude for this was best shown in throwing banquets and maintaining an open-door policy.[34] In Pompeii it was much the same, but on a smaller and more parochial scale.

Lucius Ceius Secundus stood for *duumvir* in Pompeii's latter days. He lived in a smallish house close to the town centre.[35] He and his family seem to have made a habit of supporting political candidates, and several electoral slogans (*programmata*) remain visibly daubed on the street frontage of his house. It had proved a sound investment since he served successively as *aedile*, duumvir twice, and *quinquennalis*. The latter was a particularly useful position: every five years the duumvirs were charged with the task of reviewing those eligible to vote and serve in office. It was the perfect opportunity to help cronies and push out enemies and rivals. Ceius Secundus' campaign in early 79 to become duumvir involved running alongside Gnaeus Helvius Sabinus who was standing for aedile. Helvius Sabinus instigated a conspicuous campaign for this crucial opportunity to enter a career in civic office. Sabinus was endorsed by a variety of individuals (including women who, of course, could not vote) and organizations. Being associated with Ceius Secundus was evidently seen as an advantage to Sabinus.[36]

The aedileship was the crucial entry-level magistracy because an aedile was guaranteed membership of the town council (the *curia*), the equivalent of the Senate. During his term of office an aedile had responsibility for public buildings and services. After his time was up, an aedile became a councillor (decurion) and within three years could stand for election as a duumvir.

Supporters claimed whatever they pleased about their favoured candidates, however preposterous, but were even freer in the insults they heaped on their opponents. Walls across Pompeii were routinely daubed with the name of a candidate and his alleged qualities by his supporters. Reminiscent of the public displays of election posters especially in the United States, these vote-seeking slogans were painted over and replaced with new ones in succeeding years. Some slogans bragged about the benefits a candidate might bring to Pompeii. Gaius Julius Polybius, standing for election as an aedile, was said to be a source of good bread while Claudius Verus, standing for duumvir, was vaguely said to be an 'honest young man'.[37] These slogans were frequently abbreviated. OVF appears on many of them and represented *oro vos faciatis*, 'I beg that you make [name of the candidate]' aedile or duumvir, as appropriate. Another abbreviated slogan was DDRP, short for *dicendo dignum rei publicae*, 'celebrated as worthy of public office'. Electioneering also involved knocking the opposition, sometimes in slightly subtler ways than just producing a torrent of abuse. Marcus Cerrinius Vatia's enemies painted up slogans that said those 'fast asleep, thieves, and drinkers' would be voting for him.[38]

Some of this handy support came from the guilds, local commercial associations dominated by freedmen. Unable to stand for office themselves, they served their patrons among the decurial class by helping to bankroll candidates who would serve their interests. They also found ways to manipulate the system by seeking to have their own freeborn sons elected to office, sometimes at an absurdly young, and illegal, age (see Chapter 8).

In the fifth century an anecdote was still circulating about Cicero. He was said to have mocked how Caesar ignored the usual election process in order to have his friends admitted to the senate, eventually packing in around 300 loyalists and raising the size of the senate from 600 to 900 (Augustus later restored it to 600).[39] On one occasion Cicero was being hosted by one Publius Mallius who asked Cicero to grease a path for his stepson to be admitted to the civic council, apparently of Pompeii, as a decurion. Cicero acidly responded by saying that 'if you like, he can have that in Rome, but in Pompeii it's difficult'. He was implying that at a place like Pompeii a self-serving elite routinely sewed up all the public offices for its members whereas Caesar had been indiscriminate and casual in admitting new senators in Rome.[40] The story may well be apocryphal, but the point was almost certainly a true one.

THE MOST CORRUPT OF ALL

Among the most notorious examples of corruption was the provincial governor Gaius Verres (c. 120–43 BC) who systematically bribed his way into high office. Among the crimes he was accused of was selling senatorial status to underage boys of sixteen or seventeen. That was a form of malfeasance well known at a local level in Pompeii, and doubtless everywhere else (see Chapter 8). Verres was prosecuted in 70 BC by Cicero for his behaviour while governor of Sicily from 73 to 70 BC, a post he had also secured with backhanders. Verres was accused of being (among other crimes):

a man, the embezzler of the public funds, the petty tyrant of Asia and Pamphylia, the robber who deprived the city of its rights, the disgrace and ruin of the province of Sicily ... While this man was praetor the Sicilians enjoyed neither their own laws, nor the degrees of our Senate, nor the common rights of every nation. Everyone in Sicily has only so much left as either escaped the notice or was disregarded by the satiety of that most avaricious and licentious man.[41]

Verres' misdemeanours included placing onerous charges on those who ran farms and ransacking religious monuments, becoming involved with a corrupt tax-collecting company, and forcing owners to sell works of art at knockdown prices. He was also accused of using the slave revolt led by Spartacus in 73–71 BC as a pretext for raising money. This was achieved by arresting slaves belonging to wealthy landowners, accusing them of plotting to join the slave revolt, and then offering to release them in return for bribes.[42] Cicero's first two speeches against Verres were so devastating that Verres fled Rome into exile at Marseilles. Cicero had prepared several others which survive but which were not used. In one Cicero made a great deal of how 'Roman greed and injustice' had penetrated in some way almost the whole known world and warned that Rome faced doom if people like Verres were acquitted simply on the basis that his predecessors had set precedents.[43] In c. 57 BC, Gabinius, governor of Syria, accepted a bribe from the Egyptian king Ptolemy XII Auletes (father of Cleopatra VII) to use his provincial army to restore the pharaoh, who had fled to Rome for support, to his throne which was briefly occupied by his daughter in his stead. Although Gabinius succeeded, he was prosecuted for acting without the Senate's authority, being fined and sent into exile.[44]

In 59 BC Caesar, then consul, had passed the *lex Julia de Repetundis*, which contained over one hundred provisions designed to restrict the potential for governors to become corrupt. The law is now only known from scattered references, but these show that it was designed to be all-encompassing and drew together some provisions from earlier laws, including under Sulla. Not only did the new law limit the gifts a governor could receive and require him to keep proper accounts in duplication to prevent fraud, but it also listed some of the abuses the law was designed to prevent. Cicero referred to some of them in his speech criticizing Lucius Calpurnius Piso, Caesar's father-in-law, for his governorship of Macedonia between 57 and 55 BC.[45]

THE GEMONIAN STAIRS ('THE STAIRS OF MOURNING')[46]

There were ruthless punishments awaiting anyone who fell foul of the state or the mob, including the highest status individuals. The Gemonian Stairs formed a key access route to the top of the Capitoline Hill from the Forum. Prisoners were taken out of the prison on the Capitoline Hill to meet their deaths. Being publicly executed and thrown down the Gemonian Stairs, which ran down past the prison, was an 'accursed stigma' (detestanda nota), damning the victim and his family for all eternity.[47] This made it particularly attractive as a place to do away with high-profile traitors and other enemies of the state. It was not the only execution venue on the Capitoline. The Tarpeian Rock on the side of Capitoline Hill was a favourite place for hurling prisoners and enemies off. But in a notoriously superstitious place like Rome one had to be careful. When Marius was made consul for the seventh time (in 86 BC), his first act was to have a man called Sextus Lucinus thrown off the rock. That was later seen as a powerful omen for the fact that Marius died on the seventeenth day after his consulship began. Far from heralding a new and better era, Marius' son, Marius the Younger, embarked on a killing spree of Rome's nobility.[48]

Around the same time Lucius Cornelius Cinna and Marius had ruthlessly done away with any other senators and equestrians who had opposed them. The equestrians were just murdered, but the severed heads of the senators were displayed on the rostra in the Forum for all to see. Even that was not enough. The decapitated bodies had their necks cut off too, which were then paraded in public.[49]

The deaths and displays at such places amounted to collective popular participation in ritual state executions. During the time it was on display, the corpse might be mourned by those who wished to do so. It was more likely to be mutilated before it was then removed and thrown into the Tiber, the ultimate humiliation. No one was spared on grounds of age or sex. On one occasion under Tiberius twenty were allegedly dealt with in a single day. Women and children, in most cases the families of the condemned, were also liable to be killed and left out on the stairs.[50]

Tiberius had succeeded Augustus in 14 as the second emperor, and the succession was in crisis. His nephew Germanicus had died in 19 and his own son Drusus had followed in September 23. Tiberius took the logical step of adopting Germanicus' eldest sons Nero Caesar and Drusus Caesar, whose mother was Agrippina the Elder, Augustus' granddaughter (not to be confused with her daughter of the same name who was the mother of another Nero, the later emperor). It was clear the plan was that one or other of them would succeed Tiberius. But this strategy took no account of Lucius Aelius Sejanus (20 BC–31).

Sejanus was an equestrian with high connections. Extremely ambitious, he had not only wormed his way into Tiberius' trust but also achieved appointment first as joint praetorian prefect with his father commanding the Praetorian Guard, and then as sole prefect. Eligible for promotion to senatorial status, he turned that down because he knew being prefect of the Guard gave him far more real power. The gullible Tiberius even called him 'my partner in labours'.[51]

By 23 Sejanus had engineered the relocation of the praetorian cohorts from their dispersed barracks around Italy to the brand new Castra Praetoria on the north-eastern outskirts of Rome. This increased Sejanus' power even further. He began to conspire with Tiberius' widowed daughter-in-law and niece Livilla. He planned to set aside his own wife and family, marry Livilla and father a new imperial heir. Sejanus' scheming included working up Tiberius' paranoia about Germanicus' widow, Agrippina the Elder, and convincing him that she was the leader of a rival faction. Given her popularity with the army, Tiberius fell for the story easily. By 27 he had removed himself to Capri, leaving Sejanus effectively in charge of Rome. Sejanus used the opportunity to set his spies on Agrippina and her son Nero to supply him with 'proof' of their plotting.

It was not until 31 that Tiberius woke up to how much he had been played for a fool. Rome was filling up with statues of Sejanus who had even engineered a senatorial decree for the public celebration of his birthday. Tiberius arranged for Sejanus to be tricked into believing he was about to be made heir and offered the praetorian prefecture to a former prefect of the night watch (the vigiles) called Macro if he helped bring Sejanus down.

The Senate gathered at the Temple of Apollo on the Palatine Hill, right next to the former residence of Augustus, on 18 October 31. Sejanus turned up in the gleeful belief that a letter from Tiberius was about to be read out that would declare he was to be given the honour of the powers of a tribune of the plebs, a special hybrid title devised by Augustus for the emperor, and which had later been given to Tiberius to earmark him as heir apparent. The letter started out innocuously enough but then proceeded to denounce Sejanus.

In a moment the mood changed dramatically. Sejanus was abandoned by his senatorial supporters and the Guard. Some of the senators pounced on Sejanus and attacked him on the spot. The whole assembly moved fast to dissociate themselves from a man who only hours before they had been keen to flatter. Outside the Senate made their way down the hill and gathered in the Temple of Concordia Augusta where they condemned the praetorian prefect to death.

The point about Sejanus' fate in the context of this book is the graphic and public horror of what came next. In a vivid display of brutality, designed to advertise that Sejanus had fallen from grace in the most dramatic way possible, he was killed. To round off the occasion, his body was dragged with a hook to the top of the Gemonian Stairs and thrown down.[52]

This was only the beginning of the spectacle. Under such circumstances the Romans applied 'collective prosecution'. His children, innocent parties and whom Sejanus had planned to spurn, were murdered six days later, adding to the gore spattered on the Gemonian

Stairs. His daughter Junilla had been first raped by the executioner to overcome the law against executing a virgin.[53] They were followed by anyone else believed to have been a family member, supporter, or associate of Sejanus. His wife Apicata committed suicide on 26 October, knowing she had no future.[54]

With so much at stake, it is hardly surprising that violence was routine in Rome and served as a backdrop to everyday life. But Rome was a frightened city in many other ways. All sorts of threats stalked the streets. Even returning home by foot from dinner was a potentially fatal mistake.

6

THE FRIGHTENED CITY

*When your house is closed, and your shop locked up with bar and
chain, and everything is quiet you'll be robbed by a burglar, or
perhaps a cut-throat will wipe you out quickly with his blade.*

Juvenal[1]

Violence against the person was rife in ancient Rome in all
sorts of contexts. This included the endless threat of theft
or murder on the streets at night. Here thugs and robbers
roamed at will mugging people for valuables, their preferred weapon
being the concealed short sword known as a *dolo*, 'I cut like an axe'.[2]
The culprits even included the emperor Nero (see below).[3] There were
the notorious and mysterious cases of the needle killers. Break-ins
were another hazard. Accidents such as floods or fires were also constant dangers.

THE SENATE'S REVENGE

By the middle of the second century BC the late Republic was dissolving
into unprecedented political violence, with echoes in modern times.
Tiberius Sempronius Gracchus was elected to be one of the ten tribunes of the plebs in the summer of 134 BC.[4] Late the next year he would

136

be beaten to death by a senatorial mob for trying to stop senators seiz-ing the land of ordinary Roman citizens who had been sent on military service. Some of the senators were amassing huge slave-run estates and by dispossessing the free peasants there was a potential critical shortage of manpower for future wars.

The sudden withdrawal of men from the land to serve in the army meant that it was difficult to operate farms in any reliable or efficient way. Unfortunately, the use of slaves in that context simply made more sense if the farms were going to be viable. The rich might also have been greedy and acquisitive, but compromising Rome's existence by threatening the routines and procedures on which agriculture depended threatened the state.[5] Of course, had Rome not persistently engaged in greedy wars of conquest the problem might never have arisen.

The result was rival political factions building up around Tiberius Gracchus and his opponents, the latter led by another tribune of the plebs and former friend of Gracchus called Marcus Octavius. For the moment debate remained civil. Gracchus modified his law more in tune with popular demands.[6] To begin with the prospects for com-promise looked good.

When Gracchus put his law to the Council of the Plebs (*Concilium Plebis*), bypassing the Senate, he pulled no punches by saying how seri-ous he believed Rome's predicament to be. Tribunes had the power of mutual veto and Gracchus was immediately thwarted by Marcus Octavius who, as it happens, also held some of the disputed land. As the tension rose, Gracchus used 'conceal-carry' and kept a short sword hidden under his garments.[7]

Repeated vetoes and arguments were only temporarily abated while Tiberius Gracchus suggested that either he or Octavius stand down. Octavius refused. Tiberius Gracchus continued to rely on the Council of the Plebs, changing tactics by prioritizing a vote on whether Octavius was entitled to act against the interests of the people. He won the vote, toppling Octavius who was replaced by a more acquiescent tribune and the new agrarian law was passed.[8] Together with Tiberius

Gracchus' father-in-law Appius Claudius Pulcher (consul in 143 BC) and his younger brother Gaius, the division of the land commenced. Dark threats, though, began to circulate about what would happen to Gracchus when his year as tribune was up and his legal inviolability expired.[9] A contemporary historian claimed that Gracchus never went around without three to four thousand men in attendance. If true, it was an understandable if provocative precaution, but, of course, it would have suited senatorial propaganda to depict Gracchus that way.[10]

Inevitably, the rich who had most to lose tried to rig the election of the next tribunes in the summer of 133 BC. Gracchus decided that if he was not re-elected bad things would follow. He succeeded in drumming up enough support for the first two tribes to vote for him, while his senatorial land-holding opponents protested that he was breaking the law.[11] With his supporters fearing permanent servitude and therefore backing him, Gracchus took the extraordinary step of trying to take over the Capitol where the comitia (the assembly of the people where the election was taking place) was meeting while tribunes and senators blocked votes on his re-election. Gracchus was surrounded by his unofficial bodyguards, and the senators and tribunes were driven out.[12]

Gracchus' actions immediately gave rise to the allegation that he had toppled the other tribunes and declared his tribunate renewed without an election. It was a short distance from there to being accused of seeking monarchical powers, and that soon followed. The senators promptly organized themselves around Cornelius Scipio Nasica, the pontifex maximus, and headed for the Gracchans in the nearby Temple of Jupiter Capitolinus.

A confrontation followed which dissolved into murderous violence. The Senate, that great esteemed Roman assembly of elders, degenerated into a gang of thugs. Senators grabbed weapons from the Gracchans, took them from their own attendants, or smashed up furniture to make them and started beating and killing the Gracchans. Gracchus himself was among the dead. The first blow came from a bench and the second a club. His body and those of any of his supporters who had died with him were ordered to be thrown into the Tiber, rounding off the grisly events of a day that would go down in infamy in the most humiliating and demeaning way possible.[13]

Just twelve years after Tiberius Gracchus' death, his younger brother Gaius was dead too. He committed suicide as another senatorial mob closed in on him for carrying on trying to bring in reforms. Tacitus, that arch supporter of the Senate and a senator himself, dismissed the Gracchi brothers as 'agitators' of the plebeians. In other words, they had in his view deliberately stirred up dissent and got what they deserved.[14]

ARSON AND ANARCHY

With no formal or reliable police force to protect them, Romans were often left to look after their own security. A key feature of Roman society was the relationship between patron and client. The patron, a man of substance and some wealth, surrounded himself with his clients. These men were often business associates but of lesser status and in many cases the patron's freedmen (see Chapter 8). They owed him their freedom, and often their livelihoods. In return they gave him their loyalty and sometimes their muscle.

Ceratus was a freedman who supported a member of the local decurial elite called Publius Vedius Nummianus in a Pompeii election. Nummianus was almost certainly his former master and therefore patron.[15] This sort of arrangement turns up across the Roman world, showing the close ties between local government and business. At Ostia the corn merchant Publius Aufidius Fortis served as a duumvir, the senior civic magistracy similar to the consulship, five times. He was president of the corn measurers and patron of the corn merchants. He was also a councillor at Hippo Regius, a corn trade centre in North Africa. Some of the men holding office in the guild and bearing the name Publius Aufidius in later years were his freedmen. They paid their former master the sort of respect he expected by dedicating a statue to him.[16] For a man like Aufidius Fortis, surrounding himself with advocates, whose loyalty to his family would last after his death, was clearly attractive.

Such examples represented a normal part of Roman commercial and social life that helped hold people together in a web of common interests. Actively promoting their patron's electoral prospects could take on a more sinister tone. The patron, or indeed anyone who had the necessary resources, could hire their own heavy mobs. This practice reached its dangerous climax in the late Republic. Partisan gangs became especially useful in more disturbed times when the stakes were high.

In 100 BC the usual consular elections for the following year took place in Rome. One of the two available consulships was contested by the senators Glaucia and Memmius. Memmius was much more distinguished, making his election a foregone conclusion – on the face of it. Glaucia and his tribune sidekick Apuleius had a simple solution to this threat to his own political advancement and power. While the election was in mid-throes, they arranged for a crowd of supporters to attack Memmius in the comitia. They beat Memmius to death in plain view of everyone else. This enraged the people who the next day set out to kill Apuleius but he had rounded up another gang of supporters and with Glaucia seized the Capitol.

With tension at fever pitch, the Senate declared Glaucia and Apuleius to be public enemies. Marius, an outgoing consul, had to weigh in. He planned to institute legal proceedings but was overtaken by events when persons unknown severed the water supply to the Capitol. Glaucia and Memmius surrendered, hoping Marius would protect them. Instead, he locked them in the Senate House to make it look as if he was preparing proceedings against them. This enraged the crowd who started attacking the building before stoning Glaucia and Memmius to death along with several other magistrates.[17] So much for democracy in ancient Rome, reminiscent of some of the political violence of the twentieth century.

In 87 BC the consul Lucius Cornelius Cinna garnered support from disaffected plebeians in the newer tribes of Rome, who came far down the order of priority for voting. Cinna revived a scheme of Marius' in which their votes would be distributed among the old tribes to make for a fairer system. A story went around that Cinna had been bribed to the tune of 300 talents, a vast sum, to support the plan. Meanwhile, the older tribes looked to the other consul for the year, Lucius Octavius, to support the status quo. Armed supporters from both camps ended up in the Forum and the scene was set for a showdown. Most of the tribunes of the plebs vetoed the proposal so the aggrieved new citizens promptly pulled out their daggers and attacked them. Octavius dashed down the Via Sacra into the Forum with a band of his own supporters, separated the victims from their assailants and drove Cinna away while his men attacked the new citizens, killing some and driving the rest out of Rome.[18]

In 82 BC the dictator Sulla seized Rome. He was, apparently, the first to create a formal list of his enemies to be punished with a further threat of penalties for anyone who concealed those on the roster. To this he added rewards for assassins and informers. He began with forty senators and 1,600 equestrians on his hit list, adding more senators shortly afterwards. 'Many people were killed because of purely personal feeling.' This was not because he cared much about them but to please those among his supporters who had scores to settle. His henchmen set to work, grabbing their victims wherever they could be found, whether at home or in public places such as the streets and temples. The killers gleefully totted up their murder tally by identifying each victim according to where he had been put to death, such as 'by his large house' or 'by his hot water system'. Others were allegedly 'thrown through mid-air' to land at Sulla's feet. Anyone who could tried to escape but even those who fled out of Rome were hunted down wherever possible by Sulla's spies. Thus, said Appian, 'Sulla became king, or tyrant *de facto*, not elected but holding power by force and violence'.[19]

According to Dio, certain senators had been told to gather at the Temple of Bellona, believing Sulla was going to try and justify himself. When they were killed and thrown in the Tiber, a 'great uproar and lamentation' erupted, 'their cries and wails' being heard in the Senate House by the other senators who were now petrified. Dio noted that the terrible massacre inflicted on Roman tax collectors and settlers in Asia by Mithridates VI, king of Pontus (120–63 BC), 'was of slight importance in comparison with the number now massacred and their manner of death ... such calamities encompassed Rome'.[20] In 88 BC Mithridates had secretly instructed the cities of Asia, on pain of death, to rise up on his orders and specifically targeted creditors as well as anyone else of Italian origin. He called the Romans 'the common enemy of all'.[21] When the rising came, Roman settlers were pursued into temples and killed. Eighty thousand were said to have died.[22]

Sulla had other ideas. 'A certain longing came over him to go far beyond all others in the variety of his murders.' He produced tablets with names of those to be proscribed written on them, which were published. 'There was no safety at all for anyone outside of Sulla's circle', particularly frightening for those who had learned in advance that their lives were threatened. In a revolting twist, regardless of where anyone was slaughtered his head was added to others displayed on the rostra in the Forum.[23]

The ordinary people of Rome were left either as stunned bystanders or as willingly complicit in the shameful goings-on. By the 50s BC, when Roman politics was becoming increasingly polarized during the age of the imperators Caesar, Pompey, and Crassus, violence was being routinely used to further political agendas. The candidates would do anything necessary to secure their interests. In 57 BC the notorious Clodius Pulcher rounded up a gang of gladiators to rush those assembled to vote on a measure. They attacked and killed some of the crowd. His nemesis was another senator called Titus Annius Milo, clearly inspired by such a ruthless way of pursuing political interests to use the same tactic. The year before, Clodius had revived the old collegia guilds to help provide him with the necessary brute force. They had existed long before but had been abolished. Now they were back with a vengeance and in the late Republic played a significant role in political violence.[24]

Politics had degenerated so far in Rome that by November in the turbulent year of 57 BC Cicero reported that his brother Quintus' house had been set alight by some of Clodius Pulcher's thugs. On 3 November they began their work by climbing up onto the top of Cicero's house so that they could throw stones at Quintus' residence and damage the roof before chucking in firebrands. Perhaps the most astonishing part was how brazen the attackers were. To do this they had forced their way into Cicero's house which was undergoing building work, driven off the labourers, and for good measure had destroyed the Porticus of Catulus (built c. 102 BC), currently being restored after a senatorial decree on a contract issued by one of the consuls. Eight days later, on 11 November, Cicero was caught by surprise and chased down the street by a Clodian gang who threw stones at him and threatened him with cudgels and swords. He had to duck into a friend's house for safety. The following day Clodius ordered his henchmen to attack and try and burn down Milo's house. A friend of Milo's, Quintus Flaccus, was at the ready with Milo's own thugs who burst out and managed to kill several of Clodius' mobsters.[25]

The result was that 'bloodshed occurred throughout practically the whole city', said Dio. It is difficult now to appreciate just how far elite Roman society had degenerated that such an affair was possible. It was as if two rival congressmen had formed armed gangs to run riot in Washington DC though perhaps events at the US Capitol in early 2021 make this seem less implausible than it might once have been. The ordinary people of Rome were being treated to the extraordinary sight of the shameless abuse, not only of power but also the patron–client relationship. Traditionally, aristocratic homes in Rome had served as political bases. These were where candidates met their clients and friends (*amici*) to plan campaigns. Now these homes were serving as the garrison headquarters for armed gangs where blatant acts of violence were planned, and which were just as likely to be attacked by their enemies.

The bitter rivalry between the two men continued until 52 BC when Milo, seeking election to the consulship, ran into Clodius Pulcher on the Via Appia and attacked him. Fearing that would lead to Clodius seeking revenge, he finished the job and killed him. That provoked an uproar in Rome where Clodius was hated, but Milo more. The mob set some of the city on fire and organized Clodius' funeral pyre in the Senate House which was burned down as a result. Next, they set off to burn down Milo's house, but it was saved by his supporters loosing a hail of arrows from inside the house.[26]

Not long afterwards, Milo was put on trial for Clodius' murder. He moved fast. He freed all his slaves, instantly exempting them from being tortured into testifying against him. Cicero, who defended him, insisted that he was merely giving them the reward they had long deserved.[27] It was precisely this sort of chaos that led to Caesar's first dictatorship a few years later in 48 BC, and eventually the coming of Augustus. Under him such private gangs were banned.

Meanwhile, the horrors were a taste of things to come in Rome as the Republic remorselessly fell further under the control of rival generals. Once they had been formally recognized by the Senate in law in November 43 BC, the triumvirs Antony, Octavian, and Lepidus reached Rome. In the first instance they ordered the execution of senators who were dangerously powerful, their personal enemies, or whose estates could thus be confiscated, and the money used to fund the war against Brutus and Cassius.[28] They swaggered into the city over a period of three days, each triumvir allocated a day of his own to arrive with one legion and his praetorian cohort. Another 280 executions of their enemies were ordered, demonstrating that the soldiers brought into Rome were not just there for show (see Chapter 3 for the impact on certain individuals).[29] The people had seen soldiers in the city and must have realized that even more waited outside Rome. Appian alludes to the horrors of the killing that went on but ruminated with the benefit of hindsight on the paradox that one of the triumvirs (Octavian, who became Augustus) turned out to be the one who would establish government on a 'firm foundation' and left a lineage and a supreme name.[30] The deaths were far from the last purges in Rome.

DANGEROUS STREETS

Rome was a tense place in which to live, even for ordinary individuals trying to go about their everyday business. Many of them were crammed into dangerously crowded and badly built tenement blocks. Contrary to the popular belief that the Romans were magnificent town planners, Rome had expanded without any controls.

The only protection from crime and violence was provided by the urban cohorts, created by Augustus to act as a police force. The urban cohorts, sometimes with the help of the Praetorian Guard thereafter, made Rome a slightly safer place. There was a limit to what they could do, especially as they lacked any form of surveillance equipment or high-speed pursuit vehicles, and there were too few of them. By 69 there were four cohorts, at most amounting to 3,600 men, under the control of the urban prefect. They did not function, so far as we know, in any comparable capacity to a modern police force setting out to prevent and solve crime, but they could step in to take control of disorder.

Men and women alike were vulnerable to attacks on the streets of Rome or any other city, though custom and the paternalistic society did mean that women were much less likely to be out alone after dark, especially women of high status. Lethal violence could erupt without warning, to say nothing of the Roman habit of hurling broken pots out of the window. Oddly, the available evidence suggests that many of the most dangerous cutthroats were often young men from aristocratic families.

Juvenal said that there were so many such hazards in Rome that anyone who went out to dinner without making a will first was guilty of sheer negligence.[31] He regarded Rome as a much more dangerous place than a remote province, especially at night. Having served in the army as the commander of an auxiliary unit in Britain he knew what he was talking about. Juvenal's Rome was a place crowded with thieves of every sort and some of them dangerous. 'Whether you try to say anything, or escape silently, it all comes to the same thing: they hit you, and next in a fit of anger take surety from you.' The word Juvenal used

145

for surety was *vadimonia* (plural) which means 'bail'. In other words, the mugger treated the victim like a criminal who was forced to stump up cash to enjoy some temporary liberty – until the next time. Horace mentioned how easy it was to be taken for a fool by a beggar loitering at any one of Rome's numerous road junctions pretending to be lame.[32]

In *The Golden Ass* (or *Metamorphoses*), the novelist Apuleius described how the prefect of the night watch in a provincial Italian town was accustomed to making nightly rounds to check all was well. On the night in question, he had come across a young man armed with a sword who had killed three people and then hidden out in a house to wait for morning. The prefect had waited too, and caught him. Apuleius, who lived in the early second century AD, had written his work in the first person about the adventures of Lucius. Earlier in the story, a woman called Photis had warned Lucius about a gang of young aristocrats who were killing at will in the streets and leaving the bodies of their victims where they fell. She pointed out a crucial problem: the town was too far from an army barracks for there to be any chance of catching them. Lucius assured her he would be going out armed with his own sword for protection.[33]

'By night, thieves hide themselves', said Catullus.[34] A few decades later, the young emperor Nero was one of the nocturnal thugs. As soon as night fell, he would disguise himself with a hat or a wig and set out into the dark in search of violent diversions. His targets included men returning to their homes after dinner, and presumably the worse for wear – Nero was always a coward – and beat them up. Anyone who fought back was liable to be stabbed to death by Nero's stooges and thrown into the drains. These were a favourite way of disposing of corpses because they were washed out into the Tiber and lost for ever. Nero also allegedly operated shop break-ins, selling his loot in the palace. Some of his victims did fight back. One was a senator whose wife Nero had assaulted. Thereafter the emperor took care to bring praetorian officers on his nocturnal exploits. Following behind him at a safe distance, they were able to pounce on anyone who decided to resist and beat them up on Nero's behalf.[35]

Even locking oneself up at home or at work was no guarantee a burglar would not force his way in and possibly even kill you. Petronius' famous *Satyricon* from the time of Nero includes a reference to a break-in at an inn by a pair of Syrians who were trying to take advantage of a party where the revellers were in a drunken stupor.[36] So bad was the problem that Juvenal claimed the manufacturing of chains to deal with thieves was the principal use of iron in the city, and to such an extent that it was compromising the production of agricultural equipment.[37] He was exaggerating, of course, but there had to be some truth in what he had said.

There are, of course, echoes of Victorian-style moralizing in rants by Juvenal and others. Although a large proportion of the urban masses in Rome were entitled to the monthly grain dole, amounting to 200,000 people in Augustus' time alone, the reality for most ordinary Romans was extreme poverty and hard work. The inevitable result for many was resorting to crime of some sort. In a city where extravagance was flaunted by the elite glitterati, whose retainers flung passers-by out of the way as they pushed and shoved their way through Rome's streets, the temptations were there for all to see.

THE STRANGE CASE OF THE NEEDLE KILLERS

During the reign of Domitian (81–96) there was an outbreak of a sinister new offence, not only in Rome but also elsewhere. The perpetrators' modus operandi was to spread poison on needles and then prick anyone they could with them. The extraordinary story sounds like something from Sherlock Holmes, but Rome had no celebrated sleuth, fictional or otherwise, to solve the crimes. The result was that many victims died, most of them unaware of what had happened to them.

Some of the needle killers were informed on, caught, and punished. The mystery is what the motive was. Dio, who recorded the story, suggests it was some sort of crooked business, but there is no suggestion that the murderers were after money. The wave may have been driven by nothing more than a malicious desire to spread panic. If so, it succeeded.[38]

Incredibly, perhaps inspired by tales of the fear the needle killers of Domitian's time had provoked, a fresh wave broke out a century later in 189 during the reign of Commodus, and at the same time as a plague had spread across the Empire. Domitian had been unpopular but was in many ways a sound administrator. Commodus was anything but, and his serious dereliction of duty was of far more concern to the Romans. Despite managing to kill a large number of people, the new needle killers found their actions went largely ignored and they disappeared from the news.[39]

MURDERED FOR HER JEWELLERY

Roman tombstones rarely record the cause of death. Usually, the text makes a bald statement of the deceased's name, and sometimes family information, and age at death. To find an exception we have to divert on this occasion from Rome to the city of Salona in the province of Dalmatia (equivalent to most of Croatia and parts of certain neighbouring countries).

Julia Restituta was ten years old when she died, her tombstone describing her as *infelicissima*, 'the most unfortunate'. She had been 'killed on account of her jewellery'. Her grieving parents, Julius Restitutus and Statia Pudentila, commissioned the text for her memorial.[40] Its style suggests a date in the third century AD. Unfortunately, the couple said nothing about whether she was attacked at home, in a city street, or on the open road out in the countryside, though it is unlikely she was outside her home on her own. Wherever it happened, it was a terrible shame she had not been discouraged from having her precious possessions on show. The same hazards must have faced anyone, especially wealthy women or girls wearing valuables, in Rome which was why for the most part they only ever ventured out with a band of household retainers and in a litter.

Men were more likely to be attacked, as Juvenal had so graphically described. A freedman called Flavius Kapito was unlucky enough to be mugged and killed by robbers while travelling between Viminacium and Dasminium in Moesia Superior, again probably during the third century. His grieving mother erected his tombstone and called her son's death 'most atrocious', as it behoved her to do.[41] The key phrase was that he had been *interfectus a latronibus*, 'killed by bandits/brigands'. Publius Aelius Ariortus was a civic magistrate in Dacia aged fifty when he lost his life the same way.[42]

The most conspicuous example of institutionalized and everyday brutality in Rome was slavery, which dominated all walks of life in the Roman Empire. Slaves led variable lives, some enjoying relative autonomy and even luxury. But for the vast majority, slavery meant the constant threat of injury from the sheer hard work to being beaten up by a mistress taking out her frustrations on a maid, or arbitrary execution when an entire household of slaves was put to death after a single one of their number committed a capital crime.

7

SLAVES

Joking aside, I believe the slaves, bought by me on your advice,
are seemly. It remains to be seen if they are worthy because a
judgement is formed better by what one hears than what one sees.

Pliny the Younger[1]

I n the short letter quoted above, Pliny the Younger complimented
his father for his judgement and joked that this was only because
his own judgement was the same. Pliny was, by the standards of
his day, courteous and humane. This was a man who made over vast
sums of his own money for the benefit of Comum, his hometown. He
enjoyed what passed for a sort of friendship with some of his slaves.
Pliny recorded in another letter a long description of daily life in his
country villa. This included a reference to his most senior slaves whom
he engaged in convivial conversation. There is no suggestion that he
felt disturbed by being a member of a society in which slavery was an
integral part of how it functioned. Pliny accepted the way things were
and took it for granted that the purchase of human beings was routine,
treated as we might buy a piece of household equipment. Indeed, that
was what domestic slaves were regarded as.

A huge proportion of the population in Rome was made up of slaves,
former slaves, or the descendants of slaves. They were merely the tip
of an iceberg – untold numbers of other slaves worked on vast landed

estates and in mines across Italy and the Empire, out of sight and out of mind. Even in and around Rome slaves were both visible and invisible; visible in the sense that they were to be found in every home, factory, farm, and setting, and invisible in the sense that for most of those in the slave-owning class they were simply part of the background noise of life. Just as we ignore the hum of our fridges, the buzz of electric fans and the other machinery which surrounds us, so the Romans often took little notice of the human beings whose servitude and labour made their lives possible.

Being seen to have an unnecessarily large number of slaves, especially if they came from somewhere exotic, played a part in flaunting wealth. Umber sent his friend Martial a collection of items as gifts for the Saturnalia, including toothpicks and a sponge. They were carried over to Martial's home by a detail of eight Syrian slaves from Umber's household. Estimating the total value of the presents to be a measly 30 denarii, Martial suggested how much more convenient it would have been just to send over one slave with the money. Another of his friends, Lupus, also had eight Syrian slaves but they carried round Lupus' mistress, which Martial resented.[2]

Those who consorted with slaves on an equal basis were liable to face the force of the law. In the year 52, 'the emperor Claudius proposed to the Senate that women who married slaves should be penalized. It was decided that a woman who demeaned herself like this should be made a slave herself if the slave-owner was unaware of the arrangement and reduced to the status of a freedwoman if he had known.'[3] Under Vespasian (69–79) the position seems to have been strengthened. A new law was passed that said a free woman who formed a liaison of any sort with a slave would then become enslaved herself.[4] That also meant her children would become slaves too.

Slaves might be owned by individuals and households, the state, or by organizations which in a provincial town could mean a civic council. Their duties, which were interminable, therefore ranged from the mundane and domestic to brutal hard labour. For many slaves, life was brutal and short, their servitude having perhaps begun by being taken during one of Rome's great wars of conquest. These could result in tens or even hundreds of thousands of slaves swiftly entering the labour market through the network of slave traders and markets across the Empire. From the second century BC on the latter became the most important source of new slavery in the Roman world with millions of individuals being involved. The scale as a proportion of the Roman Empire's population is difficult now for us to contemplate. In December 54 BC Cicero was offered slaves by his brother Quintus who had been campaigning in Gaul and Britain with Caesar, and which he must have acquired as his share of the booty. 'Of the slaves that you offer me, I am greatly obliged to you and I am, just as you write, understaffed in Rome and on my estates', he wrote to Quintus.[5] Others became slaves in different ways, for example abandoned children who were collected by slave dealers and reared until they were of saleable age.

The coming of machines played a huge role in the ending of most slavery in early modern times. In the Roman Empire, and throughout antiquity, slaves were often treated little better than pack animals – with which they were casually compared – and sometimes worse. In an era in which mechanization was virtually unknown, there was neither the ability nor the will to end slavery. It is no exaggeration to say the Roman world would have collapsed without slave labour. The super-rich of the Roman world were likely to own huge numbers of slaves. In 8 BC Gaius Caecilius Claudius Isidorus 'declared in his will, that though he had suffered great losses by the civil wars, he was still able to leave behind him 4,116 slaves, 3,600 pairs of oxen, and 257,000 head of other kinds of cattle, besides 60 million sesterces in cash'.[6]

Emancipation movements did not exist, apart from slave rebellions. In a letter, Seneca explored the relationship between masters and slaves, observing that 'we maltreat them, not as if they were men, but as if they were beasts of burden'.[7]

The simplest way into slavery was being born to slave parents in their master's household. These slaves were known as *vernae* (as slave children they were called *vernulae*), perhaps related to the verb *vernare* 'to bloom' or 'to be young', suggesting they were a sort of home-grown product, hence other meanings of being native or indigenous. Such slaves were notorious for being over-familiar with their masters and were sometimes brought up to serve as jesters or fools to entertain the household.[8]

The division between slave and free was blurred by the fact that so many people in Rome who were free had been slaves themselves or were the sons or daughters of former slaves. Unlike slaves in so many other eras, Roman slaves could be freed or even buy their freedom. This was a distinction of enormous importance, as well as being attractive to some owners who that way recouped something of their original investment and saved ongoing costs.

Slaves and freedmen (for the latter, see next chapter) traditionally presented themselves twice daily to their master or former master, now their patron, once in the morning and once in the evening. This old custom fell into disuse but the emperor Galba (68–9), a stickler for tradition, kept it going in his household.[9] One slave called Euaretus was so grateful to his master Gallus, or at any rate wished to appear so, that he commissioned and paid for a herm sculpture (see Glossary) of Gallus together with its inscribed marble pillar and dedicated to Gallus' *genius* (spirit). The inscription, dated on style to the first century AD, was found on the site of a rural villa on the Via Cassia about 7 miles (12 km) from Rome where Euaretus presided as *magister* (a type of priest in this context) over the household cults, among other duties.[10] The brief text is a fascinating one because of how the master had been deified in the same lateral way that emperors were obliquely deified by using the idea of an individual's *genius*. This was a form of spirit that avoided deifying a living individual but suggested he had a form of divine parallel existence in his qualities. Whether Euaretus really held his master in such esteem is not clear, but it would appear he had made enough money out of his being Gallus' slave to owe him some sort of gesture of fealty.

BUYING SLAVES

Slaves in Rome worked in an unlimited range of capacities in vast building projects, private houses, small businesses, and right up to the imperial palace. The market value of a slave was not inconsiderable but obviously the price was determined by the skills an individual slave could offer, level of education, and potential longevity, as well as location and availability of slaves.

Slaves arrived for sale in Rome and Italy from all over the Roman world. They formed a huge part of the booty from wars of conquest and could then be used or sold on by the generals responsible, with some soldiers also receiving an allocation. Caesar had a reputation for collecting slaves of 'exceptional figure and training' and this had supposedly attracted him to invading Britain.[11] There was, of course, a vast and ceaseless second-hand market in slaves. Pliny the Younger received a recommendation from Plinius Paternus, probably a relative. Having looked at them himself, he wrote to say, 'I think the slaves you recommended I buy look fine. The only other thing I care about is that they are honest. On this, I can only rely on their reputations rather than their appearance.'[12]

A writing tablet from Pompeii refers to the sale of slaves 'on 13th December next . . . at Pompeii in the Forum publicly in the daytime'.[13] Slaves for sale could expect to be stripped and inspected by a slave dealer, usually known as a *venalicius*.[14] Pliny the Younger referred to slaves casually, using the related word *venalibus* which was a synonym for saleable, and in this case sentient, commodities, and is the origin of our word venal, which now means something associated with corruption and indeed the trade was notorious for sharp practice (see below).[15] When Caligula inspected the wives of his dinner guests to choose those whom he would force to sleep with him, he was described as doing so as if he was buying slaves.[16]

A slave girl in Roman London was sold for 2,400 sesterces and that conforms well with a general picture in imperial times of around 2,000 sesterces being the going rate for an ordinary slave.[17] Martial sneered at his friends Quintus and Tucca who paid out 100,000 or even 200,000 sesterces for slaves. It would be unsurprising if especially able or experienced slaves could command far higher prices than a slave girl; but Tucca had apparently shelled out the large sums for his 'young favourites'. Elsewhere Martial refers to where the 'lower class of house slaves' could be purchased, calling such places 'greed platforms' (*avarae catastae*), a colloquial term for the general slave market where slaves were displayed on a dais for buyers to view.[18]

A slave trader could also be known as a *mango*, a pejorative term that implied someone trying to make something he was selling look better than it was. It came from a verb that meant 'to adorn' and was used by Pliny to refer to a well-known dealer called Toranius. Toranius had sold Mark Antony two handsome boy slaves who were so similar he could pass them off as twins, receiving 200,000 sesterces for them. When Antony complained, Toranius successfully argued that the resemblance between two unrelated boys was far more astonishing than a couple of identical twins, successfully convincing Antony.[19] The word mango and the verb *mangonico* were used by Pliny for any commodity, positioning slaves in another way along with any goods with a commercial retail value. He seems to have been the only writer who deployed the word like this.

Slave dealers had plenty of tricks on hand because there was a vast amount of money to be made from the trade. Hyacinth root could be placed in sweet wine to help delay signs of puberty (how this worked, if indeed it did, is not clear) and was clearly designed to help sell a slave to a buyer interested in having children either as a decorative orna-ment or for sexual purposes.[20] Castration was another method. Resin dissolved in oil made an ointment used by slave dealers to rub all over the limbs of slaves, the idea being that it would help loosen them up and make it possible for them to take in more food and thus appear better fed.[21]

It is easy to see why a slave trader might invest time and money in any means that might improve his profit. One trader, Gaius Sempronius Nicocrates, detailed on his tombstone how troublesome and arduous long sea and overland journeys with slaves were. Aulus Caprilius Timotheus, who died around the end of the second century BC, was depicted on his tombstone showing his chained slaves being pulled along like mules. At least two children were involved.[22]

Vespasian was nicknamed 'The Muleteer' because after coming back from governing Africa he was so out of pocket that he had to start trading in mules – or so Suetonius said. The word was probably a metaphor for human slaves, traded *as if* they were mules. It is, after all, difficult to imagine that a trade in real mules would have been particularly lucrative, whereas according to the satirist Persius slave-dealing was a way to *duplica rem*, meaning to double one's money.[23] Suetonius' tone implies Vespasian's personal prestige was dented by having to recover his affairs that way. The Vespasian reference might also be to castrated male slaves who commanded a premium, 'mutilated by the grasping slave-dealer's art', since in essence a castrated male was sterile like a mule. His son Domitian was later to prohibit the practice and had to place a cap on the price of remaining stock.[24] The practice continued. The law had to be reinforced under Nerva in 97, the year after Domitian's death and again under Hadrian:

> ... no one has a right to castrate a freeman or a slave, either against his consent or with it, and no one can voluntarily offer himself to be castrated. If anyone should violate my Edict, the physician who performed the operation shall be punished with death, as well as anyone who willingly offered himself for emasculation.[25]

A slave's clothing was sometimes a clue to identifying one – Mark Antony was once able to escape from Rome by wearing a slave's outfit, whatever that was, and join Caesar.[26] Conversely, Seneca reported that 'a proposal was once made in the Senate to distinguish slaves from free men by their dress; it was then discovered how dangerous it would be for our slaves to be able to count our numbers'.[27] In other words, the slaves would discover how numerous they were compared to the free, suggesting that under normal circumstances they were hard to tell apart. The proposal is sometimes said to have occurred in Nero's reign, but Seneca does not specify when the idea was mooted. It could have happened generations, even centuries, before Seneca wrote.

Of course, some slaves did run away. The legal principle was simple: since the slave belonged to a master or mistress, if he ran away then he had stolen himself from his owner; if he was stolen by someone else, then the thief had stolen the slave from his owner. The Romans had the equivalent of a stun gun available to tackle runaway slaves, so long as they had not yet fled beyond Rome's boundaries: a popular belief was that the Vestal Virgins had a spell that could 'root to the spot' a fleeing slave.[28] Cicero's friends included a tragic actor called Aesopus who owned a slave called Licinius. Licinius absconded in Athens after posing as a freedman. He was caught in Ephesus and locked up. Cicero asked his brother Quintus, then propraetor in Asia, to bring or send him to Rome for the sake of Aesopus who was upset by his slave's 'wickedness and audacity'.[29] There is no indication of what punishment awaited the errant Licinius.

COMMODITIES

Slaves were referred to in everyday speech as saleable commodities. Marcus Terentius Varro wrote a treatise on agriculture in the first century BC. He began with the land and its cultivation and only then moved on to how the land was tilled. He divided that part into three: the 'articulate, the inarticulate, and the mute'. The mute were the inanimate tools like carts, the inarticulate were any animals involved, and the articulate were the slaves. The slaves were thus seen by him purely as a class of equipment, a capital investment like any other with a practical purpose. He proceeded to make recommendations about their supervision before repeating Cato the Elder's mathematical calculations to help work out how many slaves would be needed per unit of land.[30] Varro's description exemplified the Roman capacity to dehumanize the slave. Although it was possible in certain circumstances for slaves and their owners to become close, the fact remained that slaves were just commodities.

The fictitious freedman Trimalchio in Petronius' celebrated satire of the vulgar and over-monied ex-slave who had made a fortune in trade depicted him boasting that 'there's something rather safe about a large ship, you know. I obtained another cargo of wine, bacon, beans, perfumes, and slaves.'[31] Once more the slaves came last on the list, but this time we learn a former slave had no scruples about owning slaves himself. Far from it. Successful freedmen often adopted the trappings of wealth enthusiastically, including the ownership of slaves. In Roman terms, slave-owning showed how far they had come.

Like any other piece of equipment, a slave would eventually grow old and become less useful or even completely useless. While some owners may have felt compassion for some of their slaves, Cato was not among them. He instructed landowners to sell off old or defective animals, old wagons and tools and then, last on the list, 'an elderly slave, a sickly slave, and anything else that is superfluous'.[32] Exactly who an old or sickly slave was going to be bought by is not clear, but the important point is that Cato could see absolutely no basis for any sentimentality towards another human being of servile status.

By the reign of Claudius (41–54), if not before, owners had found another solution for dealing with useless sick or elderly slaves, but the emperor was considerably more sympathetic to their plight. Suetonius recorded that 'when certain men were exposing their sick and exhausted slaves on the Island of Aesculapius [the island on the Tiber, named after its Temple of Aesculapius] because of the trouble of treating them, Claudius decreed that all such slaves were free. If they recovered, they should not return to the control of their master; but if anyone preferred to kill such a slave rather than to abandon him, he could be charged with murder.'[33]

Augustus had already followed a similar principle during a time of shortage in Rome, ordering that slaves currently for sale be expelled from the city, along with a proportion of the household slaves, gladiators, and foreigners unless they were working as doctors and teachers. He had slave doctors on his own staff.[34]

PUNISHING SLAVES

'We Romans are exceptionally arrogant, harsh, and insulting', said Seneca about the treatment of slaves.[35] Mark Antony's grandfather was long on generosity, but short of means. When a friend asked him for money, Antony senior resorted to giving him a silver shaving bowl and told him to make what use he could of it. His wife was furious when the bowl was discovered to be missing and immediately set about searching the slaves and was about to interrogate them individually, her immediate assumption being that one of them had been responsible. Antony senior had to come clean to save them from punishment.[36] In a Roman household the servile staff were seen as a potential threat to such an extent that they were automatically believed to be culprits. Of course, in practice they probably often were since theft was one way of supplementing their marginal existences.

Slaves might be punished by being sent to an *ergastulum* ('slave prison' or 'workhouse') throughout Italy where they had to work in the fields in chains. The managers of these establishments also increased their labourers by capturing travellers, or those trying to dodge military service.[37]

Slaves were subject to a variety of other vicious punishments, including summary torture and death. Any mutiny within the household or an attack on an owner could result in all the household slaves being executed. Hadrian had to ban masters from killing their slaves and ordered that a slave who had been accused of a capital crime should be tried by the courts instead.[38] That he felt the need to do this at all showed how vulnerable slaves were to arbitrary domestic executions.

Belonging to the wrong person turned out to be a crime, especially a bitter political enemy. After the Battle of Pharsalus (48 BC), Caesar saw to it that all of Pompey's slaves and freedmen were killed.[39] He was equally ruthless when it came to far more trivial matters. He had his baker thrown into irons just for serving him a different type of bread from that chosen for his guests, the implication that the latter had been given an inferior type.[40] This, incidentally, counted as a lenient punishment. That Augustus subjected his slave Cosmus to the same treatment for speaking about him in an insulting way went down as an example of his merciful attitude.[41] In an intriguing twist, beating a slave close to a statue of Augustus became a capital crime under Tiberius, the point being that it was part of a range of measures designed to prohibit any disrespectful behaviour towards the memory of the great man rather than an effort to improve the lot of slaves.[42]

Guests arriving for dinner at the house of the fictitious freedman Trimalchio struggled to get into the dining room when a slave 'stripped for flogging fell at our feet and began to implore us to save him from punishment'. His crime had been to lose the steward's clothes, worth a measly 10 sesterces, at the baths. The guests begged for the slave to be let off and the steward begrudgingly decided to give them the slave. Later in the same work, though, is a reference to a dinner guest called Habinnas taking home food from a dinner because 'if I do not bring some present back for my pet slave-boy there will be trouble'. It was clear what was going on and suggests that some slaves were able to control and manipulate their owners in return for being exploited, in this case probably sexually.[43]

Seneca described what it must be like for slaves forced to stand and wait on a glutton of a master:

> The master eats more than he can hold, and with monstrous greed loads his belly until it is stretched and at length ceases to do the work of a belly; so that he is at greater pains to discharge all the food than he was to stuff it down. All this time the poor slaves may not move their lips, even to speak. The slightest murmur is repressed by the rod; even a chance sound, – a cough, a sneeze, or a hiccup, – is visited with the lash. There is a grievous penalty for the

slightest breach of silence. All night long they must stand about, hungry and dumb.

He praised his friend Lucilius for being the sort of educated man who was content to sit down and dine with his slaves, pointing out that in truth they and their master were fellow slaves since 'Fortune has equal rights over slaves and free men alike'.[44]

Juvenal seems not to have thought much of women, a subject he went into in considerable detail in his 6th Satire which included such gems as 'there never was a court case in which the quarrel was not started by a woman'. He moved on to slate the woman who, despite going to adorn and decorate herself, discovered that her husband turned his back on her at night, and then by day took out her frustration by presiding over the beating of their slaves and even their executions. 'While the flogging goes on, she daubs her face, she listens to her girlfriends or considers the measurements of a gold-embroidered gown . . . her household is no mellower than a Sicilian [tyrant's] court.' He even suggested that such women, keen on their own private liaisons (and insinuating that they were acting like prostitutes) and impatient to look their best, might in their frustration tear a maid's hair and rip off her clothes to beat her with a 'thong of bull's hide'.[45]

In contrast, there was the case of the slave woman Alimma who lived and worked in Locri in southern Italy who had lived a life of *summa discip(u)lina*, 'highest training', by the time she died aged thirty. The meaning was subtler than a straightforward translation suggests: *discip(u)lina* has connotations here of docility. Her father and fellow slave set up her tombstone with their master's permission, remembering Alimma as a 'respectful and worthy woman'.[46]

'Flogging is only suitable for slaves', said the rhetorician Quintilian. He was writing about education at the time and was recommending that pupils not be beaten because it was 'disgraceful' and thus beneath them. That made it only suitable for those regarded with contempt. Quintilian also thought that if a boy needed beating that badly, he would end up becoming immune to its effects like the most intractable slaves.[47] The passage thus provides an indirect but useful explanation for how a Roman could justify the corporal punishment used for slaves.

Brutality could amount to a great deal more than merely flogging. At the end of the Spartacus War in 71 BC captured rebel slaves were crucified along the Via Appia to set an example and remind every passer-by, free or slave, of what the Roman state could and would do to maintain control over its servile population. The nature of the executions was brought home by a 2021 discovery at Fenstanton in Britain of a Roman crucifixion victim.[48] A young adult male, probably in his twenties or thirties, had been shackled for much of his life, his legs bearing the scars. He was undernourished and had finally met his end after being tied to a wooden board and then prevented from swinging by hammering an iron nail through an ankle. The nail survived to bear witness to the way the victim was killed. He is likely to have been displayed in public while he expired but, unusually, he was apparently then cut down and given something approximating to a normal inhumation burial resulting in the preservation of his body. This single instance is a vivid reminder of the visibility of cruelty in the Roman world and how every inhabitant of Rome from childhood upwards grew up accustomed to such sights.

Caligula was notorious for how he treated slaves, but what he ordered to be done to them differed not much from how he treated the freeborn. 'At a public banquet in Rome he handed a slave over instantly to the executioners for thieving a length of silver from the couches, with orders to cut his hands off and hang them round his neck on his chest. He also ordered that the slave then be led about around the guests, preceded by a notice board explaining the reason for his punishment.'[49] We must be careful, though. Such anecdotes may have been contrived as part of the rhetorical depiction of a tyrant, even if they fit the general background of the time.

One traditional form of execution for a criminal was to be stripped and held fast by being tied to a fork-shaped yoke. He was then beaten to death with rods. Some Roman officials were a great deal more imaginative. Vedius Pollio was an equestrian and a close friend of Augustus'. He also enjoyed inflicting cruelty. Pollio discovered that moray eels were capable of tearing human beings to pieces, especially if they were whipped up into a frenzy by tasting vinegar. Realizing this made for an opportunity to put on a spot of theatre for wider entertainment, he allegedly organized demonstration executions in which condemned slaves were hurled into pools filled with moray eels. Pollio was probably using the Mediterranean moray which can reach 1.5 metres (5 ft) and is known to bite human beings. The particular appeal to Pollio was the sight of seeing a man ripped up in an instant.[50]

STAYING ALIVE

At the end of the third century BC, the comic playwright Plautus included a speech by a slave character called Messenio. Messenio described the best way for a slave to behave in order to survive. The first priority was to take care of his master's affairs whether his master was at home or not. The second was to remember what happened to lazy or dishonest slaves: whippings, chains, treadmill, exhaustion, hunger, and bitter cold, 'suitable recompense for idleness. Being a good slave is thus much better than being a bad one.' Messenio's philosophy was simple. Carrying out his master's orders efficiently and with care was to his own best advantage. He looked forward to being rewarded in the future, by which he almost certainly meant being freed.[51]

Some slaves, especially under certain emperors, were able to become extremely rich as a result of gifts, kickbacks, and other forms of corruption. Before he became emperor himself in 69, Otho managed 'to extort a million sesterces' from a slave of Galba in return for finding him a post as a steward.[52] Cleander was another who rose from complete obscurity to become one of Commodus' chief sidekicks. He 'had formerly been sold in a group of slaves and had been brought to Rome with the others to be a pack-carrier; but in the course of time he advanced to such a point that he became Commodus' cubicularius, married the emperor's concubine Damostratia, and put to death Saoterus of Nicomedeia, his predecessor in this office, together with many others'. Cleander was accused of selling offices of any kind from senatorships to provincial governorships, making an unprecedented fortune for someone in his position. He used some of the money to help bankroll Commodus' excesses. Much good did it do him (see p. 201).

In an intriguing twist, when Commodus was assassinated on the last day of 192, the man chosen to succeed him was Pertinax, himself the son of a freedman and thus the first of all the emperors to be the son of a former slave. He was killed just three months later, on 28 March 193, by the disgruntled Praetorian Guard for failing to stump up his accession donative and also because of his love of military discipline. Theocritus was a freedman who had been born a slave and brought up in the theatre. He used his skills to teach Caracalla to dance. His theatrical career in Rome was disappointing so he took himself off to Lyon where a less discerning provincial audience appreciated his skills. By some extraordinary twist he managed to keep Caracalla's favour, incongruously rising to the position of prefect of the grain dole, and then to a senior military command.[53]

One option for a slave was to try and not only escape but also pass himself off as free. Claudius Pacatus did just that, enlisting in the army and doing so well that he rose to the centurionate. Sadly, he was rumbled and, despite his rank and success, Pacatus was returned by Domitian to his master to resume his career as a slave.[54]

A SLAVE'S LOT

Slaves, of course, also cost their masters dear. They had to be fed, clothed and housed. The surviving houses at Pompeii and Herculaneum usually have little obvious evidence for slave quarters. In some cases, such as the House of the Stags at Herculaneum, there seems to have been nowhere for them to sleep apart from the kitchen area or the floors of corridors.

On the Palatine Hill side of the Forum are the remains of the *horrea* Vespasiani ('the storehouses of Vespasian'). They had been built over aristocratic houses of Republican date which had gone through at least two phases, finally being destroyed in the fire of 64. The last houses on the site had basements comprising dozens of cubicles, one totalling fifty and all opening off narrow corridors. These were just big enough to accommodate a stone bed. One theory is that the house was one owned by Marcus Aemilius Scaurus, an ambitious and successful politician of the mid-first century BC, given to extravagance on an epic scale. Bent on living in a style which he felt befitted his station, Scaurus bought a house on the edge of the Palatine and later acquired 'an attractive and imposing house' next door belonging to Gnaeus Octavius which he demolished so that he could enlarge his original home.[55] The house was embellished with four giant marble columns taken from his notoriously extravagant temporary theatre (see Chapter 12). In 53 BC Scaurus sold it to Clodius Pulcher for 14.8 million sesterces, apparently to help pay off his debts.[56] The contrast between the tiny slave cubicles and the house above could not have been more pronounced. Tibullus had men like Scaurus in mind when he wrote about the pillager (*praedator*) whose greed led him to covet expensive foreign marble turned into columns, each of which needed a thousand teams of animals to haul it through the city.[57]

The House of the Menander at Pompeii unusually had a complete slave and service quarters accessed down a narrow opening at the corner of the peristyle garden which was overlooked by the prestige rooms (see the plan of this house in Chapter 3). But the house's footprint was large enough to spare the space. Slaves at Pompeii's House of the Vettii had a suite with its own atrium hall and other rooms. Perhaps the freedmen owners, the Vettii brothers, had in mind their own lives as slaves and wanted to give their own staff better facilities. The Villa of Civita Giuliana just outside Pompeii had a small room (16 square metres) that was apparently used as slave quarters and for storage. There were two wooden beds with rope and fabric webbing just long enough for small adults at 5.5 feet (1.7 m) long, and a third only big enough for a child at 4.5 feet (1.38 m). This makes it possible that a slave family was accommodated in there. Amphorae, jugs and a chamber pot were packed under the beds. Eight more amphorae were stacked in the room along with a wooden chest that seemed to contain components of horse harnesses. A tiny window let light in. If this was a slave bedroom, it is a remarkable survival but may represent a considerably better facility than most slaves were ever offered.[58]

In his book about the Latin language, Varro discussed the utility of having an inflected language. Having learned to inflect a noun, that is to change the form of the word according to the case or agreement of the word, the same principle could be applied to any number of nouns. The example he decided to use was when slaves were purchased and brought into a large household, they 'quickly inflect all the names of their fellow-slaves in the oblique [i.e. other] cases' so long as they had heard the name in the nominative form, whatever it was.[59] The reference to slaves here is incidental, an unconscious and blasé acceptance of the everyday reality of a society where slavery was no more than a basic fact of life. Varro probably referred to slaves here to emphasize his point because a slave's personal name was likely to be unusual or a nickname and possibly Latinized from a foreign one.

In Plautus' comic play *Pseudolus*, an oppressive master called Ballio berated his slaves in a manner showing that he expected loyalty, devotion, and hard work, all in return for abuse and brutality. 'Now you lot stand here, members of a race born to be whipped! Listen to what I say. You man, with the jug, fetch the water and make sure the kettle is filled instantly. You with the axe, set about chopping the wood.' A slave protests that the axe is blunt. Ballio retorts, 'So what if it is? You're blunted with stripes, but is that a reason why you shouldn't work for me? I'm ordering you to clean up the house. You know what your duties are, hurry up inside.' Ballio proceeds to itemize a litany of tasks his slaves need to carry out, including polishing the silver and preparing a showcase dinner.[60]

Ballio one day set off to the market but instructed a slave to take the lead as security against being mugged. Slaves were used to run before the litters of rich and powerful people. They carried torches to light the way and make sure the general crowd dodged out of the way. An unfortunate slave of Augustus' was killed instantly while performing this duty when a bolt of lightning struck him.[61]

Slaves were useful tools and that could mean finding themselves in important jobs, especially those who had education and skills. Recognizing the enormous importance control of money production could give him, Caesar placed the mint and state revenue under the management of his own slaves.[62] On the other hand, their duties could be dangerously menial. Domitian liked to have a slave stand up with one arm outstretched and fingers spread for target practice. He would then fire an arrow at the gaps between the fingers.[63] Luckily, Domitian was an expert marksman, but either way the slave would have had no choice but to stand there.

A PRIVILEGED SLAVE

In the second century AD a slave known as Callippus performed the duties of *actor* (agent, or perhaps better, business manager) in the service of Lucius Caecilius Iovinus. Iovinus is otherwise unknown, but he was important and wealthy enough to count an agent on his establishment. Callippus was therefore an important administrator for his master's economic affairs, this position becoming distinct from the more traditional general position of farm manager (*vilicus*). One of Callippus' jobs would have been to collect money in place of his master, such as the rents owed by tenants, taking down payments, earning interest by using cash for loans, and accounting for all the transactions.

In Pompeii a slave called Diognetus was in the service of Gaius Novius Cypaerus, who was probably a freedman. In 37, at the start of the reign of Caligula, Diognetus rented out his master's Puteoli warehouse number 12 to another slave called Hesicus. Hesicus was on the staff of a freedman called Primianus Evenus. The arrangements were a little complicated. Another individual, Eunus, was in debt to Hesicus'

167

master and had provided a consignment of Alexandrian wheat, as well as 200 sacks of vegetables as security for the loan. That presented Hesicus with a storage problem and he had turned to Diognetus for help. Both slaves were therefore acting as the agents for their masters' affairs. That Primianus Evenus is additionally described as the freedman of Tiberius Julius Augustus makes it likely the latter also had a finger in the pie.[64]

In law, if the slave agent committed any act of malpractice, then that counted directly against his master and could harm his reputation.[65] It was normal for the agent to be a slave, even though the duties gave them intimate knowledge of their masters' affairs, as well as the obvious opportunities to cream off a percentage for themselves. As a slave, the agent was as much at the mercy as any other slave of his master's wrath. The volatile Domitian had one crucified after pretending the day before to like him.[66]

The slave agent is most widely recorded in Rome in the second century AD. The reason seems to be that slaves in such an important job were better off than most. The reason we know about Callippus is because he recorded himself on the tombstone of his slave wife Hilara who had died at the age of twenty-seven. She was buried close to the later site of the basilica of St Paul-without-the-Walls at Rome.[67] Callippus took charge of building their tomb, also to be used by their freedmen of both sexes, and their descendants. By giving only names for himself and his wife it is clear they were both still slaves at the time, the reference to freedmen perhaps indicating that provision was being made for a more distant future when he was freed and had slaves to free of his own. Callippus made sure that his job and his master were prominently included in the inscription because this made him a more important slave and set him apart from his servile inferiors.

Epaphroditus was a slave in Domitian's service, working as a *structor*, best translated as a construction engineer. We know nothing else about him except that a slave colleague of his called Syntropus arranged Epaphroditus' burial and tombstone.[68] Conversely, Nothus enjoyed light duties for a slave. He was a *librarius a manu*, which means 'copyist', for the household of the Statilii, the family of Claudius' ill-starred wife Messalina, in the first half of the first century AD. Nothus thus spent his working life copying out books and manuscripts for the family. Tedious work no doubt, but unlikely to be arduous or dangerous. His unnamed wife set up his monument, complete with several lines in verse that read 'He was her idle hope, torn from the flower of his life by jealous Pluto. A great crowd weeps and buries him here with utmost dignity'.[69]

Columella had important advice for a slave-owner when it came to allocating slaves to the various tasks involved in running a household. He was particularly scathing about slaves who were good-looking or used to carrying out specialist jobs in a city house. Columella thought they were too used to time off which was routinely wasted at the circus and the arena, drinking, and visiting brothels. This suggests city slaves enjoyed some autonomy when it came to managing their time. It also reflects the existence of the trade in slaves or movement within an owner's properties since Columella was discussing indirectly instances where a slave had been transferred from the city to a rural establishment. Columella recommended that only a slave who had been accustomed to agricultural work all his life and had proved his competence by experience should be considered for a management job on a farm. Such a man ought to be old enough to command authority, have the personal qualities that would enable him to exercise the authority responsibly, and be 'allocated a woman to live with him and keep him under control'.[70]

RIGHTS

Slaves had few rights. 'Human rights' as we understand them did not exist in antiquity. An extreme example was the law that dealt with cases where a slave had murdered his master. Tacitus explained 'when a master was murdered by his slaves, all those who were going to be freed under the terms of his will, so long as they lived in the same house, would be executed with his other slaves'.[71] The reason was the constant state of fear the Romans lived in of slave insurrections. Their only solution was to terrorize slaves with the prospect of a mass execution.

In 61, Pedanius Secundus, prefect of Rome, was murdered by one of his slaves. One story was that the killer had been denied his freedom after agreeing the price with Pedanius. Another was that he had been infatuated with one of his master's catamites. Either way the law was clear: the household slaves would have to be executed and the recent senatorial decision had reinforced what was an ancient tradition. The prospect led to protests among the ordinary people of Rome.

The matter ended up being discussed in the Senate. A senator called Caius Cassius defended the law, pointing out that Roman households were now full of foreign slaves whose traditions and beliefs were completely different. 'You will not suppress a cesspit like that except by dread', he warned. Since none of the slaves had done anything to stop the assassin, they were by definition as guilty as him, Cassius argued. The executions were set to go ahead but a huge threatening mob gathered outside armed with rocks. Nero had to issue an edict and ordered soldiers to be stationed along the entire route along which the hapless slaves, regardless of age or sex, were to be dragged to their deaths. An idea to deport Pedanius' freedmen from Italy was also mooted, but Nero rejected that on the grounds that this additional punishment might only aggravate the protesters further.[72]

There must have been countless unrecorded occasions when individual slaves absconded. Many will have been caught and executed while others will simply have disappeared without trace, successfully changing their names, and finding a new way of life where nobody asked awkward questions. Most presumably had the sense not to draw attention to themselves, but it was possible for a slave and others who had committed crimes to seek sanctuary at certain temples, shrines, and altars, a privilege that disgusted Tacitus.[73]

In one curious incident, during the civil war of 68–9, one such slave claimed that he was the son of a senator called Licinius Crassus Frugi who had been murdered during the last part of Nero's reign. Why he should have done this is a mystery. He called himself Scribonius

Camerinus and insisted that he had spent Nero's reign hiding in Istria, being a place where the old Crassus family had owned land, and retainers, and enjoyed popularity. He was joined by a motley band of soldiers and credulous followers until he was apprehended and taken to Vitellius, the short-lived emperor of 69. There he was interrogated about who he was. His story fell apart. Once his master had identified him as a fugitive slave called Geta he was punished in the customary way for slaves, which, of course, meant execution.[74]

LOYALTY

Despite their lack of freedom some slaves lived relatively comfortable lives and were treated with what passed for kindness and consideration in a society where one human being could own another. Some were considered the favourites of their masters and benefited from privileges accordingly.[75] Their experience was probably unusual. As a result, some slaves took huge risks on behalf of their masters. During the proscriptions enacted by Marius and Cinna the senator Cornutus was saved by his slaves. They had found a dead body (easily chanced upon in ancient Rome) which they placed on a pyre, claiming successfully to Marius and Cinna's agents that Cornutus had hanged himself and they were disposing of his remains.[76]

During the proscriptions enforced against their enemies by the triumvirs Octavian, Antony, and Lepidus beginning in 43 BC, there were more examples of slave loyalty. Cicero's works survive largely thanks to his former slave and loyal freedman Tiro who published them after Cicero was executed by the triumvirs that year. Some even sacrificed their lives for their masters. These instances were even more remarkable, given that the triumvirs had offered freedom and 10,000 'Attic drachmas' (a synonym for Roman denarii here) to any slave who informed on his master.[77] The senator Gaius Antius Restio the younger was targeted. He fled, but one of his slaves followed him. Although he had been well treated, he had recently been punished for misdemeanours by being branded. Nevertheless, the slave caught up with Restio and assured his master that he remembered the kindness better than the branding. He found a cave for Restio to hide in and kept him supplied with food. Soldiers in the area seem to have got wind of Restio's whereabouts. The slave followed them and when he spotted a random old man walking in front of the soldiers, leaped out and killed and decapitated him. The astonished soldiers assumed he was a robber and arrested him, only for the slave to claim he had killed Restio in revenge for the branding scars. The soldiers fell for the ruse and took the head off to claim the bounty on Restio's life, only to discover they had been tricked. Meanwhile, the slave escorted his master to the coast and found him passage to Sicily.[78]

Around the same time, another senator called Appius was at his country house when soldiers arrived and forced their way in. Incredibly, a slave put on Appius' clothes and jumped onto his master's bed while Appius stood by dressed as a slave. The soldiers killed the slave and Appius escaped. Another, called Menenius, managed to flee to Sicily when one of his slaves pretended to be him and was carried off in a litter by other slaves. Lucretius was helped by two of his faithful slaves who carried him in a litter to Rome to seek out his wife. One slave broke his leg so Lucretius had to continue on foot, leaning on the fit slave for support. When they reached Rome they encountered soldiers, so hid in a tomb, only for tomb-robbers to turn up. The slave gave himself up to the thieves to be stripped in search of valuables while Lucretius escaped. Lucretius waited for the slave and then divided up his remaining clothing with him. They made their way to Lucretius' wife who hid her husband until friends interceded on his behalf and had him removed from the list of those to be put to death.[79]

REVENGE OF THE SLAVES

There were many slave rebellions, the most famous led by Spartacus in 73–71 BC, but slaves could also act on their own. There was always the chance that an individual slave-owner might be attacked in his own home. One of Caesar's assassins, the senator Lucius Minucius Basilus, was killed by his slaves. It might have been imagined that they were protesting at their master's actions, but they were also taking the opportunity to exact their revenge for the mutilations they had suffered when he had them punished.[80] In another instance around the same time, Ligarius was hidden in an oven by his wife. She shared this secret with one female slave who then betrayed them. One possibility is that the slave had been the subject of unwanted attention from Ligarius, something that would have been all too common in wealthy households where young female slaves were treated as sex objects by their masters.[81]

Around the early second century AD Largius Macedo, a senator, was relaxing in the baths at his country villa when he was surrounded by some of his slaves. While one grabbed him by throat, a second punched him in the face and more began to kick and trample him, including his private parts. Macedo was soon unconscious or had the wit to pretend to be. The slaves threw him on the floor of the heated bath and decided to pretend that he had been overcome by the temperature. Some of the loyal slaves turned up to try and help him recover, while the culprits made off.

Macedo only survived a few days before he expired. Most of the guilty slaves were caught and would undoubtedly have been executed. The motive is the one key factor missing from Pliny the Younger's account of the incident. But the assault on Macedo's body, and his genitals, suggests that he had gone too far with his prerogative to impose sexual demands on the female or young male slaves.[82]

FREEING SLAVES

Countless Roman slaves were freed ('manumitted') but the privilege was certainly not guaranteed. An owner had to be twenty years old before he could free a slave. Freedom came in two forms. A legal declaration of freedom took place before a magistrate, whether at a tribunal or in person, and came with the additional benefit of Roman citizenship though a freedman could not vote or hold public office. In this procedure the magistrate was 'claiming' the slave by declaring that the master did not own him. The owner for his part did not contest this claim and thus the slave went free.

Awarding freedom depended much on individual circumstances. Since slaves could play an important role in arranging their freedom, their choice was part of the process. Those in city households were more likely as freedmen to continue to offer their former masters or mistresses the same services they had performed as slaves. They were also more likely to be able to provide a replacement in the form of a *vicarius* ('under-slave', or 'proxy'), perhaps even purchasing one themselves as part of the cost of freedom. Slaves could be permitted to control a savings fund known as a *peculium*, but it remained the master's property for the simple reason that a slave could not legally own money. The master could retain the peculium as compensation if he agreed to free the slave. This became binding in law under Marcus Aurelius and Lucius Verus (161–9), obliging a master to free a slave if the slave could prove such an agreement had been made but he had not been freed.[83]

A peculium did not have to be made up just of money. Tiberius or Claudius freed a slave called Nymphodotus, who thereby became Tiberius Claudius Nymphodotus. He had lived for forty-six years with a fellow slave called Claudia Stepte, his *contubernalis* and wife who died at seventy-two. A contubernalis was more usually a military term that meant a tent companion, but was also used for a companion or mate of the same or opposite sex. In this context it was a term applied to cohabiting slaves, who were not allowed to form a legal marriage. The most likely explanation is that, when he was freed, Nymphodotus was permitted to take Claudia Stepte as part of his peculium because he referred to himself as her patron. This means that she was probably transferred to him as a slave, and that he then freed her.[84] Similar arrangements applied to an imperial freedman called Titus Flavius

Crathis who married his slave and freedwoman Flavia Sozusa at Ostia. She had been a *verna*, a slave born in a master's household (see earlier in this chapter); that she was happy to advertise this means she had evidently no shame in her origins. The term could be used to refer to men or women.[85]

Antistius Sarculo was a priest who apparently fell for one of his female slaves. His solution was simple: he freed and married her. She became Antistia Plutia. Their funerary monument, which was erected for them by two more of his freedmen, shows the two as an austere and elderly couple.[86] This was a far from uncommon practice.

Vespasian decreed that a slave woman who was sold on condition that she was not made a prostitute would become free automatically if it turned out her new owner had indeed pushed her into prostitution. If such a woman was sold without the no-prostitution condition being imposed on the buyer, that simple oversight would entitle her to freedom, making her then the freedwoman of the original owner.[87]

Revenge and greed were other ways to freedom. Under Caligula slaves could earn freedom and wealth by doing no more than give up details to the rapacious emperor of the size of their masters' estates. The information was worth one-eighth of the size of each estate. This was a way slaves found to get their own back on masters who had treated them harshly, so it is hard to feel too sorry for the owners who found themselves ruined this way. This also meant that the slaves were likely to support Caligula and were horrified when he was assassinated.[88]

Slaves could also be freed in their owners' wills or just at the owners' behest. This meant they originally retained the legal status of slave until a law change awarded them the intermediate status of being Latins. There were limits on how many slaves could be freed in a will. A sliding scale was in operation from 2 BC which began with someone who owned between two and ten slaves being able to free half, someone with ten to thirty being allowed to free one-third right up to those who owned 500 being able to free a maximum of 100.[89] By Caracalla's time in the early third century there was a tax of 5 per cent on freeing slaves. He raised it to 10 per cent as part of a programme of fiscal measures to help pay for the ever-increasing cost of the army.[90]

Latin status sat between Roman citizenship and provincial status. It was possible for slaves who had been initially freed informally this way subsequently to have their new status upgraded to the 'proper form'.[91] Until or if the latter took place the newly, but informally, freed slave was on tricky ground. In 50 BC Cicero took exception to how two of his freedmen behaved when working for his son. He was particularly disappointed by one of them, Chrysippus, whose company he had enjoyed despite his endless stealing, but whose constant running away was the last straw. Cicero dealt with Chrysippus by declaring that the informal manumission had not occurred, secure in the knowledge that there had been no competent person suitable at the time who could have made the declaration formal and binding. This was a convenient device that allowed an owner to withdraw a grant of freedom.[92]

There were numerous reasons why a slave could be freed. A slave might earn enough to save up to buy his freedom. He might be freed as a reward, or in his master's will. There were important advantages to the master because the cost of feeding and housing a slave was saved, and with even more advantages if the freedman became tied to the household in the Roman system of patron and client. Freedmen and freedwomen were indispensable to how Roman society functioned.

8

SPLENDID ACCESSORIES: FREEDMEN AND FREEDWOMEN

*Among the other splendid accessories of Caesar was a large
number of freedmen, many of them rich.*

Appian[1]

An incongruous aspect of Roman society was that slaves, surely
its greatest victims, in vast numbers coveted their liberty and
the chance to see their children grow up as Roman citizens.
The phenomenon is difficult for us to understand. This is not the place
to embark on trying to explain it beyond observing that the wholeness
and totality of the Roman world seems to have inhibited many from
even trying to envisage anything else. Instead, they looked for the best
opportunities within it. For some that meant rebellion and revolt, but
for many others they aspired to earn, be given, or buy their freedom
and make a future for themselves and their families.

Freed slaves were known as freedmen (*liberti*, singular: *libertus*) or
freedwomen (*libertae*, singular: *liberta*). Freedmen were denied the right
freeborn male citizens enjoyed to vote, or stand for office, but instead
often became important in commerce and administration. Their sons
could vote and serve in office, and in exceptional instances even rise to

high office or become emperor (Pertinax, governor of several provinces and short-lived emperor in 193, was the son of a freedman, see p. 164.) Imperial freedmen played important roles in imperial administration, scheming, and plots. With no racial or ethnic categorization of slavery, this meant once freed there was usually no obvious means of identifying someone likely to have been a slave though in practice names, behaviour, profession, and tastes easily gave them away.

Many freedmen took advantage of the Roman elite's revulsion for being visibly involved in commercial affairs (see next chapter). The senators delegated such sordid activities to their freedmen, often setting them up or helping them in business. There was a great deal to be said for this arrangement from a purely financial point of view. Seneca said 'the household staff demand clothes and food. So many bellies of extremely greedy beings are to be cared for, clothes improved, the hand of the most dishonest watched, and use made of people weeping and swearing.'[2]

Freedmen remained shackled to their former masters by new obligations of respect, and loyalty in exchange for protection. Freedmen ran businesses on their masters' behalf, provided any service their old masters and now patrons demanded, canvassed for them in elections, turned up every day to greet him at the morning *salutatio*, and were grateful for his support and help in times of need. They also bore his name. Rich freedmen were also a visible sign of a great man's prestige and fortune, their fealty and wealth acting as further proof of his status and munificence.

THE FREEDMAN AND THE FREEBORN

Martial summed up in this epigram the defining difference between the freedman and the freeborn. Martial was an equestrian, the second tier of Roman aristocracy, well-known with an international reputation but poor. Callistratus (whose name meant something like 'level footpath') was a wealthy freedman but sentenced permanently to being a social inferior, forever hamstrung by his status as an ex-slave. It was Martial's only consolation:

> Callistratus, I confess that I am and have always been, poor. Yet I am not an obscure or unknown equestrian, but am read throughout the world, and people say of me, 'Here he is'! and, what death has awarded to but few, has become mine during my lifetime. But you have halls, resting upon a hundred columns. Your coffers struggle to hold the wealth you gained as a freedman. Vast farms in Egypt's Aswan region are yours, and Gallic Parma shears countless flocks for you. This I and you are. But what I am, you cannot be. You are what anyone of the common masses can be.[3]

The idea of the freedman is perhaps the most incongruous and unfamiliar today. Tiberius Claudius Daus worked as an accounts clerk (*tabularius*) on an imperial estate and lived till he was fifty-nine.[4] He was a freedman and was probably freed by Claudius. He thereafter remained in the imperial service. Freedmen were excluded from holding political office or voting, but their sons would be able to do both when they came of age. Most importantly, they were free to run businesses and some amassed considerable fortunes, and owned slaves themselves. Their assets made it possible for them to bankroll the political ambitions of the freeborn elite either in Rome or provincial communities. Today, the evidence for this survives in its greatest quantities in Ostia, Pompeii, and Herculaneum.

Many successful freedmen enthusiastically involved themselves in guilds and religious associations where they could hold office, wield influence, and participate in local politics indirectly (see next chapter). For freedmen, then, the biggest priority could often be to line their nests and pave the way for their sons' political careers and propel the family forward.

WHO PAID FOR POMPEY'S THEATRE?

The Theatre of Pompey was the first large-scale permanent public entertainment building in Rome (see Chapter 12). It was dedicated in 55 BC and most people would have assumed that it was paid for by the eponymous general out of his massive proceeds from war and office. Dio reported that it was in fact bankrolled by Pompey's freedman Demetrius 'with the money he had gained while making campaigns with the general'. Demetrius had allegedly given his patron's name to avoid any embarrassment or criticism that a freedman of Pompey had become so fabulously wealthy.[5]

This reads like an apocryphal tale; it seems unlikely that Demetrius, having been so rich, would have spent his money in a way that did not benefit his own reputation, but he may have become notorious for having done well out of working for Pompey. Certainly, the tale of an ex-slave becoming so disgustingly rich that he could pay for a vast public facility would have tapped into a particular type of Roman prejudice about, and loathing for, the over-grown and suddenly moneyed freedman. Demetrius was said to have left a fortune of 4,000 talents, which probably means an Attic talent. At approximately 6,000 drachmas per talent, that meant he had the equivalent of about 24 million denarii or 96 million sesterces. There is no meaningful way of comparing that sum with modern values, but Demetrius was clearly extraordinarily rich.[6] He was not alone. Caesar could boast of having plenty of rich freedmen among his supporters. Clearly, the richer the patron, the richer his freedmen could hope to be if they played along – this was another way of amplifying someone like Caesar or Pompey's status. No wonder Appian called Caesar's freedmen his 'splendid accessories'.[7]

FREEDMEN IN BUSINESS

Many freedmen had been given business opportunities by their former masters who freed them in return for loyal support in elections for themselves or their sons. They were set up sometimes in commercial enterprises. Some did well with an eye for the market and benefited from the financial and practical support that came from their former owners who could that way avoid dirtying their own hands with any direct involvement in such vulgar dealings. Seneca commented on how some freedmen operated their baths, targeting the market in Rome for luxury leisure experiences. 'Take a look at their rows of statues, the clusters of functionless columns there only for decoration, all for the sake of spending cash. Look at the noisy torrents of water splashing down from one tier to the next. We've reached the stage of such fussiness that we moan if we have to walk on anything other than precious stones.'[8]

A mystery surrounds the origins of Cicero. His stellar legal and political career, for which so much evidence survives in his extant writings, makes him an important figure not only in late Republican Rome but also all Roman history. Plutarch recorded one story that Cicero was descended from Tullus Attius, a king of the Volsci (an ancient Italian people whose territory lay to the south-east of Rome). Plutarch also recorded that 'some say he was born and reared in a fuller's shop'.[9] It would have suited Cicero's enemies to put about a rumour like that, a means of cutting him down to size by implying that he came from lowly origins that would inevitably have involved descent from a freedman and thus a former slave. Either way, Plutarch was unable to find out anything certain though he said Cicero's father had risen to equestrian status.[10]

A freedman had to watch his back. His former master still had considerable power over him. Caesar had a freedman of his executed when he discovered the man had committed adultery with the wife of an equestrian, a woman who was way above the freedman's station.[11] Freedmen also discovered that their liberty came at an ongoing price on top of what it had cost them to be freed in the first place. Their former owners became their patrons, to whom they owed a legal obligation of service. It was, for example, specified in law that a freedman pantomime actor or a doctor (and it is interesting that the two professions could be so casually lumped together) was expected to provide his services for free to his patron. The operating principle was that the former slave had acquired his expertise at his master's expense and on his master's clock.

The freedman was also expected to provide his services for his patron's friends, or anyone his former master hired him out to. The operating legal principle was that the obligation was continuous. In this respect the freedman was not free at all, his life likely to be permanently constrained by these obligations. The law did recognize that 'services should not be required of a freedman without giving him certain days upon which to perform them, allowing him sufficient time for earning enough to support himself'. A freedwoman was also caught up in this web of limitations. If she had two patrons and one gave her permission to marry, she was still obliged to perform services for the other (but not once she was fifty years old).[12]

Freedmen depended on their former masters for more than just being put into business. They relied on regular handouts of food and money. This is more reminiscent than anything else today of being on the mob payroll though in fact the arrangement was generally more innocuous than that comparison suggests. The relationship was a two-way street.

Investing in the right freedmen could be a matter of life and death. During the proscriptions of 43 BC at the hands of the triumvirs, a wealthy freedman called Philemon hid his former senatorial master Vinius in an iron money chest, which would have been on open display in the building. Vinius was supplied with food at night and remained there until peace was restored. Freedmen could be bought. A senator called Varus was unlucky. A freedman of his gave him away and he was captured.[13] The same happened to another called Naso around the same time. To his horror he was betrayed by a favourite freedman.

Doubtless, the freedman was attracted by the thought of the 25,000 drachmas on offer for a freedman who shopped anyone on the proscription list. It did him no good. Naso grabbed a sword from a soldier who had come for him and killed the freedman before giving himself up. Another called Lucius gave money to two of his freedmen to help him. Instead, they abandoned him and absconded with the cash.[14]

During the reign of Septimius Severus (193–211) a band of outlaws spent two years roaming Italy, robbing and plundering at will under the leadership of an Italian called Bulla. Although his gang included slaves freed from prisons, Bulla also had a large number of disgruntled imperial freedmen on his roster who had either not been paid by the emperor or had received little money at all. When soldiers were sent out to tackle Bulla, he confronted one of the centurions and told him to take a message to his masters: 'feed your slaves so that they do not turn to brigandage!' Bulla was a serious embarrassment. He was eventually caught by a unit of the Praetorian Guard and thrown to wild animals. His rise showed the dangers of overlooking the transactional obligations of Roman society.[15]

FREEDMEN AND THE GUILDS

Roman trade guilds were notorious for their factionalism, rivalry, and their increasingly dominant role in day-to-day urban politics in the last days of the Roman Republic in the first century BC when political leaders like Caesar and Pompey used them as hired gangs of thugs. Augustus crushed the more dangerous guilds and placed strict controls on those which were approved. They remained nonetheless a potent force with equivalents in every Roman city with a thriving mercantile base.

Guilds are well known at Ostia and the later Trajanic harbour at Portus just to the north, mainly from the tombs of members. They were involved in all commercial activities, working as builders, fullers, shippers, shipbuilders, bakers, wine merchants, and corn measurers.

Each was fundamental to keeping Rome supplied and serviced. Those on the shipbuilders' guild roll based at Portus numbered over 350 by the early third century, though it was by no means the largest guild known at Ostia and Portus.

Publius Celerius Amandus was freeborn and had been elected a decurion at Ostia by special decree when he was only eighteen (he should have been twenty-five at the youngest).[16] His premature death resulted in a detailed tombstone that itemized his short career and also depicted the tools of his trade: two oars, an adze, and a pair of dividers. Crucially, his father was a freedman; we can assume he too was a shipbuilder and his influence in the guild had brought him civic influence too, and the special privilege granted his son.

The guilds were organized around a formal membership, a constitution, and a leadership structure that emulated the civic hierarchy of magistracies. Each guild met in its own dedicated headquarters. In practice membership was often hereditary and often involved each member's freedmen. In this way they acted as the commercial link between a patron and his clients. The guilds courted the membership of wealthy and powerful men who could offer their members protection and an ear in government, and fund occasional donations to members or annual celebratory festivals.

Guilds were led by their own class of officials (*magistri*), who were elected to serve for varying periods but usually five years (the *quinquennales*). The exact numbers of these men serving at any one time varied from guild to guild. They were assisted by elected treasurers. Men who had served as a quinquennalis were eligible for life status in the position. Freeborn members of guilds were still eligible for civic office. Cnaeus Sentius Felix at Ostia was not only a senior member of Ostia's town government during Hadrian's reign but also belonged to a guild of shippers and was a patron to many others, including grain measurers. His main commercial activity seems to have involved marine transport and ferry services in and around the harbours.[17]

Among these organizations was the Guild of Father Liber and Mercury, a pair of deities who respectively looked after vines and merchants, in Rome. An imperial slave called Cinnamus, who worked as a cashier of the warehouses in the emperor's financial administration, commissioned a dedication in the year 102 to them. Tiberius Claudius Zosimus and Sextus Caelius Agathemerus, who were officials in the same guild serving in their first year, probably as presidents (magistri), took charge of placing the dedication with which Cinnamus expressed his gratitude to the college of wine merchants operating in the Nova and Arruntiana warehouses.[18] The most likely explanation is that Trajan had taken over some of the formerly privately owned warehouses to create an imperial wine store managed for him by the guild.

Guilds legal and illegal certainly existed at Pompeii where there is a great deal more everyday evidence for their activities. The deadly riot in Pompeii's amphitheatre in 59 during Nero's reign which involved rival associations from Pompeii and Nuceria was promptly followed by senatorial sanctions that included the compulsory dissolution of illegal guilds in the city (see Chapter 12 for more on this remarkable episode).[19] Evidently the Pompeian guilds had played an important part in organizing the violence towards the visiting Nucerians, perhaps founded on simmering commercial rivalries and settling scores, which no doubt dated back over generations.

The most important guilds were also closely involved in local politics, with the freedmen members playing active roles in making sure their preferred candidates were elected to office and would thus promote their interests. They worked together in different ways, but one method was to operate in the name of a local cult that they supported. The Iseum (Temple of Isis) at Pompeii is among the best recorded, but in the backstreets of Rome similar cults acted as fronts for political pressure groups. Electoral slogans at Pompeii's Iseum show that members of the cult made their affiliations clear. They had doubtless been bribed or leaned on by the candidate concerned who had promised them some sort of advantage in return.

By the mid-first century AD during Nero's reign a prominent local in Pompeii called Numerius Popidius Ampliatus had grown wealthy and influential, though we know nothing about his business interests. It is certain that he was a freedman because he was clearly unable to stand for office himself, or else he would have. The most likely explanation is that he was freed by the affluent local Popidii family and proceeded to do well. He clearly had expectations of how he and his family should progress. The most obvious route was to see his freeborn son being voted into office.

The city fathers of Pompeii were anxious to see Ampliatus rewarded for his success, or perhaps more likely for his kickbacks. To do this they made a mockery of the rules. Numerius Popidius Celsinus, his son, was freeborn. Inconveniently, he was aged only six (making him nineteen years too young to stand for office). His father provided the funds in his little boy's name to rebuild the Iseum after it was wrecked in the earthquake of 62. Celsinus was thus promptly elected a town councillor, regardless of his age, bypassing the normal requirement of having been an aedile first. The grand occasion was recorded on an inscription affixed to the street entrance to the temple precinct.[20] This way his father was awarded with the proxy prestige of a status he could never legally hold, through his son. The restoration work conducted on the temple was extravagant and extensive. It must have been, in Pompeian terms, extremely expensive.

Among the most intriguing figures in the world of Pompeii's commercial guilds was Eumachia, a member of a family of the decurial elite. The remains of her once magnificent porticus building beside the town's forum bear witness to the importance of these organizations, their prestige, and the patronage of wealthy individuals. Eumachia's porticus faces the forum but its southern side wall flanks the main commercial thoroughfare that linked the western and eastern parts of the city. The porticus was built under Augustus or Tiberius by Eumachia, acting as a businesswoman and guild patron in her own right, and thus what might seem to be an incongruous figure in Roman society. While it is true that women could neither vote nor serve in office, it was possible for a woman to serve in certain honorific positions such as public priesthoods, and to own property on which commercial businesses were run. The brickworks run by Publilianus at Rome or Ostia were on an estate owned by Aemilia Severa, a woman of senatorial status.[21]

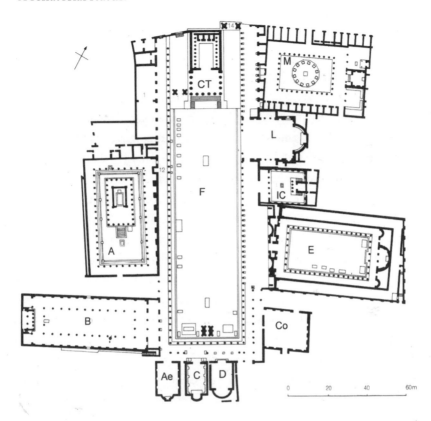

Figure 3: Pompeii forum

Pompeii's forum area emulates in miniature what was to be found in Rome: an open piazza surrounded by public buildings and temples. Key (clockwise from the top): CT = Temple of the Capitoline Triad (Jupiter, Juno, and Minerva); M = Macellum; L = Temple of the *Lares*; IC = Temple of the Imperial Cult; E = porticus of Eumachia; Co = *comitium* (voting hall); D = office of the *duoviri* (?); C = *curia*(?) (council chamber); Ae = office of the *aediles* (?); B = Basilica; A = Temple of Apollo. The little squares and rectangles in the forum mark the location of statues and monuments to local worthies. These included those of the decurial class, many the sons or descendants of freedmen, while existing freedmen played an important part in supporting freeborn candidates for magistracies.

Eumachia was the daughter of Lucius Eumachius Eros who is known from stamps to have manufactured brick, wine amphorae and presumably also the wine they contained, in the Pompeii region.

187

His products have been found in North Africa, Gaul, and Spain.[22] His business is likely to have been the source of at least part of her wealth, propelling her into a marriage with a member of the local elite, though his manufactories were probably located on an estate owned by someone of much higher status. Eumachius Eros' original status is unknown but since he appears to have played no part in town politics the likelihood is that he was a freedman. His cognomen Eros certainly suggests that he might have originally been a slave, possibly of Greek ancestry. If so, his daughter, her marriage, and her son showed just how swift Roman social mobility could propel a family forward from slave origins into the most prestigious political positions in a provincial city.

Eumachia was later buried in an exceptionally large tomb in a Pompeian cemetery that was dominated by the monuments to freedmen. She evidently wanted to ensure her prominence was remembered in Pompeii. The memorial advertised her relatively exalted station in life to those of her probable milieu above whom she had risen in her parochial context. It also suggests she had not been fully accepted by the Pompeian elite though she otherwise only appears in the record as a well-established and prominent member of the decurial class. Inscriptions on her porticus record that she was a public priestess and responsible in her own name and that of her son, Marcus Numistrius Fronto, for the structure with its elaborate entrance porch from the forum, covered walkway, and colonnaded walkway. From this we can deduce that the Marcus Numistrius Fronto who was a duumvir of Pompeii in the year AD 3 was Eumachia's husband and that he must have died by the time the building was completed.[23]

Eumachia was clearly important enough to maintain a prestigious and prominent public position as a woman in her own right, though it was also the case that her honours were a way of honouring her husband and son. The position of public priestess was the highest formal accolade that could be paid to a Roman woman in a town like Pompeii. By associating her son with the building, Eumachia labelled him also as a benefactor to Roman society. This was intended to ensure his future standing and political status in Pompeii, but the younger Numistrius

Fronto's fate is unknown. Neither he nor his father was mentioned on Eumachia's unusually large tomb. He is likely to have died young, disappointing his mother's hopes both for him and her enduring status. Indeed, Eumachia's tomb inscription was limited only to saying that she was 'daughter of Lucius'.[24]

The inscriptions on Eumachia's building also stated that the porticus was dedicated to Augustan Concord and Piety. This explicitly associated it, and therefore also Eumachia and her family, with the imperial regime in Rome. The design was based on the much larger Porticus of Livia in Rome. A visitor from Pompeii's forum passed through an elaborate architectural pronaos to be greeted by a façade decorated with niches containing statues of Aeneas and Romulus, linking Eumachia to Roman foundation myths, echoing similar arrangements in the Forum of Augustus. A doorway through the façade led to an open court in the porticus proper surrounded by a two-storey colonnade with a much larger apse at the far end probably housing a statue of Augustan Concord. Behind that is a further niche containing a statue of Eumachia dedicated by the fullers.[25]

The fulling trade was an important commercial activity at Pompeii but the fullers' association with Eumachia is unexplained. One possibility is that her deceased husband had been their patron and perhaps they had supported his political career. A number of guild inscriptions from Ostia record women known as *mater* (mother) and *filia* (daughter), perhaps because they were wives or daughters of guild magistri or patrons, and this may have been how Eumachia became associated with the fullers.

The Eumachia building was far too elaborate to have been used for the mundane trade of the fullers. Instead, it may have been partly honorific and used on occasions by their corporation to celebrate their annual calendar of festivals. It may also have functioned as a repository of records and as a meeting place for the owners of the respective fulling businesses. Other suggestions include a cloth market, or even a slave market.

In Volsinii (now Bolsena), an old Etruscan city north of Rome, a woman of the local aristocracy called Ancharia Luperca was selected for a special honour. The Volsinii quinquennales magistrates decided to commission a bronze statue of Ancharia to stand alongside one of her husband Laberius Gallus in the *schola* (meeting house) of the guild of engineers. Their purpose was to celebrate her as an *honestam matronum* ('a lady of honourable reputation'), as well as her husband and father.[26]

Eumachia's building and memorials, and the statue commissioned for Ancharia Luperca, are ample proof that in a provincial town a woman, despite her lack of political rights and privileges, was able to function in an important public and commercial role. Eumachia in particular seems to have been fairly autonomous. Although the position of women in Roman society was constantly afflicted by the rigid Roman belief in gender-based roles there was clearly a significant element of flexibility.

FREEDMEN AND LOYALTY TO THE STATE

Freedmen were eligible for membership of the priesthood of one branch of the imperial cult (the *seviri Augustales*), with a board of such priests in each town. Honouring the emperor was an important expression of their allegiance to the state. Indeed, membership was among the few routes to high status open to freedmen and was an office in which they could serve alongside freeborn men. Although election was involved, it also seems that cash payments played a part in buying one's way into the hierarchy of the priesthood. This limited the candidates to prosperous and successful men and formalized their identity as members of the freedmen elite. Although nominally a religious organization, in the Roman world formal religion was inextricably linked with social, political and financial status. The seviri Augustales functioned much as the commercial guilds did and naturally its most prominent members were conspicuous in their own trade guilds.

The prestige of membership of the seviri Augustales reflected the honours customarily heaped on prominent freeborn councillors and magistrates. Lucius Mammius Maximus, an Augustalis and freedman at Herculaneum, was awarded a life-size bronze statue of himself by the 'citizens and other residents', displayed in the theatre. He also made a number of dedications at his own expense, for example to the deified Augustus.[27]

At Pompeii, Gaius Munatius Faustus, who had been voted the honour of a special place for his tomb by the council of Pompeii, was a successful freedman who served as an Augustalis.[28] The tomb outside Pompeii's Herculaneum Gate of Munatius Faustus' freedwoman wife Naevoleia Tyche bragged that her Augustalis husband had been awarded a prestigious honorific *bisellium* ('double seat') in the theatre. This was an enduring honour that allowed even provincial freedmen to ape the privileges enjoyed by the aristocracy in Rome. The sculptural decoration of the tomb showed that their business interests involved shipping and includes a scene of the couple handing out largesse to the people of Pompeii. They had also reached the position where they were wealthy enough to free their own slaves, though there is no mention of any children.[29]

Their names are good examples of the sort given to slaves, either from birth or when they became enslaved, which often survived into their lives as freedmen and freedwomen. Faustus means 'lucky' or 'prosperous', and Tyche was the term for the tutelary goddess of a city, meaning 'god-given fortune'. Lucius Sessus Successus was a potter in the pottery owned by Publilianus, either in Ostia or Rome. Sessus Successus was almost certainly a freedman (and Publilianus too), his optimistic cognomen's meaning being obvious still today.[30] Publilianus' name may allude to his having once been a public slave owned by the state. At least two male members of Livia's staff bore the rare name Sponsianus or Spo(n)sianus, which translates as something like 'the one who is pledged'. This might mean that when they were slaves they had been handed over in fulfilment of a debt, or as security for a bet.[31]

The inscriptions on their tombs describe Naevoleia and her husband Munatius Faustus as being resident in Pompeii's 'Fortunate Augustan Suburban Country District', a zone outside the town. Its magistri had direct links to and interests in the city government. Unlike the civic magistracies, presidencies of the Suburban District at Pompeii were open to freedmen. The Suburban District could pay for statues and other honours for prominent individuals. Its officials seem to have been equally expected to pay for seating in the amphitheatre, or to put on games. An inscription from Pompeii's amphitheatre records that *pro ludis* ('in place of games') seats had been installed by the suburban magistri, fulfilling a decree by Pompeii's town council that they do so.[32]

TRADESMEN

There are several surviving tombs in the Isola Sacra cemetery for Portus at Ostia that still bear decorative panels depicting the tools used by the deceased. These tombs were preserved by drifting sand, but in antiquity all the streets radiating from Rome were lined with countless similar examples, among them that of Demetrius and Philonicus. Demetrius was a former slave with a lean and drawn face reflecting a life of hard work. Philonicus had a rounder, softer face with close-set eyes, and looks surprisingly well-fed. Their names suggest they were of Greek origins. They had laboured as slaves in the household of one Publius Licinius who had freed them. Their former master would, if he followed custom, have set them up in businesses and in return expected their loyal service and practical support for his affairs, whatever they were. The two men were eventually buried together with a monument bearing their portraits and an inscription that recorded only their names.[33] But the stone carries depictions of the tools of their trades. Demetrius was a carpenter, while Philonicus worked in the mint striking coins. Since their skills were unconnected it is unclear why they were buried together, unless it was a simple matter of friendship, economy, and convenience though it is likely they died at different times.

The Via Appia (Appian Way) is the most famous of all Roman roads. It was originally built on the orders of the censor Appius Claudius

Caecus to connect Rome with Capua in 312 BC so that soldiers could travel as fast as possible during the Second Samnite War of 326–304 BC. It was later extended to Brundisium by 264 BC, but the name stuck. Like all Roman roads it became lined with tombs within the vicinity of Rome. They vary in size and extravagance, reflecting the status in life of the occupant, and range from simple cremated burials in amphorae to elaborate architectural statements. Most are long destroyed or survive as weathered stumps of stone and brick, but here and there some memorials survive to commemorate past lives. Among them are the more successful freedmen.

These include the tombstone of Gaius Ateilius Euhodus. He was a freedman dealer in pearls (*margaritarius*) who lived and worked in Rome in the second or first century BC. Euhodus left no obvious legacy of any sort, and we have no idea whether he was thought well of or not by his family and descendants, though he was undoubtedly impressed by himself. His epitaph reads:

> Stranger! — stop and look at this mound to the left where the bones of a good, compassionate man and friend of those of modest means are contained. I ask that you, traveller, do nothing bad to this tomb. Gaius Ateilius Euhodus, freedman of Serranus, pearl seller on the Via Sacra, is preserved in this tomb. Farewell traveller. Under the terms of the will, it is not lawful to preserve or bury anyone in this tomb except those freedmen to whom I have granted and assigned [this].[34]

Euhodus' name was Greek so he probably came from the eastern half of the Empire, perhaps being sold in a Rome slave market as a child or youth. The Via Sacra ran through the Forum in Rome, a prime location that brought Euhodus sufficient success that he could afford to have his tomb and epitaph prepared, free his own slaves, and offer those whom he specified in his will a place in his tomb too.[35] He was typical of the well-to-do freedman class in Rome who made their livings in commerce. He dealt in a luxury product, relying on trade brought to him by or on behalf of the wealthiest women in Rome. He will undoubtedly have had obligations to his former master (Gaius Ateilius Serranus) and his former master's family.

REVENGE

There was always that sense of fear of how a former slave might exact revenge. The Romans were troubled by the idea of wealthy and ostentatious freedmen. They compensated by depicting them as figures of fun, vulgar figures obsessed with flaunting wealth, and displaying pretentious symbols of learning and their artistic taste. One former slave called Callistus used his new-found freedom and wealth not only to rub his old master's face in his success but also to humiliate him, as Seneca recalled:

> I have seen Callistus' former master standing in the line outside Callistus' door. I have seen the master himself shut out while others were welcomed, – the master who once fastened the 'For Sale' ticket on Callistus and put him in the market along with the good-for-nothing slaves ... The slave, too, in his turn has cut *his* name from the list and in his turn has adjudged him unfit to enter his house. The master sold Callistus, but how much has Callistus made his master pay for that?![36]

One point was always worth remembering, though few Romans did. A slave might just as easily have been born free, and a freeborn person might just as easily have been born a slave, as Seneca pointed out with a stoic's eye for the valueless nature of temporal status:

> Kindly remember that he whom you call your slave sprang from the same stock, is smiled upon by the same skies, and on equal terms with yourself breathes, lives, and dies. It is just as possible for you to see in him a free-born man as for him to see in you a slave.[37]

194

9

DINING OUT
AND EATING IN

Where various things are sold at the cornelian cherry tree grove
(in Rome) is the Forum Cuppedinis ('Luxury Market'), named
after the word for delicacy out of contempt. Many people refer to
it as the Forum Cupidinus ('Greed Market').

Varro[1]

Rome might have been an exceptionally wealthy city but inevitably the food available to individual Romans depended entirely on whether they were rich or poor. But there was much more to the subject than that. Describing an emperor like Vitellius as a grotesque glutton was a popular rhetorical device, just as much as depicting a senator of the old Republic as admirably abstemious. Cato the Elder, for example, was famed for his strictly modest diet. On campaign it was said he only drank water. If he was parched he might add a dash of vinegar and if exhausted a little wine. At home he drank the same wine as his slaves and bought his food in the public market, so he could always be ready for military service. Cato exclaimed one day 'How can we expect to save a city, where people are prepared to pay more for a fish than an ox?' The point here was that an ox could be used to pull a plough, whereas buying an expensive fish

195

was frivolous – a society that valued the fish more highly than an ox was, in Cato's view, a lost cause.[2] Nothing changed. Allegedly, on one occasion during the reign of Caligula the proconsul Asinius Celer paid 8,000 sesterces for a single red mullet.[3]

Food came to symbolize Rome's moral crisis. Extravagance was proof of Rome's success but indulging in it was seen as confirmation that Roman society was descending into the abyss. References to food abound in our written sources, but the exceptional deposits at Pompeii and Herculaneum have also provided the physical evidence. One major sewer at the latter was found still filled with effluent from latrines from nearby apartments and shops. This produced significant quantities of cereal and fruit seeds, fish bones, eggshells, and even seasoning which add to the extensive array of other evidence for food importation, production, and cooking in the form of containers, animal bones, millstones, griddles, ovens, bakeries, and olive and grape presses.[4]

THE GRAIN DOLE

Grain was the most contentious food issue in Rome. The ordinary Roman poor were dependent on the grain dole. They were prone to erupt into violence if the supply was disrupted either by pirates, incompetent storage, or officials and emperors trying to blame an enemy. In 188 BC grain dealers were fined for hoarding grain in the hope that prices would rise so that they could cash in.[5] The tribune Gaius Gracchus introduced the monthly distribution of grain to each citizen at a fixed price subsidized by the state in 123–122 BC. 'Thus, he quickly gained the leadership of the people', said Appian.[6] Grain had become a political weapon. Four decades later, Sulla attempted to end grain distribution by repealing the law, but this experiment backfired, and the system had to be restored.[7] Once grain distribution had been taken on as a state obligation, any plan to end it or any disruption to the supply meant the state was held responsible in the form of anyone deemed to represent the state at that point. Consequently, for example, when grain shortages became intolerable in 75 BC a mob chased the consuls to the house of one of them (Gaius Aurelius Cotta).[8]

By 67 BC the grain supply had become seriously disrupted by the uncontrolled Cilician pirate menace, even to the extent that the pirates landed at Ostia to burn ships and steal from the port.[9] The tribune Aulus Gabinius proposed that Pompey be given special powers to tackle the pirates, plying Pompey with moral blackmail and reminding him of his duty to Rome: 'for [Rome] you (Pompey) were born, for her you were reared. You must serve her interests, shrinking from no hardship or danger to secure them.'[10]

The suggestion was extremely popular except in the Senate which vacillated, fearing the power it would give Pompey. An outraged mob rushed the Senate, bursting in and attacking the senators which caused them to reconsider their decision. Pompey was put in command and pulled off the job in short order, transforming Rome's food security.[11]

The senators knew that whoever controlled the grain supply was master of Rome. The interests of the 'grain-exporting provinces' were of little concern. The beneficiaries of the handouts were increased in 62 BC with the addition of 'the poor and landless multitude'. The cost to the state was by then 1,250 talents.[12] By 58 BC Clodius Pulcher, then serving as tribune (although a patrician, he had arranged to be adopted by a plebeian so that he could be elected a tribune), had made the grain distribution free, a development that was politically impossible to reverse without risking popular insurrection and also made Rome even more dependent on exploiting its provinces.[13]

When Pompey was placed in charge of the grain supply in 57 BC at Cicero's behest, Dio described him as holding 'sway over the entire world then under Roman power', just as he had when he had cleared the Mediterranean of the Cilician pirates.[14] Cicero had rejected himself as someone able to provide corn in abundance and low prices but recommended Pompey as someone with the qualities capable of doing so.[15] By Caesar's time the number of people receiving the free grain had risen to 320,000, and he reduced this to 150,000 by holding a census to assess entitlement.[16]

In 49 BC Cicero talked about the prospect of starvation in Rome during the impending civil war of the late Republic if the *frumentarias provincias* ('grain-exporting provinces') were occupied and 'Italy's supply lines cut off'.[17] Although Alexandria was among the sources of grain he cited, Egypt was not yet a Roman possession. By 'grain-exporting provinces' he meant principally Sicily, North Africa, and probably Sardinia, and shows how they were classified. According to him, in 73 BC Rome took 20 per cent of Sicily's harvest, doubling its normal take.[18]

In 40–39 BC Octavian was stoned by starving rioters in Rome when the grain supply ran low due to the disruption on the seas caused by the civil war, and only just escaped with his life.[19] He had unwisely decided to confront the mob with only a few attendants and had to be saved by Antony who brought troops in. The incident showed how potentially suicidal it could be for a Roman leader to expose himself to the mob without armed protection.

As Augustus, Octavian was more concerned with consolidating the new Roman imperial state than finding a permanent solution to the grain supply problem which still depended hugely on the port at Puteoli near Naples. From Augustus on, the grain dole was managed by one of the most senior equestrian officers of state, the *praefectus annonae* ('the prefect of the Annona [grain dole]'). Supplying Rome's population with the handout became a fundamental service by the state and one that could lead to violence if it was disrupted. Augustus toyed with the idea of doing away with the dole on the basis that it had led – unsurprisingly – to a decline in farming (in Italy) to the detriment of farmers.[20] He gave up on the idea, realizing that it was inevitable a successor would reintroduce the dole for the sake of easy popularity.

One of the reasons Puteoli was so important was that the Tiber was narrow at Ostia (around 100 metres) and it was silting up. By the mid-first century BC something had to be done. Small and medium-sized ships could enter and be towed upriver to Rome. The largest merchant ships were forced to ride at anchor out at sea and be offloaded by smaller vessels, potentially disastrous in winter which shippers preferred to avoid, but in practice ships still made the perilous journey. The only other option was to be part-unloaded so that they could navigate their way upriver to Rome without fear of running aground on the shallow riverbed.[21] Julius Caesar planned various works, including breakwaters and clearage of obstructions to reduce the risk to shipping arriving at Ostia, as well as to build a new harbour, but none of these was ever executed.[22]

Ostia had to wait until Claudius (41–54) came to power as the fourth emperor of Rome. Claudius identified, correctly, that fulfilling Caesar's thwarted ambitions might improve his image, which was affected by his reputation for being mentally backward and physically infirm. Invading Britain was a scheme he dreamed up to prove his worth as an emperor. Another was dealing with Ostia. Claudius knew only too well that a shortage of grain could compromise his regime. Suetonius said Claudius always gave 'scrupulous attention ... to the supply of grain', and explained how quickly the population of Rome could turn:

> When there was a scarcity of grain because of long-continued droughts, he was once stopped in the middle of the Forum by a mob and so pelted with abuse and at the same time with pieces of bread, that he was barely able to make his escape to the Palace by a back door; and after this experience he resorted to every possible means to bring grain to Rome, even in the winter season. To the merchants he held out the certainty of profit by assuming the expense of any loss that they might suffer from storms, and offered to those who would build merchant ships large bounties, adapted to the condition of each.[23]

Claudius decided that the state would underwrite any losses from winter storms, and he offered subsidies to merchant shippers who continued to bring in grain. Building a new harbour was a much more far-reaching and permanent solution. It would also reduce the dependence on Puteoli. Claudius was responsible for creating the first proper harbour facilities known as Portus, which were begun in 42 a couple of miles to the north of Ostia and connected them to Rome by road.

This was achieved by 'building up curved breakwaters on the left and right and in front of the entrance a mole in deep water'.[24]

In the meantime, Puteoli remained vital. One day Seneca spotted the arrival of a fleet from Alexandria. First were the faster boats carrying the mail, and behind them the grain freighters, all making their way to the harbour at Puteoli:

> Suddenly there came into our view to-day the Alexandrian ships. I mean those which are usually sent ahead to announce the coming of the fleet. They are called 'mail-boats'. The Campanians are glad to see them. All the rabble of Puteoli stand on the docks, and can recognize the 'Alexandrian' boats, no matter how great the crowd of vessels, by the trim of their sails.[25]

The new Claudian port was not completed until the reign of Nero and was later supplemented by the hexagonal harbour area added by Trajan for the new facilities at Portus.

For all the resources thrown into guaranteeing the grain supply, Rome remained at the mercy of the elements. In 69 the Tiber rose higher than ever before, even though it happened at a time of year when it was expected to be at its highest. The result was a catastrophe because the river burst its banks in Rome, flooding a large part of the city and, most devastatingly of all, the grain market. The result was an immediate 'dire scarcity' of food.[26]

Providing free food for the population of Rome remained a permanent part of the emperor's responsibilities. A special type of ticket (*tessera frumentaria*) was distributed so that those entitled among the masses could present one to collect their share. One issued by Antoninus Pius bears abbreviations referring to the sixty-first monthly grain handout, probably since his accession, and the emperor's 'second largess'.[27] Persius called it a 'ticket for mangy corn', suggesting that what was handed out was usually substandard, which was probably only to be expected.[28]

In 190 during the reign of Commodus, Rome was hit by a grain shortage, for which the prefect of the corn dole had the wit to blame the emperor's chamberlain, Cleander. Cleander set the Praetorian Guard on protesters but Pertinax, then prefect of Rome, ordered the night watch troops to confront the praetorians. In the confusion Cleander fled to Commodus while a mob trailed after him screaming for his head. Commodus, who never showed loyalty to his staff, abandoned Cleander and had him executed, after which Cleander's head was carried round the city on a pole.[29]

The state's self-imposed obligations continued to increase. Septimius Severus later added olive oil to the free handouts, and Aurelian (270–5) was said to have introduced a pork allowance to the population of Rome.[30]

DIETS AND COOKSHOPS

The diet of the poorest was limited mainly to wheat, bread, and some vegetables. If they were extremely lucky, they might have the cheapest possible cuts of meat, washed down by diluted vinegar. For the rich, recklessly sumptuous dinners were available, cooked and served by slaves, and consisting of multiple courses dominated by meat and fish, and delicacies such as oysters, stuffed dormice, and sow's udder. The Romans were thus enthusiastically omnivorous and untroubled by the sort of dietary and nutrition obsessions of our age which have made eating as much a source of anxiety as pleasure. Of course, the Romans did lack our access to abundant sources of fat, carbohydrate, and sugar, saving them from some of the worst consequences of over-indulgence.

It takes a visit to Ostia, Pompeii, or Herculaneum to appreciate just how many places there were to eat and drink in a Roman town, just as in any modern city. The streetside café (*thermopolium* or *taberna*) was ubiquitous. They were crammed into almost any premises large enough to accommodate a few customers, a kitchen, and the serving bar itself with large built-in earthenware containers from which the food could be served. Surviving examples in Pompeii and Herculaneum show that their walls were often decorated with colourful and vivid paintings depicting mythological scenes, the food for sale, and sometimes humorous scenes featuring patrons engaged in activities such as gambling.[31] A recently discovered café in Pompeii features a picture of a slavering dog, complete with graffiti caption *Nicia cinaedae cacator*, 'Nicias is a shameless shitter'. This is thought by some to be a customer's reference to the proprietor or a member of staff but is perhaps more likely to be a comment on the owner's cur of a dog and its repulsive habits.[32]

With no formal postal address system in force, like most businesses these establishments were referred to by local landmarks. One such café known to Catullus was 'at the ninth pillar from the Temple of the Brothers in hats'.[33] This meant it was nine columns along from the Temple of Castor and Pollux, the heavenly twins, in the Forum in Rome, the pair often each depicted wearing the *pileus* felt cap, sometimes worn by the freedman to celebrate his manumission.

Not that one could rely on enjoying a tavern meal in peace, even in such a prominent location. In or about 89 BC a praetor called Asellio allowed the revival of an ancient law prohibiting the levying of interest on loans. While he was sacrificing at the Temple of Castor and Pollux one morning he was attacked by an irate lender. Asellio made a dash for the nearby Temple of Vesta but was stopped by a crowd of moneylenders. He fled into a nearby tavern but was set on by the gang and had his throat cut, doubtless to the dismay of diners who must have lost their appetites.[34]

These businesses were often operated from the street frontages of well-appointed private townhouses. They were probably rented from the owner, and perhaps run by one or other of his freedmen. These establishments were also known as *popinae*, best translated as streetside bistros or cookshops. Horace called them *unctae popinae*, 'greasy cookshops'.[35] The notoriously gluttonous emperor Vitellius was fond of grabbing a quick bite from these places as he passed by, despite enjoying several full meals a day as a matter of course. It might also have occurred to Vitellius, but not Suetonius who recounted the anecdote, that he was a great deal less likely to be deliberately poisoned by any food he picked up at random stops since his enemies would have had no idea when or where these would be.[36] In a ditty penned by Hadrian when a friend of his, the historian and poet Florus, mocked him for his peripatetic lifestyle the emperor said he preferred to avoid the 'fat round insects' to be found in Rome's cookshops.[37] With no hygiene laws, Romans needed hardy stomachs. Vitellius' tastes were echoed by Juvenal who regarded such establishments, particularly in Ostia, as picaresque and egalitarian places frequented by anyone from a general to a priest of Cybele and where even fugitive slaves could find sanctuary, all lounging around on the same couches.[38]

Early Roman frugality was a custom maintained by the law. Juvenal looked back to the restraint exhibited by Manius Curius Dentatus (d. 270 BC), the general who had brought the Samnite Wars to an end and defeated Pyrrhus, king of Epirus. Dentatus had been content to use the simple herbs grown in his own garden.[39] In 161 BC a law was passed that obliged the senatorial hosts (a job shared by rotation) to take an oath that they would limit the expenditure per senator on dinner at the Megalensian festival to the sum of 120 asses, not including vegetables, bread, and wine. The same law also required them to swear they would not serve up foreign wine or use more than 100 lb in weight of silverware.[40] That at least represented an improvement on earlier times. An ancestor of the future dictator Sulla called Publius Cornelius Rufinus (consul in 290 BC) had been thrown out of the Senate when it was discovered he had broken the law by having more than 10 lb of silver plate, plunging the family into modest means.[41]

Further laws enforcing restraint followed. They included one passed by Sulla as dictator which allowed 300 sesterces to be spent on a dinner during certain festivals, but only 30 on any other day.[42] Before too long they were being ignored in an age when 'many men of abundant means were gormandizing and recklessly pouring their family and fortune into an abyss of dinners and banquets', said Aulus Gellius. One dish was called 'Trojan pig', meaning the pig was stuffed full with other animals as the Trojan horse had been packed full of warriors. Force-feeding animals to fatten them, even hares, became popular.[43] When the orator Quintus Hortensius threw a banquet to celebrate the beginning of his priesthood he became the first Roman to serve up a peacock. By the 60s BC Marcus Aufidius Lurco was running a business fattening peacocks for this luxury market. Country villas servicing the peacock meat market ended up with aviaries bigger than villa buildings used to be. Yet more laws were brought in that tried to stem the tide. By the early first century AD a vast rise in the legal allowance for a festal day from 300 to 2,000 sesterces per head was allowed so 'that the rising tide of luxury might be contained *at least* within those limits', said Gellius.[44]

Extravagance played an important role in social hierarchy. The *cena recta* was a formal dinner where guests lay on couches around a dining table. As far as Juvenal was concerned, a dinner date meant being determined to 'receive payment for all your past services' from one's patron, especially as such invitations were rare and should be instantly accepted if the opportunity arose. The main worry was being fobbed off with inferior wine that would end up with the freedmen attending getting blind drunk and the whole event degenerating into fights.[45] At the other extreme there were public handouts of food to the people to which the word *sportula* was applied by Claudius, being a term more generally applied to gifts of food and money by a patron to his clients.[46]

RECIPES

Availability of spices was limited (and costly) and cooking facilities were basic. Flavouring relied on salt, herbs, honey, vinegar and fruit, and the addition of fermented fish sauce (see below). It is likely that most Roman cooks worked according to their own recipes in their heads and according to their masters' and mistresses' personal tastes. Most in households were slaves, some also operating the streetside cookshops for the general public.

Pliny referred to a famous gourmet called Apicius, 'the most gluttonous gorger', who had popularized the belief that the tongue of the flamingo had an unusually fine flavour.[47] Apicius produced a recipe book, or, rather, one was produced in his name, known as *On the Matter of Cooking*. He might have compiled it initially, but it may well have been added to over the centuries until the manuscript that survived to the Middle Ages was written up in the fifth century AD. The text has proved to be a popular record of the Roman world. It can still be used even though unlike modern cookbooks it does not provide quantities of ingredients. The following are just a few selections from the many dishes listed.

This first recipe used the bowel membrane (the caul). Since this part of an animal's body played an important role in soothsayers 'reading' the entrails (a custom acquired from the Etruscans), its name reflects the interest in the omens they contained:

Omentata are made in this manner: lightly fry pork liver, remove skin and sinews first. Crush pepper and rue in a mortar with a little broth, then add the liver, pound and mix this pulp shape into small sausage, wrap each in caul and laurel leaves and hang them up to be smoked. Whenever you want and when ready to enjoy them take them out of the smoke, fry them again, and add gravy.[48]

This recipe provides instruction on how to make one type of thick gravy:

Grind pepper which has been soaked overnight, add some more stock and work it into a smooth paste; thereupon add quince-apple cider, boiled down one half, that is which has evaporated in the heat of the sun to the consistency of honey. If this is not at hand, add fig wine concentrate which the Romans call 'colour'. Now thicken the gravy with roux or with soaked rice flour and finish it on a gentle fire.[49]

This seafood dish gives a hint of the more exotic flavourings available to a Roman cook. Malobathron leaves came from Syrian and Indian variants of the tree.

Real boiled lobster is cooked with cumin sauce essence and, by right, throw in some whole pepper, lovage, parsley, dry mint, a little more whole cumin, honey, vinegar, broth, and, if you like, add some bay leaves and malobathron.[50]

SHOWCASE DINING

There was a great deal more to the dinner than the food. At Trimalchio's fictional dinner in the *Satyricon* a large circular plate is delivered to the table decorated with the twelve signs of the Zodiac. Food had been laid out appropriate to each of the signs:

> on the Ram ram's-head peas, on the Bull a piece of beef, on the Twins fried testicles and kidneys, on the Crab simply a crown, on the Lion African figs, on a Virgin a sow's womb, on Libra a balance with a tart in one scale and a cheesecake in the other, on Scorpio a small sea-fish, on Sagittarius an eye-seeker, on Capricornus a lobster, on Aquarius a wild goose, on Pisces two mullets. In the middle was a sod of green turf, cut to shape and supporting a honey-comb. Meanwhile an Egyptian slave was carrying bread around in a miniature oven of silver, crooning to himself in a horrible voice a song on wine and the silphium plant.[51]

According to Pliny the most prestigious table services were made of silver, and that ever-changing fashions marked the rise and fall of individual silversmiths and their factories. He referred to patterns, such as the 'Delos', much as our own antique reference works discuss the 'willow' pattern on eighteenth-century china. Pliny described the subject matter of the decoration as trademarks of the craftsman responsible, for example 'goblets engraved with Centaurs and Bacchants by Acragas', whose hunting scenes were also highly prized:

Fashions in silver plate go through the most extraordinary changes, thanks to the whims of people's tastes, and not one single style of workmanship stays popular long. On one occasion Firnian plate is sought after, then Clodian, on another occasion Gratian ... It's remarkable that gold-working has failed to make a celebrity of anyone whereas celebrated silversmiths are numerous.[52]

According to Pliny, the desire to display silver in sheer quantity 'used for decorating sideboards' had become an obsession. There was 'an almost violent passion for works of fine handicraft', and looked back to when Attalus III of Asia had bequeathed his kingdom in 133 BC to Rome as the most 'serious blow to our morals', beginning with the auctioning off of the king's effects in Rome. After the final defeat of Carthage in 146 BC Scipio Aemilianus Africanus had personally left his heir just 32 lb (10.5 kg) and paraded 4,370 lb (1,437 kg) of silver in his triumph through Rome, all the silver that Carthage owned by that time. 'Yet', said Pliny, 'afterwards beaten by the splendour of our dining tables!'[53] Mark Antony appalled popular sensibilities by having golden drinking cups carried before him when he left Rome as if he was participating in some religious procession.[54]

The eventual outcome had been people like Drusillanus, a slave of Claudius' who was also known as Rotundus. He allegedly owned a silver dish weighing 500 Roman lb (165 kg) and eight more weighing 250 lb (82.5 kg) each as its side dishes. Pliny wondered how many slaves had been necessary to carry them in. Up until 82 BC there were only two silver dining couches in Rome, but this marked a time when silver became increasingly used as a decoration.[55] Silver's properties go unmentioned but the preference for its use in this context may have been based on observations that it was less associated with food poisoning and other infections. Viruses and bacteria struggle to live on silver, which is toxic to them. Herodotus had recorded how Persian kings travelled with water jars made of silver carried in carts because the metal prevented the liquid going bad, and Hippocrates knew that silver could help prevent disease.[56]

Juvenal ruminated on how, back in the old days, tables made of Italian wood were considered good enough to dine off. But by his own time in the early second century rich men were completely dissatisfied with their lavish meals unless they were eaten off an exotic ivory table, even silver being no longer considered acceptable. 'A table with a leg of silver is like a finger with an iron ring.' He contrasted this with his own modest dining arrangements for an 'elm-wood dinner', the meat cut up with blunt knives, the local wine served in plebeian cups and all served by slaves of rural origin and who had only had their hair tidied up because of the occasion. There would be no chance of girls from Cadiz with 'quivering buttocks' dancing; instead, the *Iliad* would be read. He was intrigued at the hypocrisy in a society that would condemn gambling and adultery among men of modest means but treated them as refinements when the rich indulged in such vices.[57] On the other hand, Juvenal might have been amusing himself at reactionary bores droning on about how in the old days everyone lived in brutal poverty and was grateful.

For all the extravagance that might have been seen in the houses of the rich in Rome, the vast majority of the population made good with bronze and pottery vessels for cooking and eating out of. Pliny considered pottery vessels and their 'unfailing supply' to be a gift of the 'ineffable kindness of the Earth'.[58] Earthenware was treated in antiquity as we treat paper and plastic disposable containers. In use it rapidly became contaminated by foodstuffs and was freely discarded. Today the astronomical quantities of shattered potsherds found on every Roman archaeological site bear witness to the extraordinary levels of production necessary to service demand, best proved by the cluttered kitchens of Pompeii and Herculaneum abandoned when the eruption struck.

A FAVOURITE CONDIMENT

An unusual favourite in the Roman diet was fermented fish sauce (*garum* or *liquamen*), manufactured in vast quantities and shipped round the Roman world. Elaborate presentation was common in the richest households, as were specialized condiments. Aulus Umbricius Scaurus was the head of a family that operated a highly successful and ostentatious fish sauce concern in Pompeii. Garum was made from the fermented guts of fish and was an extremely popular condiment in Roman cooking. It was manufactured in various places, but Pliny said the most popular was made from mackerel in New Carthage in Spain and was more expensive than any other liquid apart from perfume. Garum also yielded a waste product known as *allex*, which was consumed as a delicacy in a multiplicity of different varieties 'to suit all palates'.[59] Today there is no direct equivalent, except perhaps for Worcestershire sauce or Asian fish sauce, both of which contain anchovies.

Aulus Umbricius Scaurus was thus only one part of a huge industry, but he happens to be one we know about. He was almost certainly a freedman. He watched with pride as his freeborn son rose to become a civic magistrate in Pompeii off the back of the family wealth though Scaurus the younger was to die in office and was buried by his father. The Umbricii had been established at Pompeii since the early first century BC and may have been involved in the garum trade for generations. The family used several of their freedmen and freedwomen to operate the concern which involved at least six production locations, servicing a widespread market in Italy and beyond. One at least was operated by an imperial freedman called Martial, suggesting that perhaps his products went off to houses owned by the imperial family.[60] Inscribed containers have been found in and around Pompeii, testifying to the business's success. Many begin with the abbreviation GF for *garum flos*, 'prime [or flower of] fish sauce', and occasionally adding *optimum*, 'the best'.[61]

There is no doubt about where Umbricius Scaurus lived. His house lies on the west side of Pompeii in a prestigious location that overlooked the coast in antiquity (the coastline has been pushed west by the fall-out from the eruption). Like any important man's home, the house of Umbricius Scaurus was as much a public place as it was private. The atrium had a mosaic depicting miniature amphorae known as *urcei* and their inscriptions with the same business slogans as his real containers. Even his name may have been part of the promotion and linked him directly with his trade as was often the case with slaves and freedmen. Scaurus was a common enough name, but the Latin word *scarus* means the wrasse, a kind of fish which the Romans cultivated and caught in huge quantities off Italy.[62] This may be pure coincidence, but it is no less likely that an ancestor of his who began in the trade was nicknamed scarus and the name stuck, the spelling being later modified to a more conventional name form, added then to his master's name, Aulus Umbricius, when he was freed. It is hard to see how Scaurus could have failed to notice the humorous association of his name and his trade, which can only have helped remind people what his business was.

THE FISH TRADE

The freedwoman Aurelia Nais was a *piscatrix*, 'seller of fish', in Rome, which was only appropriate given that she was named after a water nymph. She worked at the *horrea* ('storehouses') of Galba, a huge complex of warehouses surrounded by shops in southern Rome and close to Monte di Testaccio, the mound of broken oil jars.[63] The warehouses stored huge quantities of food, and the fish trade was an important part of that. There was, of course, a professional guild association, known as the *corpus piscatorum et urinatorum alvei Tiberis*, 'the corporation of fishermen and divers of the Tiber riverbed'.[64] The word for a diver, *urinator*, came from the verb *urinare*, 'to plunge under water', the latter finding its way into modern English as the term for bodily liquid waste. The job of the divers was to plunge into the Tiber and rescue any goods dropped into the water during the loading and unloading on the quayside.

210

According to Varro, the Forum Piscarium (or Piscatorium, the fish market) was one of several forums dealing with essential provisions eventually brought together in one large marketplace.[65]

Aurelia Nais seems to have run her own business, but probably did so under the auspices of a patron who had perhaps freed her for the purpose. Aurelia Nais had a reputation in the trade. She is probably the woman referred to by Juvenal when writing about the market for fish:

> The mullet will be for the master, which was sent from Corsica or the rocks of Taormina, for in the rage for greed our own seas have failed, the nets of the fish-market are forever raking nearer waters, preventing Tyrrhenian fish from thriving. Therefore, the provinces supply the household, from here is sourced what the legacy-hunter Laenas buys, and Aurelia sells.[66]

Clearly, Aurelia was well-known enough to the extent that she could be referred to so casually by name. Perhaps the most interesting aspect of the extract is the revelation that Rome's rapacious levels of consumption were causing serious environmental damage through over-fishing, resulting in increased dependence on supplies from the provinces. This was likely to be reflected in many other parts of the food market.

Rome had countless food markets of all sizes, but little is known about them now. There was a large *macellum* ('provision market') in the area later occupied by the Forum of Nerva which had been around since the third century BC but is unknown after Claudius' reign. Nero built a new macellum on the Caelian Hill which he commemorated on a special issue of dupondius coins.[67] Its exact location is unknown now.

GREEDY EMPERORS

Not surprisingly, certain emperors led the field when it came to dining or were alleged to have done. The point here is how important it was to indulge in tales of imperial excess and gluttony during an era when most people were far from being guaranteed a meal, let alone a nutritious and balanced one. Colourful anecdotes abounded of spectacular profligacy, all treated as contemptuous examples of degeneracy but viewed, it seems, with a certain amount of prurient jealousy. For writers of the time these stories made for excellent copy, all adding to a rhetorical image of rottenness and decay at the top.

Augustus, despite his attempts to pass laws enforcing improved morality, was said as a young triumvir before he became emperor to have held a dinner called the 'Twelve Gods'. Guests turned up in fancy dress as gods and goddesses, with Augustus posing as Apollo. The information about this came from Mark Antony who by then was keen to use any pretext to slate his former colleague and friend.[68] Antony's own reputation was far from spotless. As a young man he had notoriously run up astronomical debts because of his 'drinking bouts, affairs with women, and reckless spending'.[69]

Augustus continued to have regular dinners as emperor, offering three courses normally and six if he was feeling extravagant. The entertainment included music, actors, circus performers, and storytellers. He also had fun with his guests by auctioning off lottery tickets for which the prizes were of unequal value or paintings of which only the back was visible. The result was that the guests were either overjoyed by their luck or hideously disappointed. Participation was compulsory.[70] Some guests just helped themselves to goodies. One went off with a gold cup but Claudius had spotted him. The man was invited back the next day and pointedly given a pottery cup from which to drink instead.[71] Vespasian threw frequent dinner parties, but he was an important part of the entertainment with his pithy observations and dirty jokes.[72] Sometimes official business was conducted at dinner. When Nero's reign was collapsing, he was brought dispatches bearing bad news while he was eating. He tore them up in fury and smashed two extremely expensive crystal cups decorated with Homeric scenes.[73] The gesture was a symbolic one; it was a way of showing that he could deny anyone else the wealth and power he was about to lose.

Not surprisingly, such dinner parties could be expensive affairs. The tight-fisted Tiberius had a solution, ostensibly to encourage frugality. He often served up leftover meat from the previous day, which in an age without refrigeration must have been both unpleasant and dangerous. His other cost-cutting wheeze was to serve up half a boar, claiming it was just as good as a whole one.[74] Nero's solution was simply to force his friends to pay up. One of them stumped up an extraordinary 4 million sesterces for one where silk turbans were the order of the day. Another paid up even more to attend a *rosaria*, which probably means a dinner either held in a rose garden or serving drinks flavoured with rose petals.[75]

Caligula's barbarities included inviting to dinner the parents of a man who had just been executed, and couples with the sole object of forcing the wives to sleep with him before returning to the meal where he slated or praised their bedroom performances. None of that was enough to put off the ambitious social climbers who wanted the prestige of having attended a banquet of Caligula's. A rich provincial bribed Caligula's staff 200,000 sesterces for admission. For light relief an entertainment on offer was Caligula's uncle and successor Claudius, who was habitually treated as an idiot and figure of fun thanks to his stammer and physical ailments. He routinely fell asleep after dinner so the other guests threw olive and date stones at him, and the jesters would go over and hit him with sticks for fun.[76] Or so the story went.

Claudius, who enjoyed eating and drinking at any opportunity, made up for the humiliation when he became emperor by throwing frequent dinner parties, but seems to have chosen venues where up to six hundred guests could be invited at any one time. This backfired on one occasion when he chose a spot by the Fucine Lake, which was prone to flooding. He had ordered the construction of drainage works, but unfortunately the outlet was opened during the dinner party and swamped it with water.[77] Dinner would be the death of Claudius, or so it was alleged. It was generally believed that his fourth and final wife, his niece Agrippina the Younger, had killed him with poisoned mushrooms in 54 so that her son Nero could become emperor and she could rule through him.[78] Nero's notorious Golden House palace in Rome featured 'dining rooms with fretted ceils of ivory, whose panels could turn and shower down flowers and were fitted with pipes for sprinkling the guests with perfumes. The main banquet hall was circular and constantly revolved day and night, like the heavens.' Remarkably, some of this building survives including some of these dining rooms and possibly even the revolving one, the remains of which might have now been identified in Rome.[79]

Galba was said to be so gluttonous that he left piles of unconsumed food in a heap which was then shared out among his attendants. As the short-lived first emperor of the civil war of 68–9 he was popularly regarded as tyrannical, greedy, and cruel. The allegations were thus inevitable.[80]

Vitellius, the third emperor of that disturbed period and who only reigned for three months, went down in Roman lore, as we have already seen, as the epitome and caricature of avarice. His defining evils were, said Suetonius, 'luxury and cruelty', proceeding to itemize the emperor's eating extravagances as part of the stock picture of a degenerate ruler, which even involved helping himself to the remains of sacrificial meals on altars. Nonetheless, the emperor's coin portraits gave some credence to the tales for they are clearly those of a corpulent man. As well as his drop-ins to streetside cookshops, Vitellius reputedly had four feasts a day, starting with breakfast and finishing with an evening drinking bout. In order to manage all that food he used emetics and saved money by ensuring he was invited to other people's homes, each having to stump up a minimum 400,000 sesterces a time. The most extravagant was a dinner thrown by his brother to celebrate Vitellius' arrival in Rome when supposedly 2,000 fish and 7,000 birds were served up.

Vitellius eclipsed even this at the dedication of a platter, which on account of its enormous size he called the 'Shield of Minerva, Defender of the City'. In this he mingled the livers of pike, the brains of pheasants and peacocks, the tongues of flamingos and the milt of lampreys, brought by his captains and triremes from the whole empire, from Parthia to the Spanish strait.[81]

The notoriously perverse and religious fanatic Elagabalus (218–22) was also the subject of tales of legendary gluttony, some of which were not written down until the fourth century. These, of course, apocryphal or not, reinforced other tales about his excess and confirmed his historical image of a reckless and self-indulgent emperor. One story was that he was liable to order 10,000 mice, 1,000 weasels, or 1,000 shrew-mice. 'So skilful were his confectioners and dairymen, that all the various kinds of food that were served by his cooks, either meat-cooks or fruit-cooks, they would also serve up, making them now out of confectionery or again out of milk products', said his biographer. Elagabalus had a sense of humour, or what passed for one, ordering that his hangers-on were served with dinners made of glass or pictures of the food rather than anything edible. As much food as he and his friends ate would also be thrown out of the palace windows.[82]

Not everyone was given to such gluttony. A senator called Ulpius Marcellus was sent to govern Britain, once more proving troublesome, by Marcus Aurelius in 177 where he remained until the early 180s. Marcellus was noted for his refusal even to fill himself up, evidently subscribing to more traditional values. He had his bread sent from Rome wherever he was, not because he could not eat the local bread, but because he wanted it to be so stale that he would be unable to eat any more than the bare minimum.[83] As it happens, Marcus Aurelius warned of the temptations caused by bread splitting open in the oven while baking, 'and in a peculiar way stimulates the desire for food'.[84]

DINNER DATES

Inscriptions on the wall of the dining room of the House of the Moralist at Pompeii provided advice for guests about appropriate behaviour. This may mean the house was a private dining club rather than a personal residence. Guests were asked to allow a slave to wash their feet and dry them, and to accept that a cloth would be placed on the couches to protect the linen. Diners were requested not to eye up other men's wives or come on to them, and either to postpone any quarrels or to leave and take them home.[85]

The large 'House' of Julia Felix at Pompeii seems also to have been a private dining enterprise that featured baths and a garden. It included various suites that were only suitable for persons of *nongenti* status to purchase the use of, according to an advertisement affixed to the property which occupied a whole block. The nongenti were a class of 900 equestrians in Rome who supervised elections. The Pompeii advertisement cannot possibly be referring to them, so the term must have been deployed as a metaphor to make it clear only people of that sort of status and above could take out a five-year lease on any of the facilities. It might just as well have said 'no riff-raff' or 'only persons of quality'.

Nearby in Pompeii was the so-called House of Loreius Tiburtinus (or Octavius Quartio) which had little in the way of living accommodation. A large part of its plot was given over to an exceptionally elaborate townhouse garden with a T-shaped canal and fountains running through a formal garden and overlooked by a triclinium featuring paintings of the Trojan War. The most likely explanation is that the building was operated as a dining business, providing patrons with a miniaturized version of the palatial country villas owned by the super-rich in the region. Petronius' satirical portrait of the vulgar and wealthy freedman Trimalchio features a discussion of his pretentious household decoration. This featured scenes from the *Iliad* and the *Odyssey* in the atrium, the main entrance hall which guests arrived in first.[86]

People attending such dinners might turn up in their *vestimenta cubitoria*. This meant their 'lying-down clothes', referring to the smart dress considered suitable for reclining at dinner on couches in a triclinium dining room where these were arranged around three sides of a table. Trimalchio's steward was proud of his Tyrian-dyed (purple) lying-down clothes given him by one of his clients.[87]

Martial set out to entice a friend of his called Julius Cerealis into joining him for dinner. Martial proposed meeting at the eighth hour, which meant the early afternoon, at the Baths of Stephanus near his home. The meal was to start with lettuce and leeks, followed by tunny fish garnished with eggs and rue leaves and served with olives and cheese. That was only the starter with further dishes to follow including more fish, oysters, and sow's udders, and fowl. Martial promised not to start reciting his own verses but was happy to hear Cerealis' compositions among which were his *War of the Giants* and *Georgics*.[88] The freedman Trimalchio, for all his pretentious literary-themed frescoes, laid on a troupe of acrobats at his dinner who performed to the sound of popular tunes, saying he only enjoyed trumpeters and acrobats.[89]

Such occasions could be costly. Keen to save money, Catullus told his friend Fabullus not to expect a good dinner unless he brought it himself.[90] Pliny the Younger dined with an acquaintance who prided himself on his 'sumptuous thriftiness', administered by grading his friends. This turned out to involve the host and a 'chosen few' being served the best dishes while everyone else was presented with 'cheap scraps' and inferior wine. Writing to a friend about the occasion, Pliny pointed out that the host could have avoided insulting his guests by showing restraint and eating the same as them.[91]

Literary readings at dinner were an opportunity for an educated man of status to display his knowledge, learning, and literary skills by producing his own version of myths or indulging in that most popular of Roman subjects, wistful poetry about the countryside. They took turns to showcase their compositions at social engagements like dinners. Catullus wrote a poem recounting when he and a friend called Licinius had taken turns to compose verse in different metres while laughing and drinking.

Tiberius Claudius Tiberinus was the type of poet who might have been hired for special dinners. He died in his early twenties. His admiring mother commissioned for him a tombstone with this epitaph which marked the spot where his cremated remains were deposited. It belongs to the mid-first century AD and was found in a columbarium tomb on the site later occupied by the Baths of Caracalla. Its pretentious text includes a reference to the Pierian spring of Macedonia, sacred to the Muses, and Maeonia, the mythical home of Homer, whose works were therefore sometimes called Maeonian:

> You, traveller, whoever you are who ride by the threshold of my tomb, please check your hurried journey. Read this through, and so may you never grieve for an untimely death. You'll find my name attached to the inscription. Rome is my native city, my parents were ordinary plebeians, then my life was defiled by no evil. Once I was well known as the people's favourite. Now I am the few ashes of a mourned-over funeral pyre. Who did not see good parties with a cheerful face, and stay up all night with me and my topics? Once I was skilled in reciting the works of poets with Pierian tunefulness and swanlike rhythm, skilled in speaking poems that breathed with Maeonian verse, poems well-known in Caesar's Forum. Of my body, which my parents sadly strew with tears, love and a name are now all that's left. They place garlands and fresh flowers for me to enjoy. That is how I remain, laid out in the vale of Elysium. My fates gave me as many birthdays as the stars that pass by in the Dolphin and winged Pegasus.[92]

Although in antiquity the Dolphin constellation was attributed with nine stars, Pegasus was awarded a range from fifteen to twenty which means the best we can say is that Tiberinus died when he was between twenty-four and twenty-nine. The epitaph belonged to a wider rhetorical tradition indulged in by poets and emulated, for example, a poem of Ovid's in which he wrote about the skills of other poets and how he had first read his youthful songs in public.[93] Tiberinus' father was probably a freedman, his name suggesting his father had been freed by Claudius. His fame, or lack of, is impossible to assess now but he was probably a jobbing entertainer who among other bookings was commissioned to turn up at dinners and perform famous works – there is no reference to his own compositions – his efforts in the Forum of Julius Caesar doubtless having earned him a following.[94]

Martial found an acquaintance called Menogenes particularly annoying. At the baths Menogenes was irritatingly ingratiating, constantly following people around and paying them unwarranted compliments like 'he will insist you have arranged your hair like that of Achilles' and even mopping people's brows. All Menogenes wanted was a dinner invitation and he carried on until the unwilling host caved and asked him to come and dine.[95]

Another annoying guest was Caecilianus who turned up for dinner ridiculously early during the fourth hour of the day. Martial was obliged to shout for his slave Callistus to put out the dining couches. He also had to tell Caecilianus that his daily water delivery had not yet arrived, and the stove had not been lit so there was no warm water. He sarcastically asked why Caecilianus had taken that long to turn up – he should have come at dawn if he was hungry, 'for breakfast, Caecilianus, you come late'.[96]

Caecilianus was annoying for a variety of other reasons. His habits included helping himself to piles of food which were then wrapped up in his *madente mappa* ('soaked napkin') for his slave to take home, leaving nothing for anyone else. Martial itemized the dishes, providing us with more evidence for what might be set on a Roman table. They included pork, woodcock, mullet, pike, lamprey, chicken, and a wood pigeon. On another occasion while other guests looked on Caecilianus helped himself to all the truffles.[97] Catullus was irritated by Asinius Marrucinus who had a reputation for stealing napkins from other guests while they were not paying attention.[98]

Martial was not alone in having unreliable friends. When Septicius Clarus failed to show up at Pliny the Younger's for dinner he was sent a humorously chiding letter pointing out that dinner had been on the table and asking Clarus to pay Pliny back. The dishes featured a lettuce each, three snails, two eggs, wheat-cake and a special delicacy consisting of snow-chilled wine flavoured with honey. Clarus would have been able to eat all this while listening to a comic play, a reader, or a singer, or even all three if Pliny had been feeling generous, or so he said.[99]

CATERING SERVICES

Laying on a lavish dinner was expensive enough just on the odd occasion. It would have been even more extravagant to maintain the necessary staff on a permanent basis. Professional catering businesses run by *ministratores* ('suppliers' or 'servers') were available to rustle up the dishes and table service. Publius Vibius Quintio was a ministrator with premises in the Forum on the Esquiline Hill in the late first century.[100] Ateius Capito described in the late first century BC how it was still common in his time for people to hire cooks on an ad-hoc basis from the provision market (macellum).[101]

A ministrator traditionally meant an attendant or a servant in a domestic context, but in Quintio's case the term was being used in a commercial context. He was probably providing a full catering and waiting service for those who wanted to lay on a dinner, probably similar to those described by Martial, on a one-off contract arrangement. Plautus refers to the 'cooks' Forum' in his play *Pseudolus*. In one scene a character called Ballio finds only one cook left available in the market, who explained why: 'in fact, directly people come to hire a cook, no one enquires for the man that's the best and the highest priced: rather do they hire he who's the cheapest. Through this have I today been the only sitter in the market. Those wretched fellows are for a drachma a-piece; not any person is able to prevail on me to rise for less than 2 drachmas.' The reason, the cook explained, was that the other cooks all packed their food with herbs that even animals do not eat and would kill those who ate it, whereas 'for those who shall eat of my victuals which I have seasoned will be able to exist two hundred years even . . . I confess that I am a very high-priced cook; but I make the results of my labour to be seen for the price, hired at which I go out'. The cook turns up with his assistants, Ballio worrying about what they might steal from his house.[102]

Pliny reports how at one point there were complaints about how a cook cost more than a horse, but that in his own time the price had risen to the equivalent of three horses – 'almost no human being has come to be more valued than one that is most skilful at overwhelming the wealth of his master [i.e. bankrupt him]'.[103]

Quintio was clearly operating a private home catering or banqueting service from the Esquiline Forum. This was probably a specialized 'go-to' area for anyone wanting to hire a cook and staff for a special occasion. It is possible that Plautus' 'cooks' Forum' was one and the same place. Publius Saenius Arsaces was another ministrator in Rome, in his case operating 'by Hercules Primgenius', evidently a locality identified by contemporaries from the presence of a now-lost altar or shrine to the god.[104]

THE POOR

In his *Metamorphoses* the poet Ovid described a peasant's meal. The setting in Phrygia was fictitious and involved an elderly couple called Philemon and Baucis who fed Jupiter and Mercury, the gods being disguised as travellers. Philemon and Baucis pulled out all the stops they could to feed their visitors, serving up cabbage and a boiled piece of smoked pork that had been kept for special occasions, olives, berries preserved in vinegar, radishes, cheese, and eggs, with fruit for afterwards. The feast counted as a great extravagance for the rural poor but also fitted the Roman urban fantasy of modest and traditional rural life which they so admired.[105]

In one house in Pompeii, connected to a streetside food bar by a doorway, was found a list of food for two days. The most noticeable fact is the limited amount of meat, with just one small sausage (*botellus*) listed and a possible reference to beef. The word *botellus* is rare in Latin (though Martial mentions it). This means it was probably a lower-class form of food. Apart from a reference to whitebait, the food list is dominated by bread, oil, onions, porridge, cheese, wine, and dates, as well as several instances of *panem puero* ('bread for boys') but here with *puer* being used in a subsidiary way to mean 'slave'. The ingredients were probably intended for use in the streetside bar, but because only bread was earmarked for slaves it is likely to indicate the basic diet they had to subsist on.[106]

The Romans were equally obsessed with health and disease but lived in a culture where medical skills and knowledge were in their infancy. Superstition and ignorance abounded, with remedies and care of all sorts available from practitioners, some of whom were more likely to kill their patients than save them or even do any good at all. Cynics thought doctors the most egregious example of a corrupt profession. Nonetheless, there were also medical writers like the encyclopedist Celsus who managed within the context of the era to make major contributions to knowledge. For the ordinary Roman afflicted with some ailment there was little chance of finding anyone capable of making any difference to the outcome.

10

DOCTORS AND DISEASE

In their hunt for popularity by means of some novelty, physicians
did not hesitate to buy it with our lives. Hence those wretched,
quarrelsome consultations at the bedside of the patient, none
agreeing with another lest he be seen to acknowledge a superior.
Hence too that gloomy inscription on monuments, 'he died from a
mob of doctors'.

Pliny[1]

T he people of Rome benefited from the advantages of piped
water pouring into the city and feeding streetside fountains
with a continuous flow, the sewers, and public latrines, as well
as – depending on income – access to food devoid of modern additives,
sugar, and other unhealthy components. It would be a mistake to
believe that such facilities and habits made the city a safe place to live
and where disease was kept at bay. It would be many centuries before
the arrival of tea and coffee, for example, involved the far safer practice
of routinely boiling water before making a drink. Sickness of all sorts
was rife in Rome and so were medical practitioners with a litany of
treatments to call on, ranging from the efficacious to the ludicrous.

For the Roman traditionalist, medicine was another sign of decadence. Pliny said that Roman degeneracy was due more to that than
anything else. He was puzzled by the remarkable achievements and

durability of the Roman state when set against the way 'good men give authority to the worst', and the 'stupid convictions of certain people who consider nothing beneficial unless it was expensive'.[2] Conversely, hardened traditionalists extolled the virtues of basics. Cato the Elder was keen to point out the medicinal properties of the humble cabbage, among which were improving digestion and encouraging the production of urine that is 'wholesome for everything'. Other benefits in his long list included cabbage poultices for dislocated joints.[3]

Roman names were often descriptive of an individual but ended up being handed down. These cognomens, the third part of a citizen's name, sometimes referred to physical appearance and even ailments. Eye conditions contributed 'Strabo' ('squinter') and Paetus ('blinker'). A prominent member of the senatorial Nonii clan in Herculaneum and benefactor of the city in the late first century BC, was called Marcus Nonius Balbus, where *balbus* means 'stammerer'.[4] This could easily have applied originally to an ancestor but either way his descendants continued to bear the name, just as Caesar, who was bald, bore a name that meant 'hairy'.

AN UNHEALTHY ENVIRONMENT

Rome's sewers were used to dispose mainly of sewage and excess rainwater, but waste of all sorts ended up in them too including the corpses of animals and people. An adult can produce at least 400 g (0.9 lb) of faecal matter per day, and a child somewhat less. Allowing then, say, an average of 325 g per head daily Rome's population of up to around one million at its height could generate at least 325,000 kg per day or 325 metric tonnes (358 US tons), which makes for 118,625 tonnes annually. The figures are only estimates and obviously in Rome's earlier days the totals were far lower. At times they were higher. But they give an idea of the scale of the problem this vast ancient city created. Of course, the figures take no account of animal faecal matter which was probably at least as great and probably higher, adding to the waste matter generated by slaughter for food though in practice probably much of that waste such as bone was reused somehow.

Much of the rubbish was thrown into the streets where it festered in a sludge washed slowly away by rain or cleared by scavengers. Vitellius was among the emperors murdered and thrown into the Tiber, but in his case only after he had been pelted with dung, presumably readily available, and then murdered.[5] Justinian's *Digest of Roman Law* contained this provision which dated back to the jurist Ulpian in the third century. Clearly, hurling waste out of windows was a serious issue, with the underlying principle being that people were responsible for building and maintaining the streets outside their houses, and cleaning out the gutters:

> The Praetor says with reference to those who throw down or pour out anything: Where anything is thrown down or poured out from anywhere upon a place where persons are in the habit of passing or standing, I will grant an action against the party who lives there for twofold the amount of damage occasioned or done.[6]

Another law stated that 'the aediles must not permit any quarrelling to take place in the streets, nor any filth, dead animals, or skins to be thrown into them'.[7]

The law was all very well, but observing or enforcing it were other matters entirely. Rome's streets could yield all sorts of horrors. In around 275 BC a series of worrying omens appeared. They included the arrival of three wolves in Rome which brought with them a half-eaten body, which they must have picked up from the street or off a rubbish dump. Startled by people shouting at them they dropped the grisly remains in the Forum.[8]

One day around 350 years later Vespasian's breakfast was disrupted when a stray dog burst into the palace carrying a severed human hand.[9] The dog had come from a trivium road junction which almost certainly means it had found part of a disintegrating execution victim, probably a criminal or a slave, who had been crucified there (see p. 26 for the trivium, and p. 162 for crucifixion as a means of punishing slaves).

The streets of Pompeii and Herculaneum provide a good impression of what Rome's alleys must have been like. Raised pavements flanked the road surfaces which served as open sewers and were crossed on stepping stones so that pedestrians could make their way over without treading in the horrors floating a few inches away, or tumbling past in a rainstorm which washed the mess away at least temporarily. Until such a storm it compacted slowly into a rotting and glutinous mass of the type that spattered over Juvenal's legs in Rome.[10] The houses of the affluent were turned inward to their peristyle gardens and dining rooms, avoiding as much as possible the noise and smell of the effluent from the streets.

Occasional floods might have helped clear out some of the filth in Rome like the disaster of late autumn in 54 BC. Today the Tiber's course through the city is contained by huge embankments. In antiquity the river was wider and the banks lower, clustered with buildings and wharfs, making Rome far more susceptible to floods than it is now. On that occasion the Tiber burst its banks, either because of heavy rains upriver or a huge onshore gale or both (but it was blamed on divine intervention). The rising waters poured into Rome, flooding even some of the higher ground and causing numerous houses to collapse, while weakening the rest. The disaster happened so quickly that many people were caught unawares; if they had failed to make a dash for safety they were drowned.[11] Cicero heard the news at Tusculum (near modern Frascati) and wrote to tell his brother Quintus how 'the promenade of Crassipes' had been washed away, along with public pleasure gardens and many shops.[12]

Much the same occurred over a century later in 69 during Otho's reign when another flood hit low-lying areas, undermining some of the cramped tenement blocks and leaving behind huge quantities of mud and rubbish when the water subsided. The result was that many of the blocks collapsed, and the general disruption and damage led to famine.[13]

These low-lying areas were already prone to disease, something the

Romans understood but not why. Columella had pointed out how dangerous such places were because no one, including the doctors, had any idea what caused them: 'Water that always remains stagnant in a swamp is laden with death.'[14]

Rome and Ostia were equipped with public and private latrines. These relied on a constant flow of water from the aqueducts. One particularly fine example survives almost intact at Ostia near the Forum Baths. The marble seating consisted of a series of keyhole recesses ranged around three sociable sides of a rectangular chamber without any divisions. Patrons therefore relieved themselves in the company of any other walk-ins. Water arrived from an aqueduct or rainwater tank and ran round a shallow channel beside their feet, into which a sponge could be dipped to clean their behinds, before running off into a channel beneath the seats where it was supposed to carry off the human waste into the sewers and out into the Tiber. Roman toilets must have reeked of excrement. The application of vinegar might have been one solution to neutralize the odour since there were no proprietary chemical cleaners available.

Martial wrote about a generic thief who spent his life stealing from the aristocracy, only to end his days lurking among beggars and scrounging crumbs of stale and rotten bread. He died in the street with scavenging dogs and birds gathering around him, trying to wave them off with his rags, but with no relief as he then entered a punitive torment in the afterlife. The reader is left to imagine the body being torn apart by the animals and its remains left to be washed away and eventually end up in the Tiber.[15] Juvenal left less to the imagination when he described a cart accident that resulted in a load of marble crushing passers-by, obliterating them in the rubbish. 'Who can identify the limbs, who the bones? The cadaver of the common man vanishes completely, just like his soul', who was thus denied a proper burial.[16] No wonder the dog that disturbed Vespasian's breakfast had been able to steal from a decaying corpse.

As if filthy streets were not bad enough, the Romans breathed an atmosphere blued by the smoke emanating from ovens, furnaces, kilns, olive oil lamps, sacrifices, and burning incense, whether in private homes, temples, or industrial premises.[17] Seneca complained about the 'poisonous fumes' and 'clouds of ashes' caused by cooking in Rome, and his relief at escaping to his vineyards.[18] When clients hurried over to their patrons' houses to collect their share of the sportula handouts they each took a slave carrying a heated container with its own miniature furnace to keep the food hot, every one of them belching out fumes to add to the suffocating murk that enveloped Rome.[19]

SICKNESS

Infectious conditions, including plague and venereal disease, were as rife as fatal conditions like cancer and heart disease. Doctors (*medici*) existed, but their medical knowledge was rudimentary compared to today and they had limited treatments at their disposal. Their training was generally on the job. Only in the Roman army was healthcare of some sort routinely available. Doctors were attached to most military units and many forts had a dedicated hospital called a *valetudinarium*. For the average man or woman in Rome, Ostia, or Pompeii, the options were different. Other medical benefits, preventative measures, and assistance were minimal. Invalids were, for example, allowed the exclusive use of the baths before the eighth hour of the day by Hadrian's time but that cannot have made much difference to their lives.[20]

Infection from contaminated food and water was one threat, but so also were respiratory conditions and fractures caused by accidents or violence. There was also the basic question of nutrition (see Chapter 9). Many Romans, especially the poor and slaves, were unlikely to have been able to maintain anything like a healthy diet. The average Roman was therefore susceptible to viral and bacterial disease transmitted through contaminated water (see Cicero below, this chapter), food that had been kept at a temperature that promoted the growth of bacteria or fungus, and the easily transferred parasites such as lice and worms.

The Romans knew nothing about micro-organisms. With few

reliable descriptions of the symptoms of individual cases, it is impossible usually to form any specific conclusions about the precise nature of any disease. Diseases also mutate into different forms, and different populations for a variety of epidemiological, environmental, and genetic reasons have varying degrees of susceptibility. Visitors to Rome, for example, were likely to fall foul of some diseases and infections that long-term residents had developed resistance to, and the latter were obviously equally susceptible to being infected by one of the thousands of foreigners who arrived weekly.

While some Romans reached remarkable lifespans, the vast majority died before their time. The maximum potential length of human life has not changed since antiquity, merely the chances of reaching it. The tombstones of the Romans record the brevity of many of their lives, most poignantly those of the children. There was nothing unusual about this in antiquity any more than it would have been in medieval and early modern times. Nevertheless, the Romans, depending on class, probably had a moderately better chance of living a reasonably healthy life well into adulthood than people of most other ancient civilizations. But we have no means of making a meaningful comparison since no contemporary society left an archive of tombstones that tell us how old the deceased were. Not even all Roman tombstones bear that information. Many people, especially slaves, are unlikely to have been certain about their ages.

Roman tombstones virtually never record the cause of mortality, usually carrying only perfunctory statements for the most part about a deceased's name, age at death, profession, and family connections. Eutyches, a trainee charioteer at Tarraco in Spain, died aged twenty-two, afflicted by a disease that consumed him. 'The doctors could not cure it', bemoaned his tombstone.[21] His fate must have been all too common thanks either to a wholly wrong diagnosis, a lack of any effective treatment, or an inability to form any diagnosis at all apart from inventing one. In a society where death at all ages was commonplace, not knowing the cause was more readily accepted, however tragic the event for the deceased's family and friends.

229

We do usually have some idea about the causes of death of the emperors and sometimes members of the imperial family. Unlike the general population, few expired from illness as Hadrian did after suffering many years of failing health (see below). Many had violent or unnatural deaths, whether murdered in the palace, in an uprising, on campaign, or killed on the battlefield. Of the first eleven emperors from Augustus to Domitian, only three died natural deaths for certain (Augustus, Vespasian, and Titus). While the position improved in the century following Domitian, the accession of Commodus in 180 heralded an era when most emperors were murdered or died in battle.

Of those who died deaths from disease or old age we know really little about why. Augustus' father Gaius Octavius had 'died suddenly' in 59 BC, from which we can only surmise that a heart attack or aneurysm might have been responsible among several possible causes.[22] Augustus wished for himself a swift and painless death, envying anyone he heard of who had died that way. In the event he had the good fortune to expire that way when he was seventy-five and in the same room in Nola as his father had.[23] Vespasian was hit by a sudden attack of diarrhoea. Fearing he was about to die, he struggled to his feet in the belief that an emperor should die standing but expired in the arms of those who were helping him. His son Titus followed him two years later after having been hit by a fever.[24] Hadrian spent the last two years of his life afflicted by a 'severe illness', which appears to have profoundly demoralized him and involved a fever before he died. Dio says Hadrian had lost blood, become consumptive and developed dropsy, but other possibilities include heart failure.[25] These examples illustrate how difficult it is to know why any individual died unless they were murdered.

Two small brothers in Rome had the misfortune to fall ill and die. Torquatianus and Laetianus were both described as a *pupus*, a term of endearment that meant 'puppet' or 'doll', perhaps equivalent to 'moppet' or 'poppet' today. Their funerary inscription from Rome, set up by their grieving parents Gaianus and Eucharis, records that on 11 September one year both children became sick, with one dying on the 21st and the other lasting till the 29th. Both seem therefore to have caught an infectious disease, which is now unidentifiable.[26]

In 57 BC Cicero came down with a bad bout of probable dysentery which he had contracted in Rome, apparently at a banquet being held by a friend who had just been made an augur. The most likely explanation is that Cicero caught this infectious condition from food prepared by a slave (in this case beetroot and mallow) who had passed it on through a simple lack of basic hygiene. Cicero blamed sumptuary laws that had prohibited luxury foods in preference to basic root vegetables which were then lavishly dressed with herbs. There was no proper understanding of the value of sterility or everyday cleanliness (but see Chapter 9 for the use of silver in dining). Cicero was so ill with pain in his bowels that he took himself off to his country villa near Tusculum. His lack of knowledge about the condition is evident from the fact that although he fasted he also spurned drinking any water. That would have led to a dangerous level of dehydration thanks to the chronic vomiting and diarrhoea from which he was suffering.[27] Pliny recorded that in superstitious tradition any food dropped during a meal had to be picked up and restored, and that it was forbidden to blow off any dirt.[28]

Catullus suffered from 'a bad cough' which he put down to having over-indulged in extravagant dinners, but which had probably been transmitted by a virus from a fellow diner or in some other social context. He said he was glad to have escaped to a friend's suburban villa, which means a farm in Rome's rural hinterland. His powers of self-diagnosis were questionable. He said the writings of Sestius had made him ill too.[29]

Seneca was occasionally struck down by something he called *suspirium*. The word meant sighing or deep breathing but could also mean shortness of breath. Seneca was probably writing about asthma, perhaps exacerbated by Rome's smoky air. He was by his own account accustomed to suffering from a variety of conditions, but he found the breathing difficulties to be the most distressing because he felt like his soul was expiring. For this reason, he recounted how doctors called it a *meditationum mortis*, a 'rehearsal for death'. Seneca was badly shaken but was relieved as the attack gradually slowed down and stopped, leaving him still with a sense that there was an obstruction. He was a Stoic philosopher and treated the whole experience as an important event in preparing himself for death one day. 'Now I am prepared, I look forward to nothing all day', by which he meant he took one day at a time.[30]

CURES

Medicines, potions, and lotions were widely available on a casual basis in general commerce. Today it is impossible to know what these really were or whether they worked. The trade was obviously lucrative. Most were produced by quacks for sale on to middlemen or women who touted them in the marketplace. One house in Pompeii had a pottery jar containing North African 'flower of lotion from donkey milk, Utica'. The place of origin was doubtless some sort of desirable trademark, and possibly fake. Another refers to honey made by thyme-fed bees marketed on the name of the producer, Gaia Severa, but whether she was a real person or just a brand name like certain modern foods, or where she supposedly worked are unknown. Numicia Primigenia's lotion, a jar of which was also found at Pompeii, was sold as *verax*, 'truthful', perhaps in today's sales terms 'the authentic' or 'the original'.[31]

Despite his cynicism about doctors, Pliny was happy to itemize various remedies. He featured the revelation that an epileptic who fell over could cure his condition by allowing his head to drive in a nail as he collapsed. Pliny listed off several powers of urine, starting with how 'great power is attributed to urine, not only natural but also religious, by the authorities who divide it into types, even that of eunuchs to tackle the sorcery that prevents fertility'.[32] Others included the intriguing anecdote that urine could relieve gout, which he pointed out fullers never suffered from. The reason for this was the use of urine in clothes washing because of its ammonia content. Various other applications such as dealing with sores, burns, or stings were cited. The explanation, of course, is urine's antiseptic properties, not understood in antiquity. Pliny was also aware that the colour of urine was a giveaway. 'A bad symptom is red urine . . . the worst of all when it is dark', perhaps a reference to porphyria. Asses' urine mixed with water from a blacksmith's could be used to treat 'delirious raving'.[33]

Pliny's account was typical of even the most educated works of antiquity for its quaint mix of useful information and myth. Superstition took on unlimited forms and Pliny was keen to supply numerous examples which he appears to have accepted at face value. These often veered into the world of medicine, blurring superstition with religion. For example, the smell of burned women's hair supposedly helped fend off serpents and slow down the breathing of a woman suffering a bout of hysteria, as well as tackle cavities caused by ulcers. To these Pliny added the powers of women's milk in the treatment of fever and coeliac disease. For broken bones one practice was to use the ashes from a burned wild boar or pig jawbone, or bacon fat, to help healing, while goat droppings in old wine were supposedly perfect for dealing with broken ribs.[34]

The hand of someone who had died prematurely was said to cure scrofulous sores and other conditions. Apparently, someone with his hands behind his back who then bit off a piece of wood that had been struck by lightning could use it to deal with toothache. An alternative was to use a canine tooth from an unburied corpse as an amulet.[35] Grudgingly, Pliny acknowledged that the 'profiteering Greeks' had produced some important remedies by using the *sordes ex gymnasio*. These were the scrapings from the skin of athletes which produced a potent mix of flesh, sweat, and oil to create an ointment used to treat inflammation and contractions of the uterus, as well as other conditions. He roundly dismissed 'shameless' claims that male semen could be used as an antidote for scorpion stings.[36]

While some ancient remedies seem absurd, others were the result of sound observation and experience. Saliva was believed to protect against the evil eye. Older women might take a baby from its cradle and apply their saliva to the child's forehead and lips, and then mutter an incantation praying for the child's fortune and strength.[37] The basis for this seems to have been the discovery that the saliva of a fasting woman could help bloodshot and inflamed eyes. This formed only one of the powers of women's bodies, Pliny noting that 'after this, there is no limit [to the power of women]'. What Pliny and his contemporaries, of course, had no idea about was that saliva contains a receptor protein now called epidermal growth factor (EGF) which has some healing and protective properties.

Pliny proceeded to supply the invaluable information that hailstorms and whirlwinds are driven away by exposing menstrual fluid to lightning flashes, along with some other bizarre claims that a menstruating woman walking round a cornfield would lead to pests like caterpillars, worms and beetles dying.[38]

Roman eye doctors marketed patent salves known as oculists' stamps which turn up around the Empire. These retrograde-inscribed small blocks of stone were used to stamp cakes of their lotions or applications, but by the time any of these reached customers they were almost certainly being used by secondary or tertiary itinerant practitioners passing off their products as being more esteemed than they really were. The inscriptions give an idea of the medication available such as *diapsoricum*, 'itch salve', and *opobalsamatum*, 'sap of the balsam tree', sometimes adding suitably catchy epithets like 'invincible' and 'inimitable'.[39] They read like the sort of patent remedies sold off the backs of wagons in the muddy streets of frontier towns in the American Old West like 'Gaius Valerius Valentinus' mixture for clear sight'. Some added the catch-all claim 'for all pains' to whatever had been stamped, or just 'infallible'.[40] Mark Twain's writings are filled with references to his willingness to try any similar sounding remedy on offer in the America of the mid-1800s, even inventing his own. His scepticism about doctors matched Pliny's.[41]

According to Juvenal, a woman discovering an itch in her eye was likely to consult her horoscope first before calling for any eye ointment.[42] There were other measures available for the worried and credulous. Having a haircut only on the 17th or 29th of every month was supposed to prevent it falling out. Those who feared ophthalmia could wear a piece of paper round their necks with the meaningless formula in Greek letters ρα or a live fly contained in a white linen bag.[43]

DOCTORS AND HEALING

Doctors tended to be Greeks, and were often slaves or freedmen, sometimes on the establishment of a more senior and well-heeled doctor. Augustus, for example, had slave doctors.[44] Eros Spo(n)sianus was a *constans medicus* ('faithful doctor') on his empress Livia's staff. His name was Greek and with no reference to him having been freed, he must still have been a slave when he died.[45] There was also Eudemus, said by Tacitus to have been both the doctor and friend of Livilla, Augustus' great-niece and Livia's granddaughter (see below, this chapter).

The early emperors were inclined to pay their doctors well. A salary of a quarter of a million sesterces was routine and some made half a million out of their imperial patrons.[46] It was not the same for lesser doctors. One might have considered the commercial value of a doctor to be fairly sound, but in Justinian's *Codex*, which was compiled in the year 531 from much older laws, an unskilled male or female slave aged over ten years was valued at 20 solidi (the solidus being the late Roman gold coin which had replaced the aureus under Constantine I). Remarkably, an older eunuch was worth 50 solidi, and one with a skill came in at 70 solidi. A doctor was valued at 60 solidi, the same price as a midwife.[47] Freedmen doctors were obliged by law to treat their patrons, their families, and their patrons' friends for free (see Chapter 8).

Augustus' great-nephew, the general Germanicus, had a personal doctor who was a Roman citizen, Tiberius Claudius Melitone, son of Athenodorus.[48] Athenodorus was almost certainly Greek, which means he was probably a doctor whose son followed in the profession but unlike his father was given Roman citizenship as a reward. Melitone's funeral urn was made of astracane, a highly sought-after and valuable form of shell marble from North Africa. Melitone had apparently done well in his career, either being able to afford this material himself or it was donated by Germanicus (who died in Syria in 19) or his family. The doctor Alcyon was on hand in the Palatine's temporary theatre when Caligula was assassinated, and people were wounded in the chaos that followed. On the pretext that he needed medical supplies, he managed to send people away from the theatre, his real purpose being to save them from Caligula's enraged German bodyguards.[49]

Sometimes the line between the medical profession and religious superstition was blurred, especially at a time when the physical world was believed to contain within it portents of the future. Vespasian's son Titus was brought up at court with Britannicus, the ill-fated son of Claudius who would be murdered by his stepbrother Nero. For reasons unknown, a *metoposcopus* (physiognomist) was hired by Claudius' freedman Narcissus to inspect Britannicus which involved studying his forehead to predict the future. The verdict was that Britannicus would never rule, but that Titus surely would.[50] The story is typical of Roman self-fulfilling prophecies and its veracity is therefore prone to doubt, but in the context of the era it is entirely possible that a professional physical examination would be sought for such purposes.

Doctors were regarded with deep suspicion in a general sense, but there were instances where the patient developed trust and respect for individual practitioners. This was particularly common among the elite who were able not only to afford the best but were also able to reward them, sometimes with an offer to help them obtain citizenship. Nevertheless, many doctors had little professional knowledge and expertise. There was no formal training or recognized standard, just as was the case with almost any other profession in antiquity. Learning came on the job, usually by starting out as a pupil of an established practitioner. Symmachus was a doctor called out by Martial one day. Symmachus allegedly turned up with a hundred of his own students, obviously an exaggeration, who proceeded to prod and feel Martial who claimed that as a result of this consultation he contracted a fever he had not had to start with.[51]

Doctors operated largely as individuals, relying on personal reputations and their own specialisms, but could also be attached to specific places or events. Tiberius Claudius Callicrates, an imperial freedman in the late first century AD, was a 'doctor of the Great Games'. His cognomen was of Greek origin, so he appears to have been a Greek doctor rewarded with his freedom.[52] Titus Aelius Aminias, another imperial freedman (probably of Antoninus Pius), was a *medicus auricularius* ('ear doctor'). Over a century earlier Tiberius Lyrias Celadianus, 'a slave of Tiberius Caesar Augustus', worked as a *medicus ocularius*, 'eye doctor', an ophthalmologist. Gaius Terentius Pistus was another, labelled as such on his tombstone, dedicated by his freedman Gaius Terentius Helius. He lived in the first century AD, surviving to a precisely enumerated (and remarkable) 87 years, 5 months, 24 days and 10 hours.[53] Pistus was therefore at the least a freedman, but it is possible he was freeborn, though that would have been unusual.

Celadianus might have worked on Tiberius' personal staff. Tiberius would have had good cause to be concerned about some of his doctors. Charicles, again obviously a name of Greek origin, was 'distinguished for his skill', doubtless the reason his advice was sought on the emperor's state of health in March 37. Charicles claimed to be leaving on personal business but grasped Tiberius' hand to check his pulse. The emperor was not fooled but behaved as normal. Charicles was in cahoots with Macro, by then prefect of the Praetorian Guard, and quickly told him that Tiberius had only two days to live. This enabled Caligula and Macro to prepare for the succession when Tiberius duly apparently expired but then Tiberius abruptly recovered, obliging Macro to have the emperor suffocated since Caligula had already announced his succession.[54]

Pliny saw two reasons to be concerned about doctors: their mercenary attitudes, and their ignorance. The result was their arrogance and quackery. He was intrigued by the problems created because no two doctors ever produced the same diagnosis, a phenomenon familiar to many modern patients. He also cursed the mercurial state of a profession that changed its claims daily. He was particularly critical of the 'vacant words of intellectual Greeks' and noted that few Romans ever practised medicine. Even today it is not unusual for someone afflicted by a serious condition to be presented with an array of varying explanations and diagnoses, sometimes as many as the number of medical practitioners they have consulted.

Pliny looked for his inspiration back to the words of Cato the Elder, a man whom he regarded as having the highest authority. Back in the Republic, Cato had advised that Greek literature should be explored but not in detail because 'they are the most villainous and intractable people ... whenever that nation shall bestow its literature upon us, it will corrupt everything, and all the sooner if it sends its physicians here'. Cato had a simple explanation for this: the Greeks were mercenary murderers, and their doctors were the vanguard. 'They have conspired among themselves to murder all foreigners with their medicine, a profession which they exercise for money in order that they may win our confidence and dispatch us all the more easily.'[55]

Cato's words cut no ice with many Romans who were easily beguiled into accepting Greek medical practice. Greek dominance of the profession helped create a requirement that anyone wishing to have medical authority had to publish his work in Greek. Pliny noted the 'new fashion of using hot water for sicknesses' among doctors. Pliny had plenty more to say but he ultimately blamed the prevalence of quackery on popular credulity, and the desire of people to place faith in something they did not understand.[56]

None of this meant that medical science was not taken seriously. Cornelius Celsus was a man in Pliny's mould. He wrote prolifically on a range of subjects but only his *On Medicine* has survived. It was a serious attempt to compile a thorough textbook on the theory of medicine, knowledge of diseases, diagnosis, prognosis, and treatments including pharmacology and surgery. For example, one chapter tackled parasitic worms and their treatments, another diseases of the womb and their cures.[57] He began by explaining that even the most uncivilized communities had knowledge of herbs and other substances that could be used to treat disease, but that it had been the Greeks who had developed the 'art of medicine', attributed in myth to Asklepios (Roman Aesculapius), a son of Apollo whom the god had educated in the subject and who was subsequently made a god himself. Doctors routinely made dedications and offerings to Aesculapius who had become their patron god.

Some of Celsus' remedies exposed his lack of understanding of infection. They included suggested treatments for a person who had been bitten by a rabid dog. 'Some presently after the bite of a mad dog order such a patient into the bath and allow him to sweat there as long as he is able, with the wound bare, that the poison may the more readily be discharged. Then they refresh him with plenty of strong wine, which is an antidote to all poisons. And when this method has been pursued for three days, the patient is thought out of danger.'[58] Celsus was unaware of the possibility that contaminated water might invade the wound and infect it. Nor did he suggest a process of experimentation and elimination that might have contributed a more accurate explanation. This illustrates a drastic difference between his time and during the Renaissance and later when scientific investigation through hypothesis and experimentation was pioneered.

Nonetheless, Celsus produced a remarkable record of the state of medical knowledge at this time during the early first century AD. Whether or not he practised as a doctor himself is unknown, but he had clearly been closely involved with the application of medicine and been an attentive observer. He also had detailed knowledge of individual patients. He noted that an active man who exercised and spent most of his time in the country and on a farm should ordinarily have no need of any medical attention. Conversely, Celsus noted, a large proportion of the weak (*imbecillis*) were those who lived in cities. He provided a range of practical recommendations on activities and habits that would serve as preventative measures before embarking on his more comprehensive exploration of the application of medicine.[59]

Celsus was pragmatic and brutal about the disadvantages of having to rely on dissecting corpses to find out how the human body worked. In this passage he pointed out the advantages of beginning a dissection while a man was alive, explaining that victims of the spectacles were ideal candidates. There are echoes of how Nazi doctors experimented on people, making this an uncomfortable reminder of how similar the Romans could be when it came to regarding some humans as lesser beings. Celsus' justification was simple — the suffering of a few criminals was nothing compared to the benefits for all:

> Only when a man dies are his chest or insides opened to the view of the killer doctor and these are therefore those of a dead, not a living, man. Consequently, the doctor is just acting as a murderer and learns nothing about our insides as they function when we are living. But if anything can be seen while he is still breathing, a lucky break can mean those treating him get to observe it. Occasionally, a gladiator in the arena, a soldier in battle, or a traveller attacked by highwaymen, is wounded so that some part of his insides is exposed ... Nor, as some say, is it cruel that executing criminals, and then only concerning a few, we ought to find cures for innocent people for all time.[60]

There were, incidentally, other uses for the bodies of criminals. Suetonius claimed that when cattle became too expensive to feed to the carnivorous wild beasts destined for the arena, Caligula ordered criminals to be used instead. The emperor allegedly inspected the miscreants but ignored the charges and ordered them to be led off to their fate.[61]

The existence of Celsus' work, and that he was able to write it at all, shows that the people of Rome existed at a time when there was some recourse to professional levels of knowledge within the limitations of the era. He was followed over a century later by another Greek doctor, Claudius Galen, whose first professional appointment was as surgeon to gladiators, a job that doubtless gave him an excellent opportunity to examine human anatomy and the effects of injury and infection. He rose to work for Marcus Aurelius. His *On the Natural Faculties* as well as other works became the most significant medical writings in antiquity.

He believed in using language that everyone could understand, and in the concept of motion, by which he meant where a body passed from its existing state to another. This included the conversion of food into blood, or the processes of growth and decay and ultimately destruction.

Galen's experiences demonstrated just how precarious the transmission of ancient writings down to our own time has been. Some of his work was kept in a storeroom in Rome's Temple of Peace on the Via Sacra. A massive fire broke out in 192 and destroyed the storeroom and its contents, such as the first version of a treatise he had written on the composition of drugs. Galen was not the only victim. The works of other authors were lost too.[62]

Galen's disdain for most of the medical profession, whom he regarded as ignorant and dangerous frauds, led him to be forced out of Rome in 168. He even refused the emperor's plea for him to come and assist in the war on the Rhine and thereafter disappeared into retirement. Galen was an enthusiastic experimenter who used vivisection on animals to explore processes like digestion in action. Nonetheless, he subscribed to the views of Hippocrates, Aristotle, and others that the body was defined by the condition of the four states: warm, cold, dry, and moist, manifested in the four humours: blood, bile, black bile, and phlegm.[63]

Galen's cynicism had some foundation. There was no guarantee that men working as doctors in any capacity were either up to the job or even had their patients' best interests in mind. Doctors were certainly not above helping people to die if the price was right and depending on where the orders came from. Livilla, Germanicus' sister, used her friend the doctor Eudemus as an accomplice in the plot to kill her husband and cousin Drusus (Tiberius' son) in 23 when she was conspiring with her lover Sejanus to kill Tiberius. A poison was secured and administered by a eunuch called Lydgus.[64] Having had his mother Agrippina the Younger assassinated in 59, Nero turned next to his paternal aunt Domitia. He paid her a visit and she said fondly, stroking his beard, that she would be happy to die when he first shaved it and thus symbolically became a man. Nero turned to his companions and joked, 'I'll take it off immediately', and then ordered his doctors to give her an overdose, helping himself to her property before her body was even cold and keeping her will secret.[65] Since they were likely to have been either his slaves or freedmen, they had no choice but to obey.

Seneca explored from a philosophical point of view what a patient really purchased from a doctor. There was the straightforward question of the fee, but he pointed out that 'some things are of greater value than the price which we pay for them. You buy from a doctor life and good health, the value of which cannot be estimated in money.'[66] Seneca evidently believed in the connection between a doctor and a cure. Varro was less sure. He used doctors as an analogy in his work exploring the meaning and origin of Latin words, 'I shall watch out for a conjecture because also with our health the doctor makes one sometimes when we fall sick'. He also recorded a standard practice of a doctor who carefully monitored the first seven days of a person's illness, paying particular attention to the fourth day which marked a turning point in whether the condition was about to worsen or start improving.[67]

While serving as governor of Bithynia and Pontus, Pliny the Younger became so ill that he feared for his life. He was treated by a freedman *iatraliptes*, an 'ointment doctor' but also translated as a 'medical therapist', called Harpocras who was an Egyptian. The job seems to have combined physiotherapy with anointing. Pliny was so impressed with the care he received that he asked Trajan to give Harpocras citizenship as a reward. He was also greatly impressed by his doctor Postumius Marinus who had helped him through what must have been the same illness. Pliny wrote to Trajan to ask him to confer citizenship on the doctor's various relatives which gives us an idea of this doctor's relatively low status, though unlike Harpocras he must have already been a citizen himself. Trajan's replies do not survive, though a later letter of Pliny's shows that Harpocras was given citizenship.[68]

An acquaintance of Martial's called Parthenopaeus (another made-up name which meant something like 'looks like a maiden', and therefore suggested he was effeminate) suffered from a sore throat, exacerbated by a bad cough. His doctor prescribed honey, nuts, and sweet cakes, according to Martial, which were remedies more normally given to difficult children. The treatment had made absolutely no difference, observed Martial, because Parthenopaeus was just greedy.[69]

Martial had a generally acerbic take on doctors of his acquaintance. 'Diaulus was a surgeon, now he is an undertaker', going on to suggest Diaulus was now merely carrying on as he had in the medical profession. Martial wittily used the word *clinicus* for Diaulus. Clinicus can mean a physician but could also mean gravediggers or bearers of the bier at a funeral.[70] As so often with Martial's cast of characters, 'Diaulus' was invented, which would have been obvious at the time but not necessarily to us. It was a Latinized version of the Greek word δίαυλος which meant a racecourse based on running a length, turning around, and running back. Metaphorically, it meant retracing one's steps and was thus an allusion to Martial's observation of Diaulus' career change: as an undertaker he was retracing his steps as an incompetent surgeon who killed his patients.

Martial found another opportunity for a pun when he wrote a short epigram on the same subject, this time about an anonymous offender, 'you are now an *oplomachus* (a type of gladiator), before you were an *opthalmicus* [an eye doctor]. You did as a doctor what you now do as a gladiator.' In other words, the offending individual's career had consisted of poking people's eyes out.[71]

It is impossible to know whether Martial was targeting known individuals, even with disguised names, or was just enjoying himself in a more general sense about the medical profession, but the jokes would only have had currency if there was some basis in truth. The message seems to be that a lack of sound professional knowledge or training was commonplace. Martial claimed to have dined with a friend called Andragorus who had just been to the baths. The next day Andragorus (whose name just meant 'man of the marketplace') was found dead. Martial had an explanation, 'in his sleep he had seen Hermocrates the doctor'. Martial also mentioned an acquaintance called Cotta who

243

had lived for sixty-two years without ever getting ill and had made a point of ordering three doctors called Alcon, Dasius, and Symmachus to keep their distance from him. He went on to consider how large a part of the average person's life was lost to fevers, weakness, or pain.[72]

THE ANTONINE PLAGUE

On and off for over twenty years in the 160s to 180s the Roman Empire was hit by plague. Today little is known about the disease because there is no surviving detailed record of the symptoms, but smallpox is often suggested. By 166 the plague had reached Rome.[73] The contagion struck Marcus Aurelius and Lucius Verus' army on campaign against the Marcomanni across the Danube in late 165 or early 166. It was, as our own age knows only too well, the movement and mingling inherent in an urban and cosmopolitan society that meant widespread transmission was easy. Once the disease reached the congested population of Rome it was bound to take off rapidly.

The plague clung on, apparently recurring with a major outbreak in Rome again in 189 during the reign of Commodus when Dio said as many as 2,000 people died in a single day, making it the worst of any plague he had any knowledge of. He cited no others, but the crucial section of his text from the 160s is lost. Herodian also referred to this incident, describing it as having hit the whole of Italy 'but it was most severe in Rome which, apart from being normally overcrowded was still getting immigrants from around the world'.[74]

The most important authority for the original outbreak is Galen who was in Rome in 166 when the plague arrived but left soon afterwards. In the winter of 168–9 he was at Aquileia with the army of Marcus Aurelius and Lucius Verus when an outbreak occurred. Lucius Verus' sudden death in the spring of 169 was attributed by later Roman sources to 'apoplexy' though today some suspect that the disease, whatever it was, was to blame.[75] Although Galen wrote in enormous detail about other conditions, he recorded little about the plague, being more interested in treating it than providing a detailed account of its nature and spread. He did make a reference to internal and external ulcerations as a symptom, but that is among the few clues he provided.[76]

A favourite myth about the Romans is that thanks to their aqueducts and baths they were, by pre-modern standards, exceptionally clean and thus healthy. Roman baths were nothing like as clean as is often imagined now. They were also seen by conservatives as a quintessential example of immorality and the descent into excess, threatening the survival of the Roman people as they sank into the indolent and narcissistic culture of the bathing establishments.

11

ENFEEBLED BY BATHS

*It was what Cato foresaw . . . that destroyed the moral fibre of
the Empire. I refer to treatments we undergo when in good health
[including] hot baths, which doctors have persuaded us cook the
food inside our bodies, but which leave everyone enfeebled.*

Pliny[1]

Doctors might have promoted washing for health reasons, but Romans like Pliny thought bathing had the reverse effect on people's health. He was fighting a losing battle. Most Romans were not listening. The Roman world was unusual among ancient civilizations for investing in free or cheap mass leisure facilities and entertainments. Rome's public baths were where the people could meet to gamble, talk business, exercise in the *palaestra* (an open space, often surrounded by a covered arcade, used for running, wrestling, or gymnastics), or while away the hours progressing through the warm, hot, and cold baths. The intimate settings and the acoustics made them ideal places for confidential discussions, gossip, and plotting.

Monumental public bath facilities were usually called *thermae*, referring to the heated features, and originating in a Greek word. Pompeii's public Stabian Baths were operating by at least the late second century BC and were improved and enlarged in 80 BC. Bathing as a form of mass leisure in Rome only started to take root under Augustus when Agrippa's baths were built in the Field of Mars. They were later supplemented by the various baths of Nero, Titus, Trajan, Caracalla, and ultimately by the truly spectacular Baths of Diocletian, large parts of which can be seen in central Rome today near Termini station. These facilities were open to anyone and were either free or cost a trifling amount, usually only a quadrans. This coin was worth ¼ of a copper *as* and the smallest Roman coin, perhaps equivalent to the old farthing (a quarter of a pre-decimal English penny) or a post-1856 US small cent.[2]

Even the emperor might on rare occasions turn up to be found mingling freely with the crowd, as Hadrian was known to do.[3] Countless smaller private bathing establishments were known as *balnea*, 'baths', and were to be found all over Rome in side streets. They were run as small businesses, often aimed at local or more exclusive clienteles and were priced accordingly.

Roman reactionaries regarded baths as a sign of the descent of the Roman people into the enervating and effeminate attractions of luxury and excess. Their moaning was ignored by the people of Rome and countless other cities around the Empire in which baths had become an integral part of everyday life, particularly in the afternoon, which was the favourite time for a visit.[4] Private baths were usually only open to paying customers, which made it possible to restrict the clientele and keep out the riff-raff. There were also baths in private houses, but in towns these were generally restricted to the richest homes.

Baths famously involved the progression from warm (*tepidarium*) to hot (*caldarium*) suites, and then to the cold plunge pool (*frigidarium*). Although the baths were supplied with astronomical quantities of clean, fresh water from the aqueducts, the evidence from the best-preserved facilities at Pompeii and Herculaneum is that the water was allowed to stand in the various individual baths, occupied by numerous people who came and went. They were therefore appallingly unhygienic. At times mixed bathing was allowed, but public baths were also constructed with separate suites for men and women.[5] It all depended on the prevailing custom and the law, and personal choice. Some women seem to have favoured certain establishments, perhaps if they meant less chance of harassment, but others were more interested in the opportunity to pick up sexual partners.[6]

Although Rome today still has the remains of several colossal public baths, such as those of Caracalla, this tends to overshadow the fact that Rome had dozens of other bathing establishments of all shapes and sizes, their furnaces adding to the pollution that fouled the city's air. One was known as the *balnea Caenidianii*, thought to have been named after a freedwoman called Caenis who was Vespasian's mistress and after his wife's death effectively his common-law wife. The baths were operated by a foreman called Onesimus, perhaps under Caenis' ownership and giving her a source of income.[7]

Martial refers to one low-life part of town where there were various taverns 'in the area of the four baths'. Both types of such establishments were clearly all part of Rome's backstreet attractions.[8] Martial also described a malodourous woman called Thais who apparently smelled worse than a jar used by a fuller to collect urine for washing. She did everything possible to remedy the problem:

> In order to replace such a smell with another one, whenever she undresses to enter the bath she is coloured green by a depilatory, or is hidden by a layer of chalk and vinegar, or covered by three to four layers of sticky bean unguent. When by a thousand different tricks she thinks she has made herself safe, whatever she does, she still smells of Thais.[9]

The poor woman's name was yet another of Martial's cruel jokes. A θαίς was a type of bandage and was presumably therefore a reference to a soiled, perhaps menstrual, dressing she wore.[10]

Baths were places for politicians to meet, as well as providing opportunities for casual socializing, or exercising in the open-air palaestras that were attached to the larger establishments. These also had a range of peripheral facilities like food bars, multi-purpose rooms, gardens, and even shrines, for example at the Forum Baths in Ostia. Baths were home to gambling with dice or knucklebones, despite the risk of cheats. In one knucklebone game the aim was to throw all three and hope each showed a different number out of 1, 3, 4, and 6 (two sides on each piece bearing no number). This was known as the *iactus Veneris*, 'the throw of Venus'.[11]

Martial was irritated by the very healthy Cotta mentioned above. Cotta seems only to have issued invitations, presumably to his home, to people he had met at the baths, thus explaining why Martial had never received an invitation himself.[12] Perhaps the reason was that Martial could not always afford the sort of baths Cotta patronized. As a lowly client he depended on handouts from his patron which only came to 6¼ sesterces, probably a daily retainer and a little less than double a legionary soldier's pay at the time. This meant, he moaned, that it was hopelessly inadequate for a good time at the resort town of Baiae in the Bay of Naples. He longed for the dingy gloom of the baths of Lupus and of Gryllus, probably both grotty downmarket establishments in the backstreets of Rome and of the type usually run by freedmen on behalf of wealthier owners or as their own businesses.

Emerging from the baths had its own hazards. Vibbenius and his son were notorious clothes thieves at the baths. Catullus called the anonymous son a *cineaedus* ('sodomite'), which might simply have been an insult or instead implied that perhaps the son distracted selected willing members among the clientele while his father emptied out the lockers and made off with the loot.[13]

With so many visitors involved, baths were noisy places. The most memorable sensations of exploring a surviving building, for example the remarkable suburban baths at Herculaneum which still stand intact on a terrace below the town, include the distinct acoustic, caused by the claustrophobic effects of the vaults and which must have been affected by the splashing water. This made it possible to have remarkably quiet and intimate conversations that were inaudible to anyone else, even a short distance away. Nonetheless, this was of little consolation to those who lived near a public bath facility. Seneca famously lived above one with the result that he recorded in one passage how he was bombarded by an all-day racket that ranged from the groans of those working out with weights, the slapping of a masseur's hands on a customer's skin, singing bathers, dive-bombers, and worst of all the sound of screeching from bathers having their hair plucked.[14]

Seneca was describing the experience from a distance, an unwilling witness to the row. Martial personally enjoyed the baths, asking 'what was worse than Nero. What is better than Nero's hot baths? . . . I prefer Nero's hot baths to the baths of a sodomite', meaning perhaps his nearest baths, those of Stephanus, which he spurned. Elsewhere he said that by the sixth hour of the day Nero's baths were so hot they were unbearable, suggesting once in an ironic insult that a rhetorician called Sabinaeus was clearly so capable of chilling a place to the bone that he even 'freezes the Baths of Nero'.[15]

Martial mentioned a wealthy woman he called Laecania (the name just means she was a Lacedaemonian, from the Spartan region of Greece), noting that when she went to the baths she took a male slave who had his genitalia enclosed in a leather covering. The purpose was to prevent the slave becoming aroused while massaging or washing her. Martial, by contrast, was keen to point out that he and his own slave were fully undressed.[16] On another occasion he made fun of a woman he called Chione who claimed to be purer than anyone else, but at the baths never veiled the part of her body she should veil. 'If you have any modesty, veil your face.' Clearly the supposedly chaste Chione was known for her oral sex skills.[17] The real Chione was probably safe from embarrassment, able to hide behind her real name, which is unknown. Chione came from the Greek χιών, 'snow', and was clearly Martial's ribald reference to the Snow White image of purity she tried to claim.

Apart from offering the opportunity of meeting one's friends and business contacts, baths were primarily an everyday personal diversion and a place to relax for part of the day. The violence and thrills of the spectacles in the amphitheatres and chariot-racing circuses are legendary. They normally formed part of a cycle of annual festivals and special occasions, but these steadily increased in numbers, filling the annual calendar.

12

SPECTACLES

The emperor did not neglect actors or the other performers on the stage, the circus, or the arena, knowing that the Roman people were held firm by two things above all: the corn supply and the spectacles.

Fronto[1]

No other ancient civilization celebrated mass leisure on the Roman scale. The ancient Egyptians had no equivalent – their only public entertainment was watching the pharaoh, his family and the elite parade past them at religious festivals or the presentation of tribute by foreign vassal states. The Greeks had developed public sporting festivals to a high art, with all major cities having theatres and stadiums, with the climax, of course, being the Olympic Games. Their facilities paled by comparison to what was available in Roman times and most especially under the emperors in the form of the chariot-racing stadium, amphitheatres, theatres, open-air exercise areas, the public porticus, and the pleasure gardens.

The spectacles were inevitably seen by conservatives as another sign of Rome's moral decline. In 69 the short-lived emperor Otho was seen to have been compromised by his men. They were, said Plutarch, 'soft', thanks to idling away their time at the spectacles, festivals, and the theatre.[2]

There were also unlimited opportunities, as we have seen, to relax in the places like the streetside cookshops and household social occasions such as banquets or enjoying a simple ball game in the street.[3] Almost any curiosity would do as entertainment, such as performing animals (see Chapter 13). During Claudius' reign a 10 Roman foot (3 m) tall man called Gabbara was brought from Arabia, while the 3-foot-tall (0.9 m) corpses of a pair of equestrians called Manius Maximus and Marcus Tullius were preserved in coffins as a sight worthy of note.[4]

ESOTERIC DIVERSIONS

There were more esoteric diversions to be had in Rome than just scrutinizing the bodies, living or dead, of people of unusual height. Paintings and statues as well as curiosities like the iron goblets in Augustus' Temple of Mars Ultor were often to be found in temples and porticuses where rich benefactors had displayed them for all to see. Mummius, who sacked Corinth in 146 BC, 'filled the city with statues'. The soldier and historian Gaius Asinius Pollio, an associate of Caesar and Antony, invested his spoils of war in various works including Rome's first public library. He actively sought out statues for that building and others 'to attract sightseers'.[5]

Among the public pleasure gardens (*horti*) were the elegant Gardens of Sallust. Its decorations included a magnificent over-life-size granodiorite statue of Tuya, widow of the 19th Dynasty pharaoh Seti I (adapted by her son Ramesses II from one originally carved for the 18th Dynasty queen Tiye). The sculpture was already well over 1,300 years old when Caligula had it brought to Rome. None of those admiring it probably had any idea who it represented. The statue was there because it added to the exotic flavour of the place and the Roman taste for Nilotica in a place that anyone could enjoy.[6] Cicero was snooty about such facilities, but he could afford to be and observed that he could enjoy the pleasures of a public garden at his own townhouse.[7]

Sometimes it was difficult to know whether to be more impressed by the quality of the material used or the workmanship, for example with the 50 Roman foot (14.8 m) high statue of Apollo in the Temple of Augustus.[8] Whether or not any of these were on view in imperial times rather depended on the emperor. Nero helped himself to a considerable number of these statues and other works of art and set them up for his own enjoyment in his Golden House palace which sprawled across the central city in the last few years of his reign. He also set up a 120 foot (35.6 m) high painting of himself on linen in the Gardens of Maius for all to see, but this act of vanity was destroyed by fire when it was struck by lightning.[9] No public paintings in ancient Rome survive today, so it is impossible to imagine how liberally distributed various pieces were. Even at the time they were vulnerable to age and decay and had sometimes to be replaced.[10]

After Nero's suicide in 68 the victor of the ensuing civil war, Vespasian, put the statues and paintings on show again in his Temple of Peace and other public buildings.[11] Once more Rome's idlers and passers-by could enjoy the works of fine art Nero had filched. There were so many works of art that it was impossible to gain any kind of expert knowledge of them. Over time the origins of many had been forgotten while the everyday needs of ordinary business meant no one had the necessary leisure time to spend on research.[12] Vespasian, though, was the emperor who had more extravagant lowbrow plans for Roman entertainment: he built the Colosseum, Rome's first purpose-built and state-of-the-art permanent stone arena.

ORIGINS OF SPECTACLES

The Latin word *spectaculum* ('spectacle') was applied to any form of public show, display, theatrical performance, amphitheatre events such as gladiatorial bouts, or races in the circus. These almost always formed part of religious festivals which were the basis of public holidays. The circus, for example, had a shrine to the sun (Sol), sometimes shown on coins driving a quadriga (four-horse chariot).[13] The rationale for holding chariot races or other events to celebrate them was usually long forgotten. This troubled no one because the festival was just a pretext, echoed today in public holidays whose religious origins have long since faded into the past. 'Next [12–19 April] come the Games of Ceres', said Ovid, when explaining one set of spectacles in his calendar of religious festivals. 'There is no need to point out the reason: the goddess's bounty and merit are obviously known.'[14]

Like most Roman religion, these festivals celebrated the deities with powers over the land, agriculture, natural phenomena such as the weather or potential disasters like plague, and more general notions of fertility. In Roman legend, Romulus had instituted the first games in honour of Neptune in his role as an equestrian deity called the Consualia, from which we can assume that horse racing formed the main entertainment, and was honoured by the water-spouting dolphin effigies used to help count laps.[15] It had a sinister undertone because the Romans were short of fertile young women. The neighbouring Sabines had turned up for the show and while they were distracted, the young Roman males carried off the Sabine women – the notorious 'Rape of the Sabine Women'.[16]

Decimus Junius Brutus, who served as consul in 292 BC, was said to have been the first to lay on a gladiatorial show in honour of his deceased father, in c. 264–262 BC.[17] In those days such events were usually organized by private individuals, but they gradually became the preserve of the emperors. Augustus set the trend with multiple gladiatorial events, three in his name and five in the names of his grandsons and (adoptive) sons, involving around 10,000 gladiators, along with other sporting events.[18]

It is a curiosity that although some emperors made much of the gladiatorial bouts they had put on (see above, this chapter), these events go almost unmentioned on imperial coinage though gladiators and beast hunts sometimes appeared on denarii in the Republic.[19] Titus celebrated the completion of his father Vespasian's Colosseum on a sestertius issued in the year 80. The coin shows a bird's eye view of the building, including part of the packed auditorium, but nothing of the shows put on there.[20] Severus Alexander restored the Colosseum around 150 years later and issued a rare sestertius of the building in which two gladiators are depicted, but it is the only such type.[21] Gladiators often appear as decorative motifs on oil lamps and pottery, for example. Pictures of them were proudly featured by local magistrates at Pompeii in their tombs to commemorate their munificence to the local community, aping the emperors. Gaius Vestorius Priscus was an aedile at Pompeii who died young. His tomb outside the Vesuvius Gate features a painting of a gladiatorial bout, presumably one he had bankrolled while seeking election, but it was only visible to those admitted into the memorial or who climbed up to look over the wall.[22]

Strange customs persisted at the games, their origins belonging to the remote past and their reasons sometimes lost in time. These included the cry *Sardi venales*, 'Sardinians for sale'. Plutarch thought it was something to do with the defeat by Romulus of the Etruscans of the city of Veii who were in legend believed to have come from the city of Sardis in Asia Minor. But the Latin phrase means Sardinians, not those of Sardis. The Veii victory does seem to have been the origin of another curious tradition, as Plutarch explained. 'Romulus also celebrated a triumph for this victory on the Ides of October . . . to this very day, in offering a sacrifice for victory, they lead an old man through the Forum to the Capitol, wearing a boy's toga with a bulla [an ornamental metal boss] attached to it.'[23]

NEW FESTIVALS

As Rome's power grew other festivals were added, for example those seeking divine favour for a war or to give thanks for a great victory, often celebrated annually thereafter, or the Saecular Games which celebrated the passage of an era. On 6 October 82 BC, for example, the *Ludi Victoriae Sullae* ('the Games of the Victories of Sulla') commenced after Sulla had seized power in Rome in an orgy of violence that left him unchallenged and effectively in the position of a monarch. The year concerned was the 175th Olympiad but the Greeks were left having to watch unexciting stadium races. Sulla had transported the athletes and all the main events to Rome to celebrate his various victories 'under the pretext that the masses needed a breathing spell and recreation after their toils'.

Putting on the games was, of course, the perfect way to anaesthetize any sense of horror at his proscriptions which had seen hundreds of his political enemies among the elite killed in Rome, to say nothing of the tens of thousands killed in Italy in the recent war. It also helped brush over the way he changed the law, including reducing the power of the tribunes of the plebs. He freed 10,000 slaves and made them Roman citizens with his name to ensure he had a solid block of loyalists.[24]

The spectacles of Rome were a barometer of the people's mood, and sometimes a dangerous one. In 32 during the reign of Tiberius the audience, emboldened by their numbers and the opportunity to address the emperor in person, took the opportunity to protest over several days about disruption of the grain supply. Tiberius was furious because the Senate and the magistrates had failed to use their authority to keep the people under control. Nevertheless, he pointed out which provinces were providing grain and that he was responsible for the supply being greater than under Augustus.[25]

A major appeal of the spectacles was that they were free at the point of use. Although the cost was originally borne by the Senate, the aediles (junior magistrates) responsible for organizing the festivals and spectacles were able to use their own resources or go into debt to outdo their predecessors and thus invest in their own careers. Caesar was curule aedile in 65 BC. He took advantage of this to launch a programme of public shows to secure 'the goodwill of the masses'. He plugged the events in major public buildings, put on theatrical plays, 320 gladiatorial bouts, and animal fights and did so variously in his name and in association with the other aedile, Marcus Bibulus, with the result that it was generally assumed the occasions were all down to Caesar, which, of course, was precisely his intention. The 320 gladiators represented a reduction of Caesar's intentions. He had organized such a large number that his political opponents in the Senate were terrified by the thought of so many armed men in Rome on Caesar's payroll; they promptly passed a law putting a cap on the numbers. According to Plutarch, Caesar 'washed away all memory of the ambitious efforts of his predecessors in the office'. It was also essential since he had dug deep into his own resources and borrowed lavishly to make sure his time as aedile would be unforgettable.[26] This was matched in cities across the Roman Empire where it was expected that the local annually elected civic magistrates would lay on games as a matter of course, with many paying for the erection of theatres, amphitheatres, and stadiums in an effort to buy popularity for themselves and their descendants.

Women and young men allegedly particularly enjoyed the gladiator shows put on by Caligula. The savagery of his events seems to have been amplified by his fondness for, and the crowd's appreciation of, handouts of meat during the bouts.[27] Such gladiatorial shows were given a form of immortality by commemorating them in paintings which were shown in public, much in the way that today a celebrated football match might be reshown on television or sporting heroes are depicted in photographic galleries.[28]

In the late Republic the average Roman could already look forward to about one-seventh of the year being given over to such holidays, but by the fourth century AD that had expanded to almost half the year. The *Ludi Romani* ('Roman Games') alone lasted a fortnight from 5 to 19 September. Later, the individual festivals themselves were liable to be extended as part of an emperor's personal largesse, with the public entertainments gradually subsuming whatever had been the original purpose and focus. Any excuse would do. When Nero was made heir to his stepfather Claudius and married Claudius' daughter Octavia he put on games and beast-baiting in the circus. As emperor he laid on one festival to celebrate the first time that he shaved his beard.[29]

The fact that the state and the elite could afford to allow so many people so much time off and pay for these entertainments reflects the resources available. Under the emperors, this reached unprecedented levels, especially when the emperor concerned had a taste for such occasions and the common touch. Nero famously put on a wide variety of shows, including an imaginative twist on chariot racing with teams of four camels being used instead of horses. Fun though that might or might not have been (but probably not for the camels), the idea was the result of desperately trying to find novelty slots in a desperate attempt to satisfy a crowd becoming increasingly bored by the endless repetition of similar events.

Nero therefore turned some of the entertainments into game shows, the only difference being that no skill of any sort was needed. He dreamed up the idea of the *Ludi Maximi* ('the Greatest Games'), choosing a title designed to suggest they were unsurpassable, and said they were for the 'eternity of the Empire'. The fun featured a vintage play from the late Republic called *The Burning House* which involved setting light to the house on the stage set. To jazz up the action and inspire the cast to act out the disaster in as authentic a way as possible, the actors were allowed to keep any furniture they rescued from the flames. Those who turned up discovered that gifts were handed out, such as a thousand birds every day, food, tickets for grain, precious metals and jewellery, slaves, animals, and then the jackpot in the form of ships, city blocks with houses, and farms. Always with an eye for pleasing the masses, Nero had even obliged some the most senior senators and aged matrons to take part in some of the events, though this was something Augustus had tried out with equestrians on the stage or taking part in gladiator fights until the Senate banned the practice.[30]

Other events involved naval battles which to begin with were staged by excavating pools near the Tiber so that the river could fill them. Seats were erected round the edges. Augustus had created such a lake and put on naval battles as part of a range of public entertainments that included gladiator fights in the Forum and other places and athletics contests in the Field of Mars. Domitian was one emperor who used the specially equipped Colosseum for sea battle re-enactments and had a lake excavated near the Tiber, but this was perhaps a restoration of the one made by Augustus.[31]

The protests under Tiberius about the grain supply (see above, this chapter) were a reminder of how volatile a large Roman crowd could become. The prefect of Rome was in charge of security, using soldiers drawn from the urban cohorts and the Praetorian Guard stationed at key spots around the venues.[32] A riot had broken out in the amphitheatre at Pompeii in 59 during Nero's reign. Citizens of Nuceria, a neighbouring town, arrived to support their favourite gladiators in a show put on by a disreputable senator called Livineius Regulus and soon became engaged in a slanging match with the Pompeians. The words turned to stones and then swords were drawn. Unfortunately for the Nucerians there were many more Pompeian supporters and the result was a number of dead and injured visitors, even children. News reached an outraged Senate in Rome, clearly highly perturbed by the thought of anything similar happening in Rome. Further gladiatorial displays at Pompeii were banned for a decade, leaving the local impresarios with nothing better to put on than athletics events. Livineius and his associates, among them presumably the presiding Pompeian magistrates, were forced into exile.[33]

THEATRES

By the late third and second centuries BC Roman playwrights such as Terence (Publius Terentius Afer, possibly of North African origin but not certainly) were already writing plays, in his case comedies, for what was evidently a growing market in Rome. At the time temporary wooden structures were used, and these continued in use in certain contexts. Plays were only one form of entertainment put on in a theatre. The Roman theatre was more akin to music halls of the nineteenth and early twentieth centuries, offering an eclectic range of turns including boxers and acrobats as well as plays, all the while trying to compete with the other shows on offer in the city such as gladiatorial bouts. Terence specifically described the challenges of competing for an audience and trying to put on a performance for raucous and impatient crowds of Romans.[34]

Roman tradition spurned the theatre because it smacked of degeneracy and indulgence and, worse, Greek influence. In 154 BC the building of a theatre in Rome was stopped because of the threat to public morals, and the structure torn down.[35] In Campania, not far to the south and where many of the cities had Greek origins, Pompeii had had a stone theatre since the second century BC. Appropriately enough, the Latin word *theatrum* was directly derived from the Greek θέατρον, which meant 'a place for seeing' from the verb θεάομαι, 'to gaze upon as spectators'.

The most notorious theatre of all was the temporary one built by the monstrously extravagant Marcus Aemilius Scaurus, curule aedile in 58 BC. Pliny described it as 'the greatest building ever constructed by man' (not that he had ever seen it) and which outclassed even those intended to last for ever. It had a stage in three tiers, the lower made of marble, the second out of glass and the third from wood. It made for a dramatic contrast with Rome's earliest auditoria when 'no awnings hung from the marble theatre, no saffron perfumes stained the stage ... the audience sat on tiers made from turf, and covered their shaggy hair, as best they could, with leaves'.[36] Scaurus' stage tiers were embellished with 360 columns, at a time when just six columns was enough to outrage traditional Roman sensibilities, interspersed with 3,000 statues. The columns on the lowest tier were 38 Roman feet high (11.25 m). The whole edifice accommodated 80,000 spectators, only a little less than the 90,000 Wembley Stadium in London has space for, and twice the claimed capacity of Pompey's theatre. The theatre was later dismantled. Four of the large columns found their way to Scaurus' house on the Palatine, but the remaining fittings and paraphernalia were taken to his house in Tusculum. When that burned down, he was said to have lost 30 million sesterces.[37]

During the height of his power Pompey, like many prominent men of Rome, had seen fit to provide the city with an extravagant public facility to emphasize his importance. As we saw earlier (see Chapter 8), it may have been paid for by one of his spectacularly wealthy freedmen. Pompey ordered the construction of Rome's first permanent theatre and other buildings that formed a huge public complex in the Field of Mars.

Plutarch called Pompey's theatre 'famous and beautiful'. The inspiration was the Greek theatre in Mytilene on Lesbos which Pompey had greatly admired. Pompey's version supposedly had a capacity of 40,000, though the reality may have been rather less than half that. It was opened in 55 BC to great celebrations which included music and gymnasts, and animal contests (see Chapter 12). Conservatives were appalled because it smacked far too much of the degenerate Greeks, but otherwise it seems to have cheered the Romans' hearts. The structure, whoever stumped up the funds, was still celebrated for its magnificence more than two centuries later, though it had by then already gone through at least two major bouts of rebuilding and restoration work under Augustus and Tiberius (see below).[38]

Pompey's complex faced several Republican temples, the ruins of which are still visible in a square called the Largo Argentina. Between the theatre and the temples was a porticus. Little of Pompey's work is visible today but its layout and size are known from the Marble Plan of Rome created in Severan times, and because modern streets preserve some of the original setting. The Via del Grotta Pinta, for example, follows the curve of the theatre's orchestra and other minor streets follow the sides of the porticus.

Pompey's huge theatre burst into flames in the year 22 during the reign of Tiberius. The fire was contained, thanks to quick work by the praetorian prefect Sejanus, and spread no further. Tiberius heaped praise on Sejanus for his assiduous efforts in controlling the conflagration and thereby delivering Rome from what could have been a catastrophe.[39]

Rome eventually had several other permanent theatres but today only one is visible in any recognizable form. The Theatre of Marcellus was named after Augustus' nephew Marcellus, the son of his sister Octavia and his first intended heir. The theatre had been begun by Julius Caesar, but it still represented a relatively late development.

Every year a temporary theatre was erected on the Palatine Hill outside the imperial palace for the Palatine games held there annually, beginning on 17 January. The building had two main doors. One led outside, allowing spectators in and out. The other led into an attached porticus, the idea being that those in the porticus would not be disturbed by anyone passing through the other entrance. There were also separate access points for actors and performers, which was obviously a practical solution but also prevented those who considered themselves to be persons of status to find themselves passing such social inferiors. This was the theatre in which Caligula was assassinated on 24 January 41 (see below for the performance on the day).[40]

An extraordinary revolving double theatre was built by Gaius Scribonius Curio, tribune in 50 BC, which allowed two audiences to see two separate performances. After midday the theatres were swung round to face each other and form an amphitheatre so that the audience, some of whom had been able to remain seated, could watch a gladiator fight.[41] The theatres were built of wood so without Pliny's description, which he must have obtained at second or third hand, we would have no idea the contraption had ever been created or the extent of the ingenuity applied to entertaining ordinary Romans.

Where you sat in a theatre and amphitheatre mattered a great deal. For example, the Vestal Virgins were allowed to sit opposite the praetor's tribunal in the theatre. Augustus deemed that Livia should sit with them.[42] This formed part of a series of regulations he devised which set aside the front-row seats for senators, restricted most women to the back rows and made special arrangements for married plebeian men, and boys who sat beside their tutors. Augustus only used the imperial box sometimes, while on other occasions he was happy to watch from the upper tiers occupied by his freedmen or one of their houses.[43] Once Claudius had become emperor, his pretentious and ambitious wife Messalina had her status advanced closer to that of Livia by allowing her to ride through Rome in a carpentum carriage, a special vehicle used mainly by imperial women, and to be seated in the front row in the theatre.

Since no theatre seating survives in Rome, it falls to Pompeii to provide evidence of just how important where you sat, or after your death where you had once been seen to have sat, was. By the end of the first century BC Pompeii's theatre provided the perfect opportunity for the powerful and wealthy Holconii family to bestow their favours on the city by commissioning a freedman architect called Marcus Artorius Primus to design improvements. An upper seating area was added, boxes over the side entrances, and seating for Pompeii's elite in the lower rows of seats and in the orchestra, recorded in an inscription which credits the work to Marcus Holconius Rufus and Marcus Holconius Celer.[44] In return for this act of generosity, seating areas for the Holconii brothers(?) were marked out with bronze letters. Honorific double seats (*bisellia*) were set aside either for personal use by Marcus Holconius Rufus or as symbolic places to mark his prominence after death. They were perhaps intended also for use by descendants but had the curious effect of making the place seem more like a cenotaph than a place of entertainment.

The Holconii were perhaps also reflecting new laws brought in by the Senate in Rome where it had been decreed that senators would have the front row of seats, and that representatives of Rome's allies would no longer be entitled to sit in the orchestra.[45] Whether local laws were brought in to enforce similar privileges and exclusions in towns like Pompeii is unknown but it seems likely that the Pompeian elite might well decide they ought to accord their own magistrates and councillors similar privileges.

In such provincial backwaters, the double-seat honour could also be earmarked for the most successful freedmen who had contributed to a town in some way. The seating hierarchy proved enduring. Herodian, writing about the reign of Commodus over a century later, after Pompeii and Herculaneum's destruction, describes how a theatre in Rome 'filled with people, who went to their places in an orderly way, nobles to their special seats and each person to the place allocated for him'.[46]

Impresarios organized some of the shows, either operating on their own account or on behalf of others such as electoral candidates.

Aurelius Nemesius was a magister ('master') of chorus, dance, and pantomime in Rome where he died aged fifty-three, probably during the third century.[47] He is likely to have been a freedman. His tombstone was set up by his wife, Aurelia Eutychiane. The second half of her name, which comes from the Greek for 'lucky' or 'successful', was typical for a slave. The pair therefore are likely to have belonged to the vast numbers of enterprising freedmen and freedwomen who found business opportunities in the teeming city, in their case in the entertainment industry.

ACTORS AND THEIR FANS

Actors and other performers, even if freeborn, were generally considered of such low status that they were not allowed to vote. They could nonetheless court attention in the highest circles. The dictator Sulla as a young man had started a long-term attachment to an actor and female impersonator called Metrobius, met among the various performers and dancers he encountered at drinking parties. Even once he was married, Sulla continued to keep company with female dancers, musicians and others from the theatre. 'They lay drinking together on couches all day long.' Sulla paid a heavy price. It appears he contracted some sort of venereal disease or other serious infection as a result of his constant indulgences. Plutarch described Sulla as having intestinal ulcers and skin erupting with worms, but like many Roman historians he was determined to paint Sulla in the worst possible light to emphasize his degeneracy as proof of his tyranny.[48]

A few years earlier a clown called Saunio enjoyed a great deal of popularity on the stage in Rome. His reputation and skill saved his life in 91 BC when he was on the bill at Asculum. Asculum was an allied Sabine town on the point of erupting in rebellion against Rome in that febrile time. Saunio, a Latin — and thus below the status of a Roman citizen — was waiting to go on and entertain an audience full of Romans, but a comedian was in the process of making a big mistake.

The unnamed comic started complaining, presumably about the Romans. The Roman crowd took exception to the insult and killed him, resulting in chaos and fear erupting in the theatre.

In what must go down as a supreme example of 'the show must go on', Saunio ventured out to begin his act. The local Picentes people in the audience wanted to kill him too, so that the Romans would miss his show. Saunio was equal to the occasion. 'My spectators', he began, 'the omens are favourable. May this evil turn into good luck. I am not a Roman, and I am subject to the fasces [the bundles of rods carried by magistrates that symbolized Roman authority] like you. I travel through Italy, searching for favours by making people laugh and giving pleasures. So, spare the swallow, which the gods allow to nest safely in all our houses, for it is not fair to do anything that would make you upset.' He continued to crack jokes which calmed everyone down and saved his life, though it must have remained astonishing that all this followed the murder of the preceding performer.[49] Saunio might have saved himself, but his ready wit did the Romans of Asculum (in the modern Marche region) no good. The city rebelled, triggering the Social War (91–87 BC) when Rome's Italian allies revolted, and the violence led to all the Roman inhabitants being killed.[50]

Volumnia Cytheris enjoyed a stellar reputation in the mid- to late first century BC, like that of a modern movie star. The Cytheris part of her name, and the one she was most commonly known by, was an epithet or nickname for Venus. She recited Vergil's messianic sixth Eclogue with such aplomb that Cicero was said to have been staggered (*stupefactus*) by the experience.[51] She was the freedwoman of Publius Volumnius Eutrapelus, himself probably a freedman, but thanks to her talents and charms her lowly status did nothing to affect her rise to fame. She attracted high-profile male attention, counting among her lovers not only Caesar's assassin Brutus but also Mark Antony. In the context of Roman society there was a darker side to this. As the freedwoman of a man who had friends in high places, Volumnia was also liable to provide favours for her former master and patron, who was therefore in a position to make her services available for his friends and associates. Cicero, for example, explicitly cited the presence of 'the mime actress Volumnia' in a procession of Antony's.[52] She was followed by a carriage of pimps, whom he dismissed as 'the most worthless of companions'. As an actress, Volumnia was firmly positioned as a symbol of degeneracy and of Antony's descent into effeminacy and lack of self-control. Volumnia's career had brought her fame, but not autonomy and freedom. The powerful men who were entranced by her also trapped her.

In Caesar's time there was a good-looking and witty slave called Publilius. Thanks to his humorous and spontaneous ripostes he was freed and educated. He toured Italy with his mime show and on one occasion appeared at some of Caesar's games. He challenged the other performers to match his prowess at improvised scenes, each of them taking turns to come up with a theme. He won hands-down, even beating the celebrated Laberius, a Roman knight, well-known for his improvisation skills. Caesar, who admired Laberius, was delighted by Publilius.[53]

In 18 BC Augustus restored a celebrated dancer called Pylades who had been exiled for sedition. Augustus once told him off for arguing with a fellow performer called Bathyllus who was a favourite of the emperor's friend Maecenas. Pylades tartly retorted with 'it is to your advantage, Caesar, that the people should devote their spare time to us', an observation many a modern politician has probably considered.[54] Pylades was a popular sensation and innovative entertainer in his own time, comparable in every way to a modern movie star. In 2 BC, towards the end of his career, he bankrolled a festival which he organized but did not perform in, made noteworthy by it being the first time equestrians and 'women of distinction' were brought onto the stage.[55]

Not long afterwards, and still during the reign of Augustus, a celebrated singer called Galeria Copiola was brought out of retirement to sing at the games held in the year 9 after the emperor had recovered from illness. She was an *emboliaria* ('actress of interludes'), which means she came out on stage to perform during the interludes between acts of a play. The occasion was all the more remarkable because she was believed to be 104 years old. Her career spanned the entire era of the rise of the imperators, the civil war of the late Republic and the dawn of the age of emperors. Copiola is a diminutive of *copia*, which means 'abundance' or 'riches' and provides our word 'copious'. The name therefore translates as something like a 'small sized package of plenty'. She might have been called that at birth, but it is more likely to be a stage name that referenced her being physically small but having an enormous presence on stage.

Most female stage roles were acted by men, but the emboliaria role represented a rare opportunity for women to pursue a professional entertainment career. Galeria allegedly performed first in 82 BC when she was thirteen, hired by the aedile Marcus Pomponius. She was already considered old when she sang for Pompey at the dedication of his new theatre in 55 BC. Galeria Copiola was not alone in treading the boards so late in life. Lucceia, a famous actress of unknown date, appeared when she was 100, though the Latin might be implying her stage career had lasted a century. Pliny is our source in a passage in which he discussed the remarkable phenomenon of several long-lived performers.[56] In both cases the advanced ages are probably approximations; Pliny is unlikely to have been able to verify his source.

Among the allegations made about Caligula was that he had had an affair with a pantomime actor called Mnester, who also performed the tragedy *Cinyras* on the day the emperor was assassinated in January 41 during the Palatine Games.[57] Caligula was killed after leaving the theatre to watch a choir of boy singers from Asia. They had arrived in Rome to participate in mysteries that Caligula was celebrating and to perform 'Pyrrhic' dances, a version of myth set to ballet.[58] Their presence in Rome that day, and their unintended ringside seats to history, must stand for countless other artistes who made their way to the great city to perform in the most prestigious venues in the Roman world. The theatre was shortly to erupt in panic when the news broke that Caligula had been hacked to death by conspirators, reaching a dramatic climax when his furiously loyal and outraged German bodyguards surrounded the theatre and trapped the audience

267

inside. A massacre was only averted when a professional auctioneer called Arruntius used his powerful voice to announce the emperor's death and full details before talking down the Germans and calming the crowd.[59]

When Caligula's coinage was melted down, as a result of the damnatio memoriae that followed his death, Messalina had the bronze recycled into a statue of the same actor, Mnester, with whom she had become obsessed. Mnester declined her advances, so she persuaded Claudius to tell Mnester that he was obliged to do whatever Messalina wanted, Claudius presumably not suspecting what his wife meant. Mnester then gave in, believing he was acting on Claudius' express instructions. It was a useful threat. Messalina claimed to other conquests that she was acting with Claudius' approval.[60]

EXPLOSIVE AUDIENCES

More than twenty years before Caligula became emperor, theatres in Rome were becoming more frequently associated with violence. The trouble was blamed not on the spectators but the performers who seem to have been given to bitter feuding. In 14, not long after the death of Augustus who had been inclined to indulge them and just after the accession of Tiberius, fighting broke out at the Augustal Games thanks to the rivalry between the actors who had their gangs of supporters in the audience. They were emboldened by the knowledge that Augustus had once said actors were immune from beatings. The troublemakers included a praetorian soldier called Percennius who led a theatre claque of hired fans and used his knowledge of the infighting between actors to whip up audiences.[61] These claques were also tied up with the commercial guilds (see below) and indeed probably served as covers for them.

In one incident in the year 15 an unnamed tribune of the Guard was injured and a centurion and a number of soldiers, presumably also praetorians, were killed. The Senate discussed the problem and decided that praetors could order performers to be whipped, over-turning Augustus' statement. A tribune of the plebs, Decimus Haterius Agrippa, vetoed the proposal as was his privilege and was tacitly backed up by Tiberius. Nonetheless, various provisions were enacted to prohibit senators from going into the homes of pantomime actors, equestrians from being around actors when they went out, and forcing actors only to perform in theatres, with the praetors enforcing exile on spectators out of control.[62]

The problem proved to be intractable. Consequently, anyone turning up to a public show with plans to cause trouble, or even look bored, had good reason to be worried. In 56 under Nero the praetor Vibullius had locked up some unruly supporters but Antistius, a tribune of the plebs, released them. This occasioned a quarrel about their respective prerogatives, but the episode shows that the authorities were still struggling to keep supporters under control.[63] The fact that the emperor himself was one of the performers complicated the issue even more, not least because he too was concerned about his fan base. Praetorians dressed in togas or tunics could mingle with ordinary people and try to inveigle them into criticizing the emperor by starting the abuse themselves. Once someone fell into the trap the praetorian could break cover and arrest the unsuspecting civilian. This comes from an account by the philosopher Epictetus in the early second century. That makes it likely he was basing his description on how some praetorians had been used by the notoriously paranoid Domitian, but several decades earlier in Nero's reign theatre audiences at the emperor's own performances were infiltrated by spies. They not only checked off names but also kept a keen eye out for evidence of a lack of enthusiasm, hostility, or anyone foolish enough to fall asleep.[64]

PATRONS OF PERFORMERS

Gaius Norbanus Sorex was a self-professed actor of 'second parts' at Pompeii. In mime, an actor of second parts would customarily imitate the main actor's movements and words. His name means 'shrew-mouse', an animal considered to be a bad omen because it was heard interrupting soothsayers.[65] It is possible Norbanus' name alludes to the type of role he might have played, perhaps a comic turn undermining priest characters, but this is pure speculation. The most important piece of information we have about him was that he was honoured by the presidents of the Augustan Country District outside Pompeii with a bronze bust (a herm) of himself in Eumachia's porticus, while another was set up in the precinct of the Iseum. Both structures were closely involved with local guilds and political factions which Norbanus was probably tied up with in some way, thereby illustrating another facet of the complex web of business interests in Roman civic life.

Given the social status of actors, it is hardly surprising that Nero's love of performing was regarded with horror by the senatorial elite. They were appalled by the ignominy of a member of the aristocracy demeaning himself by treading the boards. Domitian expelled a senator called Caecilius Rufinus for having the gross indignity to act in pantomimes.[66]

Looking down on performers as social inferiors did not mean the upper classes were above going to the theatre, or even becoming actively involved. Ummidia Quadratilla was a wealthy aristocrat who lived to the age of seventy-nine at the beginning of the second century. She perplexed Pliny the Younger because of her luxurious tastes which were inappropriate for a woman of her class. She possessed her own personal troupe of pantomime actors whom she 'cherished with a greater level of extravagance than befitted a woman of her standing'. Her husband had declined to watch any of the shows, whether in public or at home, something his wife apparently accepted without question, and nor does he seem to have done anything to stop her.[67] In another instance, Publius Vinicius Laces was a freedman of, probably, the Publius Vinicius who served as consul in the year 2 under Augustus.[68] He died aged thirty-five, a *comoedus*, or 'comedy actor', and was probably attached to the consul's household.

Thanks to a description by Apuleius in *The Golden Ass* we have an idea of why Ummidia's husband and Pliny the Younger might have been disapproving of a Roman pantomime. The performance concerned the Judgement of Paris which provided various titillating opportunities in the form of a pretty boy playing Mercury, and an unclothed actress as Venus attended by a large number of dancing maidens while she moved sensuously along with the music to entice Paris to choose her.[69] The fictitious and supremely vulgar freedman Trimalchio had bought a Greek comedy theatre company and then told the players only to perform Latin works, another way of suggesting he had unrefined tastes.[70] Tertullian said that thanks to the 'evil character of the place, the theatre is, strictly speaking, a shrine of Venus', whom he regarded as the source of 'sex perversion'.[71]

Appropriately enough, the Latin word *obscaenus* ('obscenity') was applied to anything shameful or disgraceful which could only be said openly on the stage (from *ob scaenam*, 'on the stage'), thereby giving us a hint that a Roman audience could look forward to hearing filth on a visit to the theatre.[72] Alternatively, they might have heard an actor recite Aesop's fables, taken from the Latin edition produced by Phaedrus, a freedman of Augustus. Phaedrus told his audience that his little book had two benefits: laughter and wise advice.[73]

Having fans in high places could do wonder for an actor's career but could also backfire. Lucius Aurelius Apolaustus Memphius was a celebrated pantomime actor during the joint reign of Marcus Aurelius and Lucius Verus (161–9). Born Agrippus and a Syrian, he was brought to Rome in 166 by Lucius Verus when he returned from his Parthian campaign, freed, and made a citizen, along with other favourite performers the emperor had found in the East. Verus called him Apolaustus which was an artiste's nickname that meant 'of which one can enjoy', also used by other actors. The Memphius part of his name probably means that his speciality was a form of Egyptian pantomime from Memphis. He enjoyed considerable fame, not least for his exposition in dance of Pythagoras' philosophy of the transmigration of souls, but was executed by Commodus in 189 along with several other freedmen of the imperial court. Verus had also brought many other performers with him, the *Historia Augusta* saying that they included players of the harp and the flute, actors and jesters from the mimes, jugglers, and all kinds of slaves in whose entertainment Syria and Alexandria find pleasure, 'and in such numbers, indeed, that he seemed to have concluded a war, not against Parthians, but against actors'.[74]

BACKSTAGE

Actors and performers would have been lost, though, without the backstage crew. Marcus Vipsanius Narcissus was probably a freedman of Augustus' friend and son-in-law, Marcus Vipsanius Agrippa. Narcissus was a *rogator ab scaena* ('stage manager').[75] The word *rogator* had various meanings, for example someone who proposed legislation, or an electoral officer requesting votes. In this unique context it seems that Narcissus' job was to chase up actors needed on stage, or perhaps also looking out props and other equipment necessary for the scene in question. There must have been similar staff in the theatres but were perhaps of such lowly status that they were unlikely to be commemorated as Narcissus was on a marble tablet from a columbarium tomb. In 99 BC Appius Claudius Pulcher (later consul in 79 BC and father of the infamous Publius Clodius Pulcher and his sister Clodia; they changed their names respectively from Claudius and Claudia) laid on theatrical shows with scenery paintings so realistic that they included depictions of crows trying to land on the roofs of painted buildings.[76]

On the day Caligula was killed in 41, special arrangements were in place for the tragedy *Cinyras*, which he had attended just beforehand (see above). The drama involved the death of the eponymous hero and his daughter, as well as a crucified chieftain. To make this as realistic as possible (especially in Rome where the audiences were all too accustomed to real blood), 'a great quantity of artificial blood was shed', which added to the duties of the stage crew responsible for props.[77]

CHARIOTS AND CHARIOTEERS

Rome's largest open space for much of the imperial period was the Circus Maximus, which, it was claimed, could accommodate 250,000 spectators, or around a quarter of the city's population. The racetrack was 540 metres (590 yards) long and 80 metres (87 yards) wide and was surrounded by banks of seating on the long side and the curved (east) end. The twelve starting gates were at the west end. The raised central *spina*, embellished with trophies such as obelisks and lane counters, ran down the middle and defined the 'up' and 'down' tracks. The Circus Maximus lay between the Palatine Hill to the east and the Aventine Hill to the west. It was probably earmarked as a public space from Rome's earliest days.

The Circus Maximus reached its greatest size and development under Trajan (98–117). There were other such facilities in Rome, such as the Circus Flaminius, the Circus of Domitian (now fossilized in the layout of the Piazza Navona), the Circus Vaticanus (or Circus of Caligula, or Nero) on the site of the Vatican City, and the well-preserved Circus of Maxentius (306–12) down the Via Appia not far to the south of Rome. There was also the circus built by Caracalla (211–17) in the gardens of the Temple of Spes Vetus ('Old Hope') which at 577 metres in length eclipsed the Circus Maximus for scale, but not in architectural complexity.

Chariot racing had all the appeal and ritzy glamour that international football enjoys today. According to Josephus, chariot racing was a 'spectator sport to which the Romans are fanatically devoted. They gather enthusiastically in the circus and there the assembled crowds make requests of the emperors according to their own pleasure'.[78] This included, for example, demanding relief from taxation.

There were originally four chariot-racing teams in Rome known as factions: the Reds, the Whites, the Greens and the Blues, all privately owned. Similar factions were found across the Empire. Successful charioteers could make enormous amounts of money for themselves and their teams, but that also attracted greed. Nero's father, Gnaeus

Domitius Ahenobarbus, among other examples of his loathsome personality had cheated some charioteers of their prizes.[79] This probably means that he had owned charioteers and helped himself to their share of the winnings. There were, it seems, even child charioteers. Florus was one such *bigarius infans* ('child charioteer') whose desire to race fast was even more quickly overcome by 'the shades'; unfortunately, his tombstone tells us nothing about his exact age at death.[80]

The Circus Maximus was so large that each faction could field three teams per race. Each obviously had full back-up for servicing the chariots, and also training the horses. A freedman called Marcus Antonius was a *conditor*, 'horse trainer', with the Greens.[81] A race involved seven laps hurtling up one side of the stadium, making a viciously tight and lethal turn at the end and then coming back down the other side to turn again. The turns offered the best chance of chariots colliding and turning over, whipping the crowd up even further. As a boy, Nero had talked about a charioteer of the Green faction who had fallen out of his chariot but been caught up in the reins and dragged along by his horses. He presumably died before he was able to cut himself free. Nero grew up desperate to perform as a charioteer in public, practising in private in the palace. His most famous appearance was at Olympia on his tour of Greece in a chariot pulled by ten horses.[82]

The factions all had enthusiastic bands of supporters. The stakes were high. Caligula was a fanatical follower of the Greens and was said sometimes to have spent the night in their stables. Caligula was desperate to see the Greens win, so he sent soldiers out the day before a race date to stand guard around the stable neighbourhood to keep the noise down to prevent the horses being unsettled.[83] Supporters posted inscriptions around the city with slogans such as the one that said 'May victory of the Blues remain forever unchanged! Good luck!', but they were also liable to wish death and ruin on the rival factions, echoing the abuse heaped on rivals during electioneering. At Hadrumetum in North Africa (now in modern Tunisia) the Greens and Whites were damned to oblivion by a supporter of the Reds and Blues who wanted an unnamed demon to kill the horses and cause the rival charioteers to crash and die.[84] There can be no doubt that the fans in Rome involved some who felt just as strongly about their rivals.

CHARIOTEERS

Like Nero, Caligula was also a keen charioteer, occasionally even appearing in public as one. They were not the only charioteer emperors. Commodus, over a century after Nero's death, was in love with the glamour of the arena and the stadium and was another Green supporter. He acquired special chariot horses and dressed as a charioteer (as well as living with gladiators) but preferred only to go out in a chariot at night, apparently feeling rather self-conscious about adopting the trappings of such a lowly profession.[85]

Some chariot racers were superstars, some celebrated across the Empire, their reputations enhanced by the exceptional danger they were exposed to. Most were slaves in the ownership of the businessmen who had a stake in one or other of the factions. Thallus was a slave charioteer in Rome of a man called Lucius Avillius Planta, for example, who must have been among those who had invested in the sport.[86] Caligula was so impressed by the Green driver Eutychus that he gave him 2 million sesterces.[87] A chariot racer was also known as an *agitator*, a word related to terms for movement or activity. Until the reign of Nero, charioteers were so famed that they enjoyed a special class of legal immunity from prosecution which meant they spent some of their time robbing and cheating people with impunity. Nero ended this privilege, despite his love of the sport.[88]

Just as today not everyone enjoys football or motor-racing, not every Roman was enthusiastic about chariot racing. Pliny the Younger took the view that if you'd seen one race you'd seen them all. Nevertheless, he regarded race days as a positive benefit because the result was that while hundreds of thousands of fans were enjoying the action and excitement, that meant the rest of Rome was comparatively quiet. He was particularly fascinated by how the fans were fixated by the team

275

colours, their loyalties determined by nothing else, regardless of the drivers. Pliny described all this in a letter to a friend, the purpose, of course, being to look down on lesser mortals for enjoying such an 'inane, dull, and incessant' carry-on.[89]

Around the time Pliny the Younger wrote, a young Iberian made his first appearance in Rome driving on that occasion for the Whites. He was later transferred to the Greens, and then to the Reds with whom he remained. He had probably started his life as a slave, but he was so successful that he eventually became a millionaire, winning in total almost 36 million sesterces on the track after coming first 1,462 times in 2,900 races, and in 815 of them he led from the very beginning. He was given his freedom, taking the name as a citizen of Gaius Apuleius Diocles.[90] The most remarkable fact about Diocles was that he survived.

Skill played a large part, but Diocles had obviously also been lucky. Polynices was another success story on the track, and he lived long enough to father two sons who followed him into the potentially lucrative profession. Both boys were born into slavery. One called Macaris (a colloquial contraction of Marcus Aurelius), lived to the age of twenty-nine and had won 739 races, the majority for the Reds, but he had driven for the other three factions. His brother Tatianus (perhaps a colloquial version of Titus Vespasianus) lived only to the age of twenty. They had evidently been freed since both bore the full names of citizens, but they were 'snatched away by Fate' at the height of their success which may or may not mean they died as the result of accidents in races.[91] Another great loss to the profession was Flavius Scorpus who was killed in his twenty-sixth year while making a dash for the finish line. The names of some of the horses he drove are known and seem to have been as important to the enthusiasts of the day as famous racehorses are now. They included Pegasus, Elates, Andraemo, and Cotynus.[92]

Epaphroditus did well while his career in Rome with the Red faction lasted. He had chalked up a relatively modest 178 wins by the time he died, his wife Beia Felicula seeing to his burial.[93] Marcus

Aquilius Nutius started driving chariots when he was twenty-two but was dead by thirty-five.[94] Death from natural causes in both these latter cases is eminently possible but given their ages and professions it is all too likely they had come to a sticky end on the track, or been seriously injured.

OBELISKS

Rome possesses today the largest number of standing Egyptian obelisks in the world, even more than in Egypt. Many were once installed in the chariot-racing stadiums on the central dividing line, the spina. These tapering, square monolithic pillars were carved out of Aswan granite on the orders of Egyptian kings as monuments of the sun god Ra. They were usually erected in pairs outside the entrances to temples.

To the Romans obelisks were the perfect trophies of their conquest of Egypt. After Actium in 31 BC, Egypt became Octavian's personal property. The process of harvesting the obelisks as trophies for the city of Rome began. As Augustus he brought several to Rome, for example one dating to the reign of Seti I in the thirteenth century BC. It was found at Heliopolis, transported to Rome and installed on the spina of the Circus Maximus in 10 BC on the twentieth anniversary of Octavian's conquest of Egypt. It was later joined by one from the temple complex of Karnak at Thebes (see below). Just bringing it to Rome at all was considered a feat worthy of permanent commemoration. To that end the ship used, probably for his obelisk, was preserved in a dedicated dock at Pozzuoli where it was visited by tourists keen to see such a remarkable example of Rome's capabilities.[95]

Caligula brought an uninscribed obelisk to Rome to be installed on the central axis of his Circus Vaticanus, though it was finished by Claudius. Nothing of that venue is visible today. The obelisk has survived intact and now stands in the middle of the piazza in front of St Peter's. The ship used to bring it to Rome was so impressive that it was preserved by Claudius as another great curiosity of Roman skill and ingenuity until he found another use for it (p. 291).[96] Finding ships capable of bringing obelisks into Rome turned out to be an occupational hazard with this aspect of Roman trophy hunting.

Nero, obsessed with his own sporting and artistic achievements, used Augustus' obelisk in the Circus Maximus as the place to show off the 1,808 crowns he had been awarded for winning horse races. He had them displayed around the obelisk.[97] Since Nero had announced the races himself, fairly obviously no other competitor would have dared to beat him.

The obelisk with the best story of all stands outside the great basilica of St John in Lateran. It is the tallest Egyptian obelisk ever completed and erected. It was originally commissioned by the great 18th Dynasty pharaoh Thutmose III (1479–1425 BC). The vast monolith was shipped down the Nile from Aswan to Thebes where it was landed and dragged up to the vast temple complex of Karnak. Estimates of its weight vary, one providing a figure of 522 tons and a height of 32 metres (105 ft). Thutmose apparently had no idea what to do with his single obelisk, so it was left there until the reign of his grandson Thutmose IV (1400–1390 BC). In honour of his illustrious forebear, Thutmose IV ordered it completed and erected on the central axis of Karnak where it stood until the reign of the emperor Constantine I (307–37).

Once Constantius II (337–61) was in power he was endlessly reminded by his court sycophants that this obelisk had been passed over by Augustus, partly because of its size and its especially potent symbolic location in Karnak. This had counted for nothing to his father Constantine who had decided to help himself to the obelisk and ordered it removed so that it could be installed in his new eastern capital at Constantinople. The project was so arduous that the obelisk had only reached the docks at Alexandria by the time Constantine died. For Constantius II the obelisk presented a perfect opportunity to outdo both Augustus and his father. The obelisk was, doubtless with extraordinary difficulty, loaded onto a freighter and shipped to Ostia from where it was brought slowly up the Tiber to a location 3 miles (5 km) outside the city. Thereon it was transferred to land transport and laboriously dragged in cradles along the road through the Ostian Gate on the south side of Rome.

From there the obelisk was brought further into the city and dragged down into the Circus Maximus where it was raised by numerous cranes and ropes on the spina.[98] It was equipped with a base inscription announcing Constantius II had reunified the Empire. This followed the defeat of the breakaway regime of Magnentius (350–3). Thutmose III's obelisk dominated the Circus for an unknown length of time until eventually it fell and shattered, probably lying ignominiously in fragments for as long as a millennium – the last races were held there in 549. The obelisk was found in 1587, removed and repaired (which ended up shortening it slightly), and re-erected outside the Lateran basilica, built originally by Constantine.

Since the public spectacles were so important a part of the annual cycle, an accurate measurement of the calendar was essential. Augustus set up another obelisk from Heliopolis in 10 BC, this time in the Field of Mars, to serve as a gnomon in a huge sundial known as the *Solarium Augusti*.[99] Dating to the 26th Dynasty in the sixth century BC in the reign of Psamtik (known to the Romans as Psammetichus) II, it now stood in the middle of a paved area, large enough to accommodate its shadow, with a meridian line to mark noon. The idea was to correct the new Julian calendar with its 365¼ days (mistakes had been made in the observation of leap years). By the time Pliny wrote about it, the sundial had been out of kilter for three decades, which he attributed to celestial changes. Whatever the cause, the obelisk was re-erected several times in antiquity before collapsing in early medieval times. It has been repaired and re-erected in the Piazza Montecitorio near its original location. It no longer serves its original purpose but had for centuries allowed the Romans to tell the time, or nearly so.

AMPHITHEATRE

Of all Roman entertainments, gladiators today excite the most fascination and horror, not least because of the lurking suspicion that were the sport to be revived it would rapidly pick up an enthusiastic following. Gladiators were highly trained and used a variety of different weapons, such as swords, tridents, and nets, and defensive equipment with varying styles of helmet, shields, and guards. Usually slaves or prisoners of war, they were hand-picked for their physique and potential and sold to a gladiatorial school run by a *lanista* (the owner-trainer) to be brought up to a suitable standard. The owner was then able to rent out his gladiators for shows. Gaius Futius Philargyrus was a freedman *doctor* ('instructor') of the *velites* (gladiators, 'fighters') in Rome in the first century.[100] His name was appropriately descriptive. It means 'lover of the horse-training circuit', but probably used here in a more general sense to refer to a training arena.

In the days before the Colosseum was built by Vespasian, gladiator fights took place in Rome in any public open space, or in temporary wooden arenas. Bands of highly trained armed men in private ownership were a potential threat to the state, as Julius Caesar (see above) had discovered. Earlier, the Spartacus slave rebellion had broken out at Capua when gladiators in a school run by the lanista Lentulus Batiatus erupted thanks to his brutal treatment of them.[101]

The emperors took over ownership of the gladiators, absorbing the role of the private owners in earlier years. This included the privilege of inspecting the weapons before a bout to make sure they were sharp enough.[102] By the reign of Domitian (81–96), all gladiators were apparently owned by the emperor and in Rome were housed in a special barracks right next to the Colosseum. Domitian introduced an extra frisson with bouts between women gladiators, known as Amazons, though under Nero some aristocratic women had been forced to appear in the arena.[103] A retired gladiator, one who had been lucky enough to survive all his bouts and be awarded an honourable discharge, was given a special ticket that seems to have reclassified him as a *spectator*. Cocero the gladiator was one such fortunate fighter and received his ticket in 85 BC.[104]

Gladiator bouts were not the only sport to be seen in the arena. There were also public executions, and animal hunts known as the *bestiarii*. These could be, and originally were, held in temporary structures made of wood but gladiatorial bouts had once been a form of heroic ritual held by the Etruscans at funerals, among a number of their traditions adopted by the Romans. The central feature was the *arena*, a designated elliptical area covered with sand to absorb the blood which only later became surrounded with seating.

Like its early theatre, Pompeii's masonry amphitheatre was funded by the elite, in this instance by the two *duoviri* magistrates for 80 BC who served as the local equivalents of the consuls in Rome.[105] It was 160 years before Rome had a permanent amphitheatre in the form of the Colosseum. There was no question about their intentions. The promise to provide this facility was part of how they had bought themselves into office. Such competitive munificence took place in cities across the Empire and could greatly benefit a community, even if it was at the expense of corruption. Their successors, and the junior magistrates (aediles), were able to follow in their footsteps and act as impresarios by putting on gladiatorial bouts and other events which attracted local residents and other visiting supporters from the area (see earlier in this chapter for the consequences of dangerous rival supporters gathering too close).

Pompeii's vast archive of inscriptions and graffiti shows just how much the entertainments had entered everyday popular culture. Advertisements were daubed all over the city walls flagging up forthcoming events together with pictures and sketches of gladiators. A large palaestra attached to the theatre on the other side of the city from the amphitheatre seems to have been used as a residence by the gladiators. Rome was much the same but on a far more massive scale under the emperors. Part of a late third-century tombstone from Rome preserves the name of two gladiators, Scolasticus and Damascenus, probably as part of a scene commemorating a deceased magistrate who had been responsible for gladiator shows in which the two had performed.[106]

EXCESS IN THE ARENA

Amphitheatre shows were organized in the emperor's name as part of the annual round of religious festivals. They gradually degenerated into a continuous cycle of killing for entertainment on an unprecedented scale and unmatched since. The violence was easier to understand in an era when many Roman men in the late Republic and earlier had experienced war at first hand and untold numbers had died or suffered life-changing injuries.

In the mid-first century BC and long before the spectacles in Rome reached stratospheric levels of excess, Cicero wrote to a friend called Marcus Marius to tell him how lucky or sensible he had been to miss out on attending the spectacles. 'The spectacle was so elaborate as to leave no room for cheerful enjoyment, and I think you need feel no regret at having missed it. For what is the pleasure of a train of 600 mules in the *Clytemnestra*, or 3,000 bowls in the *Trojan Horse*, or brightly coloured armour of infantry and cavalry in some battle? These things roused the admiration of the common masses. To you they would have brought no delight.'[107] Cicero went on to ask, 'What pleasure can it be to a man of refinement, when either a weak man is torn by an extremely powerful beast, or a splendid one is transfixed by a hunting spear?'

Cicero, of course, had no idea what lay in the future. A century later during Nero's reign, the blood and gore had descended into repetitive tedium. Bored audiences watched the brutality barely half awake. Impresarios trotted out the same old shows. Part of the problem was trying to please fussy audiences. Petronius, Nero's style guru, had one character in his *Satyricon* moaning about a lousy show in which only old and worn-out gladiators 'who would have fallen over flat if you'd breathed on them' were sent out to fight. So bad were they that they were all flogged at the end to punish them for a lack of enthusiasm to fight while the crowd egged on the floggers.[108]

Nero's tutor Seneca famously stopped by at one event in the hope of catching midday light entertainment in between the killing. He was disappointed to discover that not only had the killing carried on but if anything it had become more gratuitous. The animal fights that had taken place earlier in the day were 'merciful' by comparison to what followed, which he described as homicide. He described how those fighting now had no protection which meant that every blow counted. Apparently, the audience preferred this because all the armour did was slow down the killing. The crowd demanded that every man who killed his opponent should be set against another until one of them died and so on until there was single man left. Even he was earmarked for a bloody end of some sort.[109]

The most damning comment Seneca made was to say 'the whole affair is kept going by iron and fire. This goes on while the arena is practically empty.' In other words, while men died one after another the whole event was being watched by just a few people. Seneca could see that a criminal might deserve to die. He was less certain what one needed to have done to deserve watching something so unpleasant.

Vespasian commissioned the construction of the Colosseum on the site of Nero's Golden House, returning the land to public use in a pointed gesture after he won the civil war of 68–9 that followed Nero's death. When the arena was opened in 80 by his son Titus an orgy of violence followed, all designed to satisfy the public's lust for such entertainment. Nine thousand animals were killed, some by women hunters. The Colosseum was used for infantry battles and then flooded for naval ones. As if that was not enough, another venue was set up outside the city for gladiator bouts, followed by horse racing, and then more infantry and naval battles. By the end the spectacles had lasted one hundred days, during which Titus had thrown wooden balls down to the crowd, each ball being marked with the name of a gift such as food or clothing. Last on the list after cattle were slaves. Those lucky enough to catch a ball were supposed to take it to a gift distributor who would hand over whatever was on the ball (a similar story was attributed to Elagabalus, who ruled 140 years later).[110]

Whatever benchmark an emperor set, his successors were liable to try and outdo him. In 107 Trajan returned from his Dacian war and organized 123 days of games, or about one-third of the whole year. Eleven thousand animals died this time, and 10,000 gladiators fought one another.[111] Excess was becoming an end in itself though some emperors exercised restraint. At one gladiatorial event, which he was clearly attending in person, Hadrian found himself being yelled at by the crowd demanding something as a matter of urgency. Hadrian refused and told his herald to give the order for 'silence'. The herald had barely raised his hand and the crowd complied without the order ever being uttered. Nonetheless, it was a risky moment.[112] Marcus Aurelius detested violence so much he went even further, ordering gladiators to be armed with blunt weapons and to treat the bouts as if they were just athletics contests.[113]

Marcus Aurelius' son Commodus had no such scruples. He loved gladiators, so much so that he became one. The historian Dio was at pains to point out to his readers that, if for one moment they thought he was making it up, they were wrong:

Let no one feel that I am sullying the dignity of history by recording such occurrences. On most accounts, to be sure, I should not have mentioned this exhibition; but since it was given by the emperor himself, and since I was present myself and took part in everything seen, heard and spoken, I have thought proper to suppress none of the details, but to hand them down, trivial as they are, just like any events of the greatest weight and importance.[114]

Commodus had ordered the senators and magistrates across the Empire to stump up a stipend to pay for his gladiators. He would fight his opponents to the death in private in the palace, or content himself with wounding them. In public he would only use wooden practice weapons. Commodus had a special way of making an entrance when he arrived at the Colosseum. Dio continued:

> He would put on a long-sleeved tunic of silk, white interwoven with gold, and thus arrayed he would receive our greetings; but when he was about to go inside, he put on a robe of pure purple with gold spangles, donning also after the Greek fashion a chlamys of the same colour, and a crown made of gems from India and of gold, and he carried a herald's staff like that of Mercury ... He would enter the arena in the garb of Mercury, and casting aside all his other garments, would begin his exhibition wearing only a tunic and unshod.

Commodus had an easy ride with gladiators because they let him win, but he loved the profession so much that he planned to go and live in their barracks rather than in the palace. He had already declared himself to be Hercules but now set that aside in preference to being called after a long-deceased gladiator of great renown.[115]

Dio watched in person as Commodus himself killed a hundred bears on the first day of the games but, of course, the massacre was rigged. The arena and thus the bears had been divided into four by two cross walls which supported a balustrade from which Commodus had an easy task of spearing them one by one. The tiring work led him to stop and take a drink from a cup shaped like a club, reflecting his fantasy that he was a reincarnated Hercules, provoking all the senators (including Dio) and the crowd to shout out the familiar drinkers' refrain 'long life to you'. Few of them meant it since by then it had been long apparent that Commodus was a dangerously degenerate and thoroughly irresponsible ruler.

Herodian, who appears to have been an eyewitness too, was astounded by the sight of Mauretanian ostriches being dispatched by Commodus using special crescent-shaped arrows to decapitate them, resulting in the headless bodies continuing to run around the arena. On one occasion, Commodus used a javelin to kill a leopard that had just pounced on a human victim, but this paled compared to the time when a hundred lions were released from the underground pens into the arena where Commodus allegedly killed the whole lot with exactly one hundred spears, the bodies then being laid out for all to see (and count).[116]

Septimius Severus fought a bitter civil war from 193 to 197 to rid himself of his rivals, Pescennius Niger and Clodius Albinus. Once he had secured Rome, he 'tried to make himself popular with the common people by putting on continuous shows of all kinds, and slaughtering hundreds of animals from all over the world'. Rome was turned into a theme park devoted to endless entertainment. Severus threw victory games featuring mock battles and musical items performed by people hired from all over the world. Herodian, who describes all this, seems to have been in the audiences. 'We saw all kinds of different shows in all the theatres at the same time which included all-night religious ceremonies in imitation of the Mysteries.' They were celebrated as the Saecular Games, which had not been held for three generations. According to Herodian, heralds were sent out across Rome and Italy to summon the population to come and attend games 'the like of which they had never seen before and would never see again'.[117]

In 202 a boat-shaped pen holding 400 wild beasts was installed in the Colosseum as part of the games to celebrate Septimius Severus' first ten years in power. Designed to fall apart on cue, it promptly released the animals simultaneously. 'Bears, lionesses, panthers, lions, ostriches, wild asses, and bison' hurtled out to meet their deaths in an orgy of brazenly gratuitous violence. Dio, our source, goes on to say incongruously that 700 animals were involved, with one hundred for each day of the festival. Either way, the numbers mean little now – the point was bloodthirsty excess for the sake of it.[118]

Severus' wife's great-nephew, the bizarre religious fanatic Elagabalus (218–22), maintained the trend. 'He staged lavish shows and built racetracks and theatres, believing that chariot races, shows, and countless recitals would please the people, who held night-long feasts and celebrations. He placed the sun god in a chariot adorned with gold and jewels and brought him out from the city to the suburbs.'[119]

And so the spectacles went on. It is rare to hear much about the individual fighters involved. Gaius Tutilius Rufinus was a *venator* (hunter) in Rome. Such men performed in wild beast hunts in the arena. He died, from unknown causes, but Tiberius Claudius Secundus arranged for his funeral, ordering up a fine marble coffin. He dedicated it *amico*, 'to his friend', whom he buried near the Via Appia close to the Tomb of Cecilia Metella. One might imagine that the men worked together in the arena, striking up a friendship based on their shared experiences. That two such lowly individuals have the names of Roman citizens suggest that they lived after Caracalla's edict of universal citizenship in 212, but the style of the text is so good that it points to an earlier date.[120]

Elagabalus' cousin and successor Severus Alexander (222–35) had plans to lay on so many games that there would be a new spectacle every thirty days. This plan seems never to have come to fruition, probably because the sheer logistics were beyond even the Roman world to manage at that rate. He had also had to invest heavily in restoring the Colosseum and other venues which were deteriorating with age.[121] Massive celebrations with new Saecular Games followed in Rome during the reign of Philip I (244–9) when Rome reached its thousandth year.[122] Gladiatorial bouts continued at the Colosseum into the fifth century, with animal hunts lasting until the early sixth century but within a few decades all the entertainments had stopped. The vast building was given over to a variety of other uses including industry and housing. A major structural collapse of the outer south wall in the fourteenth century led to the building being used as a quarry for several centuries, leaving it in the state it is today.

Ancient Rome was home to a million or more people, but it is easy to overlook the vast numbers of animals that lived and died there. All these massive public displays involved animals of some sort, whether as victims of beast hunts in the arena, horses for racing, or as cherished and sometimes extraordinarily valuable pets.

13

ANIMALS IN ROME

Among all the species of insects the prime position belongs to the bees. They alone among insects have been created for the sake of man. They collect honey . . . They model combs and wax that serves a thousand uses, they endure toil, they construct works, they have a government.

Pliny[1]

The Romans treated animals as another facet of the munificence that destiny had bestowed on them to use as they wished. They were capable of venerating individual animals as pets or for the remarkable features of individual species. After all, the she-wolf had suckled and saved Romulus and Remus at the dawn of Rome's mythologized history. In the festival of the Lupercalia priests stripped naked at the supposed site of the wolf's cave on the Palatine Hill and then raced round the city's original boundary striking women with strips of goatskin to promote fertility.[2] The eagle became a symbol of Roman military power, decorating military standards along with other beasts (including mythological ones) chosen as the emblems of some of the legions, and appeared on coins.

In other ways animals were regarded as an infinitely exploitable resource, measured, and assessed according to their usefulness to man whether as servants, disposable features of entertainment, or as food and raw materials (such as bone and ivory). Rome was filled with pack animals, which slaves were often compared with, and the cavalry horses of the mounted wing of the imperial bodyguard. Animals were sacrificed in astronomical quantities. There were also the extraordinary arrangements for bringing in wild animals from across and beyond the Empire to be used in the spectacles in the arena.

Most Romans were untroubled by many of the moral qualms that afflict our own age. The environmental consequences of ravaging north Africa for animals to be displayed and killed in the arena were of no interest. Meat in all its forms was so integral a part of the Roman diet, at least for those who could afford it, that ideas about vegetarianism and veganism were largely limited to philosophical circles, though they did not have specific terms equivalent to ours. Seneca said he had been greatly influenced by the works of Pythagoras and a Roman philosopher of Augustan date called Quintus Sextius, especially in their various reasons for adopting a vegetarian diet. Sextius, for example, believed that man had enough available food anyway; shedding blood to obtain more only served to create a habit of cruelty.

Seneca became interested in the idea that souls could be transferred between all living beings. 'I began to abstain from animals', he said. He enjoyed the experience, believing that he had become more mentally agile as a result, but came up against an unexpected problem. Certain 'foreign religious cults', some of whose adherents spurned eating meat, arrived in Rome. Seneca was probably referring to Christianity. Some (but by no means all) early Christians chose to reject meat. Spurning meat risked accusations of being a member of such cults. Seneca's father, who his son said disliked philosophy, persuaded him to resume a normal diet which he did, apparently, with enthusiasm. Evidently, the ideology had had little enduring effect on Seneca, but either way the vegetarian ideas he had toyed with were not really connected to modern reasons for vegetarianism.[3]

PREHISTORIC MONSTERS

Fossils have always been available for discovery even if it was not until the nineteenth century that their true nature was properly identified. Discoveries in Greece of huge disarticulated mammoth bones were almost certainly responsible for myths about races of giants, and the mammoth skull for tales of the one-eyed Cyclops. During Tiberius' reign, earthquakes in Sicily threw up large bones and teeth. The local people were far too scared to do anything with most of them but one of the teeth was sent to Rome for the emperor's attention. Phlegon of Tralles, who wrote during Hadrian's time a century later, recorded the story. It seems that in Roman times, curiosity about such phenomena was guarded:

> The tooth was not just a whole foot in length but even longer. The messengers showed it to Tiberius and asked whether he wanted the epic corpse brought along. Tiberius acted wisely by avoiding the impiety of robbing dead bodies but at the same time found out about its size. He ordered Pulcher, the well-known geometrician, and told him to reconstruct the face based on the tooth's scale. Pulcher worked out what the proportions of the whole body and face would have been from the tooth. He made a replica up quickly and brought it to Tiberius.[4]

Tiberius expressed his interest at having seen the tooth but played safe by ordering it to be taken back to the findspot. Palaeontology would have to wait.

THE OSTIAN WHALE

During the reign of Claudius, a killer whale arrived off the coast at the port of Ostia. Claudius had commissioned the construction of a large new harbour with a protective mole to make up for the rapid silting of the Tiber. The larger ships were having to moor out to sea for smaller vessels with a shallower draught to come out so that the cargo could be laboriously unloaded into them and taken to the quayside. A shipload of hides had arrived from Gaul, but the ship sank at the mouth to the new harbour. The whale had been attracted by the prospect of the free food but lingered so long at the wreck that it sank into the seabed and became trapped by sand banking up against it. Claudius ordered nets to be thrown across the entrances of the harbour, and then took out a flotilla of boats with praetorian soldiers on them armed with spears to attack the whale for the purposes of a public spectacle. A boat was sunk when it filled with water from the whale's blowhole.[5] The whole occasion seems to have given Claudius an idea. The huge ship that had brought the uninscribed obelisk from Egypt for Caligula (see Chapter 12), which now stands in the Vatican piazza, was sunk on his orders at the mouth of the new Ostian harbour to create the mole.

EXOTIC ANIMALS

Exotic animals were another of the fruits of conquest, despite the complex logistics of storage and transportation. As Rome's power and sphere of control expanded, ever more unusual animals could be hunted and captured to entertain the crowds. Such beasts made for magnificent theatre in the arena and in triumphal processions, amply demonstrating Rome's unprecedented power.

By the second and third centuries AD the number of animals involved was becoming ludicrous. The first elephants had been seen in Rome in 275 BC after they had been captured from the army of Pyrrhus five years earlier.[6] Others followed in later years. As a young general, too young still to be a senator, the precocious Pompey had his chariot drawn by a team of elephants yoked together. No one had measured the elephant teams, which turned out to be too wide to go through the gates of Rome.[7]

Pompey followed this up in 55 BC with a staged fight between twenty elephants and Gaetulians (north-west Africans) wielding spears to mark the dedication of the Temple of Venus Genetrix in Caesar's Forum. One animal covered itself in glory when, badly wounded, it still summoned up the strength to flick away the spearmen's shields and hurl them up in a parabolic arc to the wonder of the crowd. The mood soon changed. An elephant was killed by a javelin that entered its skull. The surviving elephants rushed their compound's iron fence but were thwarted. Allegedly, the distressed animals gave up but put on such an extraordinary display of mourning and wailing that the spectators were profoundly moved and, uncharacteristically for a Roman mob, filled with compassion. The result was that the whole event backfired, with the people cursing Pompey.[8] Cicero watched a similar event around this time, and was struck by the crowd's reaction:

> The last day was that of the elephants, on which there was a great deal of astonishment on the part of the vulgar crowd, but no pleasure whatever. Nay, there was even a certain feeling of compassion aroused by it, and a kind of belief created that that animal has something in common with mankind.[9]

Elephants continued to be an important sight in Rome well into imperial times. They were used in formal processions and were owned by the emperors. Juvenal mentions them in the early second century explaining that 'Caesar's herd' was 'not for sale', worked for no private owner, and did not breed anywhere in Italy but are 'fetched from the dark peoples and fed among the Rutulian trees and the lands of Turnus'.[10] This was a reference to the imperial elephant compound at Laurentum, in the land once ruled by the mythical Turnus whom Aeneas had defeated and killed in the *Aeneid*, to where elephants were brought from Africa. The ordinary Roman had the chance to use coins issued by Antoninus Pius in 148–9 that depicted an elephant on the reverse with the legend MUNIFICENTIA.AUG, 'the liberality of the emperor'.[11] In 193, as his short-lived regime was collapsing, the desperate Didius Julianus ordered the imperial elephants to be trained to carry men and turrets in order to try and terrify Septimius Severus' army then approaching Rome.[12] Elephants appeared on coins again under Philip I as part of the celebrations of Rome's 1,000th year in 248 with the legend AETERNITAS.AUGG, the 'Eternity of the Emperors' (Philip and his co-ruler son Philip II).

There were plenty of other exotic animals displayed in the arena. In 58 BC the profligate curule aedile Aemilius Scaurus laid on a procession of 150 female leopards, only to be outdone subsequently by Pompey who managed to supply 410.[13] The logistics involved in shipping such dangerous animals to Rome and keeping them alive en route can only be guessed at. Scaurus was also responsible in 58 BC for the first display in Rome of a hippopotamus and five crocodiles. They required an artificial lake to accommodate them. Pliny considered the crocodile an 'evil quadruped'.[14]

Scaurus' coup, though, was surely to have obtained in Judaea the 40 Roman foot (11.84 m) long skeleton, believed at the time to be that of the sea serpent from which Perseus had rescued Andromeda. It is impossible to know what Scaurus had really acquired, but dinosaur fossils in Israel are rare. The most likely possibility is that this was the disarticulated remains of a member of the Protocetidae, a group of four-legged ancestors of whales that mark the transition from land animals to the sea, which are known in the region (the remains of the residual legs either being lost or ignored). None of that would have mattered to the audiences who flocked to see the impressive bones shown along with 'the rest of the marvels of his aedileship'.[15]

Scaurus commemorated his aedileship and that of his colleague Plautius Hypsaeus with a most unusual silver denarius depicting an animal. One side was Scaurus' name above a camel before which the named King Aretas III of Nabatea is kneeling, recording his surrender to Scaurus in 62 BC. The coin was the first occasion on which a Roman magistrate responsible for coinage in his year of office had the effrontery to showcase a career achievement that way.[16]

Pompey also put on a show involving 600 lions. The first had appeared decades earlier in 104 BC when Quintus Scaevola as aedile arranged a lion fight at Rome. The future dictator Sulla organized a fight involving 100 lions with manes in 93 BC, but giraffes were not seen in Rome for another half-century when Caesar as dictator used them in his games.[17] Commodus was especially fond of killing animals in the arena. 'His marksmanship was generally agreed to be outstanding', said Herodian who commented also on how remarkable it was to see species brought over for Commodus that until then were only known to him in pictures. This suggests that Herodian saw them for himself. They included animals from India and Ethiopia, and, as we have seen, ostriches from Mauretania.[18]

For those climbing the greasy pole, having exotic animals for shows could be decisive in their political careers. In September 51 BC Marcus Caelius Rufus was desperate to be elected curule aedile. His friend Cicero had been sent out to Cilicia as governor. Caelius Rufus spotted an opportunity and badgered Cicero to send panthers back to Rome so that he could put on a crowd-pulling show at the games he was responsible for. 'I beg you to be taking measures about the panthers', he wailed. He grew increasingly anxious, and pointed out that his colleague in the office, Curio, had not only been given panthers by someone else but was also offering some to him. 'In nearly every letter I have mentioned the subject of the panthers to you. It will be a disgrace to you that Patiscus has sent ten panthers to Curio, and that you should not send many times more.' Caelius Rufus said that all Cicero had to do was give the order because he had already provided the necessary manpower to take care of bringing them back to Rome.[19] Cicero did his best, or at any rate claimed 'the usual hunters' were doing so on his behalf. Writing to Caelius Rufus on 4 April the following year, he excused himself by humorously explaining that there was a terrible shortage of the animals because most had removed themselves to the neighbouring province of Caria for safety.[20]

Given the costs involved, there was a vested interest in keeping the animals healthy and able to perform. Some medical professionals were devoted to animal care. In the early first century AD Apollodorus Tromentina was a *medicus equarius et venator*, 'horse doctor and hunter', which probably means that he served as a wild beast hunter in the arena but also took care of the horses he and his compatriots used.[21]

On a much smaller scale came the enterprising itinerants with their performing animals. One such trainer is depicted on a Roman lamp of mid-first century date accompanied by an ape, and a cat scooting up a ladder heading for a couple of hoops in mid-air to jump through. The scene depicts a pot, perhaps to collect gifts from the audience, and a bell which either announced his presence or was used to prompt the animals into action. Doubtless such modest troupes made their way from street to street in Rome and other cities putting on a show for a few copper coins and breaking up the monotony of everyday life.[22]

HORSES

Horses made an early appearance on Rome's silver denarii, including a pair being ridden by the Dioscuri (Castor and Pollux), or a team of four pulling a chariot driven by Jupiter. Horses were regarded in a completely different light to most animals by the Romans. Their intelligence was held in considerable regard, and they were highly valued. Being mounted of course made a Roman leader appear more considerable, the notion of being in charge and control of a powerful horse conveniently resonating with the heroic exploits of the warrior ruler Alexander the Great (reigned 336–323 BC) who was greatly admired by the Romans. Alexander had won over at the age of twelve his stallion Bucephalus, an animal regarded as being uncontrollable.[23]

The Romans became accustomed to the sight of their leaders in Republican and imperial times riding on horseback and the appearance of equestrian statues in public places, a custom aped by local worthies in provincial cities. In 56 BC the magistrate and moneyer Lucius Marcius Philippus (and, incidentally, the stepbrother of the future emperor Augustus) issued a silver denarius commemorating his ancestor Quintus Marcius Rex who had built Rome's Aqua Marcia aqueduct in 144 BC. The coin design featured a section of the aqueduct

295

on top of which was an equestrian statue of Marcius Rex, probably a real statue once displayed in Rome. In the later Roman Empire, the arrival of the emperor on horseback in Rome or certain provincial locations became a motif adopted for coinage with the legend *Adventus Aug(usti)*, 'the coming of the emperor'.

Caligula's favourite horse was Incitatus (which means 'swift' or 'at full gallop'). He provided the animal with lavish quarters, purple blankets, a collar studded with precious stones, and his own house and household slaves so that the horse could 'invite' people to parties. Incitatus was also the source of the famous story that Caligula made him consul, usually described today as if that was what had happened. This is a good example of an ancient source being elaborated on and not being checked. In fact, Suetonius recorded that 'he [Caligula] is also said to have *destined* the consulship [for the horse]'. While this makes for gratifying proof of Caligula's unbalanced state of mind, the story is much more likely to have originated in Caligula setting out to make fools of the senators by suggesting that he *might as well* make his horse a consul. He had also been known to force senators to drive chariots in the races. By humiliating the senators, Caligula, who had no special qualifications or achievements of his own to justify his position as emperor, had found a way to flaunt his rank and remind them that he could do as he pleased.[24] Needless to say, this backfired when he was assassinated in 41.

In 47 Claudius put on the Saecular Games that marked the 800th anniversary of Rome. Corax ('Raven'), a charioteer in the White faction, was in the lead shortly after the race started but was flung out of the chariot. To everyone's astonishment, his horses carried on regardless, leading the field, but stopped dead at the finishing line. Pliny put this down to them being ashamed of outdoing human beings.[25]

WORKING ANIMALS

Horses were bred with donkeys to create mules, a vital tool in antiquity for hauling loads. These beasts were to be seen in the streets of Rome performing all sorts of tasks. These included the job of pulling the car-pentum carriage, used by the women of the imperial family. Caligula issued a sestertius to commemorate his mother Agrippina the Elder with a design on the reverse featuring such a vehicle with its mules.[26] Mules were also used to transport vehicles carrying imperial officials and post. A mule sold at Pompeii in 15 during the reign of Tiberius cost 520 sesterces, at the time more than half a legionary's annual pay.[27]

The cost of providing such animals was imposed on local commu-nities as the imperial traffic passed through and was known as the *vehiculatio*. Nerva remitted this impost in Italy and publicized his gen-erosity on a sestertius struck in 97 that showed mules grazing on the reverse, no longer harnessed to a cart which appears in the background tipped up. This must be a reference to how local mules had been alle-viated from the possibility of being requisitioned.[28]

DOGS

The cast of the body of a dog found at Pompeii has always been regarded as among the most poignant relics of the buried city. The hound had been tethered to a post and left to its fate, gradually being asphyxiated by fumes as the ash and pumice accumulated around it. Pompeii's House of the Tragic Poet has in its entranceway a mosaic depicting a snarling canine and the inscription *cave canem*, 'beware of the dog'. Although Martial never hesitated to write cruelly about the various human characters he came cross in his everyday life, he wrote with charm and affection about a dog called Issa who belonged to an acquaintance of his called Publius. He said she was more to be valued than gems from India, more loving than any woman, and described how Publius had had her painted so she would be preserved in an image after her death.[29] Some of his other references, though, allude to Rome's stray dogs that fought over rotting hides and dug up the bones of the dead.[30]

There is a small bronze statuette of a dog found in Egypt and now in the British Museum. The animal is clearly shown wearing a disc attached to his collar. One such identifying tag from Rome, and probably of fourth-century date, reads, 'Hold me, lest I flee, and return me to my master Viventius on the estate of Callistus'.[31] Another has a similar message but in this case retains the metal ring worn round the animal's neck, and asked in this instance for the wearer to be returned to the lord Zoninus with the promise of a reward of one gold solidus coin.[32] These are thought by some to have been identifying discs worn by slaves as a precautionary measure because traditionally runaway slaves who were caught had their foreheads branded or tattooed, but in 316 Constantine outlawed such practices.[33] The Egyptian statuette makes it far more likely these discs were attached to dog collars. It is hardly likely that a runaway slave would make off while still wearing an incriminating identity tag inviting someone to arrest them.

Nothing can compare with the tombstone of a white dog, appropriately named Margarita ('Pearl') who died in Rome during the second century AD while giving birth to a litter of pups:

Gaul was my birthplace. The oyster from the rich water's waves gave me a name suited to my beauty. I learned to run boldly through treacherous woods and to pursue shaggy beasts in the hills. Heavy chains never restrained me, nor did my snow-white body ever suffer any blows. I lay in my master's and mistress's soft laps and curled up on their bed when I was tired. I talked more than I should, with my dog's dumb mouth, though no one feared my barking. But alas, misfortune befell me when whelping, and now this little marble slab marks where the earth enfolds me.[34]

It appears from the text that Margarita was a type of Gaulish dog bred for hunting and for which there was a market in dogs with such skills. She must have been both expensive and deliberately sourced for the owner. We know nothing about the owner except that he or she was prepared to invest in an expensive tombstone for an animal who had clearly been much loved and spoiled. There were others. Amminaracus was a dog who was given a marble tombstone bearing his name and a carving of him crouched and ready to leap up.[35]

A gravestone dedicated 'to Helena, foster daughter, incomparable and worthy soul' is harder to interpret. Instead of a carving of a girl there is a depiction of a Maltese breed dog, raising the question of whether it is a memorial to a pet or a child. The latter is more likely, possibly a favourite child slave called Helena (since there are no other names or titles given, or parentage) with the dog perhaps being her companion.[36] The choice of a Maltese dog may simply have been a motif unless it genuinely reflected a preference for the breed. Another marble funerary monument that once served as a cover for a sarcophagus, and had been modified to fit, depicts a reclining girl with another Maltese dog. Her name is lost but the surviving inscription starts 'Here beauty and splendour lie, tragically young ...'. This Hadrianic-era sculpture is unfinished, raising the possibility that it was a standard item and was perhaps pressed into service as old stock.[37]

BIRDS

Birds were popular pets, whether they were ordinary or exotic types. The poet Catullus wrote about a pet sparrow that belonged to a paramour 'whom she loved more than her eyes'. When the bird died, those eyes were left 'heavy and red with weeping'.[38] At the Palatine Games in January 41, on the day Caligula was murdered there, rare birds were among the gifts thrown out to the spectators. Caligula enjoyed watching them fight over the animals.[39]

In the year 49 Agrippina the Younger, sister of Caligula, married her uncle Claudius. She was already wealthy but among her wedding presents was a white nightingale costing 600,000 sesterces. This was a vast amount of money that was enough to pay 666 legionaries for a year. Agrippina added the nightingale to a collection of birds that went on to include, if it did not already, a thrush that supposedly mimicked people. Pliny recorded that at the time he was writing down the story about Agrippina, her son Nero and his stepbrother Britannicus (Claudius' son by his previous wife Messalina) owned a starling and nightingales that could speak Greek and Latin words.[40]

The most prominent relics in the Forum today include the Temple of Castor and Pollux. Earthquakes and time have destroyed most of the building, but three columns have withstood the centuries and still stand, attached at the top by a small piece of the original entablature. It is hard now to visualize the great classical temple they once formed part of. At night they are lit up and make an especially conspicuous sight. During the reign of Tiberius, who rebuilt the temple between 14 BC and AD 6 under Augustus, there was a raven in the Forum that had an optimistic take on the imperial family's prospects. Optimism was no bad thing. Death had already carried off several potential heirs. Tiberius, Augustus' stepson, had been something of a last resort.

This raven had hatched somewhere within the temple structure, and when grown up moved into a cobbler's shop nearby. Roman temples were often used for a variety of apparently unrelated purposes, businesses and other enterprises finding accommodation in any handy niche or open vault in the podium. The result was that a temple in such a prominent place as the Temple of Castor and Pollux was filled with an endless throng of people wandering through. Here the bird had the opportunity to listen to them talking and soon learned to mimic the words it heard. Every morning the raven flew the short distance to the rostra that overlooked the central piazza where more usually Rome's politicians and demagogues declaimed to the crowds that gathered. Here the raven squawked out the names of Tiberius, his son Drusus and his nephew Germanicus to passers-by and then returned to the cobbler's.

The raven continued this morning salutation for many years throughout Tiberius' reign, long after both Drusus and Germanicus were dead, and became a famous sight. Unfortunately, in the year 36 the ageing bird's popularity, or more likely its toilet habits, caused a neighbouring cobbler to kill the bird. This gratuitous violence caused a riot among the raven's fans, and the bird-killing cobbler was forced out of his shop and sent away. A major funeral for the bird followed with a procession that led two miles down the Via Appia to a specially chosen burial spot. Pliny, our source for the tale of the raven, mused on the irony that many Roman men of note had been awarded nothing like the same degree of honour at their deaths.[41]

There was money to be made from talking animals for those enterprising enough to train them to flatter the vanities of the elite. There was another famous talking raven. A fan of Caesar's had taught it to squawk *ave Caesar victor imperator*, 'Hail Caesar, victorious general', and brought the bird to show him. Unable to resist, Caesar handed over 20,000 sesterces to buy his avian admirer, only to be told by the fan's friend that the fan had another, but this time one that praised Mark Antony instead. Caesar told the fan to split the money with his chum.[42]

LIVESTOCK

Marcus Antonius Teres was a *negotiator suariae et pecuariae* (a trader of pigs and livestock) who lived and died in the second century AD. He came from Misenum on the north side of the Bay of Naples, where he had filled several public offices, but was buried in Rome where he made most of his money.[43] He seems to have specialized in trading in animals from Campania, for which he became (at least according to his tombstone epitaph) *celeberrimus*, 'most celebrated'. He was involved in a trade dominated by the guilds known as the *boarii* (oxen), the *pecuarii* (cattle) and the *suarii* (pigs). In an era without refrigeration, the only practicable option was the movement of live animals on foot to be slaughtered, butchered, and sold in Rome. The roads that led to Rome must have been packed with constant animal traffic.

ALLEGORICAL TALES

Stories about animals also served as important allegorical moral guidance for the Romans. The *Aesopic Fables* remodelled and published in Latin by Augustus' freedman Phaedrus are dominated by tales about animals, like the 'vainglorious jackdaw' who dressed himself up in fallen peacock feathers and tried to pass himself off as a peacock. The other peacocks stripped him of his acquired finery and chased him off. The other jackdaws lectured him on the value of being content with his station in life, a topic of obvious appeal in a society built on a rigorous hierarchy.[44] In the other fables apes and foxes make frequent appearances, the fox usually being depicted as mean-minded and sly. The more depressingly memorable include the tale of the ass who was made to carry round the baggage of the Galli (priest adherents of Cybele) until it died from exhaustion and beatings. The ass's hide was then used to make tambourines for the Galli who with perverse self-satisfaction observed that although the ass might have looked forward to relief from the abuse heaped on him, he merely continued to experience renewed blows in death. The moral tale here, such as it was, was that those born to ill luck in life continue to experience misery after death.[45]

This chapter has barely scraped the surface with the stories of animals in everyday Roman life. Untold numbers of animals were sacrificed as part of the endless annual cycle of religious festivals. There was a huge industry engaged in supplying them. The practice had its origins in Roman rural prehistory and survived long into the historical era until Christianity outlawed pagan practices. Cato the Elder recounted the method necessary to purify a farm with the *suovetaurilia* procession which involved leading a pig, lamb, and calf around the fields, and all to the sound of the ubiquitous flute players who accompanied processions, rituals, games, and funerals. The tradition was maintained within the city with the *ambarvalia*, a word that meant 'walking round the ramparts', in honour of the farmers. Although Jupiter and Juno were addressed, the prayers were directed at Mars and his remoter and more traditional role as a protective agricultural deity. The climax of the occasion came when the animals were killed with a special knife and incantations offered to Mars. In the urban version the gods invoked were Bacchus and Ceres.[46]

14

GODS, SHRINES, AND OMENS

A god gives the sign.

Tibullus[1]

If you want advice, you will allow the gods themselves to provide what is good for us, and what will be fit for our affairs.

Juvenal[2]

Traditional Roman religion was primarily transactional and contractual, as was usually the case in antiquity. This meant that people sought services and protection from deities in return for offerings and sacrifices, perhaps handing over a copper as fee for the privilege.[3] This normally took the form of a request along with a vow or promise. Subsequently the vow was fulfilled by making the sacrifice, or erecting an altar with a suitable dedication, or both. Religious inscriptions often refer to the fulfilment of that vow, but it is rare to find the original requests. 'Happy then shall I be, and, as your [Apollo's] debtor for the fulfilment of my prayer, will lead to the rustic altar a young steer with golden horns, as a sacrifice to you', said Martial.[4] There were endless opportunities or pretexts for sacrifices.

One was known as *propter viam* ('on account of the road', perhaps better in English 'one for the road'), performed just before setting off on a journey.[5]

'There is no place, whether streets or marketplaces or taverns or even our own homes, that is completely free of idols', moaned the moralizing Christian writer Tertullian.[6] Effigies and pictures of gods were everywhere, including on coins. Rome was filled with temples and shrines of all sizes. Augustus claimed to have restored eighty-two temples alone.[7] The biggest dominated public spaces, crammed side by side with basilicas, markets, and theatres. They were mainly used for the practising of highly politicized state cults (including the imperial cult which honoured deified past emperors and the imperial house), the public rituals of which took place outside. Cult statues were housed inside in the *cella*. These buildings were outnumbered by the smaller temples and shrines, frequented by locals or passers-by keen to have some recourse to spiritual sustenance in the face of everyday jeopardy. Side streets and junctions were home to countless shrines. Even the open space dedicated to a god alongside a temple counted as part of a 'shrine' (*delubrum*), such as the one dedicated to Jupiter Stator at the Circus Flaminius.[8] The word delubrum meant '[the place] of expiation', or in other words where actions or other mechanisms could be used to avert or avoid something.

In and around the Forum of Rome on nearby hills were the great temples of the major state and traditional deities. These included the Capitoline Triad of Jupiter, Juno, and Minerva, as well as the other great deities of Venus, Mars, Diana, Ceres, Vulcan, and others who corresponded with Greek Olympian gods. There were also Rome's own deities, such as Romulus and especially Vesta, goddess of the hearth and symbol of home, and favourites like Castor and Pollux, and Hercules. Their cults underpinned Roman society because those gods guaranteed the perpetuation and security of the Roman state. In the year 70, following the civil war of 68–9, Vespasian restored the Capitol in Rome. The area was purified with the sacrifice of a pig, sheep, and an ox. Their entrails were offered on an earthen altar to Jupiter, Juno and

305

Minerva to protect the building. On the instructions of the soothsayers unrefined lumps of raw gold and silver were hurled into the foundations.[9] At the other end of the scale on the banks of the Tiber stood the Temple of Fors Fortuna ('Lucky Fortuna'), a goddess favoured by the plebeians because in legend her cult had been founded by a plebeian, and countless other minor streetside and household shrines.[10]

Roman gods were usually visualized in human form and depicted as such in statuary, in reliefs, and on coins. They were perceived as acting on and being involved with human affairs and therefore needed propitiating to ensure that influence was for the good. Temples were not ponderous places devoted merely to the observances of cult. They were often used as public art galleries, landmarks, shopping arcades and thoroughfares, and meeting places. A Caecilius Metellus (there are several possible candidates from the family who all held the same name) decorated the Temple of Castor and Pollux with statues and paintings. These included a portrait of a high-class prostitute called Flora who was celebrated for her beauty and had been well-known to Pompey in her younger days (p. 111).[11]

Julius Caesar and Augustus both promoted the idea that their family, the Julii, were descended from Iulus, the son of Aeneas who in myth had come from Troy, founded the Roman people and was also the son of Venus. Julius Caesar built the Temple of Venus Genetrix ('Venus the Progenitor') in his Forum which lay just to the north of the main Forum. This story conveniently allowed the first imperial dynasty to pose as having divine origins without its members claiming to be gods themselves, at least during their lifetimes, which would have been a stage too far. The posthumous deification of Julius Caesar was followed by the posthumous deification also of deserving emperors, beginning with Augustus. This concept repositioned the temporal identity of the Roman emperor somewhere between the gods and ordinary mortals by allowing living emperors to pose as the son of a deified predecessor. There were temples also to the cults of individual deified rulers, such as that of the Deified Claudius on the Caelian Hill where it had once overlooked the site of Nero's Golden House.

In the Forum of Rome were also the Temple of Vespasian and Titus and that of the deified Julius Caesar. Today the temple to the deified Antoninus Pius and his empress Faustina is among the most prominent surviving buildings thanks to it being incorporated into a medieval church (San Lorenzo in Miranda) by the seventh or eighth century, among the most prominent original monuments in the Forum. It serves as a reminder of how conspicuous the cults of deceased members of the imperial family could be and the idea that the emperors and their wives could become gods.

Nearby stood the Temple of Vesta which had had a fraught history. Like many major temples in Rome, it was destroyed by fire more than once. During the reign of Tiberius, it went up in flames, no doubt assisted by the presence of the perpetual hearth burning inside it. The emperor's dowager empress mother Livia raced down to encourage soldiers and civilians who were fighting the flames. It was the perfect gesture for an empress the poet Ovid had called 'the Vesta of chaste mothers', a goddess Livia and the Augustan regime had actively identified her with.[12]

The Temple of Vesta burned down again during another major fire in Rome in the reign of Commodus, on this occasion exposing the secret statue of Pallas (the Palladium) reputed to have been brought to Rome by the Trojans. It had to be swiftly taken by the Vestal Virgins up to the imperial palace for safety. The credulous Herodian claimed his generation was the first to have seen it since it had arrived from Troy. Moreover, the statue – regardless of its true age – had been rescued by Caecilius Metellus when the building burned down in 241 BC. According to legend, Metellus had been heading for Tusculum but turned back when two squabbling ravens blocked his way.[13] Fires, accidental or deliberate, were endemic in Rome. Temples with their wooden roofs, and the fires used in ritual, were inevitably particularly vulnerable.

There were also temples to more abstract, but highly politicized, divine concepts. Rome's Forum included a temple to Concordia Augusta, a personification of the Harmony inherent in the rule of

Augustus and transmitted through the person of later emperors. These buildings dominated the centre of Rome. Every person going about his or her business in the city saw and experienced these structures as an indelible part of everyday life, along with the formal ceremonies that went on outside them. The surviving temples of the Forum Boarium, close to the Tiber, give a rare flavour of the smaller scale local examples that must have covered Rome at one point. One, in classical form, was probably dedicated to the harbour deity Portunus. The other is circular and was probably originally dedicated to Hercules. Both are no later than the early first century BC. Of their original benefactors nothing is known now, the temples only having escaped destruction because they were converted into churches.

The major cults were an integral part of the state's identity and were inseparable from it. Martial described what went on after Domitian's campaign in Pannonia in 92:

> While the newly acquired glory of the Pannonian campaign is the universal theme of conversation, and while every altar is offering propitious sacrifices to our Jupiter on his return, the people, the grateful knights, the Senate, offer incense; and largesse from you for the third time enrich the Roman tribes.[14]

Horace would have approved. As far as he was concerned there was a direct cause and effect relationship between traditional piety and Rome's wellbeing. A century before Martial praised Domitian, Horace explained how in the latter part of the civil war of the late Republic he wrote about how the Roman people would pay an endless price for their predecessors' sins unless they restored the burned and crumbling temples, shrines, and statues that had suffered so badly during the decades of civil war, in large part from sheer neglect. The connection in the Roman mindset was obvious. By failing to honour Rome's traditional gods, the powers that had brought Rome an empire, calamities had come about. These included, as Horace pointed out, two major Roman defeats at the hands of the Parthians in 53 (against Crassus) and

40 BC (against Antony) and how Ptolemaic Egypt had taken advantage of the disorder. Cleopatra VII had supported Mark Antony's feud with Octavian, risking the whole Roman world splitting apart. Horace looked back to Rome's struggle with Carthage, wars fought by 'a manly brood of peasant soldiers', and bemoaned how 'our times, teeming with sin, have defiled marriage, our kind and homes'.[15]

Minor and local cults could be sometimes as local as the Lares gods of the street corner in a neighbourhood, represented by a streetside shrine (see Chapter 1). Such guardian deities existed everywhere, especially in homes (see Chapter 3) and business premises. They all belonged to the same tradition as the state cults of stability, security, and continuity, and were treated with the same reverence for ritual and tradition. There was complete freedom to believe in any one or as many as a person wanted, or none.

Martial sold his farm one day but wrote an epigram importuning the new owner to respect the pine trees, the oaks, and the altars dedicated to Jupiter and Silvanus on which countless lambs and kid goats had been sacrificed. He also remembered his devotion to Diana, Mars, and Flora, and wished to be remembered whenever the new owner made his own sacrifices.[16] The personal opportunities and choices for interacting with the gods were limitless, and on any pretext from the profound to the trifling. 'When the loving mother passes the Temple of Venus she prays in whispered breath for her boys, more loudly and entering into the most trifling particulars, for her daughters, that they may have more beauty', said Juvenal.[17]

Many Romans believed that the gods were all around them everywhere, serving as spiritual manifestations of everyday objects like doors, a street corner, a stream or a tree, to the might of Jupiter Optimus Maximus who presided over all other deities and who both protected and directed Rome's destiny. There were also deities like Hilaritas who personified joy and Pudicitia who personified chastity and moral purity, and the divine personifications of places like Roma herself and even the Tiber, as well as the full classical pantheon. Gods even had multiple manifestations. Mars was a god of both healing and war, for example Mars Ultor, 'Mars the Avenger'. Juno was the queen of the gods but was also Juno Moneta, the goddess of the mint.

Rome was filled with depictions of gods in every possible context. These were often private benefactions commemorating something of personal significance. In 58 BC, Cicero was forced into exile in Sicily where he remained until the following year. Before he left, he climbed the Capitoline Hill to dedicate a statue of Minerva, labelled as 'protectress'.[18] Under the late Republic and the emperors most of the coins the Romans handled featured divine figures, sometimes reflecting an emperor's personal preferences. Domitian (81–96), for example, was especially keen on Minerva who appears as a type on many of his coins from the time they were first issued during his father Vespasian's and brother Titus' reigns when he was heir apparent.

Much later, St Augustine looked back from a Christian perspective on what he regarded as the extraordinary Roman habit of having a different god for almost everything, even though Christianity developed a veneration for saints believed to have special powers of influence over divine intervention in specific areas. In particular, Augustine found it amazing that three gods had separate protective duties over a door: Forculus for the doors, Cardea for the hinges, and Limentinus for the threshold.[19] Augustine was intrigued by the idea that no one god could be 'entrusted' with the guardianship of a broad portfolio by 'men who loved a multitude of gods'.

RITUAL

The protection of all pagan cults was sought through the accurate performance of rituals according to custom. Cato the Elder advised on appropriate rituals for propitiating the spirits of woodland groves when the trees were thinned for agriculture.[20] On 25 March came the beginning of the Hilaria festivals which celebrated the mother goddess Cybele. Herodian described the event in the early third century. 'All the tokens of people's wealth and the treasures of the imperial house – items of marvellous material and workmanship – are paraded in honour of the goddess.' Revellers were permitted to dress up as whoever they wanted which turned out to be unexpectedly risky. A disaffected soldier called Maternus who had formed a large and dangerous band of criminals was bent on killing Commodus. He took advantage of the festival to disguise himself as a praetorian soldier so that with his armed compatriots he could make a dash for Commodus and kill him. He was betrayed by some of his own men who disliked the idea of being ruled by a gang leader rather than an emperor. Maternus was beheaded and Commodus resumed the festival, which involved sacrifices and a procession in Hilaria's honour.[21]

Ovid's unfinished *Fasti* recounted the Roman year in religious festivals. He described for 25 April the feast of Robigalia (Robigo: the deity Mildew, an enemy of crops) who had to be propitiated:

> As I was returning to Rome from Nomentum with the light [of that day], a white-robed priest blocked my way in the middle of the road. A *flamen* priest was going to the ancient grove of Robigo to offer up the entrails of a dog and sheep into the flames. I came forward immediately, not to be ignorant of the ritual.[22]

Ovid then proceeds to quote the priest's prayer which implored Robigo 'to spare the sprouting corn ... and take thy scabby hands from off the harvest' among other invocations, and asked Robigo to be satisfied only with the *power* to harm; or, in other words, to desist from using the power. The priest added wine and incense to the entrails which he placed on the fire. Ovid asked him why something as lowly as a dog was suitable. The explanation was fabulously arcane. In myth the dog Maera had led Erigone to the body of her murdered father Icarius. Erigone hanged herself in distress and the dog threw itself over a cliff. Zeus and Dionysus honoured all three in the sky, Icarius becoming Boötes, Erigone was Virgo, and Maera was the star Procyon in the constellation of Canis Minor ('the lesser Dog') and was known as the Icarian dog. The latter first rises in the northern hemisphere in early November, a time associated with the earth being 'parched and dry', causing the crops to ripen too soon. The sacrificed dog was a substitute for the stellar Maera and thus an attempt to offset the problems with drought.

In Roman legend, claimed Ovid, a countrywoman was plagued by a vixen which had killed many of her chickens. Her son caught the animal and killed it brutally by wrapping it in straw and hay and setting the animal alight. The fox raced off through the crops, which burst into flames. At the Games of Ceres (the Cerealia) in March and April, foxes were allegedly punished in perpetuity by attaching torches to their backs and sending them into the circus to die agonizing deaths.[23] This pyrotechnic revenge ritual was a complex tradition with obscure links Ovid was probably unaware of; with only his word for the custom it is unclear where truth gave way to myth and whether it really happened in the way he described. In the Old Testament Samson supposedly destroyed the Philistines' crops by tying firebrands between the tails of 150 pairs of foxes and sending them into fields, vineyards, and olive groves.[24] In either case, it is difficult to imagine how successful anyone could have been at managing to control animals celebrated by the Romans for their cunning and uncontrollability; Vergil used the idea of yoking foxes as a metaphor for something that was impossible, linking it with milking billy goats.[25]

Ovid's tall tales could stand for so many other similar rituals, lost in obscure associations and which were followed year after year in countless locations. Livy endlessly recounted the omens that had materialized and caused alarm. In 99 BC 'when an owl was sighted in Rome, the city was purified', only for another owl to appear the following year, this time over the Capitol. Offerings were made to expiate this alarming incident but a bull being prepared for the occasion dropped dead without warning. On the plus side 'it rained white chalk in the theatre; this foretold good crops and good weather'.[26] Anything that seemed deviant was recorded and scrutinized, whether it involved a meteor falling from the sky, a talking cow, a swarm of bees, a maidservant giving birth to a boy with only one hand, or anything else that looked or sounded peculiar.[27] In many instances the stories must have been hearsay, but they were added to the catalogue just the same.

By such signs, promising or ominous, the Romans ruled their lives. Particularly popular was the examination of entrails of sacrificial victims for appropriate indicators of impending doom or great prospects (see below). Cicero wondered whether the superstitious observations and the attention paid to omens and their interpretation amounted to self-induced imprisonment. A comet was, for example, 'the evil sign of war'.[28]

Not all Romans bought into the culture. Pliny, when describing the power of the Vestal Virgins to stop runaway slaves in their flight (see Chapter 7), said if it was accepted as a truth the gods would listen to prayers or ritual in this instance then one would have to accept it was a universal truth in all contexts.[29] Pliny seemed ambivalent, though, and was disinclined to refute the notion out of hand.

SATURNALIA

For all the theology and ritual, religious festivals were also, and perhaps primarily, about entertainment. They formed the pretext after all for the public spectacles and games (see Chapter 12). The Saturnalia was the great mid-winter festival held in December and inherited by Christianity, but unlike many other festivals it did not involve games or spectacles. Instead, the focus was on making merry in the depths of winter, and a modest reversal of roles. Slaves, for example, in the more enlightened homes might be given a day off while their masters waited on them instead. In its original form the Saturnalia had taken place only on 17 December. As Seneca commented, though, times had changed and the Saturnalia had been allowed to take over the whole month:

It is the month of December, and yet the city is at this moment in a sweat. Licence is given to the general merrymaking. Everything resounds with mighty preparations, — as if the Saturnalia differed at all from the usual business day! So true it is that the difference is nil, that I regard as correct the remark of the man who said: 'Once December was a month; now it is a year'.[30]

The killjoy Pliny the Younger customarily hid in a bedroom apartment in his country villa, enjoying the seclusion 'especially during the Saturnalia when the rest of the building resounds with the row of holiday freedom, for I am not disturbing my household's fun and nor they my work'.[31] Those who were prepared to participate in the festive merriment dressed up, even the emperor wearing the *pileus* liberty cap. Lots were drawn for presents which ranged from trifles like a clothes brush to something more substantive like a pig reared on acorns.[32] As it happens, the Saturnalia was barely over when another festival began, this time the Compitalia, which celebrated the guardian spirits of property boundaries.

THE PRIESTHOOD

The priesthood normally formed part of a suite of honours a man of substance held. It was not a separate profession, but there were several different types of priests. Most were organized into collegia with a fixed number of members. The most senior were members of a college that included the sixteen pontifexes (*pontifices*) and the fifteen flamens (*flamines*). The *pontifex maximus* ('chief priest') or head of the college, was a post adopted by the emperors from Augustus on. The flamen priests were attached to the worship of one god each, starting with Jupiter.

The derivation of the word pontifex puzzled Varro who cited Quintus Scaevola as saying it came from *posse* and *facere* and thus meant 'to be able to do'. His own theory was that it meant 'building of bridges' and came from an early bridge over the Tiber where rituals were held on either side and which required constant repairs.[33] Officials and magistrates also served as priests in various capacities, a prestigious role that formed part of a man's status. Women were also able to hold priesthoods, a rare instance in which they could occupy a formal position comparable to men. Freedmen, who could not hold political posts, still organized themselves into guilds with a religious identity and priesthoods.

Pliny the Younger was appointed to the college of augurs by Trajan. It was a mark of the esteem in which Trajan held him because of its antiquity and also, unlike other priesthoods, once granted it was apparently for life and could not be taken away.[34] An augur's duties consisted of interpreting signs for evidence of the will of the gods, such as the activities of birds, entrails of sacrificial animals, and natural phenomena. Pliny was far more concerned with the importance of the office for a man of his station in wider society. This is borne out by other religious roles which their holders flaunted in Rome or other cities around the Roman world. Marcus Lucretius Decidianus Rufus was a magistrate in Pompeii and had held the duumvirate, the most senior position, several times. Inscriptions recording his impressive civic career listed his offices which included the priesthood alongside the incongruous 'military tribunate', a purely honorary title which had nothing to do with the army. Like his priesthood it was more of a title than anything else.

Marcus Holconius Rufus was an equestrian and therefore an unusual instance in Pompeii of a man with pretensions to the real Roman aristocracy, albeit of the second tier. He was a 'priest [*sacerdos*] of Augustus Caesar' showing that above all holding the post expressed his affiliation to the state.[35] Marcus Holconius Rufus' position in Roman society was nothing when compared to a senator in Rome, but in parochial Pompeii he was an important man. Like all prominent locals, he and his family had a lurking wish to appear considerable in their native place. Rome provided the template. This helps explain the incongruous pretension of his statue, sited close to a major crossroads in the heart of the town, which was probably erected after his death. He was shown as a senator and successful general, despite being neither, on a statue that had clearly been adapted from one that had formerly

315

represented an emperor. The figure, dressed in military costume, had had its bust replaced with that of Holconius Rufus. The unwitting donor was almost certainly the hapless Caligula, whose monuments and statues had been toppled or usurped after his assassination in 41.

No one was going to question the local worthy being reincarnated as an emperor, at least so long as the family clung on to a high profile in the city. For their part the family of Marcus Holconius Rufus and their friends and clients could enjoy the benefits of association. His status in life was thus seamlessly absorbed by them into their own personal standing both then and thereafter. The statue would also have automatically become a landmark in Pompeii, another example of an address detail used to identify the location of businesses and residences and help when giving directions.[36]

At Ostia, Marcus Umbilius Maximinus, ' a renowned boy', was also a 'priest of the Genius of the Colony [of Ostia]', commemorated on a statue base's inscription in the Serapeum which means he was also probably involved in the cult there.[37] Not far away at the Temple of Hercules in a small streetside precinct which included several temples, Gaius Fulvius Salvis, a *haruspex* (soothsayer), made a gift of a relief carved on a piece of imported Greek marble around 150–80 BC that depicted the recovery of a statue of Hercules at the mouth of the Tiber by fishermen. This had almost certainly been the reason behind founding a temple to him in the city. Hercules was also able to provide oracular services through the drawing of lots (*sortes*) and this is shown on the relief too.[38] Fulvius Salvis, whose other roles in Ostia are unknown, clearly had enough resources to be able to pay for the relief. As a haruspex his priestly role was to read the entrails of sacrificed animals (see below, this chapter) and interpret their signs.

CONFUSING CULTS

Roman deities might be confusing to us but even the Romans were little less bewildered by the array of gods and goddesses and their various powers. Cicero was frustrated by theologians who had come up with three different versions of Jupiter's origins, but appeared amused by the contradiction in the name of the sun: Sol. By definition this meant the only one, the sole, solar deity, but he listed five different myths of how the sun god had come into existence. There was also the question of whether gods born to gods by mortal mothers, such as Hercules and Aesculapius, were true gods.[39]

Seneca was intrigued by how and where gods existed, particularly in a natural setting. His feelings help explain why the Romans found it so easy to find gods all around them in every possible place, and also why the Romans had no problem in finding gods everywhere their power extended. He thought a 'sense of wonder' at the sight of an ancient forest was bound to make it seem a god lived there. He went on:

> Any cave with a mountain above where the rocks have been eroded deep into it, hollowed out into an impressively cavernous space caused only by natural forces and not human labour, will strike into your soul a suggestion of something divine. Sources of important rivers are venerated by us. Altars are provided in places where great rivers suddenly escape from their hiding places. Hot springs are worshipped. Pools with water which is dark or bottomless has made them sacred.[40]

Pliny described one such place perfectly. The source of the River Clitumnus (now the Clitunno) in Umbria was a rural shrine which had also become an elegant rural retreat:

> You can count glistening pebbles and the coins, which have been thrown in, lying on the bottom ... Nearby is an ancient temple in which stands a statue of the god Clitumnus, dressed in the splendid robe of a magistrate ... You may examine the innumerable inscriptions written on every wall and pillar surface which honour the spring and the god. Some will impress you, others will make you laugh.[41]

Many Roman shrines, large and small, must have been similarly festooned with messages soliciting favours, such as asking for hideous punishments to be meted out on the pilgrims' enemies, and thanking the gods with offerings and sacrifices.

NEW GODS IN ROME

The Romans were equally sensitive to the needs and interests of new gods whether they were found in conquered territories or had been imported by private individuals. The Christian Marcus Minucius Felix, writing in the third century AD, commented on how one could see nations and empires worshipping their own gods, but that the Romans accepted them all. He thought this was the secret to Rome's success, 'even at the first moment of victory, they worship the conquered gods in captured citadels'.[42] As late as the beginning of the fifth century, Macrobius recorded a traditional veneration even for the gods of Rome's ancient enemy, Carthage.[43] Even so, a Christian writer like Lactantius believed that Roman civilization debased itself by welcoming barbaric gods. This was not a simple expression of unconditional tolerance. The Romans hoped they presented a more attractive prospect to the new gods and could appropriate their protective powers instead.

The result was that worship of novel deities arrived in Rome from all over the ancient world. The most radical were the mystery cults, which initially were dominated by the worship of Serapis and Isis from Egypt, and Mithras from Persia. Traders and soldiers were the most dynamic components in the chain of transmission. Christianity followed these earlier eastern cults and eventually supplanted all of them, but to begin with it was just one more new cult among many in the city.

There was no legal compulsion to worship any one god above another, though making sacrifices to the official cults and the spirit of the imperial house was an essential part of personal loyalty to and recognition of the state. This was important in formal settings and in the army but did not preclude a wider personal choice of other cults.

This was to cause considerable problems with Christians who, unlike other Romans, belonged to a religion that refuted the existence of all other deities. Since these included the imperial cult, to which many refused to swear allegiance even if only for show, they were subjected to episodic bouts of persecution until Christianity was legitimized by Constantine I in 313. Religious intolerance otherwise did not normally exist unless a cult included human sacrifice in its rites. Unfortunately, Christian liturgical practices involving the symbolic eating of the body and blood of Christ gave rise to the idea in some quarters that human sacrifice was involved.

The official cult of the Magna Mater ('Great Mother', in Greek Cybele) began in the later part of the Second Punic War when Rome was almost on its knees following the catastrophic defeats at Trasimene (217 BC) and Cannae (216 BC) by the Carthaginians. The war had dragged on so long that by 213 BC there had already been an outbreak of religious hysteria in Rome with many people turning to foreign cults and abandoning traditional cults. 'Phony priests and fortune-tellers had taken hold of men's minds.'[44] Profoundly rattled by this, the Senate placed an urban praetor in charge of banning the activities. But eight years later with Hannibal at large in Italy, the oracular Sibylline Books were consulted and the advice discovered that bringing in the Magna Mater could rid the Romans of this scourge.[45]

A Roman deputation went to Phrygia to secure the silver cult statue with its head made out of a piece of a meteorite from Pessinus. They brought it home to save Rome on the advice of the Sibylline Books. It took until 191 BC for a temple to house the goddess to be built on the Palatine Hill. The structure was rebuilt several times, including in AD 3, a project commissioned by Augustus. This helped the cult's development over the next century and its importance to Roman culture, the Magna Mater eventually being incorporated into the canon of Roman state cults.[46]

Cybele's lover Atys had been unfaithful to her and in remorse emasculated himself.[47] Her male followers, known as the Galli, did the same to themselves and became another of the curious sights of Rome.

Martial, who called them mutilated, described how one troupe of the priests happened upon a veteran soldier and his good-looking slave on whom they had designs to make one of their own. The slave had the wit to trick them so that they castrated the old soldier rather than him.[48] Martial was clearly fascinated by the Galli and mentioned them on several occasions. In one instance he compared them to a lethal barber he knew of called Antiochus: 'The knives with which, when the maddened troop of Cybele's priests rage to the sound of Phrygian measures, their white arms are lacerated, are less cruel than the razor of Antiochus', and used them as a synonym for someone who had had too much sex and was shrivelled up.[49]

SERAPIS AND ISIS

Egyptian deities were being worshipped in Italy by 105 BC. An inscription from Puteoli records in a matter-of-fact way the building of a wall 'which is in front of the Temple of Serapis', here being simply used as means of locating the plot.[50] Serapis was a conflation of Osiris and the Apis bull, a cult popularized in Egypt mainly by the Ptolemaic pharaohs who followed Alexander the Great). If Isis was not already being worshipped too, she followed soon after and became well-established but not initially among the Roman elite. She had already been absorbed into Greek mythology as the deified Io (the priestess of Hera and mortal lover of Zeus), 'now with fullest service worshipped as a goddess by the linen-robed throng'. Isis was described as such by Ovid with her 'crescent horns upon her forehead' and with her associates Anubis, Bastet, Apis and Osiris – the latter two who had been combined as Serapis by the time of the Ptolemaic pharaohs.[51] Tibullus celebrated Osiris whose 'cunning hand first made ploughs and vexed the young earth with the iron share'.[52] Horace referred to Osiris as a god someone might swear by in everyday speech.[53]

Isis was a mother goddess, and the central mystery that separated her from traditional Roman cults lay in much more ancient Egyptian tradition. Her appeal also lay in the fact that as the principal agency in bringing back her brother-husband Osiris to life she was therefore associated with rebirth and immortality, reinforced by her role as the mother of their divine child Horus, heir of Osiris and a complex deity identified with the sky and the sun and of whom the pharaoh was the living embodiment.

The Serapis cult became immensely popular, especially under Septimius Severus (193–211) and his son Caracalla (211–17). Caracalla was particularly interested in the god, who therefore appears on some of his coins. Minucius Felix one day visited Ostia around that time in the company of a pagan friend called Quintus Caecilius. They took a stroll along the beach, enjoying the sensation of sand between their toes, when Caecilius spotted a statue of Serapis. Caecilius immediately raised his hand to his lips to kiss it and then pressed his hand to the statue to transfer the kiss 'just like the superstitious mob used to do', said Minucius.[54] The fleeting gesture is a vignette of an old pagan practice which was, as so often, transferred to Christianity where it subsists to this day in some countries.

Isis was regarded as a benevolent and compassionate goddess. Her nurturing and maternal interest in her followers was symbolized in her caring for the infant Horus and the way her tears of sorrow at hardship in Egypt caused the annual inundation of the Nile which restored fertility, growth and prosperity. Compared to the often petulant and vengeful classical deities of the Roman pantheon, her appeal was obvious. This was reinforced by the belief that she took a specific interest in each of her adherents, regardless of that person's station in life. The similarities to Christianity are obvious, not least in the Isis-Horus relationship. Her cult formed part of a much wider trend that would lead to the supplanting of paganism in the Roman world. In the meantime, Isis offered hope and solace of a type not available in the state cults, and a different type of relationship with a deity from the conventional transactional one that characterized all other Roman cults from the worship of Jupiter to the spirit of a street corner in Rome.

Mystery cults like that of Isis were associated with collegiate organizations which in the eyes of the Roman authorities were more or less synonymous with dangerous political organizations bent on subverting the state. By 64 BC they had been prohibited. In 52 BC the Senate decreed that any temples of Serapis and Isis were to be demolished, some of which had apparently been erected as private ventures. Even once the deities had been publicly accepted, they were excluded from Rome's pomerium (a defined religious zone within the city).[55] In 48 BC a series of bad omens, including a swarm of bees settling beside a statue of Hercules on the Capitoline Hill, had caused great disquiet especially as sacrifices were being made to Isis nearby at the time. Soothsayers advised that temples of Isis and Serapis be destroyed once more, a decision that implied more had been built in the intervening four years, despite the senatorial decree in 52 BC.[56]

By 43 BC the cults of Isis and Serapis had become sufficiently popular for the triumvirs Antony, Octavian and Lepidus to vote that a temple be built to both gods in Rome. The context and reason for this is not explained other than mentioning that the decision followed in the aftermath of proscribing their enemies in Rome; it was probably a populist gesture designed to endear ordinary people to them. It is also not known whether the temple was ever built but the decision to allow its construction alone must have been taken as official tolerance.[57]

SCANDAL AT THE ISEUM IN ROME

During the reign of Tiberius (14–37) there was a scandal at the Iseum in Rome, according to Josephus.[58] Paulina was a well-known woman of wealth and rank, highly esteemed, and married to a similarly well-respected man called Saturninus. Paulina was also a follower of Isis. An equestrian called Decius Mundus was in love with her, but knew she was beyond his reach. In desperation he offered her 200,000 Attic drachmas (meaning denarii) to sleep with him just once. This futile gesture was rejected, so Mundus resolved to starve himself to death, much to the horror of his freedwoman Ida. Ida insisted to Mundus that for 50,000 drachmas she could persuade Paulina to succumb. Ida went to the temple and promised the priests 25,000 drachmas if they would help. One of the priests visited Paulina, insisting that he had been sent by the god Anubis who was in love with her and wished to see her.

This greatly flattered Paulina, who agreed to visit the Iseum. Her husband acquiesced, believing her to be completely honourable. Paulina dined at the Iseum and then settled down to sleep there, the doors having been shut. Mundus, of course, was already there hiding. He emerged, pretending to be Anubis. The gullible Paulina not only slept with him but also engaged in sexual activity with him all night in the belief he was the god. Mundus then disappeared before the night was up. When she awakened, Paulina reported the manifestation of the god to her husband and her friends who initially refused to believe her, but when they took into account her personal reputation and standing decided her story must be true – somehow the notion of sleeping with the god appears to have been acceptable.

Two days later, Mundus accosted Paulina, unable to restrain himself from flaunting his triumph. He told her she had saved him 200,000 drachmas, but had still performed the service he had wanted, explaining that he had pretended to be Anubis. Horrified, she fled to her husband, told him the truth and begged him to seek redress. Saturninus went off to Tiberius who, appalled, had the Isis priests interrogated, and then crucified them and Ida. For good measure, he also ordered the Iseum to be destroyed and her statue to be thrown in the Tiber. Mundus, oddly, got off with exile on the basis that his crime had only been one of passion.

ISIS ENDURES

Tiberius was generally not keen on imported exotic religions and tried to ban them, focusing especially on Egyptian cults and Judaism. Adherents of either were told to burn their vestments and other religious items. Jews of military age were sent off to the provinces to serve in the army, 'the others of that same race or of similar beliefs he banished from the city, on pain of slavery for life if they did not obey. He banished the astrologers as well but pardoned such as begged for indulgence and promised to give up their art'.[59]

Worship of Isis went on unabated, despite the measures. The Iseum in Rome was rebuilt, and worship of the goddess was once again established later in the first century. The 'bareheaded priests of Isis clad in linen vestments, and the choristers who play the sistrum' were a familiar and distinctive sight by Martial's time under Domitian.[60] Visitors to the Capitoline Hill in Rome today pass a pair of distinctive Egyptian granite lions in either side of the huge staircase that leads up to the summit. They are of Ptolemaic date (the last three centuries BC) and once belonged to a shrine in Egypt. They were brought to Rome, probably by Domitian, to embellish the Iseum and belong to a group of surviving but dispersed sculptures known to have been displayed there.[61]

Today, not far from the Piazza della Minerva in what was once the Field of Mars is a huge male marble sandaled foot by the side of a narrow street called the Via del Pie' di Marmo ('the street of the Marble Foot'). The stone is unidentified but is thought now to have belonged to a colossal statue of Serapis, and which had once adorned the nearby Iseum. Nothing today is visible of the temple, but a small Egyptian obelisk in the Piazza della Minerva was found on its site. Originally from Sais in Egypt, it bears the names of an obscure 26th Dynasty pharaoh called Wahibre who reigned in the early sixth century BC. None of this would have been of the slightest interest to the worshippers. The obelisk and the statue, among the others found in the area which must also have come from the temple, were more of the collection of accessories that gave the Iseum its identity and exotic appeal. It was an excellent example of the way in which Rome displayed its dominance of the world. Triumphal arches were blatant expressions of military power. A building like the Iseum was a subtler illustration of how Rome had absorbed and assimilated other cultures and religions.

With the exception of Christianity, these exotic cults were by no means exclusive when it comes to other deities. The Iseum at Pompeii, for example, featured depictions of other Egyptian deities, also a statue of Dionysus/Bacchus, and in one streetside painting Isis was combined with Aphrodite, the patron goddess of Pompeii.

Two imperial slaves in the reign of Vespasian (69–79) had an interest in the complex web of associations and symbolisms. Spendon Consortianus made arrangements for the burial of a fellow imperial slave called Servandus Agathopodianus in the form of an elegant marble urn with figured decoration. The most conspicuous part of the design was a cloaked putto-like figure opening a basket, a *cista mystica*, from which a snake emerges to the alarm of an eagle.[62] The snake was closely associated with Isis. She was able to protect against snakebites and in myth created a snake to bite the sun god Ra. This made Ra ill, so Isis offeed to cure him in return for being told his secret and true name. Eventually he gave up the name which Isis took to her son Horus to bolster his royal authority.

Vespasian and his son and successor Titus (79–81) had some interest in the worship of Isis, and it seems likely from the decoration on the urn that household staff shared this affiliation. Rome's Iseum appears on a rare coin of Vespasian issued at Rome in 71, the year in which his joint triumph with Titus was held for the Jewish War. Overnight in mid-celebrations the pair spent the night in that temple.[63] The cista mystica was more often associated with Dionysiac/Bacchic mysteries, originating in Greece and therefore an alternative possible and probably more likely association. At the top of the urn in its pediments are two snakes in the style of those that were often seen on the silver cistophori coins struck at Ephesus, flanking a cista mystica on top of which sometimes stood a figure of Dionysus. The urn's decoration also includes a pair of stands, each topped by two heads that resemble those of Cybele's lover Atys.

Isis was believed to watch over the interests of seafarers, celebrated annually on 5 March in the *navigium Isidis* ('the vessel of Isis') with a procession that carried a model ship from a waterway to the temple.

The date marked the commencement of the annual sailing season after winter. Isis was therefore unsurprisingly popular in Ostia. Lucius Valerius Fyrmus was both a priest of Isis and of Cybele at the port town, probably in the second century.[64] There was undoubtedly a Serapeum though it is not recorded until 24 January 127 when it was dedicated, a day that happened also to be Hadrian's birthday.[65] Indeed, most of the evidence for Egyptian cults at Ostia belongs to the second and third centuries. The Serapeum still exists but in a ruinous state, long stripped since late antiquity of most of its original dedications.

Despite the lack of evidence for a temple there, Isis is better known at Ostia than Serapis. Several inscriptions have been found which demonstrate the open following of the cult by persons associated with Ostia's local government as well as imperial officials. Their concentration suggests that the Iseum was in the western part of the town close to the river and thus not far from the Serapeum. One was Publius Cornelius Victorinus, a clerk to the town decurions, who dedicated a statue of Mars to the queen Isis who had 'restored his health', adding that he was an '*Isiacus* and *Anubiacus*', an initiate of the cults of both Egyptian deities.[66] Another dedicant, a woman called Catilia Diodora, belonged to a family associated with the Hadrianic dedication of the Serapeum, and added that she was also a *Bubastiaca*.[67] Bubastis was the Egyptian city at the heart of cult of the feline deity Bastet which had become popular in Graeco-Roman times.

In the middle of the second century, Apuleius wrote his account of the Isis cult and the initiation of a character called Lucius who had had a series of adventures such as being turned into an ass (*The Golden Ass*, sometimes called *The Metamorphoses*). He was to be restored to human form through his induction to the rites of Isis. Clearly based on his own experience, Apuleius painted a picture of watching a celebratory and joyous procession led by women dressed in white, decorated with flowers. They were followed by men and women bearing lights as symbols of the goddess' birth among the stars and after them the initiates who had been admitted to the sacred mysteries. They were the visible evidence of rebirth. Crucially, he observed that these initiates were drawn from people of all ages and from all social classes. The parade involved music from flutes and also the noise from the sistrum rattles, as well as displays of other gods.

This was the occasion when the model ship was dedicated to Isis in return for her protection of seafarers (see above, pp. 325–6). The initiation at the temple where a silver statue represented Isis was presided over by the *pastophori* (the senior priests). The rites featured loyalist prayers for the emperor, the Senate, the equestrians, and the Roman people, marking out Isis as a protectress for the Roman state as much as the general population. The procedure also involved a period of ten days' fasting, now readily identifiable as likely to provoke hallucinations but which at the time were interpreted as evidence of the initiate's enlightenment. 'Lucius' described his spiritual death as the allegorical arrival at the Underworld to be greeted by Proserpina only to be born again into the sunlight.[68]

Not everyone was impressed by Isis worship, especially Christians who rejected anything similar to their own beliefs. The Christian Minucius Felix mocked the way in which Isis among other deities of mystery cults sought what they would find, 'and what they have lost they find'. Despite this, he added, 'once these were Egyptian rites and now are Roman'.[69] That indeed was the point. The cults of Cybele and Isis are examples of how exotic eastern cults were absorbed into Roman cultural tradition.

Isis and Serapis were the vanguard of an increasing interest in Rome in monotheism that would ultimately lead to the adoption of Christianity as the state religion. There was also the cult of the Persian mystery god Mithras which reached Rome, probably via Ostia with traders and returning soldiers.

MITHRAS

The worship of the Persian god Mithras was congregational and held indoors, but was open only to men, and based around an arduous series of initiation rites and a hierarchy of stages.[70] The central mystery was also focused on rebirth but with a different theology to Isis worship. The Roman version of the Mithras cult differed somewhat from its remoter origins in Zoroastrianism and represented an adaptation to new circumstances. Mithras, also identified with Sol Invictus ('the Unconquered Sun'), had killed a primeval bull in a cave. The bull's death had released blood which contained within it the essence of life. It was thus primarily a triumph of good over evil, and life over death. The mithraeum was a small basilican structure intended to emulate the cave. It contained the tauroctony, a standard depiction of Mithras killing the bull with his associates Cautes and Cautopates in attendance, and motifs such as the twelve signs of the Zodiac embellishing the scene, in painted or relief form. Worshippers gathered there to witness the ceremonies about which we know little. They climaxed in a sacred meal that symbolized the original killing of the bull. Aspects of Mithraism disgusted Christians who saw far too many similarities in its rites to their own liturgical practices, but in fact Christianity borrowed freely from the cult.

Thanks to the preference for subterranean settings to help recreate the cave, several well-preserved mithraea have been found in Rome. One lay across a road from the Circus Maximus at its west end. Publius Aelius Ur(banus?) had built it, his name suggesting he or his ancestor was freed during the reign of Hadrian, during the priesthood of Aulus Sergius Eutychus.[71] Gaius Arrius Claudianus, probably a freedman of the Arria family (the clan from which Antoninus Pius came) was the most senior priest (*pater*, 'father', copied by Christians) in the late second-century mithraeum near the Colosseum and now under the church of San Clemente.[72]

The Ostian mithraea (where at least fourteen are known) include a subterranean example under the private so-called Baths of Mithras, containing a tauroctony sculpture in the round made by an Athenian called Kriton. He was almost certainly the same man as the Marcus Umbilius Criton who donated a marble basin to another mithraeum at Ostia. He was a freedman given his liberty by the senator Marcus

Umbilius Maximus, and who may well have been the patron of a guild in Ostia that Criton belonged to.[73] The baths and the mithraeum are likely to have been for the personal use of a guild where religious observations and leisure were an integral part of its organization and hierarchy.

The mystery cults all fell officially into abeyance after pagan worship was proscribed under Theodosius I (379–95). There were many examples of their cult practices and beliefs that were quietly absorbed into Christianity, some silently enduring to this day. Among them are Mithras' birthday (25 December), the Mithraic use of the word *pater* or priests, and the depiction of the holy mother Isis nursing her son Horus on her lap.

READING THE ENTRAILS

Sacrificial victims were treated as a portal to understanding the future. Writing in the early third century AD, Herodian said of omens and entrails that 'the Italians place particular faith in this kind of divination'. The secret of the shape of things to come was enshrined in the state of the dead animal's entrails, sometimes with a serious impact on whether an important event or occasion could proceed. A haruspex priest who found 'a cleft in the lung of a victim' could cause some undertaking, whatever it was, to be 'postponed to another day'.[74]

Cicero had his doubts about the validity of these interpretations.[75] Over a century earlier the comic playwright Plautus had included a scene in his *Poenulus* ('the Little Carthaginian') in which a frustrated pimp gave up on sacrificing lambs to Venus in a futile search for good omens, expressing his irritation at a haruspex who did nothing more than foretell disaster and bankruptcy for him.[76] The joke, of course, was that those paying good money for a promising outcome expected to get just that and it was in the financial interests of the priests to deliver something suitable that their customers (for want of a better word) wanted to hear. In the transactional world of Roman pagan religion this would have seemed entirely reasonable.

Martial recorded what he thought was a hilarious story about a soothsayer, showing that in contemporary Roman culture such priests were sometimes regarded as pompous and self-important figures worth poking fun at. A billy goat was to be sacrificed to Bacchus by a Tuscan haruspex. While engaged in cutting the animal's throat he asked a handy yokel to slice off the animal's testicles at the same time. The priest then concentrated on the job in hand when the yokel was shocked to see a huge hernia exposed, 'to the scandal of the rites', emerge from the goat's body – or so he thought. Anxious to live up to the occasion and observe the religious requirements by removing this offensive sight, the yokel sliced off the hernia only to discover that in fact he had accidentally castrated the haruspex.[77]

Juvenal was disparaging about such practices in a different way, describing how wealthy women would go to a 'Phrygian or Indian augur skilled in the stars and heavens' for answers to their problems, or turn to an elders who was paid 'to expiate thunderbolts'. Poorer women by comparison had to make do with seers who frequented the circus to have their fortunes told.[78] Nonetheless, many people invested a great deal in the belief that reading entrails was a way of ensuring the future. Juvenal, for example, described the popular emphasis on hoping for a wife and children, offering up 'entrails and prophetic sausages' from a 'white pig' in the hope the offspring would have sound minds and bodies.[79]

OMENS AND PORTENTS

Omens were watched out for at any opportunity as a sign of the shape of things to come, for good or ill. They were also sought out retrospectively, especially by historians looking for tales to tell. A solar eclipse or the sight of a circling bird of prey could provoke real fear. In 83 BC, for example, a civil war broke out against Sulla who was then sailing to

Brundisium (Brindisi) where he could land and march against Rome for a second time. Appian took delight in itemizing the portents that had shown what was about to happen. Allegedly 'a mule foaled, a woman gave birth to a viper instead of a child', an earthquake toppled temples in Rome, and a mysterious fire destroyed the Capitol. 'All things seemed to point to the multitude of coming slaughters', commented Appian knowingly, exhibiting the customary credulousness of the time.[80]

Sulla was particularly fond of signs that appeared to foretell his rise to power. In his now-lost Memoirs he had recounted various signs, including how when he went to war against the Italian allies (the Social War) 'a great chasm in the earth opened near Laverna' from which flames erupted, one right into the sky. The soothsayers said this was a sign that a striking-looking man would take over the government in Rome and liberate the city from all its troubles. Sulla decided that thanks to his locks of golden hair it was obvious the man was him.[81] Conversely, Augustus was allegedly preoccupied by bad omens, and had a particular loathing of 'dwarfs, cripples, and everything of that sort, as freaks of nature and of ill omen'.[82] This was in spite of the fact that his daughter Julia had a freedwoman who was said to be the smallest ever known.[83] Conversely some women, especially the wealthier ones, set great store by populating their households with slaves suffering from various physical deformities, with the more extreme the deformity the greater the value.[84]

There was an upcoming omen in 45 and Claudius worried that it might be a bad one. An eclipse of the sun was predicted for his birthday that year (1 August). Claudius decided to publicize the impending phenomenon, adding an astronomical explanation to show that it was a purely natural event and offset any superstitious rumblings. There was indeed an eclipse that day. The path of totality passed over central Africa, so the eclipse was only partial in Italy. In Rome about 21 per cent of the solar disc was obscured by about 0828 hours in the early morning but that would have been enough to excite popular attention into considering its significance.[85]

On 7 October 218 a total eclipse of the sun commenced in south-eastern Gaul. The path of totality passed on over northern Italy, modern Bulgaria and through the middle of Asia Minor (Turkey) and eastern Syria. It was visible as a substantial partial eclipse over most of the Roman Empire. Dio regarded the event, and the appearance of a comet (which can be identified as the one known now as Halley's Comet, estimated to have appeared closest to Earth on 30 May 218), as clear indications that the 'evil and base' reign of Elagabalus had been foretold; but then he was writing with hindsight.[86]

A mysterious portent took place at Livia's home known as Prima Porta on the Via Flaminia. Pliny said an eagle dropped a white hen carrying a sprig of laurel into her lap. Livia kept both on the instructions of the augurs, the chicken proving to be the progenitor of a vast brood. The laurel flourished so that it provided the wreaths for all those celebrating triumphs. This took on great significance within the Julio-Claudian family. Nero, the last Julio-Claudian emperor, took his own life (with assistance) in 68 and the descendants of Livia's hen died along with the laurel. For good measure 'a temple of the Caesars' was struck by lightning. The end was nigh.[87] Nero's death was followed by a year of chaos in which four emperors ruled in succession during the civil war of 68–9.

Like many ancient peoples, the Romans were wedded to the idea that a significant event could be explained by a previous sign. Appropriately enough, they hunted out explanations. Anything 'odd' or that seemed like an aberration might do, despite the lack of any evidence for a direct connection. Pliny blamed the demise of the Julio-Claudians all the way back to the fact that Agrippa had had a breech birth. His name derived from *aegre partus*, 'born with difficulty'. A breech birth was thought to guarantee a problematic life; indeed, in Pliny's view, Agrippa was exceptional in having been a success, though he had suffered lameness as a child. But the real price for his breech birth was the 'unhappiness caused to all the world by his offspring . . . especially the two Agrippinas, who gave birth to the emperors Caligula and Nero (respectively), two firebrands to mankind'.[88] He seems to have changed his mind. Elsewhere, Pliny reported that Agrippina the Younger was said to have two upper right canine teeth, an indication Pliny said (though on what basis is impossible to fathom) of a woman destined to be favoured by fortune.[89] She was to begin with, but since she was killed on her son Nero's orders in 59, Pliny's evaluation of her prospects seems rather flawed.

Writing in his *Alexander, the False Prophet* in the second century, the satirist Lucian was amused at how the highly successful religious charlatan Alexander of Abonuteichos in Bithynia and Pontus, fiddled prophecies that had not been fulfilled so that it looked as if he had been right all along.[90] All that is except the prophecy that he would die at the age of 150, since he expired before he was seventy. Alexander's motivation was, of course, to make money, but he was only one practitioner among many across the Empire.

Superstition was a huge industry which ranged from the large-scale commercial enterprises operated at major cult centres in Rome, other cities, and the countryside, to itinerant fortune-tellers who clearly roamed the countryside. Columella warned that a slave manager of a farm estate should not allow 'fortune-tellers and sorceresses' onto the farm where they would inveigle 'unsophisticated people' into handing over money in return for a useless prophecy.[91] A service on offer was the interpretation of dreams by *coniectores*.[92] These seers toured the countryside, knocking on doors to tout their business among credulous slave staff managing the establishment while the owner was away.

It was no different in Rome. Martial poured scorn on people falling for Cosmus, a notorious 'dotard with staff and wallet', who loitered on the thresholds of the Temple of the Divine Augustus and the Temple of Minerva in Rome. Here 'the crowd, as it meets him, gives him the scraps he barks for', believing that his wretched appearance meant he must be a philosopher from the school of Cynics. No, said Martial, he was 'a dog', playing on the fact that 'cynic' was derived from the Greek word for a dog.[93]

COINAGE AND CULT

Pliny found the division of human virtues and vices into divine person-ifications such as Concord ridiculous and self-serving. He was especially interested how people fixated on Fortuna ('chance') believing her to be the source of all their advantages, and her caprices the cause of their disasters.[94] Other men, Pliny said, took fate a stage further and decided that God cast a die for each man before birth. He concluded, rather unoriginally, that the only certainty was that nothing was certain. He envied animals whose sole concern was food, while human beings worried themselves sick over money, injustice, status, glory and, more than anything else, death.

Roman deities and other divine personifications were the most pop-ular choice of subject for Roman coin reverses to associate them with the state and the emperor. Everyone therefore handled them daily. A popular theme on imperial coinage was the figure of Aequitas, 'equity' or 'fair dealing', suggesting that the Roman state could promise some relief from the unfairness of life. But there were dozens of others from Fortuna to Concord (Harmony), Laetitia (Joy), Pax (Peace), and Spes (Hope). Coin legends linked these notions directly to the person of the emperor. Spes was especially favoured by Claudius because Spes' feast day was 1 August, his birthday.

Coins were a cheap and easy way of making an offering, especially when marking the transition from one zone to another. Crossing a river, for example, was an important part of a journey and it is not uncommon at all to find coins on the riverbed close to Roman crossing points. Careful choice of reverse type, such as Fortuna, shows that the Romans did notice what was on their coins.

Coins are common finds at shrine sites, but the Romans were canny pilgrims. Most coins found on shrine sites are worn. It even seems likely that badly worn coins were sold in bags to pilgrims who could then share them out among family groups. In an era when the coinage system was based on the intrinsic value of the metal in a coin, a badly worn piece had reduced commercial value and so too did contemporary forgeries. It was the thought that counted. The recovery of items such as supposedly 'ritually broken' brooches takes on a different tone if one considers the possibility that using damaged pieces as votive items made more sense than writing off serviceable goods. Countless other items served as votive offerings, such as models of parts of the human body. These appear to have represented limbs or other parts that were afflicted by some disease.

One variant class of Roman coin depicted deified emperors with the prefix *divus*, for example DIVVS AVGVSTVS PATER, 'the deified Father Augustus', on a variety of types struck from Tiberius' reign on. More often, deified emperors only appeared on the coins issued by their immediate successors to commemorate their death and funeral, but there was nothing consistent about this practice. Domitian, for example, issued coins in the names of his deceased brother Titus, his father Vespasian, and his long-dead wife Domitilla, and his niece Julia, the daughter of Titus, all having been deified by him.

Antoninus Pius (138–61) issued a small number of coins in the name of his predecessor, the deified Hadrian, but astronomical quantities in the name of his deceased and deified empress Faustina Senior. This coinage was so prolific that it remains among the commonest in the whole Roman imperial series to this day.

RESILIENT PAGANISM

Engrained cultural habits often die hard. Christianity was supposed to have seen off pagan customs and superstition. Vettius Agorius Praetextatus was a pagan senator in the fourth century, a time when the Empire had officially turned its back on paganism (after Constantine's Edict of Milan in 313 which made religious toleration universal in the Roman world). Although most officials found it expedient to adopt Christianity to secure advancement, some stuck to the old ways which for some time remained legal. The fourth-century aristocrat Agorius Praetextatus served various magistracies, including the prefecture of Rome and as consul, major provincial governorships, and pagan priesthoods – for example in the cult of Vesta and of the sun as well as the augurship. His joint funerary monument also commemorates his wife of forty years, Aconia Fabia Paulina. Her inscription was a conventional epitaph for a loyal, honourable, and chaste woman, but is detailed. It features a reference to how she too was 'initiated in all mysteries', and served as a priestess of Cybele and Atys, among others.[95]

Cultures are often defined by their attitude to death, usually the ultimate expression of religious belief. Ancient Egypt is the supreme example, and the principal cause of a modern fascination with Egyptian culture. Today, most ordinary Romans are only known to us because of their funerary monuments, often bearing the key inscriptions that preserve key details about their lives, for example the baker Eurysaces with whom this book started. The Romans thought a great deal about death and the fragility of human life.

15

FROM ROME TO ETERNITY

*Since the span of life which we enjoy is short, we may make the
memory of our lives as long as possible. For the fame of riches
and beauty is fleeting and frail.*

Sallust[1]

*Of all the blessings given to man by Nature, none is greater than
a timely death.*

Pliny[2]

The Romans knew only too well that death was the great leveller, yet even in death some were more equal than others. Death was treated with great ceremony, especially for the more affluent. Graves are among the most important archives of evidence for individual lives but for much of the period cremation was the favoured (but by no means exclusive) form of burial. Few inhumations are ever recovered with accompanying inscriptions, meaning that physical remains are not commonly available for examination in association with any epigraphic evidence for the person's life.

Funerary monuments were more important than the physical remains of the body, even at the time. They created a public form of

337

immortality, and many have already been discussed in detail. Such memorials guaranteed posthumous prominence and an enduring presence as travellers and traders wandered past. For family members who had made no mark on public life and had thus not been awarded the honour of a statue at state or community expense, these figures made that deficiency good and created a proxy public presence. Portrait sculptures, at least of those who could afford them, displayed suitable qualities and virtues such as a man's *auctoritas* (a form of personal power and authority) and *virtus* (manly vigour), and a woman's virtue and matronly chastity. These effigies had a role to play as participants in the banquets held at the tomb by family members and descendants.

Not a single body of a Roman emperor exists today, or that of any member of the imperial family, even though several imperial mausolea and even tombstones have survived, for example that of Agrippina the Elder, Augustus' granddaughter and mother of Caligula.[3] One reason is that most were cremated, although the bodies of some of the more notorious were destroyed at the time by being thrown into the Tiber. Tacitus described how the body of Nero's empress Poppaea was embalmed and packed with perfumes before being installed in the Mausoleum of Augustus in direct contrast to being 'destroyed by fire, as is the Roman custom'.[4] In general, the physical remains of Romans are elusive. Only excavations, usually of late Roman inhumation cemeteries in the provinces, provide any evidence but these are not usually applicable to Rome. An exception, of course, is the discovery of corpse-shaped voids in the ash and pumice that buried Pompeii (from which casts have been made), and skeletons immersed in solidified pyroclastic mud and lava at Herculaneum, though these are without exception anonymous.

For the impoverished masses, their tomb might only be a pottery jar or box filled with their ashes and inserted on a plot, sometimes intrusively, beside the more grandiose monuments of the better-off. Many corpses were disposed of unceremoniously in communal graves. Martial described on one occasion how 'four branded slaves' carried through the streets a *vile cadaver* ('common corpse') of the type heaped in their thousands on the funeral pyres of the 'wretched'.[5]

The collective result is that it is rare to be able to associate the physical remains of a Roman with a tombstone that might bear specific information about cause of death, age at death, family circumstances and ethnic origin. Tombstones, memorial plaques, or other inscriptions can bear witness to the wide range of places from which the inhabitants of Rome came, but most are fairly perfunctory and often omit this key information, probably because of cost. Many Roman names are simply too conventionally Roman to help. For example, those who became citizens by being freed added their former masters' names to their own and unless a personal name can be specifically associated with a place we have no idea where they came from; even then that could involve making an assumption that in any one case might be wrong. Publius Claudius Abascantus ended up a prominent citizen of Ostia. Were it not for a dedication he set up in which he tells us he was a freedman of the Three Provinces of Gaul we would know nothing about his origins (see below, this chapter for Gaius Annaeus Atticus, another man from Gaul).[6]

Soldiers are often more helpful with information about their origins, especially veterans who ended their lives in Rome. Caius Vettius Collina Nigrus was a veteran of the XII legion Fulminata who settled in Rome, where his tombstone was found. The text tells us he died aged fifty-seven and was from Antioch in Syria.[7] Aurelius Mucianus, another veteran, came from Thrace.[8] Titus Flavius Maximus served thirty-three years in the imperial fleet at Misenum and lived to the age of sixty, and was buried in Rome where he presumably lived in retirement. Like many members of the Roman navy, he was an Egyptian, specified on his tombstone, but we know from other evidence that such men were made to give up their Egyptian names and adopt a Roman one in service. Without their tombstones or other documentary evidence their Egyptian origins would be lost.[9]

Slaves, unless they belonged to important and wealthy households, in general left no surviving monuments, denying us the chance to gain a fuller picture of the ethnic balance or bias among the wider population. Some had accumulated enough resources to join a burial guild (see below, this chapter). The best most of them could hope for was for their ashes to be interred in a reused amphora or jar buried in the ground outside the tomb of their master and his family, their names recorded in terse epitaphs like 'Helle, slave girl. She lived four years', who was buried at Pompeii.[10] Few are likely even to have enjoyed that modest privilege. The text is unusual in specifying that she was a slave. It is likely that tombstones recording only a single name were often those of slaves.

For those slaves owned by the imperial family, the prospects were better. Along the Via Appia outside Rome was the so-called *columbarium Liviae* ('columbarium of Livia'). This was the burial place of the cremated remains of more than 1,100 slaves and freedmen on the imperial staff from the reigns of Augustus to Claudius. Around ninety were once in Livia's service, among them doctors, dressers, footmen and craftsmen. This expression of *noblesse oblige* afforded her staff posthumous honour and allowed them to continue the status of their employment after death.[11] Even so, the information is minimal. Eros was a doctor on her staff. From his name we can guess he was Greek (which we might have assumed from him being a doctor anyway), but his origins are unmentioned on the memorial text, as is his age at death, and, of course, there are no physical remains.[12]

LIFESPANS

A common assumption today is that people in the past necessarily lived shorter lives than they do in developed countries now, thanks to most diseases being untreatable, poorer nutrition, and greater dangers. This was only partly true. Set against the bigger picture of human evolution, the two millennia or so that separate us from the Romans are certainly not enough to account for changes in absolute life expectancy. The Romans had the potential to live as long as anyone

Trajan's Markets, flanking the Via Biberatica, built into the Quirinal Hill on the eastern side of Trajan's vast new forum built from the spoils of his Dacian war. Rows of commercial premises were laid out in a semicircle that respected the eastern exedra of his forum. Although the forum and basilica have largely been lost or remain buried, the market structures remain well preserved. Part has been used for a modern museum. c. 106–117.

Ostia, public latrine at the forum. A rare survival of this essential urban facility. There were no cubicles. Waste dropped into a leat below. Clean water flowed in from an aqueduct around the floor into which patrons dipped sponges to clean themselves. This water flowed into the lower leat along with other water that washed the solid and liquid waste on into the sewers and presumably the Tiber or the sea. Rome would have been replete with numerous similar arrangements. Second century AD.

Coin reverse designs were used for state messaging, often with deities and divine personifications. Top row: Spes (Hope), 41 (Claudius); Roma 64 (Nero); Minerva 80 (Domitian); Salus (Health of the Emperors) 162–3 (Marcus Aurelius and Lucius Verus). Second row: Victory c. 80 (Vespasian, posthumous under Titus); Laetitia (Joy) 219 (Elagabalus); the Faithful Army 238–9 (Gordian III); Mars Propugnator (defender of Rome) 243–4 (Gordian III); Aequitas (Equity) 245–7 (Philip I); Uberitas (Fruitfulness) 250–1 (Trajan Decius). Third row: Fortuna with her rudder and globe 151–2 (Antoninus Pius); the Dioscuri 211–206 BC; Felicitas Publica (Public Happiness) 73 (Titus, as Caesar); the Aqua Marcia (aqueduct) of 144 BC commemorated in 56 BC; Romulus and Remus and the Wolf 142 (commemorating Rome's first millennium under Antoninus Pius). Bottom row: Temple of Jupiter Capitolinus, Rome, 78 BC; Securitas Perpetua (perpetual security) 281–2 (Probus). All struck at Rome except the last, at Ticinum.

Triumphal procession, terracotta relief from Rome. Triumphal processions amounted to spectacular street theatre and reinforced a sense of superiority and entitlement among the population of Rome. Here a pair of barbarian captives, probably Dacians, are displayed chained in a cart pulled by horses as part of a parade of prisoners and spoils. Probably Trajanic, c. 107.

Wall-painting panel from Pompeii depicting a pair of lovers, perhaps just married. The man is by convention shown with darker skin, the woman as pale and thus implying she was chaste and protected within her family household. She entertains him with a lyre. Mid-first century AD.

Antistius Sarculo was a priest who apparently fell for one of his female slaves. His solution was simple: he freed and married her. She became Antistia Plutia. Their funerary monument, which was erected for them by two more of his freedmen, shows the two as an austere and elderly couple. c. 30–10 BC.

The mysterious tomb on the Via Appia of Gaius Rabirius Hermodorus, freedman of
Gaius Rabirius Postumus, Rabiria Demaris (possibly his wife and also a freedwoman), and Usia Prima,
priestess of Isis. Although the first two can be stylistically dated to the mid-1st century BC and their
connection to the minor nobility Rabirii family, Usia appears to be unrelated. The stylistic differences,
for example her hair, and the lettering in her name, suggest the third original figure has been re-carved
to show her a century or more later. In other words, the tomb had simply been hijacked for Usia
by obliterating an earlier occupant. This was a common practice.

Ostia. Tombstone of Titus Flavius Crathis, an imperial freedman, and Flavia Sosuza, his slave
and freedwoman (and presumably wife), and their freedmen and freedwomen. By the fourth century
the stone had been removed from the tomb, which had probably fallen into ruin, to the city's House of
the Porch where it was reused as a drain cover with perforations cut through the text. No effort
was even made to conceal the surviving lettering (this displayed stone in situ is a cast of the original).

Gladiators. A painting of a bout in the arena from the tomb of the aedile Marcus Vestorius Priscus, just outside the Vesuvian Gate at Pompeii. Vestorius Priscus had probably laid on gladiatorial events in Pompeii's amphitheatre to encourage voters to support him. This was typical of his class, emulating the emperor's entertainments in Rome and before then those of the senators and imperators of the late Republic. First century AD before 79.

Theatre of Marcellus, Rome. Begun by Caesar and completed by Augustus in the name of his deceased nephew and former intended heir Marcellus. The building is the only theatre in Rome with any meaningful extant remains. The stage and seating area, or what remains of them, are still buried. Apartments occupy the upper part. Such venues featured entertainments ranging from tragic and comic plays to musical performances, pantomime, and other diversions.

Temple of Portunus (a harbour god), Forum Boarium, Rome. Apart from the Pantheon, this is one of the most complete ancient structures in Rome. It was converted into a church in the ninth century but restored to its ancient appearance in the Fascist era. In recent years it has been heavily restored, and much stonework replaced. Built c. 80–70 BC, replacing an earlier structure.

Rural shrine in a fantasy setting, Villa San Marco, Castellamare di Stabiae. Romans of all classes loved indulging dreams of rustic bliss. Wall-paintings were a popular way of creating trompe l'oeil scenes of a mythologized depiction of the countryside. Mid-first century AD before 7⁹

The three surviving columns of the Augustan-date Temple of Castor and Pollux in the Forum. Like all such temples, the building fulfilled several roles. It served as an art gallery and was home to commercial premises. Among the latter was a cobbler's where a raven lived. The bird was a superb mimic and shouted out the names of members of the imperial family during the reign of Tiberius. It was later killed by a rival cobbler who resented the attention the raven attracted.

Frigidarium (cold room) of the Baths of Diocletian, Rome. Although restored and modified (including raising the floor) by Michelangelo in 1563–6 to convert the ruins of the frigidarium into the church of Santa Maria degli Angeli, the building today gives a good idea of the vast enclosed space contained by Roman public baths, and of the natural light creeping in through the attic vault windows. Originally completed and dedicated in 305–6.

Tomb memorial of Pomponius Hylas and his wife Pomponia, made of stucco and a mosaic using glass tesserae. The couple shared their underground burial chamber a few metres from the Via Appia with at least eighteen other burials of unrelated people. All were cremated and deposited in urns. The likelihood is that they were all members of a burial club and paid subscriptions to maintain their right to a place. The association may have been a private concern, a business run by a third party, or operated on behalf of a commercial guild. There would have been a surface monument but that is long lost. Early first century AD.

Mosaic from a house in Pompeii (Region I Insula 5, building 2). On the left are symbols of wealth and on the right, poverty, suspended from a balance. The skull symbolizes how death will come to rich and poor alike.

today, and indeed centenarians are recorded, as we have already seen in Chapter 12. The early Roman statesman and military leader Lucius Quinctius Cincinnatus was around eighty-nine when he died in c. 430 BC. Augustus lived to his mid-seventies, his wife Livia to her mid-eighties. There were others, recounted by Pliny, such as Clodia, wife of an equestrian jurist called Ofilius, who allegedly clocked up 115 years after a life during which she had borne fifteen children (her lifespan is surely an exaggeration but she might have reached ninety to a hundred years).[13] The truth is that far fewer had the opportunity to live that long compared to the modern world.

Old age held no attractions for some Romans. Seneca viewed his own decline with a mixture of fascination and resignation. He wrote to his friend Lucilius, 'I was just lately telling you that I was within sight of old age. I am now afraid that I have left old age behind me. For some other word would now apply to my years, or at any rate to my body, since old age means a time of life that is weary rather than crushed. You may rate me in the worn-out class, – of those who are nearing the end.'[14] Seneca appreciated that his mind at least was intact and looked forward to a gradual fading away. In an earlier letter to Lucilius he told of how annoyed he had been to see that a house of his was falling down and needed repair. His bailiff pointed out that Seneca had built the house originally, and it was simply a question of age. Seneca wondered what must be happening to his own body since it was the same age as the dilapidated house, only to discover that plane trees he had planted were also decaying.[15]

Juvenal's painfully graphic description of old age is even more uncomfortable today in an age when ever more people live on into their dotage, constantly brought down by disease and discomfort, waning or lost faculties, and worst of all, dementia. He wondered why people prayed for longevity more than anything else when 'how great, how unceasing, are the misfortunes of old age?' He graphically described the sagging features, the 'wrinkles like those of a mother baboon', and how all young men look different but all old men the same, 'their voices shake like their limbs, their bald heads, and their noses dribbling as they had in childhood'. Even the pleasures of music are destroyed by deafness. Cold all the time except when feverish, the old man is plagued by innumerable diseases of all sorts coming at him from all sides. 'But worse than loss in body is the failing mind which forgets the names of slaves and cannot recognize the face of an old friend who dined with him last night, nor those of the children whom he has begotten and reared.' The final price of a long life was to bury his children, his wife, his brothers and sisters, and only to be able to look at their burials.[16]

Juvenal painted an irremediably gloomy image of advanced age, but he wrote at a time when anyone who lived into their sixties and beyond represented only a small part of Roman society and which became rapidly smaller, the longer they lived. An extended Roman life was therefore only too liable to feature one tragedy after another. Moreover, there was little in the way of treatment to mitigate the effects – failing sight and hearing being but two examples which today are relatively easily helped.

Pliny the Younger's friend Spurinna, who had reached his seventy-seventh year, had his own way of coping. Pliny was greatly impressed by the old man's 'peaceful and orderly' routine. This began by spending the morning in bed until the second hour. He then rose and went for a 3-mile (5 km) walk, often in conversation with his friends to stimulate his mind. An alternative was to be read to, even though both his sight and hearing were sound. In the afternoon he went for a ride in his carriage with his wife or a friend before exercising as a preamble to his bath at the ninth hour in winter and the eighth in summer. Another reading followed before dinner. Pliny hoped he would be able to follow a similar lifestyle in old age though as far as we know this did not happen; he probably died during the reign of Trajan, while still in post as governor of Bithynia and Pontus in his mid-fifties.[17]

The wealthy could, of course, afford to soften the blow of old age, especially if the elderly person was a member of a large extended family. In an era with no welfare state and the concept of a government pension unimaginable, the prospects for those who had the misfortune to be both poor and long-lived were not promising. Claudia Quinta made an offering to the gods for the sake of her paedagogus and 'guide' Gaius Julius Hymetus.[18] Hymetus, who was Greek and had clearly been freed, had become her legal guardian when she was orphaned. He had become an *aedituus* ('sacristan'), which means he was a temple-keeper and took care of the building and its contents. Hymetus was responsible for a temple on the Quirinal Hill to Diana, known as Diana Planciana because it had probably been dedicated in 55 BC by the curule aedile Gnaeus Plancius. Another paedogogus, a freedman called Gaius Gargilius Haemon, proudly said on his tombstone that he had been poor but had lived without incurring debts.[19]

Claudia Quinta had made sure her old guardian was provided with employment to see him through later life. She had also remembered Hymetus' brother Epitynchanus, her nurse's daughter Julia Sporis, and all her freedmen and freedwomen. The reference to Hymetus is only fleeting but paints a poignant picture of the loyal old family retainer going about his daily duties at the temple, letting people in, keeping an eye on them, seeing to everyday maintenance in his quiet corner in Rome, and earning a modest and respectable stipend in the latter days of his life.

Untreatable disease, accidents, childbirth, violence, and the brutality inherent in a society that relied on mass slavery and killing for mass entertainment meant that there were countless chances of dying young. The inscriptions on tombs and burials are obviously selective in the sense that they depend on someone commissioning the text and the chances of its survival. They record deaths from infancy and right on into old age, but rarely the cause of death. Since the body of the deceased is not usually available there is no chance of finding out anything more.

One exceptional instance was that of a small girl, aged no more than eight, who was embalmed and buried just outside Rome by the Via Cassia which headed north through Etruria. The child had rickets and was interred in or beside a marble sarcophagus during the mid-second century. Given the taste for Nilotica in Rome, it is possible that embalming had become an option, albeit probably an expensive one, for those unable to contemplate the physical destruction of the deceased's remains. There are other instances of mummified bodies being found at Rome. Mummification was still used in Graeco-Roman Egypt, though the techniques employed were poor compared to earlier in Egypt's history. It is possible that Romans who had lived and worked in Egypt for part of their careers came back with the intention of being mummified.[20] Nonetheless, the practice remained rare.

Lucretius' seminal work *On the Nature of Things* explored among other topics the idea that all living matter is made up of atoms, a suggestion which went back to fifth-century BC Greece, and which had been expounded also by Epicurus. Lucretius explained that death did not kill the atoms or the compounds in which they had been combined. The atoms were merely broken apart by death and would then join together with other atoms to create something new. He showed a piercing and modern sense of regeneration, and the idea that the force of life was constantly carried on that way, using as a metaphor the image of a new-born baby crying at a funeral. 'That also which once came from earth, to earth returns back again.'[21]

CONDOLENCES

When someone died, the occasion was usually treated with the same sadness and grief found at any other time in human history. Cicero's daughter Tullia died in 45 BC. A month later, on 9 March, he was still trying to come to terms with the loss by taking himself to a remote forest setting. There he isolated himself with books but constantly broke off to weep.[22] Around this time, he received a letter of condolence from a senatorial colleague and jurist friend called Servius Sulpicius Rufus. There is no doubt that the letter is sincere, but it was also a form of literary exercise, in which Sulpicius Rufus explored grief and how best to deal with it. He deeply sympathized with Cicero but was also keen to urge him to accept that Tullia's mortality was inevitable at some point, and of no consequence when set against the colossal losses of the recent civil war of the late Republic. She had been a wife, a witness to her father's celebrated career, and enjoyed life. He reminded Cicero of the advice he would have given to someone else, that time would soften the blow, but it was beneath Cicero to sit around waiting for that time to come.[23] The letter was thus underpinned by Stoic philosophy, 'even she had not died now, by being born a mortal she must nevertheless have died a few years from now'. This reads harshly to our eyes, but Cicero and Sulpicius Rufus lived at a time when experiencing the deaths of younger family members was commonplace. Finding ways to accept what could not have been avoided or undone was an important way of coping.

Pliny the Younger was greatly distressed by the death of his friend Corellius Rufus who had taken his own life in his sixty-seventh year. Pliny described his grief as 'inconsolable', contrasting it with death from disease which one could more easily accept as 'inevitable'. This was in spite of the fact that Rufus had clearly committed suicide as a form of euthanasia, thanks to suffering from a disease that caused him so much pain he could not face going on.[24] The death of a senator called Junius Avitus caused Pliny equal despair though in this case it seems to have followed a period of illness which Pliny had known nothing about because he had been away – the effect was to cause him to stop everything he was doing: 'I can think and speak of nothing else right now.'[25]

On another occasion Pliny the Younger reported the unusually tragic coincidence of two daughters of Gaius Helvidius Priscus who died in labour after both giving birth to girls. They were 'noble young women ... the victims of their motherhood'. They may well have been still in their teens. Helvidius Priscus, of whom Pliny had been fond, appears to have been executed by Domitian in c. 93. His father, of the same name, was a Stoic philosopher who had been executed by Vespasian for refusing to acknowledge him as emperor. Now only a son was left to carry on the family, which was some comfort to Pliny.[26]

Gaius Futius Onirus, a magistrate in the city of Crotone in the boot of Italy, left 10,000 sesterces to the city councillors. He was determined not to forget his deceased daughter Futia Lollliana and not to let his city do so either. The interest on the money was supposed to cover the cost of them gathering for a party on her birthday. Another 400 sesterces were provided for a public gathering, with 200 more to be distributed, Futius Onirus sternly warning that the money was not to be put to any other use.[27]

Unlike these family tragedies, when Nero committed suicide the reaction was mixed. 'Such was the public rejoicing', said Suetonius, 'that the people donned liberty caps and ran round all over the city.' But Nero had been popular with some of the general public who enjoyed his common touch and theatrical antics, as well as the way he ran rough-shod over senatorial traditions. Some of his fans propped up statues of him on the rostra in the Forum and pretended news of his death had been greatly exaggerated. When pretenders emerged who claimed to be Nero, they soon found eager followers, desperate to believe their hero was indeed still alive.[28]

FUNERALS

Death, at least for a family of some means, was likely to be followed by the laying out of the dressed corpse in the public part of the home for up to a week during which time it could be visited by mourners. The Tomb of the Haterii, found on the Via Labicana at Rome, had a marble relief showing a deceased affluent woman on a couch serving as a bier displayed in the house's atrium.[29] The tableau, which formed part of a narrative series, featured plenty of action underway to highlight the deceased's generosity. Along with other detail, a musician played a flute by the corpse's feet as her children beat their chests in mourning while three freed slaves sat by the bier to honour their mistress for granting them their liberty. Burning torches flickered nearby along with more figures in a state of mourning. Another figure read out her will, which in another little scene she was shown composing. Of course, there was a rhetorical element to the composition. We have no idea whether she was as depicted, or even her name. The only clue is the scene showing a large crane beside a temple-tomb which might suggest she and her husband owned a construction business and were probably freed slaves.

Sulla's funeral in 78 BC involved vast quantities of spices, all contributed by his fans among the women of Rome. Enough was left over to make an effigy of the former dictator out of frankincense and cinnamon. Hs ashes were laid to rest in the Field of Mars, accompanied by his self-penned epitaph in which he said he had exceeded his friends in doing good and his enemies in doing harm.[30]

Funerals were costly affairs, especially for the elite. An otherwise unknown member of the patrician Scipio family, Scipio Serapio, died in office but was down on his luck, perhaps because of the costs incurred in securing his election. At any rate, he was so popular with the plebs that they had a whip-round for small change among their number to pay for Serapio's funeral and lined the route to scatter flowers as the cortège passed.[31] The occasion was an interesting instance of deferential ordinary people being prepared to stump up the necessary cash so that an aristocrat could be buried with the pomp appropriate to his rank.

The lying-in-state over, the body was carried in a procession to the place of burial. The surviving family members of a well-to-do household went first to the cupboard containing the wax masks of the honoured ancestors which they individually wore or carried in the procession.[32] In this guise they revived the ancestors by speaking their words and acting out their deeds, including those of the person being buried. It seems that even actors could be hired to play the parts and such occasions did not need to be po-faced affairs. One called Favor wore Vespasian's mask at his funeral and took the opportunity to make a humorous reference to the emperor's legendary stinginess by pretending to find the expense of the funeral absurd.[33]

If a cremation was to take place, which was normal until the third and fourth centuries AD when inhumation become more commonplace, the body was burned at or near the place of burial. When the body had been destroyed the ashes and remaining fragments (it was almost impossible to reach the temperatures necessary to reduce it entirely) were gathered up and placed in a suitable receptacle which could be a vessel of almost any type depending on the funds available. The richest might be placed in a casket made of precious metal, the poor in a pottery jar. When Pompey's daughter died in childbirth, she was accorded the special honour of being buried in the Field of Mars, later home to the Mausoleum of Augustus where the first emperor and some of his family members were buried.[34]

Not everyone watched a funeral procession with sympathy and sadness. For some, the occasion marked an opportunity. Rufa of Bononia (a city in northern Italy), the wife of Menenius, who was known for fellating her 'dear Rufus', had a reputation for helping herself to meat and bread from funeral pyres and being attacked by the undertaker's slave for doing so, or so Catullus claimed.[35] Rufus, incidentally, struggled to find other female company thanks to his appalling body odour that made him smell like a goat.[36]

FUNERAL OF AN EMPEROR

Imperial funerals were effectively another form of public entertainment and involved grand spectacle which ordinary people looked on in awe. Josephus mentions that Caligula gave Tiberius 'a splendid funeral in the old Roman fashion'. This had included, according to Suetonius, a grand oration delivered by a tearful Caligula. Dio says the body of Tiberius was sneaked into Rome under cover of darkness, but also describes the public funeral. In his version, though, Caligula used the oration to talk about his father Germanicus and his great-grandfather Augustus, thereby reminding the people of his own esteemed lineage.[37]

Both Dio and Herodian wrote accounts of imperial funerals. Dio described how Septimius Severus honoured the murdered emperor Pertinax, whose name he added to his own. Pertinax was commemorated with a shrine, mentions in prayers and oaths, and a golden image on a carriage pulled into the Circus Maximus by elephants. Severus did not arrive in Rome until several months after the death of Pertinax on 28 March 193, following the intervening reign of Didius Julianus. Pertinax's corpse had been decapitated by his killers, but the fate of his remains is unknown; they must have been long disposed of by the time Severus arranged his funeral.[38]

Dio was more than an eyewitness: as a senator he took part. His account includes remarkable detail of the showcase event. A waxen effigy of Pertinax, accompanied by a good-looking young man with a feather to wave away flies, was placed in an elaborate shrine of gold and ivory on a wooden platform. Severus, the senators, and their wives were treated to a procession. The senators sat in the open air, their wives protected from the sun by being seated in porticoes. Dio went on:

> There moved past, first, images of all the famous Romans of old, then choruses of boys and men, singing a dirge-like hymn to Pertinax; there followed all the subject nations, represented by bronze figures attired in native dress, and the guilds of the City itself – those of the lictors, the scribes, the heralds, and all the rest. Then came images of other men who had been distinguished for some exploit or invention or manner of life. Behind these were the mounted troops and infantry in armour, the racehorses, and all the funeral offerings that the emperor and we senators and our wives, and the corporations of the City, had sent. Following them came an altar gilded all over and adorned with ivory and gems of India. When these had passed by, Severus mounted the rostra and read a eulogy of Pertinax. We shouted our approval many times during his address, now praising and now lamenting Pertinax, but our shouts were loudest when he concluded. Finally, when the bier was about to be moved, we all lamented and wept together. It was brought down from the platform by the high priests and the magistrates . . .

From there, the mourners moved on to the Field of Mars where a three-storey pyre had been erected, topped off with Pertinax's favourite gilded chariot. The effigy of Pertinax was installed and his relatives, together with Severus, kissed it. Magistrates and equestrians paraded along with the soldiers, mounted and foot, who acted out manoeuvres of peace and war. Finally, the consuls set light to the pyre and 'when this had been done, an eagle flew aloft from it. Thus was Pertinax made immortal.'[39]

Herodian added some useful colour to what was probably the same occasion which amounted to a form of entertainment and spectacle that lasted seven days. An unusual aspect of the rites that Herodian described was how the imperial effigy was treated as the living emperor in his final days. Doctors would go up every day and attend to it, pretend to make an examination and pronounce that the emperor was in the process of dying. Once it was finally announced the effigy had 'died', selected young men of senatorial status together with the most senior equestrians carried the couch to the Forum and set it down in front of the rostra where two choirs in stands, one of women and another of children, sang hymns and incantations. From there it was carried north to the Field of Mars to the highly decorated wooden pyre (see above).[40]

INFANT MORTALITY

There was little anyone could do about a high level of infant mortality, or women dying in childbirth (see above). Sextus Pompeius Justus, likely to be the man of this name who was consul in the year 14 at the end of Augustus' reign, buried his unnamed son (it was probably the same as his father's) and his daughter Pompeia. In the funerary text inscribed on their tombstone by the Via Appia he bemoaned how they had predeceased him and his sadness at having to set their pyre alight; he hoped to be reunited with them soon.[41]

The emperor Marcus Aurelius and his wife Faustina the Younger had more than a dozen children of whom only five lived to adulthood. One, and the only boy to live, was the degenerate emperor Commodus whose twin brother died aged four. Of course, most of the babies who expired as infants have left no trace, but it is safe to assume that most fertile women had to experience some or even most of their children dying before adulthood, with perhaps overall only half or less living to have children of their own. Cornelia, mother of the Gracchi brothers Tiberius and Gaius, had twelve children but only three lived to adulthood.[42]

There were some fortunate exceptions. Quintus Metellus Macedonicus had six children but along with his eleven grandchildren's spouses (all but one were married), he could count twenty-seven people who called him 'father'. On 9 April 5 BC, during the reign of Augustus, Gaius Crispinius went to the Capitol in Rome to make a sacrifice. He had made a journey from his home in Fiesole, just outside Florence, accompanied by his six sons and two daughters, twenty-seven grandchildren and eighteen great-grandchildren, and eight wives of the grandsons.[43]

There are numerous other examples of Romans experiencing the tragedy of burying their children. Sextus Rufius Achilleus died aged seven months and nine days. 'Sextus Rufius Decibalus made this for his most sweet son', recorded his father on the marble tombstone he commissioned for the child. It was decorated with a carving of Mercury depicted as a child and clearly conceived as a representation of the infant.[44] This tragic relic shows that even in an age of chronic infant mortality, the death of a child was still almost impossible to bear. Harmonius Ianuarius and his wife Clodia Trophime experienced the tragedy of losing their two daughters in succession. They were beside themselves with grief when they buried the second, Harmonia Rufina, when she was thirteen years, six months, and twenty-six days: 'We, the parents, hope to hasten to you ... nor would we hesitate to give up this troublesome life', they said on her tombstone, clearly having been reduced to total despair by the loss of their children.[45]

These monuments were sometimes not what they seem. One memorial from Rome depicts a child that looks like a boy aged around ten to twelve in a panel between two pilasters and surmounted by a pediment. The Greek inscription, however, commemorates a small girl called Agrippina, aged three. There was a thriving trade in pre-fabricated funerary monuments which means that even those which correspond with the details of the deceased are not necessarily por-traits and sometimes obviously not so. In this instance, regardless of the intended gender shown, the carving is of a much older child than Agrippina is described as. It must have been bought off the shelf, per-haps with the intention of suggesting how she might have appeared, had she lived.[46] Either way, it is a warning not to interpret these memo-rials too literally.

For poor or slave children and young people of any class, a prema-ture death was all too likely a prospect. There are countless instances of such untimely demises, but in some cases the archaeological evi-dence illustrates just how the disadvantaged lost out. A cemetery of the second century AD at Casal Bertone just outside Rome between the Via Tiburtina and the Via Praenestina was associated with an industrial complex identified as either a laundry or a tannery. The 166 burials found there, unusually inhumations which made it possible to analyse the remains, showed that significant permanent skeletal damage had been caused to both upper and lower limbs, with most of the bodies showing a reliance on female child labour for a large part of the workforce.[47] This is unsurprising, since such oppressive and dan-gerous working conditions have been the norm throughout much of human history, and continue to be so in large parts of the world today.

Among the most striking aspects of the Casal Bertone human remains is that the high rate of attrition among females under thirty was inevitably balanced by the dominance of deceased males among those of older ages. The figures probably reflect industries where girls were preferred, and the consequences of the work for their life expec-tancy, doubtless exacerbated by the risks of childbirth. Only 10 per cent of the bodies were estimated to be those who had reached at least forty years of age, while only a fifth of the burials contained any grave goods, an indication of the impoverished existences the deceased had experienced. Such contexts are likely to have been matched across the

Roman world and the rest of antiquity, just as they would have been among the slaves of the Old South or the mill workers of Manchester in the early 1800s and untold numbers of other places.

TOMBS

There was a massive contrast between the funerary monuments of the wealthy and the communal columbaria tombs shared by dozens of the deceased as repositories for their cremated remains. Within the city itself are the vast imperial mausolea built by Augustus and Hadrian for themselves and their descendants. Tombs played a central role in the annual *Parentalia* festival when the family would go out to dine in the company of the deceased (see p. 359). Ancestor worship was of huge importance, effigies of forebears being displayed in the family house and paraded in memorial ceremonies to remind the family of the great achievements of those who had come before them. In time these all gave way to the Christian catacombs of Rome and the veneration of the martyrs and saints.

Rome's celebrated sights still include today the tombs of the Via Appia, known now as the Via Appia Antica. Like most Roman roads radiating out from the city it was lined with tombs, some of which have survived. The most prominent now is the drum Tomb of Cecilia Metella which stands on a hill close to the third milestone south of the city. She probably died during the earlier part of the reign of Augustus and had been married to a supporter, Marcus Licinius Crassus the younger (d. 49 BC).[48] She was also the daughter of an ex-consul who had won a victory in Crete in 62 BC and been awarded a triumph. The substantial 11-metre (about 36 ft) high drum-shaped mausoleum sits on a prominent hill and survives because it was converted into a fortress in the twelfth century. The commemorative inscription is perfunctory, stating simply that the tomb belonged to 'Caecilia Metella, daughter of Quintus (Caecilius Metellus) Creticus, (wife of Marcus Licinius) Crassus'. Caecilia Metella, whose achievements, skills, and

353

other admirable characteristics (whatever any of those were) are lost
to history, was thus primarily celebrated only as the wife and daughter of exalted men.[49] Even though the tomb was ostensibly Caecilia
Metella's, it really served as an advertisement hoarding for her deceased
father's and husband's individual and collective status and the prestige
it brought their families thereafter. A beneficiary would have been
Crassus' son of the same name who was consul with Octavian in 30 BC.

Less prominently located, but no less conspicuous today, is the
remarkable pyramid tomb of Cestius. It stands a few metres from
Rome's Ostian Gate and was built during the reign of Augustus in c.
18–12 BC on a fork between two roads. The land on which the pyramid
stands lies just over 13 feet (4 m) below the modern road surface which
makes the tomb look less prominent than it once was. The pyramid
stands almost 120 feet (36.4 m) high and is over 98 feet (30 m) wide at
the base. Typically for Roman construction the core is concrete, but
it was faced with marble. Inside was a vault with no access once the
tomb was sealed though when it was explored in the 1600s the contents
were found to have been long since robbed out. The inspiration for the
tomb's design obviously came from Egypt but how is unknown. The
occupant was Gaius Cestius Epulo, a senator who had served as a praetor and tribune of the plebs. As a senator he would have been officially
prohibited from visiting Egypt. The province was so important that
Augustus decided it would be governed by an equestrian prefect, to
prevent it and its garrison falling into the hands of a man who might
have challenged Augustus or another successor. Another possibility is
that Cestius had served in Egypt prior to that rule being instituted, or
perhaps had even made a private visit in the latter days of the rule of
Cleopatra VII. If so, he might have seen the celebrated pyramids of the
Old and Middle Kingdoms at Giza and nearby. The tomb was a considerable investment since the inscription records that its construction
took 330 days.

Cestius rose without trace in his own time. Were it not for his
tomb he would have disappeared from history, but his careful choice
of location guaranteed that in death his memorial would be noticed.

When the Aurelian Walls of Rome were begun (270–5) the pyramid was incorporated so that it could act as a bastion guarding the approach to the Ostian Gate. At some point during its history the passers-by must have included Gaius Annaeus Atticus, an even more obscure individual than Cestius and of modest means. He, or his heirs, commissioned a diminutive brick pyramid to hold his cremated remains in the cemetery on the Isola Sacra between Ostia and Portus. The tomb's inscription says he came from Aquitania in Gaul and that he was a painter. He died aged thirty-seven but there is no mention of a wife or family.[50]

The Tomb of Cecilia Metella and the pyramid tombs of Cestius and Annaeus Atticus stood outside the religious boundaries of, respectively, Rome and Ostia, as the law dictated. In special circumstances burial within the settlements was permitted. The most obvious were the mausolea of Augustus and Hadrian but the privilege was sometimes granted to private individuals. Just below the massive edifice of the Vittorio Emanuele Monument in central Rome is a fragment of the once grandiose tomb of Gaius Poplicius Bibulus who had been tribune of the plebs in 209 BC. The extant tomb itself belongs to the late first century BC and was awarded by the Senate and people of Rome at public expense. This was a special honour, the likelihood being that the original tomb had become damaged or ruinous and had been rebuilt. The possession of such a prominent monument was a public statement of the family's importance and the expectation by Poplicius Bibulus' descendants that they be accorded the respect appropriate to people of their status. As such it was far too valuable to be allowed to fall into decay.

The Tomb of the Scipios lies by the Via Appia close to Rome and within the later circuit of the Aurelian Walls. It was built at the beginning of the third century BC by Lucius Cornelius Scipio Barbatus. By the second century BC it contained the remains of several generations of members of the famous family, unusually interred in stone sarcophagi, each with an epitaph, in subterranean chambers, and regardless of their individual achievements or obscurity. The tomb was a substantial and prominent monument with an elaborate architectural façade that fronted a side road off the Via Appia. It was decorated with paintings of military events, suitable for a family that had included Scipio Africanus, victor of the Second Punic War, and Scipio Aemilianus, an adoptive member of the family and hero of the Third Punic War, also known as Africanus. Scipio Africanus was only commemorated at the Via Appia tomb by a statue. He and certain other prominent members of the family were buried at their villa at Liternum in Campania. This is a reminder of the role the tomb played as a public memorial of a great family which could be incidental to the presence or lack of the remains of the individuals concerned.[51]

Those leaving Rome to the south down the Via Appia were bound to see the Tomb of the Scipios on the left-hand (east) side as they walked or rode past. The main line of the family had died out by Augustus' reign, and it was left to a collateral branch to take over care of the tomb. In the third century AD, Scipio Africanus was still a famous figure in Roman military lore and continued to be so for a long time afterwards, but by then the family tomb had fallen into decay. It was absorbed into the substructure of a new house, which is odd considering how often Scipio Africanus was cited by writers for long afterwards; the Romans had little sentimentality for their forebears when it came down to the need for space and stone. Even in remote provincial forts and fortresses, soldiers unhesitatingly reused tombstones of their predecessors, sometimes just as hard core fill for new walls or to incorporate in new buildings.

Prominence in life could be followed by obscurity in death. Otho, who reigned for just three months in the troubled year of 69, committed suicide after his army was defeated near Bedriacum. His remains were deposited in a modest tomb at Brescello in northern Italy. It bore an inscription that just said, 'to the memory of Marcus Otho', with apparently no further reference to his life or office.[52] His predecessor Galba, murdered by soldiers, was secretly buried by a freedman in Rome.[53] Galba had toppled Nero, but conversely Nero's burial in Rome was well-known and expensive. He was buried in the family tomb of his father's ancestors on the Pincio Hill and overlooked the Field of Mars for all to see. It was decorated for years after his death by his resilient fan base with 'spring and summer flowers'.[54]

Helping oneself to another person's grave seems to have been a popular solution to securing a burial place. Titus Aelius Euangelus, probably an Ostian freedman of the late second century, was concerned that his remains and those of his wife might be ejected to make way for someone else's burial. 'I forbid another person to be [in this sarcophagus] after me and Gaudenia Nicene', he said, though it is hard to see what he could have done about any such intrusion.[55]

Along the Via Appia still stands the late Republican tomb of Gaius Rabirius Hermodorus, freedman of Postumus, his probable wife Rabiria Demaris, and Usia Prima, priestess or devotee of Isis.[56] The inscribed aedicular relief that commemorates the three is now in a museum but a cast has been installed on the original monument. Rabirius Postumus may well be one and the same with a man once defended by Cicero, which helps date the tomb. Usia Prima's connection with Hermodorus and Demaris is not at all apparent. She is accompanied by a sistrum which fits her description but there is nothing at all to suggest any connection with the other two occupants. Her portrait bust is smaller than theirs and it is obvious therefore that she was a later inclusion in the tomb, a third and now unknown figure being re-carved to represent her, and a stylistically different inscription added. She may have had some connection by descent or had been buried there by heirs after taking over the tomb from a family that had perhaps by then died out. This practice is certainly known elsewhere, for example at the tomb of Eumachia at Pompeii.

At Ostia as elsewhere in the Roman world, tombstones were sometimes ripped up and reused in well-appointed houses rather than bother with sourcing new stone. Titus Flavius Crathis, an imperial freedman, and Flavia Sosuza, his slave and freedwoman (and presumably wife), invested in a marble tombstone at Ostia for themselves and their freedmen and freedwomen at some point in the late first or early second century. By the fourth century the stone had been removed from the tomb, which had probably been destroyed or usurped, and carted off to the city's House of the Porch where it was installed as a drain cover with perforations cut through the text. No effort was even made to conceal the surviving lettering which remains visible to this day in the ruins of the house.[57] It was not the only decorative fitting the thrifty tomb-raiding owners collected from the necropolis. In an adjacent room the opus sectile floor still includes a marble panel made from a cut-down rectangular tombstone, probably of a freedman called [Pe]scennius. The rest of the lettering remained visible, rendered unrestorable by the truncation.[58]

Near the Tomb of the Scipios in Rome was the far less prepossessing so-called columbarium of Pomponius Hylas, named today after an occupant and his wife whose cremated remains were buried there early in the first century. The burials were in a communal underground chamber once marked by a surface monument that has long since disappeared. Pomponius' ashes were interred here with those of his wife Pomponia. There were at least eighteen other burials in the various architectural niches, decorated with mosaics and paintings. Since they seem to be unrelated, the most logical explanation is that the columbarium was shared by a group of men and women who had formed a burial guild for the benefit of those who wanted to pool the costs of burial.

One such burial guild at Lanuvium, 20 miles (38 km) from Rome, was formed during Trajan's reign in 103. Membership required a joining fee of 100 sesterces and an amphora of good wine, followed by a monthly subscription of 1¼ sesterces (thus 15 sesterces annually). If the member died, then the guild would stump up 300 sesterces for the funeral. If any of them lived more than thirteen years and four months after joining, they would have paid in more than the guild would pay out, but this, of course, covered the costs of those who did not manage to survive that long. Evidently, most of them must have thought their chances of dying before then were high enough to make the subscription worthwhile.

This guild also admitted slave members and made provision

for when an owner refused to release the body for burial. On such occasions the funeral would still go ahead but using an effigy of the deceased. The members made the most of their association, treating it as a social club. They gathered regularly to celebrate dinners according to an annual calendar of events such as the birthdays of members or their divine patrons Diana and Antinous and took it in turns to make the arrangements.[59]

The annual festival of the Parentalia lasted from 13 to 21 February, at the end of which family members gathered to eat a celebratory meal of bread and wine in the presence and with the spiritual participation of the deceased family members, and to leave offerings. Among the surviving tombs at Ostia on the Isola Sacra, as elsewhere, are those with outdoor couches in the style of a triclinium dining room where the meal could take place. When Aeneas remembered the burial of his father, Vergil had him say 'the day is come that I shall ever keep as one of grief and honour'.[60]

When Flavius Agricola, a native of Tibur (Tivoli) 19 miles (30 km) east of Rome, died he was confident his son Aurelius Primitivus would take care of his parents' grave *in aevum* ('for eternity'). Agricola's previously deceased wife, Flavia Primitiva, had been a *cultrix deae Phariaes*, which translates as a 'devotee of the goddess Pharia', a manifestation of Isis as the deity of the celebrated lighthouse at Alexandria. They had spent 'thirty years of happiness' together. Agricola reminded passers-by to enjoy the pleasures of love with beautiful women and to bear in mind that after death everything would be consumed by 'earth and fire'.[61] It was hardly an original sentiment – the Romans were fond of remembering that death came to everyone – but his dead wife's interest in Isis means she at least was likely to have been attracted by the idea of being reborn in an ecstatic afterlife, something that would eventually lead to Christianity taking over.

THE UNBURIED DEAD

Some Romans never had a funeral or a known grave, even a simple one. It is impossible for us to quantify how many, though it goes without saying that many were likely to have been criminals, poor, or enslaved, regardless of the cause of death, or soldiers who died in battle. It is rare to find the body of someone of Roman date who had died by misadventure, and to be able to tell anything much about them.

There are, of course, exceptions but even these are as tantalizing as they are instructive. One example is the collection of skeletons recovered from the so-called boatsheds along the waterfront at Herculaneum. On 24 August 79 when Vesuvius erupted, some of the townsfolk burst out of their homes and abandoned their work. They raced down the streets towards the sea and made their way down steps and a track to the beach. There they flung themselves into the boatsheds and hoped for the best. They had made a catastrophic miscalculation. The pyroclastic flow pouring down the mountain's slopes enveloped the whole city and would eventually encase it in rock that pushed back the coast by hundreds of metres. The people in the boatsheds were incinerated by the thermal shock in an instant. Their brains boiled, and their flesh and muscle were obliterated in less time than it took to type those words.

Around three hundred skeletons have been found in those boatsheds. Their anonymous bodies and the goods they died with reflected the structure of Roman society. The 'wealthy matron' met her end with gold rings on her fingers and accompanied by her gold bangles and other jewellery. Another was a teenage girl, apparently in charge of a baby, whose teeth afflicted by hypoplasia point to malnutrition in her own infancy. She was perhaps a slave in charge of her mistress's child. There was nearby on the beach a man in his late thirties wearing a military belt and a soldier's *gladius* sword. He was not wearing armour and therefore must have been dressed in an everyday tunic. He was also equipped with an adze and three chisels which were slung over his back. He had suffered a serious wound to his left thigh, but the recovery and healing to the bone indicated a man who was in excellent condition and well nourished. He cannot be identified conclusively as a member of any military unit but it is, surely, more likely than anything else that he was a member of the imperial Praetorian Guard. If so, he was on duty in the region (praetorian soldiers were detached individually and in units on a vast array of tasks on the state's behalf).[62]

To these we can add the celebrated plaster casts of the dead made in Pompeii from the voids their decayed bodies left. The irony is that without exception we cannot put a single name to any of these people, even the pile of mouldering bones in a glass case displayed at the House of the Menander. They must be the remains of members of the household, but it is impossible now to say who they were or what status they held. The eruption of Vesuvius was an exceptional event and the unique circumstances have preserved human and animal remains in remarkable contexts. Nevertheless, they can serve as reminders that for every tomb and funerary inscription that has survived there were untold hundreds of thousands of others whose lives in Rome have left no trace, just as it will be for us.

Seneca wrote to his friend Lucilius about growing old and dying. As a Stoic, Seneca was focused on accepting things as the way they are. He could do nothing about death so chose instead to try and see it as a liberation:

> Epicurus will oblige me with these words: 'Think on death', or rather, if you prefer the phrase, on 'migration to heaven'. The meaning is clear, – that it is a wonderful thing to learn thoroughly how to die. You may deem it superfluous to learn a text that can be used only once; but that is just the reason why we ought to think on a thing. When we can never prove whether we really know a thing, we must always be learning it.
> 'Think on death'. In saying this, he bids us think on freedom. He who has learned to die has unlearned slavery. He is above any external power, or, at any rate, he is beyond it. What terrors have

prisons and bonds and bars for him? His way out is clear. There is only one chain which binds us to life, and that is the love of life. The chain may not be cast off, but it may be rubbed away, so that, when necessity shall demand, nothing may retard or hinder us from being ready to do at once that which at some time we are bound to do. Farewell.[63]

In an earlier letter to Lucilius, Seneca had already explained his guiding philosophy that since 'death is so little to be feared that through its good offices nothing is to be feared'. Not everyone had time to ruminate on the prospect of death. In the year 94, a boy called Quintus Sulpicius Maximus competed in a Greek poetry competition held by Domitian to honour Jupiter Capitolinus. He died in Rome aged eleven years, five months, and twelve days to his parents' understandable consternation. On his tombstone they had some of his verse inscribed, the subject being Zeus castigating Helios for lending his chariot to Phaethon. His father Sulpicius Eugramus and his mother Licinia Januaria provided their son's thoughts, among them, 'I left this contest for the land of shades. Disease and weariness carried me away'. They consoled themselves with the thought that at least the boy would not be forgotten.[64]

It was all very well for Seneca. A wealthy and influential man, he could afford the luxury of believing he was going to be allowed to slide gently towards death. He was to be disappointed. In the year 65 he was forced into suicide by Nero who believed Seneca was in some way implicated in the senatorial conspiracy to assassinate him. As for so many Romans, his death came not in the natural course of events but thanks to circumstances beyond his control. An attempt to hasten his death by poison failed, but already greatly weakened by old age and his ascetic lifestyle, he expired shortly afterwards, overcome by the steam when he was carried into the baths. Seneca was immediately cremated and had no funeral, on his strict instructions.[65] The remains of the tomb believed to be his still stand by the Via Appia, close to the villa where his life ended. Most of the Roman people have left no such trace.

EPILOGUE

Alas, the worthlessness of man!

Pliny[1]

A t the ruins of Ostia Antica, in one of the scattered, anonymous, derelict buildings most visitors stroll past and barely glance at, is a Roman brick lying in the grass that still bears the clear impression of a heel of a typical nail-studded Roman sandal. Evidently, a tile worker had carelessly walked across some of the products while they were still wet. A dog had joined in and left its pawprints. Perhaps the worker was chasing the hound. More usually, Roman tiles only bear the impression of canine paws but this time a careless human being had also left a mark. It was a fleeting moment in his, or perhaps her, life but preserved for ever, a tantalizing glimpse that symbolizes the nameless and unknown millions who passed their lives in the days of the emperors. The wearer of the sandal knew Ostia at its height and must also have known Rome in those days yet nothing else about that person's life, slave, freed, or freeborn, has survived. For every person preserved in the inscriptions and texts included in this book there were hundreds of thousands of others or even millions who have left no mark in that written record.

Pliny said that 'our civilization, or at least our written records, depend largely on paper'. He described the various techniques, and even minimum standards laid down by Claudius, and was impressed by the durability of paper prepared with special adhesives and flattened. He concluded that this should guarantee it would last 'a long time' and proudly recounted the documents he had seen with the autographs of the great men of the Republic such as the Gracchi and Cicero. He claimed that autographed manuscripts of Augustus and Vergil were seen 'constantly'. Doubtless some were fakes. Cicero chose 'ivory-polished' paper for letters to his most esteemed correspondents. By imperial times, the best-quality papyrus (*hieratica*) paper had been renamed after Augustus, while the second grade was labelled 'Livia paper'.[2]

A curious paradox of the Roman world is that while lettering was routinely reproduced on coins through the engraving of coin dies, and on manufacturers' name stamps, printing or any equivalent was never invented. There was no such thing as the book in the form we know it. Texts were written by hand on scrolls of papyrus or ultra-thin leaves of fine wood. Potsherds were often used for notes or even for writing lessons and sometimes carry extracts or quotes from famous works. Output was relatively small, and by our standards the number of copies of literary works unimaginably few. The process of manual copying was, inevitably, unreliable. Cicero bemoaned how some he had had copied for him were full of mistakes, a problem that continued throughout the Middle Ages until printing arrived.[3]

In the film version (1960) of H.G. Wells's *The Time Machine*, the Time Traveller discovers a shelf of books. Eager to grasp the learning gained in the centuries between his own time and the distant future in which he found himself, the Time Traveller seizes a volume. To his despair it turns to dust in his hands.

The greater part of the written record of the Roman world has likewise turned to dust. Private and public libraries, domestic and public archives have crumbled, been burned, lost, or otherwise destroyed. Only in the waterlogged deposits of Britain or the sands of Egypt have original private archives of any sort survived in quantity. For the rest, we are generally dependent on the happenstance survival of copies of documents that were stored and often recopied in medieval monastic libraries. Much was lost. As a result, the works of many ancient authors are incomplete (such as Tacitus) or have sections only extant now as epitomes created by later authors (such as Dio). What survived turned out to be a goldmine for the early printers of the Middle Ages. They pounced on the manuscripts and eagerly started to publish them. Over time the various versions have been collated to iron out as many mistakes and inconsistencies as possible and produce reliable editions, but nothing can make good the lost texts.

Inscriptions, such as the tombstones or religious dedications that tell us so much about the ordinary people of Rome, or graffiti involve no indirect transmission. Those that survive are the originals but, as we have already seen, many inscriptions were treated with brutal indifference even in the Roman period. In the Middle Ages they became even more vulnerable to reuse for the stone. Graffiti have had an even more precarious journey. Apart from those that survive on potsherds or tiles, only Pompeii and Herculaneum have produced significant numbers because of the survival of buildings on whose walls the texts had been scrawled or daubed.

One way of measuring the importance of Rome as a symbol of stability and power to the people who lived there is to jump several centuries further forward to a time when the city was decaying and under threat. In 403 St Jerome had delighted in how the pagan temples of Rome were 'covered in soot and cobwebs' while the people hurried out to visit the graves of martyrs. He described how the Capitol had become filthy and rundown.[4] In the year 412, almost exactly four hundred years after the death of Augustus and three hundred since the Empire reached its greatest extent under Trajan, Jerome wrote a letter to a woman called Principia. By then Jerome was living in Judaea but he recorded his reaction to the news that Rome had been sacked two years earlier in 410. 'We heard a rumour that Rome was besieged, that the citizens were buying their safety with gold ... the city which had taken the whole world was itself taken.' Jerome quoted the man who had announced the news to a crowd of horrified and sobbing citizens.[5]

Of course, Rome had not gone, and certainly not for good. The city survived and took on a new identity, but the Rome of the Republic and the Caesars gradually retreated into the past. Its mighty monuments slowly disintegrated. Only a few survived into the Renaissance period recognizably in their original form, such as Hadrian's sensational domed Pantheon ('Temple of all the Gods') which survives largely intact.[6] Artists of the period explored the ruins, such as the subterranean remains of Nero's Golden House, and found inspiration in the surviving decorations and features. By the seventeenth and eighteenth centuries folio editions of examples of ancient architecture such as columns and their capitals, and entablature, had been produced. These served as textbooks for the architects of the period who reproduced the designs in great country houses, palaces, and public buildings, mainly in northern Europe but also further afield, such as in the United States (especially Washington DC).[7]

Random fragments of ancient structures in Rome were absorbed into later buildings or for some other unaccountable reasons escaped demolition. These include the pair of columns and their entablature that remain from the Forum of Nerva (originally built by Domitian), still visible in Rome by the Via dei Fori Imperiali. Known today as Le Colonnacce ('the ugly columns') they were half buried by the time of the Fascist era. By then, the imperial forums were all choked with rubble and refuse, with the buildings having been systematically robbed out mainly for projects commissioned by the popes. Ostia became a forgotten malarial backwater but thankfully this meant that its backstreets, houses, and apartment blocks were surprisingly well preserved. Mussolini was a prime agent in ordering the excavation of the ancient remains and making them as prominent as they are today. He also ordered the clearance and display of the imperial forums in Rome, and the construction of the Via dei Fori Imperiali for Fascist military parades in the 1930s, down which thousands of tourists now wander every day.

As ancient texts started to appear in print, antiquarians and scholars scrutinized the manuscripts. Some widened out the market by beginning to produce translations too. Alongside came the study and cataloguing of inscriptions which have done so much to liberate the evidence for ordinary individuals from among the ruins. The excavations at Pompeii and Herculaneum have done more than anything else to help us understand the Roman way of life under the early emperors. All around the flotsam and jetsam of everyday life was left where it had been dropped or abandoned, from the small change in streetside cookshops to the silverware in the richer houses.

For all the compelling sense of place that the ruins of Rome invoke there is an impenetrable stillness and lifelessness in their decay. Instead, it takes closing one's eyes and imagining these places packed with throngs of people for whom the ancient city was home. For this writer at least it is the written word that fills the streets and houses of the Romans with images of colour and life, whether from the letters of Cicero or the inscription on an ostentatious tomb of a freedman and his wife beside a street at Pompeii. We can see it all, from the sordid realities of slavery and the horrors of the arena to the extravagant dinners of the wealthy and picaresque scenes from the baths or streetside cookshops, set against a backdrop of rowdy and dangerous streets, vast public buildings, and the cinematic theatre of chariot races.

There can be no better way to end this book than with the life of Agilia Prima, also known as Auguria. Agilia is recorded on her funerary text from Rome, carved on a stone tablet commissioned by her bereaved husband, Quintus Oppius Secundus. She had died following her twentieth birthday. The inscription celebrated her chastity, modesty, and frugality but went on to quote both Cato the Elder and Seneca in an elaborate message composed in meter and in Agilia's voice.[8] She exhorted her husband not to mourn her because she has preceded him to the grave, 'it is foolish to lose the joy of life while fearing death'. She told him that 'death is the nature, not the punishment of mankind. Whoever chances to be born, therefore also faces death.' The sentiments were familiar rhetorical themes the Romans were fond of utilizing in such circumstances and are unlikely to have been her own words; but they might reflect a personal choice on Agilia's part.

The grave of Agilia Prima was doubtless visited by her grieving family in the years that followed. The same was true of many others whose memory was honoured by their descendants and those of their retainers, among them their freedmen and freedwomen. In time, of course, just as happened to the Tomb of the Scipios, the mourners diminished and eventually faded away, leaving the deceased commemorated only by fleeting references and fragmenting inscriptions that recorded their names and achievements for later ages to muse upon. Their texts make it possible for us to understand something of what it meant to be Roman. They must speak for all or the rest whose fate, however blameless their hidden lives might or might not have been, was to rest in unvisited and forgotten unmarked tombs, if indeed they ever had one at all.[9]

Agilia's funerary inscription finished with a message from the grave to all those who had outlived her, including us:

Be well, those who live above, and all men and all women, be well.

APPENDIX 1: DATES

Some key dates (this is in no sense comprehensive but shows a basic outline of Roman history)

753 BC	Mythical foundation of Rome
509 BC	Last king of Rome (Tarquinius Superbus) thrown out. Foundation of the Roman Republic
494 BC	Plebeians assert rights
451–450 BC	Twelve Tables of law published
449 BC	Secession of plebs. Tribunes' rights defined
366 BC	First plebeian consul
343–341 BC	First Samnite War
340–338 BC	War against the Latin Revolt
326–304 BC	Second Samnite War
312 BC	Via Appia begun
298–290 BC	Third Samnite War
280–275 BC	Pyrrhic War
270 BC	Beginning of overseas expansion of Roman power
269 BC	First Roman silver coinage
264 BC	First gladiatorial show in Rome
264–241 BC	First Punic War against Carthage
261–260 BC	First Roman fleet built

218–201 BC	Second Punic War (Hannibalic War)
212–211 BC	Silver denarius coinage introduced
214–205 BC	First Macedonian War
202 BC	Carthage defeated at Zama
200–196 BC	Second Macedonian War
192–188 BC	Seleucid War (Antiochus III)
172–168 BC	Third Macedonian War
150–148 BC	Fourth Macedonian War
149–146 BC	Third Punic War: Carthage destroyed
146 BC	Conquest of Greece: Corinth sacked
143–133 BC	Numantine (Celtiberian) War
135–132 BC	Slave war in Sicily
133 BC	Attalus III leaves Asia to Rome. Tribunate and death of Tiberius Gracchus
123 BC	First tribunate of Gaius Gracchus
121 BC	Death of Gaius Gracchus
118–116 BC	Jugurthine War
104–101 BC	Marius' war against the Cimbri and Teutones
91–88 BC	Social War against Roman allies
88–82 BC	Civil War between Marius and Sulla
88–84 BC	First Mithridatic War in Asia
83–81 BC	Second Mithridatic War in Asia
82 BC	Civil War in Italy: age of Sulla
81 BC	Sulla becomes dictator
73–71 BC	Spartacus (Servile) War
73–63 BC	Third Mithridatic War in Asia
67 BC	Pompey's War against the Cilician pirates
58–50 BC	Caesar's Gallic Wars
54–53 BC	Parthian campaign under Crassus (Crassus killed at Carrhae, 53 BC)
49–48 BC	Civil War between Caesar and Pompey
48 BC	Caesar becomes dictator

44 BC	Assassination of Caesar, currently dictator for life
44–31 BC	Civil War fought by the triumvirs and the tyrannicides, followed by the war between the triumvirs
31 BC	Battle of Actium. End of the Republic. Octavian supreme ruler of the Empire
30 BC	Annexation of Egypt
27 BC	Octavian becomes Augustus

THE EMPERORS

Augustus 27 BC–AD 14

Tiberius 14–37

Caligula 37–41

Claudius 41–54 (43: invasion of Britain)

Nero 54–68

Galba 68–9 (Civil War: 68–9)

Otho 69

Vitellius 69

Vespasian 69–79 (70: Fall of Jerusalem)

Titus 79–81

Domitian 81–96

Nerva 96–98

Trajan 98–117 (Dacian Wars: 101–2, 105–6, Parthian War: 113–17)

Hadrian 117–38

Antoninus Pius 138–61

Marcus Aurelius 161–80 (with Lucius Verus 161–9; with Commodus 177–80) (165: plague emerges)

Commodus 180–92

Pertinax 193 (murdered, leading to Civil War of 193–7)

Didius Julianus 193

Septimius Severus 193–211 (with Caracalla 198 –211, and also with Geta 209–11)

Caracalla 211–17 (with Geta 211–12) (212: edict of universal citizenship)

Macrinus 217–18

Elagabalus 218–22

Severus Alexander 222–35

> 235–84 Third Century Crisis: Military Anarchy

Maximinus I 235–8

Gordian I 238

Gordian II 238

Balbinus and Pupienus 238

Gordian III 238–44

Philip I 244–9 (with Philip II 247 –9)

Trajan Decius 249–51 (with Herennius Etruscus and Hostilian 251)

Trebonianus Gallus 251–3 (with Volusian 251–3)

Valerian I 253–60 (with Gallienus below)

Gallienus 253–68

Claudius II 268–70

Aurelian 270–5

Tacitus 275–6

Probus 276–82

Carus 282–3

Carinus 283–5

Numerian 283–4

The 'Tetrarchy' (rule of Four Emperors):

> > Diocletian 284–305 (with Galerius 293–305)
> >
> > Maximianus 286–306 (with Constantius I 293–305)
> >
> > (followed immediately by a confusing period of abdications and overlapping reigns)

Maximianus (second reign) 306–8

Constantius I 305–6

Galerius 305–11

Severus II 306–7

Maximinus II 309–13

Maxentius 306–12

Licinius I 308–24

Constantine I 307–37

> 313 Constantine legitimizes Christianity in the Edict of Milan

THE LATER EMPIRE

337–61 Constantius II

361–3 Julian

364 Accession of Valentinian I (West) and Valens (East): the Empire now permanently ruled in two parts

375 Death of Valentinian I, accession of Valentinian II (375–92) (West)

378 Death of Valens at the Battle of Adrianople

379–95 Theodosius I (East)

383–408 Arcadius (East)

393–423 Honorius (West)

402–50 Theodosius II (East)

410 Rome sacked by Alaric

425–55 Valentinian III (West)

476 Death of the last Western Roman emperor, Romulus Augustulus

APPENDIX 2:
ROMAN SOCIETY

I
n its earliest form, Roman society was divided into the **patri-cians** and the **plebeians**. The patricians were the old nobility who jealously guarded their property-based wealth and sense of innate superiority and entitlement, ruling through the Senate after the monarchy was overturned in 509 BC and the Republic established. The plebeians were the general populace. In early Republican times the plebeians rose up and demanded the patrician abuse of power stopped, and the granting of rights (including the tribunate of the plebs). This led to the admission of the wealthiest plebeians to the senatorial class in 367 BC. Those referred to as the **nobiles** (nobles) originally meant the patricians but came to mean those descended from a man who had served as a consul. These nobles dominated the elected high offices. Men of senatorial status required a family fortune of 1 million sesterces by the time of the emperors.

Beneath the senators came the **equestrians**, traditionally men who had enough wealth to go to war and fund a horse for military service. By imperial times they needed 400,000 sesterces to belong to the class, but the label was an anachronism. Horses no longer played a part. Instead, they fulfilled a huge number of procuratorial posts and prefectures and were of great importance to Roman administration in the city and beyond. The most senior positions were the prefects of the Praetorian Guard, of Rome, the corn dole, and of Egypt. It was possible for an equestrian to be promoted to the senatorial class.

Beneath the equestrians came the vast mass of freeborn **Roman citizens** who enjoyed various rights such as voting and holding office but in practice these privileges were often limited by electoral arrangements and property qualifications.

At the bottom came the **slaves** (*famuli*) who had few rights, but could be entitled to be freed, either by the emperor, the master, or by buying freedom (with the master's agreement). If so, the slave became a **freedman** or **freedwoman** (*libertus* and *liberta*). A freedman's children, if born in freedom, could grow up to enjoy all the rights of other citizens. Freedmen held office within their own organizations, typically commercial guilds, and could become wealthy and influential. The sons of freedmen could do well, and some did. In a few exceptional cases at later dates some of these became emperors. There were also those who enjoyed **Latin** status, a form of lesser citizenship conferred on peoples in Italy and sometimes beyond, which placed them between citizens and **provincials** whose rights and status were determined within their local communities.

Throughout Roman society the **patron–client** system operated. This was founded on hierarchy and obligation. Typically, a freedman became the client of his former master who was now his patron. The patron took care of the freedman, perhaps set him up in business and protected the business. In return, the client performed services for his patron and his patron's friends and family for nothing. Clients would gather at the patron's house at the morning salutatio to show their respects. This operated at all levels. The patron himself might also be (and probably was) the client of someone else higher up the gravy chain, providing his own services to his patron while receiving respect and services from his own clients.

APPENDIX 3: SOURCES

T he following are the principal ancient written sources mined for the stories and anecdotes distributed throughout the text, along with some brief biographical details of the authors. In some cases, a reasonable amount is known about the writers, but usually only from incidental references in their texts. All too often we know very little about them. The information here will help place them in chronological context. Inscriptions form a completely different type of source. They are usually brief, formulaic and abbreviated, but can provide unique details of the lives of ordinary individuals. Each cited is referenced in the notes.

A. INSCRIPTIONS

Inscriptions carved in stone are the only true primary written sources from the Roman period, other than the rare instances of documents which only survive in exceptional conditions such as the sands of Egypt, waterlogged military deposits in northern Britain, or writing tablets in Pompeii and Herculaneum. The vast majority of ancient written sources, such as the works of Tacitus, are only known to us from copies of copies of copies that were found in medieval monastic libraries.

Inscriptions, such as tombstones and religious dedications, provide a rich record of ordinary Roman people about whom we would never have known anything otherwise. For every such person recorded on a surviving text there were untold thousands whose records have been destroyed or lost over time, to say nothing of those who were never commemorated this way. Some survive where they were originally erected but in many other instances it has only been sheer happenstance that has allowed them to come down to us, for example by being reused as a drain cover.

Roman inscriptions were routinely abbreviated. That saved money and space but can make the texts cryptic, and at worst incomprehensible. Fortunately, inscriptions were formulaic in composition, and this makes recovery of the meaning usually possible at least to some extent. Unfortunately, all too often they are broken and incomplete. Nonetheless, the existence of those that survive places us in a wholly different position compared to the medieval period when far lower literacy levels and much higher relative levels of poverty, and different customs, mean that there is no comparable record until early modern times.

For all the deficiencies of the Roman epigraphic archive, it has opened a window on the ancient world that has no equal and without which this book would have been far harder to write.

B. ANCIENT SOURCES

The following is a list of the principal ancient authors cited in the book. In the notes the relevant work is only cited where the author is known to have produced more than one. Thus, either Tacitus' *Annals* or *Histories* is specified, but in Martial's case only his *Epigrams* are extant and therefore the notes feature only his name and a numerical reference.

Ammianus Marcellinus c. 325–95
Ammianus Marcellinus wrote much later than most of the sources,

belonging to the Christianized Roman Empire. He was a Greek from Antioch in Syria and served in the late Roman imperial army. He came to Rome in later life where he settled and wrote a history of Rome in Latin from 96 to 378. Only the latter section, covering 354–78, is extant.

Appian (Appianus) second century AD
Appian was a Greek who lived and worked in Alexandria. He died during the reign of Antoninus Pius (138–61) having risen to be made an equestrian and given a procuratorship. He wrote a military history of various Roman wars in the latter half of the Republic, and much of his original text has survived.

Aulus Gellius c. 123–70
Almost nothing is known about this author apart from his surviving work *Attic Nights* though he was evidently well-educated and connected. This is a collection of material that interested the author who summarized and quoted from other works, most of which are lost. The contents included everything from law to grammar and history to literature.

Cato the Elder (Marcus Porcius Cato) 234–149 BC
Cato was the model of the old-fashioned Roman, dedicated to the Republic and traditional ideas of restraint and modesty. He was disgusted by Greek ideas and tastes. Most of his extensive works are lost though later writers often referred to and quoted from him. *On Agriculture* is his only extant book and reflects both his character and the ideals of the farmer Roman. His great-grandson was Marcus Porcius Cato 'the Younger' (95 –46 BC), a conservative senator in his famous ancestor's mould, a stoic, and opponent of Caesar.

Cicero (Marcus Tullius Cicero) 106–43 BC
Cicero was a lawyer and statesman whose brilliant career took place during the latter days of the Republic. The texts of dozens of his legal speeches survive, as well as other works and hundreds of his

personal letters. He witnessed the explosive politics of his era at first-hand, making him an exceptionally important source for the period. He was a bitter enemy of the triumvirate who proscribed and executed him.

Columella (Lucius Junius Moderatus) *fl.* c. 40–70
Columella came from Cadiz in Spain but moved to Italy where he farmed. He is known today for his *On Agriculture* which is considered to be the most comprehensive surviving Roman treatise on the subject.

Florus, Publius Annius *fl.* 120–40
Florus came from North Africa but lived in Spain and Rome in the early second century. He is known for his *Epitome of Roman History* which starts from the beginning and ends with the death of Augustus. It was probably unfinished. Like many such Roman historical works, his agenda was a moral one. Florus tracked how Rome had descended into indulgence and immorality from its far greater early days.

Frontinus (Sextus Julius Frontinus) c. 35–103
Frontinus was a senator who served in a number of senior positions, including serving as governor of Britain in the late 70s after his first consulship in 73 or 74. In 97 he was placed in charge of Rome's aqueducts and wrote a treatise about the aqueducts, the law, his duties and the uncovering of fraud and corruption.

Fronto (Marcus Cornelius Fronto) c. 100–165/70
Fronto was born at the Roman colony of Cirta in Numidia (Algeria) and was probably of Roman descent. He was of senatorial status and embarked on the traditional cursus honorum of offices, rising to the consulship in 143, becoming a tutor to members of the imperial family, including Marcus Aurelius. He subsequently became governor of Asia. He is principally known for his correspondence with Marcus Aurelius.

Herodian (c. 178–post 238)
Very little is known about Herodian except that he witnessed events in the 190s and lived on till after the accession of Gordian III (238–44). He may have come from Alexandria or Antioch. He set out to write his version of the tumultuous events that followed the death of Marcus Aurelius (161–80) over the next sixty or so years, some of which he witnessed.

Horace (Quintus Horatius Flaccus) 65–8 BC
Horace was the son of a freedman who initially supported Caesar's assassins and fought on their side in the civil war against the triumvirate. As a result he lost his property and turned to writing poetry. This brought him into Vergil's circle in 39 BC, and thereby to Augustus' friend Maecenas who gave him a country estate to support him. Horace became a supporter of Augustus. He wrote a number of works including his *Odes* and *Epistles*.

Jerome (Eusebius Sophronius Hieronymus) c. 345–420
Jerome was a scholar and priest who was born in Dalmatia. He was baptized a Christian in 360. He was ordained in Antioch in 379 and among other activities produced a Latin translation of the Bible. Jerome was a teacher of scripture, Hebrew, and monasticism and was particularly enthusiastic about encouraging Christian women to be as modest, chaste, and devout as possible. For the purposes of this book he is most useful for his correspondence.

Josephus (Titus Flavius Josephus) c. 37–*post* 97
An aristocratic Jew from Jerusalem who was a soldier and statesman who also wrote history. His *Jewish War* (an account of Vespasian and Titus' war in Judaea) and his *Jewish Antiquities* survive. Josephus was a philo-Roman who greatly admired Roman achievements and became a Roman citizen under the Flavian emperors. His accounts of Caligula's assassination (*JA*), the Roman army on campaign and Vespasian and Titus' triumph in Rome (*JW*) are particularly famous.

Juvenal (Decimus Junius Juvenalis) *fl.* c. 95–127
Juvenal was an equestrian who can be tentatively identified with a man of the same name who served as the commanding officer of an auxiliary unit in Britain. He came from Aquinum but clearly spent much of his time in Rome, an experience that contributed so much colour and picaresque detail to his *Satires* for which he is known today.

Livy (Titus Livius) c. 64 BC–*post* AD 17
Livy was an Italian senator who wrote a history of Rome from its beginning to 9 BC. Less than a quarter survives intact, along with summaries of most of the rest and some fragments and quotes. He is a key source for the mythologized history of early Rome and the Second Punic War period in particular, but even the summaries supply vital detail about some years.

Macrobius (Macrobius Ambrosius Theodosius) *fl.* early fifth century
Macrobius' *Saturnalia* is a collection of history, folklore, sayings and anecdotes, many of which are unknown in any other source. It was composed as seven books based on discussions that took place at the private house of the praetorian prefect Vettius Agorius Praetextatus. Little is known about the author.

Martial (Marcus Valerius Martialis) c. 40–c. 105
Martial was an equestrian and a poet from Spain who came to live in Rome. His *Epigrams* provide all sorts of colourful detail about life in Rome from dining to prostitutes and his own everyday experiences, prejudices, preoccupations and frustrations, making him a key source for this book.

Minucius Felix (Marcus Minucius Felix) d. c. 250
Possibly (but not certainly) a Roman lawyer, and a Christian apologist who wrote a dialogue between a Christian (Octavius, after whom the work is named) and a pagan. Nothing else is known about him.

Ovid (Publius Ovidius Naso) 43 BC–AD 17/18
A key poet of the Augustan period who grew up during the civil war
of the late Republic and early part of Augustus' reign. His poetry
includes many personal references. In AD 8 he was forced into exile by
Augustus for unknown reasons. This may have been connected with
some of his enthusiastic references to immoral behaviour, for example
in the *Art of Love*.

Persius (Aulus Persius Flaccus) 34–62
Persius was an equestrian from Volaterrae who moved to Rome when
he was twelve. He is unusual for the reason that an ancient biography of
him was appended to manuscripts of his *Satires*. He was well-educated
and connected and knew Seneca, but did not like him.

Pliny the Elder (Gaius Plinius Secundus I) 23–79
Pliny was an equestrian, auxiliary commanding officer, historian and
polymath. His greatest work is his *Natural History*, a vast compendium
of the world he knew which he collected with a characteristic lack of
critical discrimination. His curiosity was his undoing. As commander
of the fleet at Misenum in August 79 he was suffocated by poisonous fumes while leading a rescue expedition during the eruption
of Vesuvius.

Pliny the Younger (Gaius Plinius Secundus II) c. 61–113
Nephew and adopted son of Pliny the Elder. He was of senatorial status,
served as a lawyer, and rose to the consulship in 100. He acted as a phi-
lanthropist for his hometown of Comum where some of his work is
recorded in an inscription, a small part of which survives.* He was later
made governor of Bithynia and Pontus by Trajan but apparently died
in post. He is mainly known for his correspondence with his friends
and with Trajan.

---

* *CIL* 5.5262 (Milan, formerly at Como). Viewable at: https://www.livius.org/
pictures/italy/milan/st-ambrogio/pliny-s-inscription-original/

Plutarch c. 45–*post* 120
Plutarch was a Greek who studied in Athens and later became a priest at Delphi, though he also visited Rome and knew Hadrian. He is best known for his *Parallel Lives* of famous Greeks and Romans which became particularly famous in the Renaissance.

Sallust (Gaius Sallustius Crispus) 86–34 BC
Sallust was a senator whose early career was reckless but he rose to support Caesar. In retirement he wrote history, most famously an account of the *War with Catiline* and the *War with Jugurtha*.

Seneca (Lucius Annaeus Seneca) the Younger c. 4 BC–AD 65
Philosopher, statesman, playwright and writer, Seneca lived through the reigns of all the Julio-Claudian emperors and was forced to commit suicide by the last, Nero, whose tutor he had been. He was a controversial figure, implicated in various scandals, for example being accused of adultery with two of Caligula's sisters and later provoking the Boudican Revolt by making huge loans to tribesmen and recalling them abruptly. He played a major part in governing the Empire in Nero's earlier years, but was eventually marginalized and ordered to commit suicide by Nero on the spurious basis that he had been implicated in a senatorial plot against the emperor.

Strabo c. 64 BC–AD 25
Strabo came from Pontus in Asia Minor and completed his education in Rome. He travelled widely and spent some of his time in Alexandria. He wrote a history which is lost but his *Geography* has come down to us. This is an invaluable description of the known world in his time.

Suetonius (Gaius Suetonius Tranquillus) c. 69–*post* c. 125
Suetonius was born into an equestrian family, probably in Numidia, and was a friend of Pliny the Younger (q.v.). He became an imperial secretary under Trajan and Hadrian, but was sacked by the latter for allegedly having had an affair with Hadrian's empress Sabina.

Suetonius is best known today for his cycle of biographies of Julius Caesar and the first eleven emperors (*The Twelve Caesars*), an eclectic mix of history, rumour, scandal, and anecdotes.

Tacitus (Cornelius Tacitus) c. 56–120

Tacitus is generally considered to be Rome's finest historian. He famously claimed to be recording events without bias but in reality consistently judged the emperors badly against his vision of the Republic. Much of his *Annals* (covering 14–68) survives but only a small part of his *Histories* (68–96). Part of his tombstone survives.*

Tertullian (Quintus Septimius Florens Tertullianus) c. 155–220

A Christian writer from Carthage who, in his enthusiasm to condemn various aspects of Rome life such as in his *Spectacles*, provides us with invaluable detail about the very topics during Rome's height that he loathed so much. His *On the Crown* inadvertently supplies us with detail about Mithraic ceremonies that we would otherwise know nothing about.

Valerius Maximus *fl.* 14–37

Almost nothing about Valerius Maximus is known except that he enjoyed the patronage of Sextus Pompeius (consul in 14), tying to him to the reign of Tiberius. His work consists of various deeds and sayings of Romans and foreigners which he considered memorable in some way and taken from other works, many of which are no longer extant.

Varro (Marcus Terentius Varro) 116–27 BC

Varro was a scholar who wrote extensively and whom Caesar engaged to manage a projected national library. Only his *On Agriculture* (in fact the Latin means more accurately 'Rustic Affairs') and his *Latin Language* survive but the latter is incomplete. Both provide a wealth of detail

---

* *CIL* 6.1574 (Rome). Viewable at: https://commons.wikimedia.org/wiki/File:Tacitus,_Sepulchral_Inscription.jpg

even if the *Latin Language* is sometimes incorrect in its analysis of the origin of Latin words.

Velleius Paterculus (Marcus Velleius Paterculus) c. 19 BC–AD 31
Velleius Paterculus was a soldier and historian of senatorial status. His history of Rome began with the fall of Troy but is considered most useful today for his stylized and rhetorical account of the reigns of Augustus and Tiberius.

Vergil (Publius Vergilius Maro) 70–19 BC
By far and away the most famous of all Roman poets, Vergil experienced the dereliction of the late Republic at close hand and welcomed the coming of Augustus. His *Aeneid* enshrined in verse the myth of Augustus as a predestined ruler of Rome who could trace his ancestry back to the minor Trojan hero Aeneas who brought survivors to Italy and founded the Roman people. His *Eclogues* and *Georgics* bought into the myth of a bucolic utopia, and in the *Eclogues* featured a foretelling of a messianic saviour.

Vitruvius (possibly Marcus Vitruvius Pollo) c. 75–*post* 15 BC
The celebrated architect and military engineer whose treatise *On Architecture* set down all sorts of essential techniques and design details for a variety of Roman buildings and both military and civil engineering projects. This work was considered an essential textbook well into the Middle Ages and afterwards.

APPENDIX 4: VISITING THE WORLD OF *POPULUS*

R eaching Rome, Ostia, Pompeii, and Herculaneum is easy today. International flights arrive in Rome from around the world. Naples is less easy but there are plenty of direct flights from other European cities. Intercontinental flights will generally involve going, for example, via London, Paris, or Amsterdam. Although the ruins of the ancient city are scattered, the main concentration is around the imperial forums and the Palatine Hill in the heart. From this area it is easy to walk north to the Field of Mars and, for example, the magnificent experience of visiting the Pantheon. Other short excursions include the church of Santa Maria degli Angeli (close to Termini railway station), which preserves the frigidarium (cold bath) of the Baths of Diocletian, and the adjacent Museum of the Baths (Museo Nazionale delle Terme), which contains many important pieces. There are, of course, also the Capitoline Museum and the Vatican Museum. To the south of the Circus Maximus lie the vast ruins of the Baths of Caracalla. Buses stop nearby which head down the Via Appia Antica where the Circus of Maxentius, the Tomb of Cecilia Metella, and catacombs can be seen before enjoying a walk down the old Roman road. No serious visitor should venture to Rome without a copy of the late Amanda Claridge's indispensable *Rome. An Oxford Archaeological Guide*

(Oxford University Press, 2010), which provides comprehensive details of virtually all the visible remains.

A sense of daily life in ancient Rome, rather than the major public buildings such as the Colosseum, is best achieved by visiting the ruins of the ancient port of Rome at Ostia where houses, apartment blocks, and other facilities like public baths can be visited in their original context by wandering through Roman streets. Ostia is most easily accessed by taking Rome's Linea B metro to Piramide station, then walking a few yards to the Lido di Ostia station and taking the overground train out to Ostia Antica (about thirty minutes). From the station it takes about ten minutes to walk to the charming ruins which make for a pleasing half-day or full-day excursion. Rome's metro tickets are valid on both legs of the journey. Pompeii and Herculaneum (Italian: Ercolano) are equally easily reached by taking the Circumvesuviana railway that runs between Naples and Sorrento. Both sites have their own stations, though the walk down from Ercolano's station is a little further than Pompeii's. It is worth bearing in mind that at all three sites the visitor is likely to discover that certain key buildings are locked or otherwise inaccessible on an erratic and unpredictable basis. Access to many of the principal houses at Pompeii and Herculaneum is now restricted to booked groups, sometimes involving an additional ticket. For further information about Pompeii consult http://www.pompeiisites.org/

GLOSSARY OF TERMS

aedile: junior senatorial magistrate (two) responsible for the maintenance of public buildings, games and services. The word is
linked to *aedes*, 'temple', and *aedificare*, 'to build'. For curule
aedile, see under curule magistracies (q.v.).

amphitheatre: elliptical venue with seating all the way round overlooking an arena in which gladiatorial bouts and beast hunts
took place. In the most elaborate the arena could be flooded
for mock sea battles, and there were sometimes substructures
from which gladiators and animals could be brought up
straight into the arena.

arch (triumphal): a monumental arch, sometimes with flanking and
transverse passages designed to mark usually great military
victories. As such they often stood at the entrance to places
like the Forum, and frequently bore sculptures and inscriptions to commemorate the events.

as (plural in English: asses): a copper coin worth one half of a dupondius, and a quarter of a sestertius. The commonest everyday
'small change' in Roman coinage, often translated variously
(and randomly) as a 'farthing' or 'penny'.

atrium: the main hall of the *domus*, reached by the *fauces*. The main public area where guests were greeted, domestic rituals performed. Surrounded by private chambers (e.g. *cubicula*), and normally with an *impluvium* and *compluvium*.

Augusta: the formal and honorific title eventually used by the wife of an Augustus, the emperor. It denoted her special association with him and by implication shared status and privileges. Augusta was also a form of religious dignity that could be attributed to a man. Augusta was therefore an ambiguous label, probably deliberately so.

Augustus: the name adopted by Octavian in 27 BC. It had semi-religious associations and marked him out as of special status with unique authority, but without specifically referring to him as a ruler. It became synonymous with what we would call an emperor.

aureus: standard Roman gold coin unit, nominally equivalent in value to 25 *denarii*, or 100 *sestertii*.

baths: baths of all shapes and sizes were found in Roman cities, from the gigantic facilities such as the Baths of Caracalla in Rome to small baths frequented by locals or members of guilds, as well as baths in some of the wealthier houses. All tended to follow the pattern of warm baths followed by hot baths, finished off by a cold bath. Often accompanied by gymnasium facilities.

bisellium: the honorific 'double seat' awarded to civic worthies in the theatre and amphitheatre. Such an honour could continue posthumously.

carpentum: carriage originally used by Roman matrons in processions in Rome. Enjoyed as a specific privilege by some senior female members of the imperial family for private purposes.

censor: magistrate who drew up the census of those eligible to vote and hold office, but was also in charge of public morals.

circus: racetrack consisting of two parallel tracks divided by a *spina* for chariot racing. Chariots entered through gates at one end, hurtled down one side and then around the far, curved, end before racing back down the other side for multiple laps. Not all cities had a circus though Rome had several.

consul: the two most senior elected magistrates of the Roman state, the pinnacle of the senatorial career. A former consul was a *proconsul*. The Roman emperors usually held the consulship but not consistently or necessarily consecutively.

curia: the senate or town council, 'a meeting place'.

curule magistrate: these were magistrates (consuls, praetors, censors and curule aediles) entitled to sit on a dedicated chair of office.

decuriones (Eng: decurion): town councillor. To be eligible a candidate normally had to have served as an aedile first, fulfilled the local property qualification for office, reached the age of twenty-five, and been elected. The word *de curia* means '[a member] of the assembly/senate'.

denarius: the standard Roman silver coin, issued from Republican times regularly up until the mid-third century when it gave way to the double-denarius, the *antoninianus*. Purity declined during the period. Diameter typically 19 mm, weight c. 3.9 gm.

dupondius: a (usually) brass coin worth two asses or half a sestertius (q.v.).

duumvir (or *duovir*, plural *duoviri*): one of the two annually elected senior civic magistrates (*duoviri*, 'the two men') in a Roman city. They were the local equivalent of the two consuls in Rome. A duumvir had to fulfil a property qualification and had previously served as a junior civic magistrate, *aedile*.

effeminare: 'to make [someone/something] effeminate'. This pejorative term suggested weakness and degeneration through greed into luxury, vice, and decadence. It was used particularly to discredit men, such as Mark Antony, and was often associated with the influence of a degenerate woman, in his case Cleopatra.

equester (Eng: equestrian): the second tier of Roman aristocracy. Historically, an *equester* was wealthy enough to supply a horse with which to fulfil his military service. By imperial times this was completely obsolete, and all an *equester* had to possess was the 400,000 sesterces property qualification. Usually translated as 'knight'.

Etruscans: inhabitants of Etruria, north of Rome, from c. eighth to fifth centuries BC. Although their language is largely lost, many of their words and customs were absorbed by Rome.

forum: large open piazza surrounded by colonnades, temples, porticuses, and commercial buildings, serving as a thoroughfare and marketplace where much commercial and political business took place. Statues of prominent citizens and dedications were displayed all around. Ordinary Roman cities had usually only one. Rome had several.

freedman (Latin: *libertus*) and freedwoman (*liberta*): a slave freed in his master's will, in his master's lifetime as a gift, or purchased by the slave from savings. A freedman could not vote or stand for office, but his sons could. Freedmen dominated commerce, often running businesses on their former masters' behalf. For this they were obliged to stay loyal and offer free services to the master and his friends, which might include support in elections.

guilds: the guilds (*collegia*) were trade organizations found in every Roman city though we know most about them from Rome,

Ostia, Pompeii, and Herculaneum. They had formal constitutions and elected officials and sought to protect their
members' interests. Freedmen dominated guilds, reflecting
their prominent role in commerce. Guilds were usually closely
associated with specific deities who were venerated in guild
headquarters. Guilds also played an active role in politics,
turning out to canvass in elections promoting their favourite
candidates' virtues and heaping abuse on their opponents. In
more extreme instances guild members turned to violence.

herm: a sculpture, usually in stone or bronze, of a head, neck, and
central part of the torso set into or integral with a square
pillar in place of the body, sometimes with genitals located in
the correct relative place on the shaft. Originally Greek but
adopted by the Romans.

imperator: original meaning was 'general', or 'commander-in-chief', but
evolved under the principate into being synonymous with
ruling, leading to our word emperor.

imperium: the authority to control an army or other branch of the government within the scope of the holder's magistracy. *Imperium
maius*, held by the emperors, outranked others with imperium.

Latin status: in the fourth century BC, Latin rights were devised as a
compensation afforded to the members of the Latin League
after they were defeated by Rome, and created a form of intermediate status between Roman citizens and provincials. The
Latins were awarded certain rights such as an entitlement to
trade with Roman citizens on equal terms. Under the emperors, Latin rights were in the gift of the emperors. The leaders
of such communities who held municipal magistracies were
elevated to Roman citizenship.

legion: Roman army unit under the emperors of around 5,500
citizen legionaries each, divided into cohorts, subdivided

into centuries. The total fluctuated over time from around twenty-five to over thirty. The vast majority were stationed round the frontiers according to perceived threat. Britain and Syria, for example, had some of the largest numbers. Some legionaries were sent on detachment to Rome, for example on military intelligence duties. In the Republic legions were normally raised only when needed and differed considerably in organization.

materfamilias (also *materfamilias domina*): mother, mistress, of the family. The senior female figure in a Roman household with authority over the day-to-day management of the household and its staff, and the education and upbringing of her children.

obelisk: Egyptian stone tapered square column with a pyramidion-shaped top. Formerly erected in Egypt's temples, many were taken by the Romans as trophies to Rome and erected in public spaces such as the Circus Maximus.

ordo decurionum: the 'order of decurions', i.e. the body of men on the council. The local civic equivalent of the Senate in Rome. Election as a civic aedile, for example in Pompeii, meant automatic entry to the council for life and the potential election to senior magistracies.

paterfamilias: father of the family. The senior male who stood at the head of a household with supreme authority over all family members. He determined who married who, using marriage contracts to form political and social alliances. He might also selectively use adoption to extend his family's interests and contacts.

patricians (Latin: *patricii*): the most senior and oldest Roman families. In earlier times they had a complete monopoly of power over the Senate and all other aspects of Roman society. During the Republic they were forced into sharing that power with some of the richest plebs (q.v.) but their sense of privilege and status never abated.

plebeians (Latin: *plebs*): the term for the vast majority of the freeborn and freed Roman citizenry, meaning the 'crowd' or the 'mob', to distinguish them from the patrician elite. The richest plebs were also admitted to the highest offices.

porticus: the word meant a colonnaded walkway, but evolved into the generic term for a building complex of some architectural pretensions with an elaborate entrances, colonnades, niches, temples, art galleries displaying paintings and sculptures, meeting rooms, and facilities such as a library. Livia and Octavia each endowed Rome with a porticus, but there were several others (Latin singular *and* plural: *porticus*). They remained in use for centuries. Only the porch of the Porticus of Octavia survives today.

praetor: senatoral magistracy, one tier below the consuls. Praetors could have responsibility for various activities, including judicial matters and the games in Rome. A man who had served as praetor then enjoyed propraetor status and could serve as a governor or administrator in a province. Under the emperors legionary commands and some provincial governments were classified as propraetorian.

Praetorian Guard: the imperial bodyguard based in the Castra Praetoria (Praetorian Camp) in Rome from the reign of Tiberius until that of Constantine I. The highest paid and most privileged troops in the Roman army, they were notorious for their inclination to bully civilians and also topple emperors who did not indulge them to their satisfaction.

quinquennales: every five years the elected pair of *duoviri* in a Roman city were given special responsibilities for compiling a census of people who possessed the appropriate property qualification. They were known as the *quinquennales*.

senate: the principal political assembly. Men of the senatorial order were eligible to stand for a series of magistracies culminating in the consulship at Rome; these magistrates were then advised by their peers in the Senate. Such men, as part of their careers, could also expect to command legions and provinces. Under the emperors their powers and influence waned.

sestertius or (English) sesterce: the principal base-metal (brass) coin of the imperial era, produced from the reign of Augustus up till the mid-third century and briefly revived under the Gallic emperor Postumus. In Republican times it occasionally appeared as a small silver coin. Tariffed at one-quarter of a denarius (q.v.). The sestertius was also the standard unit of measure cited when sums of money were considered even though in reality larger amounts were probably paid in silver denarii. Plural sestertii (Latin) normally used for generic references to the coin, e.g. 'Nero's issue of sestertii', sesterces (English) usually used for amounts, e.g. 'it cost 100 million sesterces'. Diameter c. 30–33 mm. Weight c. 23 gm.

seviri Augustales: priests of the imperial cult. The order was open to freedmen, making it their most important route to status in urban communities.

stadium: see circus (q.v.).

theatre: semi-circular auditorium based on Greek models with the audience in tiers of seats arranged according to status and facing the stage and its backdrop. Used for all sorts of entertainment from the highbrow to comedies, concerts and pantomime. The earliest masonry example in Rome was Pompey's theatre but Pompeii, having had Greek origins, had a much older one.

Vestal Virgins: the six priestesses of Vesta, goddess of the hearth. Their prime duty was to tend the eternal fire in their temple in the Forum, which they lived next door to. Vestals were appointed as girls aged six to ten and served for three decades, taking a vow of chastity. Breaking their vows meant severe punishment and sometimes execution, which could involve being buried alive. They were influential and considered to have various special powers.

NOTES

FOREWORD AND INTRODUCTION

1   *Natural History* 35.10.
2   *CIL* 1.1203, *apparet* = 'it is obvious'. Also, Claridge (2010), 385–6.
3   Catullus 10.2 *foro otiosum*, 'idling at the Forum'.
4   Suetonius, *Caesar* 52.1.
5   Livy 1, preface 4.
6   Catullus 23.
7   Juvenal 7.138, 3.183.
8   Tacitus, *Histories* 1.4.
9   Tacitus, *Histories* 1.71.
10 See de la Bédoyère, G. (1997), *Particular Friends: The Correspondence of Samuel Pepys and John Evelyn* (Boydell Press, Woodbridge), 16.
11 The reader is advised to read Adam Sisman's *Boswell's Presumptuous Task* (Penguin, London, 2001), in particular p. 168 ff on how Boswell compiled his biography of Johnson from his records.
12 Chris Mason, BBC Radio 4 1800 News, Sunday 11 June 2023.
13 C.S. Lewis (1942), *The Screwtape Letters* no. 27.
14 Mark Twain, *The Innocents Abroad* (1869), chapter 53.
15 Dio 59.6.3. The woman's demand is not recorded, nor whether Hadrian granted it.
16 *In defence of Plancius* 14.35 where Cicero complained that he was angered when 'the sayings of other men' were attributed to him, not least because he considered himself unworthy of them. This gripe also occurs in a letter of his to Volumnius Eutrapelus (*Letters to his Friends* 7.32.1).
17 A rare exception is a sestertius of Hadrian recording the 874th year 'from the birth of the city' struck in AD 122. *RIC* (Hadrian) 609.

18 2 April 1775, as recorded by James Boswell in his *Life of Samuel Johnson*.
19 Juvenal 7.98 ff, using the word *ignavus*.
20 *Henry IV Pt. II*, Act III Scene 1.

1: CITYSCAPE

1   Horace, *Odes* 3.29.12.
2   Tertullian, *Spectacles* 16.1.
3   Josephus, *Jewish Antiquities* 19.26–7.
4   Cicero, *Handbook to Electioneering* 54.
5   Pliny 3.67.
6   Juvenal 3.182–4, 225.
7   Macrobius 3.9.
8   Cicero, *Letters to his brother Quintus* 3.4.5, referring to his brother's Greek library.
9   Pliny 3.66.
10 Plural *triviis*, see Horace, *Epistles* 1.17.58. Trivia was also the goddess of grave-yards and witchcraft.
11 Juvenal 3.235.
12 Martial 12.57.
13 Martial 6.77, and 9.22.
14 Herodian 1.17.6.
15 Pliny 37.31; Cicero, *Letters to his brother Quintus* 1.1.16.
16 Diodorus Siculus 33.28b.
17 *CIL* 1.2937a (Philae).
18 Loeb series, *Select Papyri* vol. II, no. 416, p. 567.
19 Appian, *Civil Wars* 1.58.
20 Appian, *Civil Wars* 4.7.
21 Nominal here means exactly that. In practice, the actual numbers serving were affected by all sorts of factors including sickness, being posted elsewhere, or a shortage of recruits. The men were organized into 'centuries' of 80 men each.
22 Tacitus, *Annals* 4.5.3, *Histories* 2.93.
23 The term cohortes vigilum means 'the cohorts of watchmen'. See variously Dio 55.8.6; Suetonius, *Augustus* 25.2, Strabo 5.3.7, Dio 26.4 (that freedmen were used), Suetonius, ibid. 30.1 (describing their distribution).
24 Josephus, *Jewish Antiquities* 19.266.
25 Juvenal, *Satires* 16.7–25.
26 Juvenal 16.7–17.
27 Herodian 2.4.1.
28 *CIL* 6.22355 (Rome).
29 See Chapter 8 for the story of Euhodus.
30 Martial 1.117 (the Argiletum, see Varro 5.157).
31 Aelius Aristides, *In Praise of Rome* 200, 201.

32 Portus lay just north of Ostia and serviced the Claudian harbour and subsequently that of Trajan. Its site is partly covered now by Fiumicino Leonardo da Vinci Airport.

33 *AE* 1980.84.

34 Strabo 5.3.2.

35 Strabo 5.3.7; Horace, *Epistles* 1.1.100.

36 Cicero, *Letters to his brother Quintus* 3.1.17 where he states that letters he had just received had been en route for twenty-seven days.

37 Josephus, *Jewish Antiquities* 19.1.4; Dio 55.8.3–4 for the Field of Agrippa (*campus Agrippae*).

38 Pliny 36.24, 35.

39 Pliny 36.101.

40 Pliny 36.121.

41 Pliny 36.111.

42 Strabo 5.3.8.

43 Frontinus, *Aqueducts of Rome* 1.10.

44 Frontinus, *Aqueducts of Rome* 1.16.

45 Frontinus, *Aqueducts of Rome* 2.96, 117–18.

46 Frontinus, *Aqueducts of Rome* 2.70, 73.

47 Frontinus, *Aqueducts of Rome* 2.75–6, 114, 115.

48 Frontinus, *Aqueducts of Rome* 2.88, 105, 107.

49 The FEL.TEMP. REPARATIO type which first appeared c. 348 and was struck in numerous imperial mints around the Roman world.

50 Ammianus Marcellinus 16.10.9 ff.

51 Plutarch, *Sulla* 1 specifically states 250 Attic drachmas to be equivalent to 1,000 sesterces, which made it an exact equivalent of a Roman denarius.

52 *CIL* 4 3340.142; C&C H81 (Pompeii).

53 Hobbs, R. (2017), 'Bes, Butting Bulls, and Bars: The Life of Coinage at Pompeii', in Flohr, M., and Wilson, A. (2017), *The Economy of Pompeii*, Oxford University Press, pp. 341, 343.

54 Varro, *Latin Language* 5.173.

55 Varro, *Latin Language* 5.173.

56 Pliny 33.132.

57 See L&R II, 421, involving a sudden devaluation by the state c. 300. Such declarations could (and did) result in some hoarded savings simply being abandoned.

2: THE ROMAN MINDSET

1 Vergil, *Aeneid* 1.278–9.

2 Sallust, *The War with Catiline* 53.2, 4–5.

3 Livy 1.11.

4 Florus 1.1.1–2, 7.

5 Cato, *On Agriculture* 1.4. See Appendix 3 for him and his great-grandson, Cato the Younger.

6 Martial 14.34.

7 *infirmitatem consili.* Cicero, *In defence of Murena* 27.

8 Cicero, *On Old Age* 15.51, 16.56.

9 Horace, *Epodes* 2.

10 Horace, *Epistles* 1.11 lines 29–30.

11 Martial 12.57.21.

12 Cicero, *In favour of the Lex Manilia* 22.64–5.

13 Quoted by Aulus Gellius 2.22.29, *quantum demas, tantum adcrescit.* Gellius took this from Cato's lost work *Origins.*

14 Polybius 34.9.8–11 (Strabo 3.5.7 C172); see also Diodorus Siculus 5.38.1 for the lives of slaves in the mines.

15 Livy 2.10; Valerius Maximus 3.2.1, 4.7.2.

16 Pliny 34.22.

17 Florus 1.4.3–4.

18 Livy 2.12–13.

19 Valerius Maximus 6.1.1.

20 Florus 1.7.9–15.

21 Fronto to Marcus Aurelius, Loeb edition vol. II, p. 181.

22 Seneca, *Letters* 86.

23 Zonaras, *Epitome* 7.21.

24 Vergil, *Aeneid* 1.278–9. See the beginning of this chapter.

25 Pliny, *NH* 3.17.

26 Pliny, *NH* 3.39.

27 Livy 8.40.3–5.

28 Cicero, *Brutus* 16.62.

29 Pliny 35.12–13. The Latin term for such a portrait was *imago clipeata.*

30 Juvenal 8.1 ff. By Corvinus, Juvenal means Marcus Valerius Messalla Corvinus (c. 64 BC – AD 12), a celebrated author and general, distantly related through the marriage of one of his sisters to a cousin of Augustus, and who had changed his loyalties during the wars following Caesar's assassination.

31 Livy 1. Preface 4.

32 Livy 39.6.3–9. 7.1 ff.

33 Livy 37.5.4 (booty); 37.46.3 (triumph).

34 Livy 37.57.10–15, 58.1 (censor election); 40.34.5 (temple).

35 Pliny 33.150.

36 Dio 21 (Zonaras 9.31; Loeb edition vol. II, p. 405).

37 Strabo 4.6.23. Polybius saw the destruction of art at Corinth, his observations reported by Strabo.

38 Pliny 34.6, 37.49.

39 Plutarch, *Sulla* 35.1.

40 Pliny 37.18–19, and see also Nero's crystal cups at 37.29 (Chapter 9).

41 Josephus, *Jewish Antiquities* 19.1.7–9; Suetonius, *Caligula* 22.2.
42 Pliny 9.118.
43 Velleius Paterculus 2.1.1–2.
44 *CIL* 11.1069a (Parma).
45 Petronius, *Satyricon* 32, 71, and 78.
46 Quintilian, *Orations* 2.5.12.
47 Tacitus, *Agricola* 30.4.
48 Dio 19.64.
49 Tibullus 2.3.35.
50 Dio 39.17.1–2.
51 Tacitus, *Annals* 1.2.
52 Dio 53.16.
53 Augustus, *Res Gestae* 34.
54 Dio 53.17.
55 Josephus, *Jewish Antiquities* 19.167–84.
56 Suetonius, *Augustus* 94.4.
57 Appian, *Civil Wars* 1.5.
58 Varro, *Latin Language* 5.80–81. The crucial word is *terni*, 'three each'.

3: DOMUS ET FAMILIA

1 *Digest* 1.6.4 (Ulpian).
2 Aulus Gellius, *Attic Nights* 2.15.1–2.
3 Varro, *Latin Language* 6.69–70.
4 Macrobius 1.3.9.
5 Quoted by Aulus Gellius, *Attic Nights* 1.6.3. Numidicus was censor in 102 BC.
6 *CIL* 6.34268.
7 Plutarch, *Roman Questions* 86.
8 Plutarch, *Roman Questions* 30; Pliny 8.194. Tanaquil was the wife of Tarquinius Priscus, fifth king of Rome.
9 *ILS* 8393. Translation of full text at http://www.u.arizona.edu/~afutrell/survey/laud%20tur.htm
10 Valerius Maximus 6.7.2.
11 Appian, *Civil Wars* 4.23.
12 Valerius Maximus 6.7.1.
13 Cicero, *Letters to his Friends* 16.26.
14 The girl's father, Arulenus Rusticus, had been executed by Domitian in 93. Pliny the Younger, *Letters* 1.14.
15 *CIL* 6.11602 (Rome).
16 Suetonius, *Augustus* 64.2.
17 *CIL* 6.29580 (Rome).
18 Pliny the Younger, *Letters* 4.19, 6.4, 8.10, 11.
19 *CIL* 6.20116, 20158 (Rome).

20 *CIL* 6.2527a (Rome).

21 Horace's tribute to his father is in his *Satires* 1.6.

22 ISIS 00132 (Isola Sacra). The readings here are by the author following personal examination of the stone.

23 Fronto, *Letters* 1.12 (Loeb edition vol. II, p. 173).

24 Pliny the Younger, *Letters* 7.18.

25 Aurelius Victor, *Epitome* 12.4.

26 *CIL* 11.1147 (Veleia); *Digest* 34.1.14.1, and see Pliny the Younger, *Panegyric* 25.

27 Valerius Maximus 7.8.1; Cicero, *Academica* 2.89.

28 Valerius Maximus 7.8.2.

29 Valerius Maximus 7.8.4.

30 Pliny the Younger, *Letters* 6.33.

31 *CIL* 6.10230 (Rome).

32 Valerius Maximus 2.1.6. Viriplaca is otherwise unknown.

33 Livy, *Epitome* 48; Valerius Maximus 6.3.8. There are slight differences in the names.

34 Livy 8.18.

35 Pliny 6.54, 29.26.

36 Livy 10.23.3–10. His placing of the patrician shrine in the Forum Boarium may have been a mistake. Its exact location, like the plebeian one, is unknown now.

37 *CIL* 6.19128 (Rome).

38 See also Aulus Gellius, *Attic Nights* 12.1 on the benefits of a mother breastfeeding her own child.

39 Livy 3.44 ff; Valerius Maximus 6.2.

40 Valerius Maximus 6.3–4.

41 Valerius Maximus 6.3.9 and Pliny 14.89; also called Egnatius Mecenius. For the Bacchanalian executions, see Valerius Maximus 6.3.7 and Livy 39.18.6, who provides the date.

42 Valerius Maximus 6.3.8.

43 Plutarch, *Roman Questions* 3.

44 Vitruvius 6.3.

45 Cicero, *Letters to his brother Quintus* 3.1.1–2.

46 Pliny 36.48.

47 Juvenal 3.295 ff.

48 Martial 8.14.5.

4: SEX AND PASSION

1 *ILS* 8157 (Rome).

2 Plutarch, *Sulla* 35.4–5.

3 Pliny 28.58.

4 Suetonius, *Caesar* 52.3.

5   Sallust, *The War with Catiline* 11.3, 12.1.

6   Josephus, *Jewish Antiquities* 19.5.29.

7   Dio 54.19.1–3; Suetonius, *Augustus* 69.1–2, 71.1.

8   Dio 60.22.1–2; Suetonius, *Augustus* 44.2.

9   Pliny 10.171–2.

10 Juvenal 6.283–305.

11 *CIL* 6.36819 (Rome, found near Monte di Testaccio).

12 L&R II, 48–9.

13 As reported by Aulus Gellius 10.23.4. Cato's oration has not survived.

14 Tacitus, *Annals* 13.44, in the year 58 under Nero.

15 Suetonius, *Domitian* 3, 10; Dio 67.12.1–2.

16 Juvenal 6.314–48.

17 Livy, summary of Book IX. See Loeb edition vol. IV, p. 551.

18 Dionysius of Halicarnassus 4.62.

19 Livy 22.57.2 ff.

20 Dio 26.87.3 ff.

21 Plutarch, *Roman Questions* 83, and *Life of Marcellus* 3.

22 Plutarch, *Cato the Elder* 17.7.

23 Valerius Maximus 4.6.2.

24 Plutarch, *Pompey* 48.5.

25 In 43 BC. Dio 47.7.4.

26 *ILS* 8393 (Rome).

27 Velleius Paterculus 2.45.1.

28 Suetonius, *Caesar* 6.2; Plutarch, *Caesar* 10.9; Dio 37.45.

29 Plutarch, *Caesar* 8–10. The account includes a detailed description of the affair.

30 It has been suggested that Catullus immortalized Clodia Metelli in in his works as 'Lesbia'. Apuleius, *Apologia* 10 says that Catullus used 'Lesbia' as a pseudonym for Clodia but this is not enough to specify which of the three sisters of Clodius named Clodia she was. As so often with these cases of disputed identity in antiquity there is simply insufficient evidence to provide a definitive and indisputable conclusion.

31 Cicero, *Pro Caelio* 31 ff.

32 Cicero used the rhetorical term *inpudicissimus* ('extreme sexual misbehaviour') to refer to Antony, for example, in *Philippics* 2.70, and also challenged his pudicitia at, for example, 2.3.

33 Appian 5.59.1.

34 Velleius Paterculus 2.74.2.

35 Plutarch, *Antony* 10.3.

36 Macrobius 2.5.9.

37 Suetonius, *Claudius* 36. He suggests that it was not until Silius came on to the scene that Claudius' 'ardent love' for Messalina diminished.

38 Soranus, *Gynaecology* 1.61.1–3; Pliny 29.85 quoting 'the commentaries of Caecilius'. Another plant, *silphium*, possibly associated with contraception

and certainly many other medicinal properties, had led to it being harvested into extinction in Cyrenaica, its main source, by Pliny's time (19.38–40). More information at Riddle, J.M. (1992), *Contraception and Abortion from the Ancient World to the Renaissance*, Harvard University Press, Harvard.

39 Sallust, *The War with Catiline* 24–5.
40 Juvenal 6.489 – Juvenal is only implying the association with prostitution here by suggesting a well-to-do woman was acting like one when seeking a secret liaison; Martial 11.47.
41 *CIL* 6.37965 (Rome). The other descriptions in this passage come mainly from Juvenal's third and sixteenth Satires, and Polybius 6.53.
42 Catullus 55.
43 Martial 3.93.15.
44 Aulus Gellius, *Attic Nights* 4.14.
45 Plutarch, *Roman Questions* 35, *Life of Romulus* 5.
46 Plutarch, *Pompey* 2.2–3.
47 The decree was displayed on bronze tablets in Italian cities. One from Larinum seems to refer to this measure though the relevant section is incomplete. See Sherk (1988), no. 35, n. 1, and also Suetonius, *Tiberius* 35.2. Tactus 2.85.1–3; Suetonius, *Tiberius* 35.2.
48 Suetonius, *Tiberius* 58.
49 *CIL* 9.2029 (Benevento), 116 (Brindisi), and 238 (Taranto). The modern Spanish *ramera*, 'whore', appears to preserve part of the Latin term but rather less ambiguously. *Meretrix* is the origin of the English word 'meretricious' meaning 'worthless' or 'undeserving of praise'.
50 *CIL* 6.37965 (Rome).
51 Dio 62.15.4.
52 *ILS* 7478, *CIL* 9.2689 (Isernia). For the number of brothels in fourth-century Rome see McGinn, T. (2013), 'Sorting out prostitution in Pompeii: the material remains, terminology and the legal sources', *JRA* vol. 26, 610–33.
53 Variously in this order: *CIL* 4.1751, 8536, 2178, 2188, 2213 (Pompeii).
54 VDM (2012), 74.
55 Martial 11.45.
56 *SHA* (Elagabalus) 27.7.
57 Ovid, *Art of Love* 1.10.
58 Ovid, *Art of Love* 1.5 (especially lines 135–63). He used the term *leves animos* to refer to women.
59 Ovid, *Art of Love* 1.135 ff; *Amores* 1.4.
60 Ovid, *Amores* 1.4.
61 Martial 3.93.
62 Juvenal 6.352 ff. Ogulnia was the female version of a known Roman proper name, Ogulnius, e.g. Livy 10.6.4, and seems to have had no special significance. Ogulnia was thus probably her real name.

5: CURSUS HONORUM

1   Sallust, *The War with Catiline* 3.4–5.
2   Suetonius, *Caesar* 29; Plutarch, *Caesar* 11.
3   Varro, *Latin Language* 7.30.
4   Cicero, *Letters to his brother Quintus* 1.2.9.
5   Pliny 35.23.
6   Cicero, *On Duties* 1.8.25.
7   Plutarch, *Crassus* 2.
8   Plutarch, *Marius* 2.
9   Plutarch, *Cicero* 2.1–2.
10   Seneca, *On Anger* 2.21.1–7.
11   Pliny the Younger, *Letters* 6.3. The farm was worth 100,000 sesterces when given to the nurse, a sum roughly approximate to the annual pay of eighty legionaries.
12   Quintilian, *Institutes* 1.1.4 ff.
13   Martial 11.39.
14   *CIL* 6.7767 (Rome). The female slave was called Florentina. Her age is not specified. It is not possible to know who Philaeterus taught though the date might mean the young Hadrian.
15   *CIL* 10.6561 (Velitrae). Her death is recorded by Suetonius, *Claudius* 26.1.
16   Petronius, *Satyricon* 58.7.
17   Suetonius, *Schoolteachers* 9.
18   Cicero, *Letters to his brother Quintus* 2.4.2; Plutarch, *Lucullus* 19.
19   Martial 9.68; Juvenal *Satires* 7.215 ff.
20   Pliny the Younger, *Letters* 4.13.
21   Quintilian 1.4.2–4, 10.1.2, 12.11.31.
22   Polybius 6.19.
23   Tacitus, *Dialogue on Orators* 34.1.
24   Dio 68.7.4.
25   Suetonius, *Grammarians* 16.
26   Quintilian 1.1.6, 'read not merely as an honour to her sex'. Quintilian specifies other women whose learning and literary skills had earned them enduring reputations, including Cornelia, mother of the Gracchi. See also Valerius Maximus 8.3.3.
27   Valerius Maximus 8.3.1–3, writing in the reign of Tiberius; Ulpian is cited by Justinian, *Digest* 3.1.1.5. On the importance for a man of not sounding like a woman, see Quintilian 11.3.19.
28   Cicero, *Letters to his brother Quintus* 3.9.2.
29   Plutarch, *Gaius Gracchus* 3 (123 BC).
30   Plutarch, *Sulla* 5.
31   Plutarch, *Pompey* 53.
32   Cicero, *Letters to his brother Quintus* 2.15b.4.

33 See, for example, Frontinus, *On Aqueducts* 2.129.

34 Cicero, *Handbook to Electioneering* 2–5, 44.

35 Pompeii House no. I.vi.15 (Region I, Insula vi, entrance 15).

36 *CIL* 4.1083 (Pompeii) is an instance of Sabinus and Secundus being cited together. *CIL* 4.7273 is a recommendation by the millers of Sabinus for aedile. Among the women endorsing Sabinus was Iunia (*CIL* 4.1168).

37 For Polybius and his provision of 'good bread', see *CIL* 4.429; for Claudius Verus, see *CIL* 4.3741 (both Pompeii).

38 *CIL* 4.575, 576, 581 (all Pompeii).

39 Suetonius, *Augustus* 35.1.

40 Macrobius, *Saturnalia* 2.3.11 (see also Suetonius, *Augustus* 35.1).

41 Cicero, *Verrine Orations*, 2.49.122, First Pleading 1, 4.

42 See for example Cicero, *Verrine Orations* 5.4–5.

43 Cicero, *Verrine Orations*, 3.89.

44 Appian, *Civil Wars* 2.24, *Syrian Wars* 51; Dio 39.57.3–58.1, and Strabo 17.1.11.

45 Cicero, *In Piso* 90.

46 'The wailing stairs'.

47 Valerius Maximus 6.3.3; Dio 58.5.6.

48 Plutarch, *Marius* 45.

49 Appian, *Civil Wars* 1.71.

50 Suetonius, *Tiberius* 6.3.4–6.

51 Tacitus, *Annals* 4.2.

52 Juvenal 10.66 adds the detail about the hook.

53 Tacitus, *Annals* 5.9.1–2.

54 Tacitus *Annals* 4.3.5; *BSRH* p. 47, no. 98 (Ostian Calendar).

6: THE FRIGHTENED CITY

1 Juvenal 3.302–5.

2 Plutarch, *Tiberius Gracchus* 10.7.

3 Suetonius, *Nero* 26.1.

4 Tribunes of the plebs were men of senatorial status, but from wealthy plebeian families whose wealth fulfilled the property qualification and had been admitted to the Senate.

5 Plutarch, *Tiberius Gracchus* 8.7.

6 Plutarch, *Tiberius Gracchus* 10.1–4.

7 Plutarch, *Tiberius Gracchus* 10.5–7.

8 Appian, *Civil Wars* 1.12; Plutarch, *Tiberius Gracchus* 11.2–4.

9 Appian, *Civil Wars* 1.13. This Apppius Claudius Pulcher was the probable father of his namesake (consul in 79 BC) who was father of the notorious Publius Clodius (formerly Claudius) Pulcher.

10 Sempronius Asellio, quoted by Aulus Gellius 2.13.4.

11 Appian, *Civil Wars* 1.14.

12 Appian, *Civil Wars* 1.15.
13 Appian, *Civil Wars* 1.16. Plutarch, *Gracchus* 19.5 says the senators' attendants had brought weapons. For the death see 20.2–3; see also Valerius Maximus 1.4.2.
14 Tacitus, *Annals* 3.27.2.
15 *CIL* 4.910 (Pompeii).
16 Meiggs (1960), 185, 203, 224.
17 Appian, *Civil Wars* 1.4.32.
18 Appian, *Civil Wars* 1.8.64.
19 Appian, *Civil Wars* 1.11.96, 98; Plutarch, *Sulla* 31.1, 5.
20 Dio 33.109.6 ff.
21 Dittenberger 741 (cited by L&R I, 212).
22 Appian, *Roman History (Mithridatic Wars)* 12.4.22–23; Velleius Paterculus 9.2.
23 Dio 30–35.109.11.
24 Dio 38.13.2, providing a direct Greek transliteration of collegia.
25 Cicero, *Letters to Atticus* 4.3.
26 Dio 39.7–8, 48.2 ff. But then the stakes were already very high. Not long afterwards a famine in Rome led to a huge mob rushing first into a theatre and then onto the Capitoline Hill to find the Senate. They shrieked at the senators, threatening to kill them or burn them alive along with the temples. Fortunately, under the emperors, private gangs were banned.
27 Cicero, *In Defence of Milo* 57, 58.
28 Appian, *Civil War* 4.2–3, 5.
29 Appian, *Civil War* 4.7.
30 Appian, *Civil War* 4.16.
31 Juvenal 3.268 ff.
32 Horace, *Epistles* 1.17.61–2.
33 Apuleius, *The Golden Ass* 3.3, 2.18.
34 Catullus 62.
35 Suetonius, *Nero* 26.
36 Petronius, *Satyricon* 22.
37 Juvenal 3.268–314.
38 Dio 67.11.6.
39 Dio 73.14.4.
40 *CIL* 3.2399; *ILS* 8514 (Solin, Dalmatia).
41 *AE* 1934.209 (Moesia Superior).
42 *CIL* 3.1559 (Dacia).

7: SLAVES

1 Pliny the Younger, *Letters* 21, to his father.
2 Martial 7.53, and 9.2.
3 Tacitus, *Annals* 12.53.

4   Suetonius, *Vespasian* 11. The verb is *iunxisset* which means any sort of connection or joining together, not just marriage.

5   Cicero, *Letters to his brother Quintus* 3.7.4 (Letter 27).

6   Pliny 33.134–7.

7   Seneca, *Letters* 5. Instances of modern slavery constantly emerge in the news today, for example: https://www.telegraph.co.uk/news/2022/02/04/man-exploited-slave-kept-40-years-given-18-month-suspended-sentence/

8   See, for example, the Loeb text of Martial 1.41.2, where *verna* is translated as 'buffoon'.

9   Suetonius, *Galba* 4.4.

10   *AE* 1990.51 (nr Rome).

11   Suetonius, *Caesar* 47.

12   Pliny the Younger, *Letters* 1.21.

13   *CIL* 4.3340.155 (Pompeii).

14   Cicero, *Orations* 232: *neque me divitiae movent, quibus omnis Africanos et Laelios multi venialicii mercatoresque superarunt.* https://www.perseus.tufts.edu/hopper/text?doc=Perseus%3Atext%3A2008.01.0545%3Achapter%3D70%3Asection%3D232

15   From the nominative form *venalis*.

16   Suetonius, *Caligula* 36.2.

17   Tomlin, R.S.O., 2003, 'The Girl in Question: A New Text from Roman London', *Britannia* vol. 34, 41–51.

18   Martial 3.62 (Quintus), 6.29 ('greed platforms' market), and 11.70 (Tucca).

19   Pliny 7.56; and see Suetonius, *Augustus* 69.1 for another reference to the famous Toranius.

20   Pliny 21.170.

21   Pliny 24.35.

22   The Timotheus tombstone is in Amphipolis Archaeological Museum. For these two traders and references, see Bosworth, A.B. (2002), 'Vespasian and the Slave Trade', *Classical Quarterly* vol. 51, no. 1, 351–7.

23   Persius 6.75.

24   Martial 9.6.4; Suetonius, *Domitian* 7.1.

25   *Digest* 48.8.4.2 and see 48.8.4 for the law of 97.

26   Plutarch, *Antony* 5.4.

27   Seneca, *On Mercy* 1.24.1.

28   Pliny 28.13.

29   Cicero, *Letters to his brother Quintus* 1.2.14.

30   Varro, *On Agriculture* 1.17–18.

31   Petronius, *Satyricon* 76.

32   Cato, *On Agriculture* 2.7.

33   Suetonius, *Claudius* 25.2.

34   Suetonius, *Augustus* 42.3, *Caligula* 8.4.

35   Seneca, *Letters* 47.11.

36   Plutarch, *Antony* 1.

Notes

37 Suetonius, *Augustus* 32.1, and *Tiberius* 8.

38 *SHA* (Hadrian) 18.7.

39 Suetonius, *Caesar* 75.3.

40 Suetonius, *Caesar* 48.

41 Suetonius, *Augustus* 67.1. Doubtless Cosmus was classed as a verna, one of the insultingly over-familiar household slaves. Under Galba, slaves who had spoken insultingly to their masters during Nero's reign were handed over to their masters for punishment. Dio 63.3.4.

42 Suetonius, *Tiberius* 58.

43 Petronius, *Satyricon* 30, 66.

44 Seneca, *Letters* 47.2–3.

45 Juvenal 6.242–3, 474–91.

46 *CIL* 10.26 (Locri).

47 Quintilian, *Oratory Institutes* 1.3.13.

48 At Fenstanton, Cambridgeshire, and publicized in the national press, e.g. *Daily Telegraph*, 9 December 2021. https://www.telegraph.co.uk/news/2021/12/08/first-physical-evidence-roman-crucifixion-britain-unearthed/

49 Suetonius, *Caligula* 32.

50 The *muraena Helena*. Pliny 9.76–7.

51 Plautus, *The Menaechmi*, 5.4.

52 Suetonius, *Otho* 5.2.

53 Dio 78.21 *passim*.

54 Dio 67.13.1.

55 Cicero, *On Duties* 1.138.

56 Asconius 27C, 32C; Pliny 36.103, and see also Claridge, A. (2010), *Rome. An Oxford Archaeological Guide*, Oxford University Press, Oxford, 118.

57 Tibullus 2.3.41–4.

58 Widely reported, for example: http://pompeiisites.org/en/comunicati/the-room-of-the-slaves-the-latest-discovery-at-civita-giuliana/

59 Varro, *Latin Language* 8.6.

60 Plautus, *Pseudolus* 1.2.

61 Suetonius, *Augustus* 29.3.

62 Suetonius, *Caesar* 76.3.

63 Suetonius, *Domitian* 19.

64 *AE* 1973.143 (Pompeii).

65 *Digest* 44.4.5.3.

66 Suetonius, *Domitian* 11.1.

67 *CIL* 6.33824 (Rome).

68 *CIL* 6.33470 (Rome).

69 *CIL* 6.6314 (Rome), found in the columbarium of the Statilii near the Porta Maggiore. Viewable at: https://commons.wikimedia.org/wiki/File:NOTHI_LIBRARI_A_MANU.jpg

70 Columella, *On Agriculture* 1.8.1–8.

71   Tacitus, *Annals* 13.32, for the year 57–8.
72   Tacitus, *Annals* 14.42.1–45.2.
73   Tacitus. *Annals* 3.36.2–3.
74   Tacitus, *Histories* 2.72.
75   Suetonius, *Caesar* 27.
76   Appian, *Civil Wars* 1.73.
77   Appian, *Civil Wars* 3.11.
78   Appian, *Civil Wars* 4.43.
79   Appian, *Civil Wars* 4.44.
80   Appian, *Civil Wars* 3.98.
81   Appian, *Civil Wars* 4.23. It is not entirely clear whether this Ligarius is related to the pair of proscribed Ligarii brothers referred to in the preceding passage. Both refer to hiding in ovens, so it is possible Appian has referred to the same incident twice but become confused.
82   Pliny the Younger, *Letters* 3.14.
83   *Digest* 40.1.5; in practice, the peculium was usually treated as if it was the slave's own money, see ibid., 40.1.4.1.
84   *CIL* 6.15598 (Rome). For the use of contubernalis just as a friend of the same sex, see Pliny the Younger, *Letters* 1.19.
85   See Chapter 15 and second colour plate section.
86   *CIL* 6.2171 (Rome c. 30–10 BC). On display in the British Museum.
87   *Digest* 37.14.7.
88   Josephus, *Jewish Antiquities* 19.133.
89   Gaius, *Institutes* 1.40.
90   Dio 78.9.4.
91   Pliny the Younger, *Letters* 7.16. See also Ulpian, *Rules* 6.1–10.
92   Cicero, *Letters to Atticus* 7.2.8.

8: SPLENDID ACCESSORIES

1   Appian, *Civil Wars* 3.94.9. The term is αλλα λαμπρα. This can be translated in several different ways, for example 'splendid others'.
2   Seneca, *On a Tranquil Mind* 8.8.
3   Martial 5.13.
4   *CIL* 11.3885 (Capena).
5   Dio 39.38.6.
6   Plutarch, *Pompey* 2.4.
7   Appian, *Civil Wars* 3.94.
8   Seneca, *Letters* 86.6.
9   Plutarch, *Cicero* 1.
10   Plutarch, *Cicero* 11.
11   Suetonius, *Caesar* 48.
12   *Digest* 38.1.25, 27, 28, 19, 35 (in the same order as discussed in the text).

13 Appian, *Civil Wars* 4.44, 28 (in the same order as in the text).

14 Appian, *Civil Wars* 4.26. At 3.11 Appian supplies the 25,000 figure.

15 Dio 77.10 *passim*.

16 *CIL* 14.321 (Ostia).

17 For example, *CIL* 14.5374 (Ostia).

18 *CIL* 6.8826 (Rome).

19 Tacitus, *Annals* 14.17.

20 *CIL* 10.846 (Pompeii).

21 Various recorded tile stamps, for example *CIL* 15.427 (Pompeii).

22 C&C, 172.

23 *CIL* 10.892 (Pompeii). The inscription bears a consular date from Rome for the year 3.

24 See C&C, 101 (Pompeii).

25 *CIL* 10.813 (Pompeii).

26 *CIL* 11.7217 (Volsinii).

27 *CIL* 10.1452, *ILS* 6352; *AE* 1979.172 (Herculaneum).

28 C&C G38.

29 *CIL* 10.1030, *ILS* 6373 (Pompeii).

30 Various references to this man are known, but especially *CIL* 15.420 (Rome).

31 Nicodemus Sponsian and Eros Spo(n)sianus, a doctor, *CIL* 6.3959, and 8901 (Rome). For the latter see Chapter 10.

32 *CIL* 10.853, *ILS* 5653e (Pompeii).

33 *CIL* 14.2722 (Tusculum, near Rome).

34 This man was either a member of the senatorial family of the Atilii (Aetilius is simply a variant spelling) or one of their freedmen himself. Part of the Latin text is ambiguous, hence the variant reading. Euhodus is probably from the Greek word for 'fragrant', ευωδης.

35 *CIL* 6.9545 (Rome).

36 Seneca, *Letters* 47.9.

37 Seneca, *Letters* 47.10.

9: DINING OUT AND EATING IN

1 Varro, *Latin Language* 5.146. By Varro's time, the facility had been incorporated into a general marketplace (*macellum*) along with other sellers of various different foods.

2 Plutarch, *Cato* 1.7, 4.3–4, 8.1.

3 Pliny 9.67, repeated by Macrobius 3.16.8 who gives 7,000 sesterces as the figure.

4 Rowan, E., 'Sewers, Archaeobotany, and Diet at Pompeii and Herculaneum', 112, in Flohr, M., and Wilson, A. (eds) (2017), *The Economy of Pompeii* (Oxford University Press, Oxford).

5 Livy 38.35.7–8.

6   Appian, *Civil Wars* 1.21; Plutarch, *Gaius Gracchus* 5.2. For the colonists, see Appian, *Punic Wars* 136.

7   Sallust, *Histories* 1.55.11, also given as *Speech of the Consul Lepidus* 11, as quoted by Sallust (Loeb edition of Sallust's extant works, p. 389).

8   Sallust, *Histories* (fragment) 2.42.

9   Dio 36.22.2.

10 Dio 36.28.4.

11 Dio 36.36a.

12 Plutarch, *Cato the Younger* 26.1.

13 Dio 38.13.1.

14 Dio 39.9.3.

15 Cicero, *On His House* 16.

16 Suetonius, *Caesar* 41.3.

17 Cicero, *Letters to Atticus* 9.9.2.

18 By using the provision in the Lex Terentia-Cassia. Cicero, *Verrine Orations* 2, 3.163, 173.

19 Appian 5.68.

20 Suetonius, *Augustus* 42.3.

21 Strabo 5.3.5.

22 Plutarch, *Caesar* 58.10.

23 Suetonius, *Claudius* 18.1–2.

24 Suetonius, *Claudius* 20.3.

25 Seneca, *Letters* 77.1, 3.

26 Plutarch, *Otho* 4.5.

27 Illustrated in the British Museum *Guide to the Exhibition Illustrating Greek and Roman Life* (British Museum, London, 1908), p. 10. Accession number not traced.

28 *Scabiosum tesserula far*, Persius 5.74.

29 Dio 73.12–13 *passim*.

30 *SHA* (Aurelian) 35.2.

31 Gambling scenes were found on the walls of one establishment at Pompeii VI.10.1.

32 Widely reported in the press, but especially https://www.pompeionline.net/en/news/252-completed-excavations-at-pompeii-thermopolium-in-regio-v

33 Catullus 37.

34 Appian, *Civil Wars* 1.54.

35 Horace, *Epistles* 1.14.21.

36 Suetonius, *Vitellius* 13.3. Anecdotally, President Trump was said to prefer stopping for cheeseburgers at fast-food restaurants for exactly this reason.

37 *SHA* (Hadrian) 16.4.

38 Juvenal 8.463.

39 Juvenal 11.77 ff.

40 Aulus Gellius, *Attic Nights* 2.24.2.

41 Plutarch, *Sulla* 1.

42 Aulus Gellius, *Attic Nights* 2.24.11.

43 Varro, *On Agriculture* 3.12.4–5.

44 Aulus Gellius, *Attic Nights* 2.14 *passim*; for the peacocks see Pliny 10.23, and for the enlarged aviaries Varro, *On Agriculture* 3.3.6.

45 Juvenal 5.12 ff.

46 Suetonius, *Claudius* 21.4.

47 Pliny 10.133.

48 Apicius 2.44.

49 Apicius 2.55.

50 Apicius 9.399, and for the malobathron see Pliny 12.129.

51 Petronius, *Satyricon* 35.

52 Pliny 33.139 ff, 155.

53 Pliny 33.141.

54 Plutarch, *Antony* 9.5.

55 Pliny 33.145–6.

56 Herodotus 1.18; Hippocrates, *On Ulcers* 7, referring to the use of powdered silver.

57 Juvenal 11.117 ff.

58 Pliny 35.158.

59 Pliny 31.3–94.

60 *CIL* 4.9406 (Pompeii).

61 *CIL* 4.5682 (Pompeii).

62 Pliny 9.62.

63 *CIL* 6.9801 (Rome).

64 *CIL* 6.40638 (Rome).

65 Varro, *Latin Language* 5.146–7.

66 Juvenal 5.92–5.

67 Nero's macellum is depicted on a brass dupondius. *RIC* (Nero) 187, struck in 64.

68 Suetonius, *Augustus* 70.

69 Plutarch, *Antony* 2.3.

70 Suetonius, *Augustus* 74, 75.

71 Suetonius, *Claudius* 32.

72 Suetonius, *Vespasian* 22.1.

73 Suetonius, *Nero* 47.1; Pliny 37.29.

74 Suetonius, *Tiberius* 34.1.

75 Suetonius, *Nero* 27.2.

76 Suetonius, *Caligula* 27.4, 36.2, 39.2, *Claudius* 8.

77 Suetonius, *Claudius*, 20.2, 32, 33.1.

78 Suetonius, *Claudius* 44.

79 Suetonius, *Nero* 31.2.

80 Suetonius, *Galba* 22.1.

81 Suetonius, *Vitellius* 13.

82   *SHA* (Elagabalus) 27.1–6. The source, which dates to around a century or more later, is not generally regarded as reliable in detail.

83   Dio 73.8.5.

84   Marcus Aurelius, *Meditations* 3.2.

85   *CIL* 4.7698 (Pompeii).

86   Petronius, *Satyricon* 29.

87   Petronius, *Satyricon* 30.

88   Martial 11.52.

89   Petronius, *Satyricon* 53.

90   Catullus 13.

91   Pliny the Younger, *Letters* 2.6.

92   *CIL* 6.10097 (Rome).

93   Ovid, *On Sadness* 4.10.41 ff.

94   The Baths of Caracalla lay close to the Via Appia within Rome in an area that had hitherto been dominated by cemeteries and tombs.

95   Martial 12.82.

96   Martial 8.67.

97   Martial 2.36, 1.20.

98   Catullus 12.

99   Pliny the Younger, *Letters* 1.15.

100   *CIL* 6.39659 (found near the Porta Maggiore, Rome).

101   Pliny 18.108.

102   Plautus, *Pseudolus* Act 3, scene 2.

103   Pliny 9.67.

104   *CIL* 6.9645 (Rome; see also 6.7655 for another reference to the Hercules address).

105   Ovid, *Metamorphoses* 8.630 ff.

106   *CIL* 4.5380 (Pompeii House IV.vii.4–5); see Martial 5.78.9 for the botellus sausage.

10: DOCTORS AND DISEASE

1   Pliny 29.12.

2   Pliny 29.28.

3   Cato, *On Agriculture* 156–7.

4   This Marcus Nonius Balbus was tribune of the plebs in 32 BC. He was also praetor and proconsular governor of Crete and Cyrene. He made little impact on wider history.

5   Suetonius, *Vitellius* 17.2.

6   Justinian, *Digest* 9.3.1.

7   Justinian, *Digest* 43.10.5.

8   Orosius, *Against the Pagans* 4.3.2, probably originally from one of the lost passages of Livy.

9   Suetonius, *Vespasian* 5.4.

10   Juvenal 3.247.

11   Dio 39.61.1–3.
12   Cicero, *Letters to his brother Quintus* 3.7.1. A Crassipes was betrothed to Cicero's daughter Tullia in 56 BC. Ibid., 2.5.1.
13   Tacitus, *Histories* 1.86.
14   Tacitus, *Histories* 2.93; Columella, *On Agriculture* 1.5.3, 6.
15   Martial 10.6.
16   Juvenal 3.259–67.
17   This is a shameless nod on the author's part to Charles Dickens's *The Uncommercial Traveller*.
18   Seneca, *Letters* 104.6.
19   Juvenal 3.249–50.
20   *SHA* (Hadrian) 22.7.
21   Sherk (1988), p. 168.
22   Suetonius, *Augustus* 4.1.
23   Suetonius, *Augustus* 99–100.
24   Suetonius, *Vespasian* 24, *Titus* 11.
25   *SHA* (Hadrian) 24–25; Dio 69.20.1.
26   *CIL* 6.27556 (Rome).
27   Cicero, *Letters to his Friends* 7.26.
28   Pliny 28.27.
29   Catullus 44.
30   Seneca, *Letters* 6.54.1–6.
31   *CIL* 4.5738, 5737, 5741, 10282 (Pompeii).
32   Pliny 28.65. The Latin is rather more abbreviated than the translation implies.
33   Pliny 28.63, 65 ff, 226.
34   Pliny 28.226–7.
35   Pliny 28.45–6, 52.
36   Pliny 28.50.
37   Persius 2.31 ff.
38   Pliny 28.76–8.
39   Pliny 12.111 ff. For a list of the medications available see *RIB* II, Fascicule 4, 45.
40   *RIB* 2446.2 (d), 2446.4 (b), 2446.3 (c) (Britain).
41   See Justin Kaplan's review of K. Patrick Ober (2003), '*Mark Twain and Medicine: "Any Mummery Will Cure"'* in *Mark Twain and His Circle Series* (University of Missouri Press, Columbia) (https://muse.jhu.edu/article/175812)
42   Juvenal 6.578 ff.
43   Pliny 28.29, 37.
44   Suetonius, *Caligula* 8.4.
45   *CIL* 6.8901 (from the columbarium of Livia, the burial place of more than 1,100 members of imperial staff up to the reign of Claudius). See also the discussion in Chapter 8 about slave personal names used by freedmen. Eros Spo(n)sianus as a doctor attracted attention in the Renaissance, the text of his funerary inscription being published a number of times in the 1500s and 1600s.

46 Pliny 29.7. At the time, 500,000 sesterces were the equivalent of the annual pay of 555 legionary soldiers.

47 *CJ* 6. Title 43.1.

48 *AE* 1941.64 (found on the Via Praenestina, 8.8 kilometres from Rome).

49 Josephus, *Jewish Antiquities* 19.157.

50 Suetonius, *Titus* 2.

51 Martial 5.9.

52 Livy 1.35.9, *CIL* 6.1604 (Rome).

53 *CIL* 6.6192 (found at the Porta Praenestina, Rome).

54 Tacitus, *Annals* 6.50.2–5.

55 Pliny 29.14.

56 Pliny 29.11, 17, 22.

57 Celsus 4.17, 20.

58 Celsus 5.27.

59 Celsus 1.1–2.

60 Celsus, *prooemium* 43, 26.

61 Suetonius, *Caligula* 27.

62 Galen, *On the Composition of Drugs* 1.1, and *Of the Appropriate Writings of Galen* 2 (see https://www.cambridge.org/core/journals/journal-of-roman-archaeology/article/abs/galens-storeroom-romes-libraries-and-the-fire-of-ad-192/A2126E75F947287F0F900D2C36A5B521)

63 Galen, *On the Natural Faculties* 1.2 *passim*, and 2.8.116 ff.

64 Tacitus, *Annals* 4.3.5, 8.1, 10.1 ff.

65 Suetonius, *Nero* 34.5.

66 Seneca, *On Benefits* 6.15.

67 Varro, *Latin Language* 5.8, 10.46.

68 Pliny the Younger, *Letters* 10.5 and 6 (Harpocras), 10.11 (Postumius Marinus).

69 Martial 11.86.

70 Martial 1.30, 47.

71 Martial 8.74.

72 Martial 6.53, 70.

73 *SHA* (Marcus Aurelius) 13.3.

74 Dio 73.14.3; Herodian 1.12.1.

75 *SHA* (Lucius Verus) 9.10.

76 Littman, R.J., and Littman, M.L. (1973), 'Galen and the Antonine Plague', *American Journal of Philology* vol. 94, no. 3, 243–55, provide a useful summary of the evidence.

11: ENFEEBLED BY BATHS

1 Pliny 29.26.

2 Juvenal 6.447.

3 *SHA* (Hadrian) 17.5–6.

4 Domitian favoured this time. Suetonius, *Domitian* 21.1.
5 Pliny, writing in the 60s or 70s, refers to 'women bathing in company with men' and how much that could have appalled some of those in earlier times, at 33.153.
6 Martial 11.47.
7 Caenis is in Suetonius, *Vespasian* 3 and 21. The baths and Onesimus are recorded on an inscription from Rome, see Houston, G.W. (1996), 'Onesimus the Librarian', *Zeitschrift für Papyrologie und Epigraphik*, Bd. 114, 205–208.
8 Martial 5.70.
9 Martial 6.93.
10 Galen 18 (1), 792, as cited by L&S (vol. i), 781.
11 Martial 14.14–17.
12 Martial 1.23.
13 Catullus 33, *furum . . . balneariorum*, 'thief of the baths'.
14 Seneca, *Letters* 56.1–2.
15 Martial 1.23, 59 (where the sportula is tariffed at 100 quadrans = 25 asses, or 6¼ sesterces); at 11.52 he tells us the Baths of Stephanus were the nearest to him.
16 Martial 7.35,1.59, 2.13 (making it clear the baths of Lupus and of Gryllus were separate establishments), 3.25 and 10.48 (Baths of Nero). Laecania was derived from an established Roman cognomen, Laeca.
17 Martial 3.87.

12: SPECTACLES

1 Fronto, *Preamble to History* 17 (Loeb vol. II, p. 217).
2 Plutarch, *Otho* 5.5.
3 Petronius, *Satyricon* 27.
4 Pliny 7.74–5.
5 Pliny 35.10, 36.33.
6 The statue of Tiye/Tuya is now in the Vatican Museums (https://m.museivaticani.va/content/museivaticani-mobile/en/collezioni/musei/museo-gregoriano-egizio/sala-v--statuario/statua-della-regina-tuia.html). Catalogue number 22678.
7 Cicero, *Letters to his brother Quintus* 3.1.14.
8 Pliny 34.36 (Mummius and Scaurus), and 34.43 (Apollo).
9 Pliny 35.51.
10 Pliny 35.91 when describing the fate that befell Apelles' depiction of Aphrodite emerging from the sea, placed by Augustus in the Temple of the deified Julius Caesar.
11 Pliny 34.84; for the goblets see 34.141.
12 Pliny 36.27.
13 Tacitus, *Annals* 14.75; Tertullian, *Spectacles* 7.5; coins showing Sol in a chariot mainly appeared in the third century, for example under Probus (276–82).
14 Ovid, *Fasti* 4.393–4.

15 Tertullian, *Spectacles* 4.5, 8.3.

16 Livy 1.9.6 ff.

17 Livy, summary of Book 16 (see Loeb series vol. IV, p. 553).

18 Augustus, *Res Gestae* 22.

19 For example, a denarius of 113–112 BC showing gladiators issued by Titus Deidius. Crawford 294/1; Sydenham 550, and another by Livineius Regulus in 42 BC showing a beast hunt. Crawford 494/30, Sydenham 1112.

20 *RIC* (Titus) 110.

21 *RIC* (Severus Alexander) 410.

22 The tomb is close to the Vesuvius Gate, but the interior cannot usually be inspected by visitors. The inscription is at C&C, 128, no. F88 (*AE* (1913), 70).

23 Plutarch, *Romulus* 5. See also his *Natural Questions* 53.

24 Appian, *Civil Wars* 1.11.99–100.

25 Tacitus, *Annals* 6.13.

26 Suetonius, *Caesar* 10, 11; Plutarch, *Caesar* 5.8–9.

27 Josephus, *Jewish Antiquities* 19.130.

28 Pliny 35.52.

29 Suetonius, *Nero* 7.2, 11.1.

30 Suetonius, *Augustus* 4.3, *Nero* 11.

31 Suetonius, *Augustus* 43.1, *Domitian* 4.2.

32 Ulpian, *Digest* 1.12.12.

33 Tacitus, *Annals* 14.17.

34 Terence, *The Mother-in-Law* 28 ff.

35 Livy, *Epitome* 48.

36 Ovid, *Art of Love* 1.4.

37 Pliny 36.114–15.

38 Plutarch, *Pompey* 40.5, 42.4, 52.4; Dio 39.38.1–2; Pliny 8.4. For objections to the theatre, see Tacitus, *Annals* 14.20.

39 Tacitus, *Annals* 3.72.2–4. The major fire in Rome in 64 under Nero would show how vulnerable the city remained.

40 Josephus, *Jewish Antiquities* 19.88–90.

41 Pliny 36.117. The theatre was built in honour of his father of the same name who died in 53 BC and had been consul in 76 BC.

42 Suetonius, *Augustus* 44.3; Tacitus, *Annals* 4.16.4. Also, Dio 60.22.2 on Livia's privileged use of front-row seats in the theatre.

43 Dio 57.11.5, Suetonius, *Augustus* 44.1.

44 *CIL* 10.833, 844 (Pompeii).

45 Suetonius, *Augustus* 44.1.

46 Herodian 1.9.3.

47 *AE* 1987.107 (Rome, Vatican).

48 Plutarch, *Sulla* 2.4, 36.1 ff.

49 Diodorus Siculus 37.12.

50 Appian, *Civil War* 1.38.

51 Servius, *On Vergil's Eclogues* 6.11. See also https://eugesta-revue.univ-lille.fr/
pdf/2011/Keith.pdf

52 Cicero, *Philippics* 2.58.

53 Macrobius 2.7.6–8.

54 Dio 54.17.4–5.

55 Dio 55.10.11.

56 Pliny 7.158–9; for Augustus' recovery, see Suetonius, *Augustus* 59.

57 Suetonius, *Caligula* 36; Josephus, *Jewish Antiquities* 19.94.

58 Josephus, *Jewish Antiquities* 19.104.

59 Josephus, *Jewish Antiquities* 19.17.138–18.152.

60 Dio 60.22.3–5.

61 Tacitus, *Annals* 1.16.3, 54.2.

62 Tacitus, *Annals* 1.77.1–4.

63 Tacitus, *Annals* 1.28.1.

64 Epictetus, *Discourses* 4.13.5, Tacitus, *Annals* 16.5.2.

65 Pliny 8.223. Norbanus Sorex's portrait inscription is at *CIL* 10.814 (Pompeii).
Horace refers to such actors and their imitative roles at *Epistles* 1.18.14.

66 Dio 67.13.1.

67 Pliny the Younger, *Letters* 7.24.3.

68 *CIL* 6.10102 (findspot unknown but somewhere in or around Rome).

69 Apuleius, *The Golden Ass* 10.30 ff.

70 Petronius, *Satyricon* 53.

71 Tertullian, *Spectacles* 10.3, 8.

72 Varro, *LL* 7.96.

73 Phaedrus, *Aesopic Fables*, prologue.

74 *CIL* 14.4254 (Tivoli); *SHA* (Lucius Verus) 8.10–11 and (Commodus) 7.1.

75 *CIL* 6.10094 (found on the first mile of the Via Appia, Rome).

76 Pliny 35.23. This Appius Claudius Pulcher was probably son of the man of the
same name who was consul in 143 BC.

77 Josephus, *Jewish Antiquities* 19.94–5.

78 Josephus, *Jewish Antiquities* 19.4.24.

79 Suetonius, *Nero* 5.2.

80 *CIL* 6.10078 (Rome).

81 *CIL* 6.10067 (Rome).

82 Suetonius, *Nero* 22, 24.2.

83 Suetonius, *Caligula* 55.3.

84 Sherk no. 168I.

85 *SHA* (Commodus) 2.9, 8.5; Dio 73.9.1, 17.1.

86 *CIL* 6.621 (Rome).

87 Suetonius, *Caligula* 55.2.

88 Suetonius, *Nero* 16.2.

89 Pliny the Younger, *Letters* 9.6.

90 *CIL* 6.10048 (Rome).

91 *CIL* 6.10049 (Rome).

92 Martial 10.50, 53; the horses are on *ILS* 5289 (Rome), Sherk no. 168D.

93 *CIL* 6.10062 (Rome).

94 *CIL* 6.10065 (Rome).

95 Pliny 36.70.

96 Pliny 36.70.

97 Dio 61.21.

98 Ammianus Marcellinus 17.4.12 ff.

99 Pliny 36.73.

100 *CIL* 6.37844 (Porta Salaria, Rome). Another word for a gladiator was *hoplomachus* and also *oplomachus* (the two referred to different types of gladiator); the name was derived from the Greek word for equipment.

101 Plutarch, *Crassus* 8. Lentulus Batiatus is featured as a character played by Peter Ustinov in the 1960 film *Spartacus* and has thus earned an unusual immortality two millennia after his life.

102 Suetonius, *Titus* 9.2; Dio 68.3 (Nerva).

103 Suetonius, *Domitian* 17.2, 4.1, and see Tacitus, *Annals* 15.32 for the reference to Nero's reign.

104 *CIL* 1.892 (Venice). He had perhaps retired to the area; we do not know which arena(s) he fought in. The ticket bears the names of the consuls for 85 BC.

105 The magistrates were Gaius Quinctius Valgus and Marcus Porcius. *CIL* 10.852a (Pompeii).

106 *AE* 1953.71 (found in the largo Arenula, Rome).

107 Cicero, *Letters to his Friends* 7.1.

108 Petronius, *Satyricon* 45.11–12.

109 Seneca, *Letters* 7.3.

110 Dio 66.25.5, 26.1; *SHA* (Elagabalus) 8.

111 Dio 68.15.3.

112 Dio 69.6.1.

113 Dio 72.29.1.

114 Dio 73.18.3.

115 Herodian 1.15.8.

116 Herodian 1.15.5–6.

117 Herodian 3.8.9–10.

118 Dio 77.1.4–5.

119 Herodian 5.6.6.

120 Lot 103, Timeline Auctions 24 May 2022. https://timelineauctions.com/lot/marble-sarcophagus-excavated-near-the-tomb-of-cecilia-metella-in-rome/193913/. The inscription seems not to have been recorded in the usual catalogues but see Koch, G., and Sichtermann, H. (1982), *Römische Sarkophage* (Beck, München), 73–6, and 241–2.

121 *SHA* (Severus Alexander) 43.4, 24.3.

122 Aurelius Victor 158.

13: ANIMALS IN ROME

1 Pliny 11.11.
2 Ovid, *Fasti* 2.268 ff, and especially 425 ff, for 15 February.
3 Seneca, *Letters* 108.18–24. Although the word vegetarian is often used in translations of this passage, Seneca's words were *abstinere animalibus coepi*, 'I began to abstain from animals'.
4 Phlegon, *Book of Marvels*.
5 Pliny 9.14–15, 36.70.
6 Pliny 8.16.
7 Pliny 8.4.
8 Pliny 8.20–22.
9 Cicero, *Letters to his Friends* 7.1.
10 Juvenal 12.102 ff.
11 For example, *RIC* III 862a.
12 Herodian 2.11.9; Dio 74.16.3.
13 Pliny 8.64.
14 Pliny 8.89, 96.
15 Pliny 9.11.
16 Sear (2000), nos 378–9.
17 Pliny 8.53.
18 Herodian 1.15.4–6.
19 Cicero, *Letters to his Friends* 8.2, 8.9.
20 Cicero, *Letters to his Friends* 2.11.
21 *CIL* 6.9610 (Rome).
22 The lamp is BM acc. no. 1814,0704.79 and can be seen here: https://www.britishmuseum.org/collection/object/G_1814-0704-79
23 Plutarch, *Alexander* 6.
24 Suetonius, *Caligula* 54.1, 55.2–3; for senator charioteers ibid., 18.3.
25 Pliny 8.160.
26 *RIC* (Caligula) 55.
27 *CIL* 4.3340.1 (Pompeii).
28 *RIC* (Nerva) 93.
29 Martial 1.109.
30 Martial 6.93, 9.29.
31 The dog statuette is BM acc. no. GR 2001, 0314.1, the disk BM acc. no. 1975, 0902.6 (viewable online at: https://www.britishmuseum.org/collection/object/G_1975-0902-6)
32 *CIL* 15.7194. Findspot unknown.
33 See Martial 10.56 for a reference to branding slaves' foreheads, though he does not mention them having run away.
34 BM acc. no. 1756, 0101.1126; text at *CIL* 6.29896. The translation is by the late Rev. R.C.A. Carey (1921–2017), the author's father-in-law and a classical scholar.

35   *CIL* 6.29895 (Rome).

36   *CIL* 6.19190 (Rome), now in the Getty Museum, Malibu, California, acc. no. 71.AA.271.

37   Now in the Getty Museum, Malibu, California, acc. no. 73.AA.11.

38   Catullus 2, and 3.

39   Josephus, *Jewish Antiquities* 19.93.

40   Pliny 10.84, 120. The conspicuous consumption of the super-rich remains a timeless fascination, as witnessed by modern television documentaries salaciously recounting the indulgences of today's multi-millionaires and billionaires.

41   Pliny 10.60.121–3.

42   Macrobius 2.4.29.

43   *CIL* 6.33887 (Rome).

44   Phaedrus, *Aesopic Fables* 1.3.

45   Phaedrus, *Aesopic Fables* 4.1.

46   Cato, *On Agriculture* 141; Tibullus, *Elegies* 2.1.1 ff. For flute players, see Ovid, *Fasti* 6.659.

14: GODS, SHRINES, AND OMENS

1   Tibullus 1.5.57 *dat signa deus*.

2   Juvenal 10.346–8.

3   Juvenal 10.116 refers to the as fee for a schoolboy worshipping Minerva.

4   Martial 9.42.

5   Macrobius 2.2.4.

6   Tertullian, *Spectacles* 8.9.

7   Augustus, *Res Gestae* 20.

8   Macrobius 3.4.2.

9   Tacitus, *Histories* 4.53.

10   Ovid, *Fasti* 6.771–84.

11   Plutarch, *Pompey* 2.2–4.

12   Ovid, *Letters from Pontus* 4.13.29; Newlands, C.E. (1995), *Playing with Time: Ovid and the Fasti* (Cornell), 131, discusses the Augustan association of the cult with womanly virtues and with Livia. Ovid's *Fasti* also showed the very close proximity in the Roman religious calendar between Vesta (6.249 ff) on 9 June and Matralia, the cult of good mothers (6.475 ff), on 11 June.

13   Herodian 1.14.4–5; Valerius Maximus 1.4.5, using Livy, *Periochae* for Book 19.

14   Martial 8.15.

15   Horace, *Odes* 3.6 *passim*.

16   Martial 10.92.

17   Juvenal 10.289 ff.

18   Dio 38.17.5.

19   Augustine, *City of God* 4.8.

20   Cato, *On Agriculture* 139–40.

21   Herodian 1.10.5 ff.

22   Ovid, *Fasti* 4.905–9. See also Tertullian, *Spectacles* 5.8.

23   Ovid, *Fasti* 4.679 ff (19 April); see also Babrius, *Fables* 11, which refers to a variant on the same story of the punished fox setting fire to crops. Babrius wrote a little later than Ovid, in the first century AD.

24   *Judges* 15.4–6.

25   Vergil, *Eclogues* 3.91.

26   These stories are from lost sections of Livy but were recorded by Julius Obsequens in the fourth or fifth century AD in his *Book of Prodigies* 46, 47 (see Loeb vol. XIV in the series covering Livy).

27   Ibid., 52, 53.

28   Tibullus 2.5.71.

29   Pliny 28.15.

30   Seneca, *Letters* 18.1.

31   Pliny the Younger, *Letters* 2.17.24.

32   Martial variously 14.1, 70, and 71.

33   Varro, *Latin Language* 5.83.

34   Pliny the Younger, *Letters* 4.8 *passim.*

35   *CIL* 10.788–9 (Pompeii) (Lucretius Decidianus Rufus), 10.830 (Holconius Rufus).

36   See for example, Terence's *Adelphoe*, lines 573–84, where a section of dialogue set in Athens makes reference to several local features in order to give directions.

37   *AE* 1988.214; VDM, 77 (Ostia).

38   *CIL* 1.3027; VDM, 63–5 (Ostia).

39   Cicero, *On the Nature of the Gods* 3.53, 54, and 45.

40   Seneca, *Letters* 41.4.

41   Pliny the Younger, *Letters* 8.8.

42   Minucius Felix, *Octavius* 6.

43   Macrobius 3.9.7–8.

44   Livy 25.1.8.

45   Livy 29.10.4 ff.

46   Claridge (2010), 133–4, see pp. 387–8.

47   Described for example by Catullus 63.

48   Martial 3.93, 5.41.

49   Martial 11.84, 13.63.

50   *CIL* 10.1781 (Puteoli).

51   Ovid, *Metamorphoses* 1.747, 9.687 ff.

52   Tibullus 1.7.29–30. He mentions Isis in passing at 1.3.23.

53   Horace, *Epistles* 1.17.60.

54   Minucius Felix, *Octavius* 2.3.

55   Dio 40.47.3–4.

56   Dio 42.26.1–2.

57 Dio 47.15.4.

58 Josephus, *Jewish Antiquities* 18.4.65–80.

59 Suetonius, *Tiberius* 36.

60 Martial 12.29.

61 See Claridge, A. (2010), *Rome. An Oxford Archaeological Guide* (Oxford University Press, Oxford), 265.

62 Sinn, F. (1987), *Stadtrömische Marmorurnen*, Mainz, no. 258. The urn is in the Museo delle Terme, Rome, and can be viewed at: https://db.edcs.eu/epigr/bilder.php?s_language=en&bild=$Sinn_00258.jpg;pp

63 A copper as. See, for example, BM acc. no. 1852,0609.1 (viewable at: https://www.britishmuseum.org/collection/object/C_1852-0609-1). Not to be confused with a coin of 73 showing the similar Temple of Vesta, but explicitly identified as such. For the overnight stay at the Iseum, see Josephus, *Jewish War* 7.123.

64 *CIL* 14.429, *ILS* 4406 (Ostia).

65 Ostia *Fasti* 127; see Meiggs, R. (1960), *Roman Ostia*, Clarendon Press, Oxford, p. 367, n. 2.

66 *CIL* 14.4290, *ILS* 4369 (Ostia).

67 *CIL* 14.21, *ILS* 4373 (Ostia).

68 Apuleius, *The Golden Ass* 11.7 ff.

69 Minucius Felix, *Octavius* 23.1.

70 For example, in Tertullian, *On the Crown* 15, and Jerome, *Letters* 107.

71 *AE* 1946.87 (Rome); https://www.tertullian.org/rpearse/mithras/display.php?page=cimrm437

72 *AE* 1915.98 (Rome). Sometimes given as Gnaeus instead of Gaius.

73 VDM (2012), 68–9 (Ostia).

74 Herodian 8.3.7.

75 Cicero, *On Divinity* 1.39.85.

76 Plautus, *Poenulus* 449 ff.

77 Martial 3.24.

78 Juvenal 6.585–6.

79 Juvenal 10.354–5.

80 Appian, *Civil Wars* 1.83.

81 Plutarch, *Sulla* 6.6.

82 Suetonius, *Augustus* 83.

83 Pliny 7.75.

84 Quintilian 2.5.11, 'some people place a higher value on figures which are in any way monstrous or distorted than they do on those who have not lost any of the advantages of the normal form of man'.

85 Dio 60.26.1–2; eclipse details accessed from NASA at https://eclipse.gsfc.nasa.gov/SEsearch/SEsearchmap.php?Ecl=00450801

86 Dio 79.30.1. For the eclipse of 7 October 218, see https://eclipse.gsfc.nasa.gov/SEsearch/SEsearchmap.php?Ecl=02181007. For the appearance of Halley's Comet, see Seargent, D.A.J. (2008), *The Greatest Comets in History*, Springer, 40.

87 Pliny 15.136-37. Variant versions are at Suetonius, *Galba* 1.1 and Dio 48.52.3–4.
88 Pliny 7.45.
89 Pliny 7.71.
90 Lucian's description of Alexander of Abonuteichos was once most easily accessed in the Penguin edition of his works, *Satirical Sketches*, pp. 221–48, but this is only obtainable second-hand now. Today the only ready source is in volume IV of his works in the Loeb Classical Library, 173–253.
91 Columella, *On Agriculture* 1.8.6.
92 Cicero, *On the Nature of Gods* 1.20.55.
93 Martial 4.53.
94 Pliny 2.22.
95 *CIL* 6.1778, 1779 (Rome).

15: FROM ROME TO ETERNITY

1 Sallust, *The War with Catiline* 1.3.
2 Pliny 28.9.
3 *CIL* 6.40372 (Rome). The inscription is prominently displayed in the Tabularium section of the Capitoline Museum, Rome.
4 Tacitus, *Annals* 16.6.2.
5 Martial 8.75.
6 *CIL* 14.326 (Ostia).
7 *CIL* 6.3644 (Rome).
8 *CIL* 6.3216 (Rome).
9 *CIL* 6.3110 (Rome), and see the author's *Gladius. Living, Fighting, and Dying in the Roman Army*, Little, Brown, London (2020), pp. 56–7 for the Egyptian recruit Apion.
10 C&C no. G51.
11 Treggiari, S. (1975), 'Jobs in the Household of Livia', *Papers of the British School at Rome*, vol. 43, 48–77 (https://www.jstor.org/stable/40310720). The communal tomb was excavated in 1726 but inscriptions were recovered at earlier dates too.
12 *CIL* 6.8901.
13 Pliny 7.158.
14 Seneca, *Letters* 26.1.
15 Seneca, *Letters* 12.1–2.
16 Juvenal 10.188 ff.
17 Pliny the Younger, *Letters* 3.1.
18 *CIL* 6.2210. Note that a Greek word is used for the term 'guide', making it certain along with his name that Hymetus was Greek by birth, but this was far from unusual for a man serving in this capacity. Plancius issued a denarius in his name in 55 BC. The obverse bust is identified variously as Macedonia, recalling his service there, and as Diana Planciana. Sear (2000), no. 396 but Crawford 431/1 gives Diana. The legend does not help.

19 *CIL* 6.8012 (Rome).

20 Toynbee (1971), 41.

21 Lucretius 2.575–80, 999.

22 Cicero, *Letters to Atticus* 12.15.

23 Cicero, *Letters to his Friends* 4.5.

24 Pliny the Younger, *Letters* 1.12 *passim*.

25 Pliny the Younger, *Letters* 8.23 *passim*.

26 Pliny the Younger, *Letters* 4.21 *passim*.

27 *CIL* 10.107 (Crotone, Calabria).

28 Suetonius, *Nero* 57.

29 Now in Gregoriano Profano Museum (formerly in the Lateran Collection) in the Vatican catalogue numbers 9997, 9998, see https://www.museivaticani.va/content/museivaticani/en/collezioni/musei/museo-gregoriano-profano/Mausoleo-degli-Haterii.html

30 Plutarch, *Sulla* 38.2.

31 Pliny 21.11. It is not clear what office Serapio held. Pliny stated him to be a tribune but as the Scipios were patricians Serapio should not have been eligible for the position. This is probably therefore a mistake for another magistracy, unless he held a military tribunate.

32 Polybius 6.53.

33 Suetonius, *Vespasian* 19.2.

34 For Pompey's daughter's burial, see Dio 39.64.

35 Catullus 59.

36 Catullus 69.

37 Josephus, *Jewish Antiquities* 236; Suetonius, *Caligula* 14; Dio 59.3.7.

38 Dio 74.10.2; Herodian 2.5.8. Neither specifies what happened to the body but there is no reference to it being disposed of in the Tiber either.

39 Dio 75.4.2–5.5 ff.

40 Herodian 4.2.1 ff.

41 *CIL* 6.24520 (Rome).

42 Plutarch, *Tiberius Gracchus* 1.3–5.

43 Pliny 7.59–60.

44 *CIL* 6.25572. Although from the Rome area, the exact findspot is unknown.

45 *CIL* 10.2496 (Pozzuoli). Late first, early second century AD.

46 Now in the Getty Museum, Malibu, California, acc. no. 71.AA.456.

47 Musco, S., et al. (2008), 'Le complexe archéologique de Casal Bertone', *Les Dossiers d'Archéologie*, Novembre–Décembre 8, no. 330, 32–9.

48 The son of the triumvir of the same name killed at Carrhae in 53 BC.

49 For the story of a Caecilia Metelli, i.e. '(wife) of Metellus', see Valerius Maximus 1.5.4.

50 *AE* 1947.184 (Ostia, Isola Sacra).

51 Cicero, *Speech for Aulus Licinius Archias* 22; Livy 38.56.4 for the tomb at Liternum.

52 According to Plutarch, who saw it. Plutarch, *Otho* 18.1.

53 Plutarch, *Galba* 28.3.

54 Suetonius, *Nero* 50, 57.

55 *AE* 1990.1044 (Ostia). The style and type of the monument is common in Ostia. Titus Aelius Euangelus' name suggests he was a slave freed by Antoninus Pius (138–61). Now in the Getty Museum, Malibu, California, acc. no. 86.AA.701.

56 *ILS* 4404 (Rome).

57 *T(itus) Flaviu[s A]ug(usti) lib(ertus) Crathis | sibi et Fl[aviae S]ozusae | vern[ae] e[t libe]rtae | et liber[tis] lib[ertab]usque suis | pos[terisque eor]um.* See second colour plate section. A published reference has proved elusive but the text can be found online: https://db.edcs.eu/epigr/epi.php?s_sprache=en

58 *AE* 2005.306 (Ostia). An opus sectile floor was made up of cut sections of stone of various colours and types, usually laid in patterns.

59 *CIL* 14.2112 (Lanuvium).

60 Vergil, *Aeneid* 5.45 ff.

61 *CIL* 6.17985A (Rome).

62 See Wallace-Hadrill, A. (2011), *Herculaneum Past and Future* (Frances Lincoln Limited in association with the Packard Humanities Institute, London), 123 ff and especially 130.

63 Seneca, *Letters* 26.8–10.

64 Seneca, *Letters* 24.11. For the boy poet Sulpicius Maximus, *CIL* 6.33976 (Rome).

65 Tacitus, *Annals* 15.64.

EPILOGUE

1 *heu vanitas humana*. Pliny 32.3.

2 Pliny 13.68–83; Cicero, *Letters to his brother Quintus* 2.15b.1.

3 *ita mendose*, Cicero, *Letters to his brother Quintus* 3.6.6.

4 Jerome, *Letters* 107.1.

5 Jerome, *Letters* 127.12.

6 The building was originally erected by Agrippa. Hadrian rebuilt it following a fire in 80 and again in 110.

7 Such as Roland Fréart's *Parallele de l'Architecture Antique et de la Moderne* (Paris, 1650), and issued in English by John Evelyn in 1664 and three posthumous editions.

8 *CIL* 6.11252 (Villa Pamfilia, Rome). See also: https://usepigraphy.brown.edu/projects/usep/inscription/MD.Balt.JHU.L.50/ and https://archaeological museum.jhu.edu/staff-projects/latin-funerary-inscriptions/epitaphs-for-women/agileia-prima/. The quotations appear to be from Seneca, *Letters* 99.8 and his *On Remedies for Fortunes* and *Sayings of Cato* 2.3. Agilia means 'nimble', Auguria 'prophecy'.

9 See the closing words of George Eliot's *Middlemarch* (1872) from which I have shamelessly pilfered for this paragraph.

ABBREVIATIONS
AND BIBLIOGRAPHY

(NB online references are subject to change)

AE = *L'Annee épigraphique* (Paris, 1888–) (NB some of this material is now available on the internet from the same source as *ILS* below)

BSRH = Braund, D.C. (1985), *Augustus to Nero: A Sourcebook on Roman History, 31 BC–AD 68*, Croom Helm, London (reissued by Routledge, 2014)

C&C = Cooley, A.E., and Cooley, M.G.L. (2004) *Pompeii. A Sourcebook*, Routledge, London

CIL = *Corpus Inscriptionum Latinarum* (Berlin, 1863–) in sixteen volumes (NB some of this material is now available on the internet from the same source as *ILS* below)

CJ = *Codex of Justinian*. Accessed at: https://droitromain.univ-grenoble-alpes.fr/Anglica/codjust_Scott.htm

Crawford = Crawford, M.H. (1974), *Roman Republican Coinage*

Digest = *Digest of Justinian*. Accessed at: https://droitromain.univ-grenoble-alpes.fr/Anglica/digest_Scott.htm

IGRR = *Inscriptiones Graecae ad Res Romanas Pertinentes et impensis Adademiae inscriptionvm et litterarvm hvmaniorvm collectae et editae (Paris, 1901 and later)*

ILS = Dessau, H., 1892–1916 *Inscriptionum Latinae Selectae*, Berlin (three volumes) (now available on the internet with full search facilities at http://db.edcs.eu/epigr/epi_en.php)

JRS = *Journal of Roman Studies*, published by the Society for the Promotion of Roman Studies

L&R = Lewis, N., and Reinhold, M. (1990), *Roman Civilization. Selected Readings*, Columbia, 3rd edn (2 volumes)

L&S = Liddell, H.G., and Scott, R. (various editions, 1940 used for this book), *A Greek–English Lexicon* (2 volumes), Clarendon Press, Oxford

RIB = *Roman Inscriptions of Britain*: see Collingwood and Wright (1965), revised edition Tomlin (1995), inscriptions reported 1995–2006 see Tomlin, R.S.O., Wright, R.P., and Hassall, M.W.C. (2009), and for non-stone inscriptions see Frere, S.S., and others (eds) (1990 and later, see Bibliography). The superb and indispensable online resource at https://romaninscriptionsofbritain.org/ is highly recommended and will eventually feature all of Britain's Roman inscriptions

RIC = *Roman Imperial Coinage*, various volumes mainly by Mattingly, H., and Sydenham, E.A.

Sear = Sear, D.R. (2000), *Roman Coins and Their Values. The Millennium Edition*, vol. I: *The Republic and The Twelve Caesars 280 BC–AD 96*, Spink, London

SHA = *Scriptores Historiae Augustae*, available in the Loeb Classics Series, Harvard University Press, vols I and II (also in Penguin translation, *The Lives of the Later Caesars*, trans. by A. Birley, Penguin)

Sherk = Sherk, R.K. (ed.) (1988), *The Roman Empire: Augustus to Hadrian*, Cambridge University Press

Sydenham = Sydenham, E.A. (1952), *The Coinage of the Roman Republic*

VDM = L. Bouke van der Meer (2012), *Ostia Speaks. Inscriptions, buildings and spaces in Rome's main port*, Peeters, Leuven

FURTHER READING

Although it is routine for books of this sort to provide an extensive guide to further reading, this is not necessarily of great use to most readers, and nor is a rambling and indulgent bibliographical essay. This is a book about the evidence from ancient sources, not a summary of scholarly thinking about ancient sources. The focus has been to concentrate much more on providing comprehensive references to every one of those sources used for this book.

I. WRITTEN SOURCES

For most modern readers, the best place to start with ancient sources is the available anthologies. Jo-Ann Shelton's *As The Romans Did* (Oxford, 1988, and later editions) is among the strongest but is both elusive and expensive these days, no doubt thanks in part to the decline of classical civilization and ancient history courses for which it would be, or was, essential reading. Her selection is comprehensive and extensive with an excellent commentary weaving together each extract in the thematic chapters. A great perennial mainstay is Naphtali Lewis and Meyer Reinhold's two-volume *Roman Civilization. Selected Readings* (3rd edn, Columbia 1990). This is heavier going but provides extracts that the average reader might find hard to track down. Other opportunities can be found, such as Jane F. Gardner and Thomas Wiedemann's *The Roman Household* (Routledge, 1991), Valerie M. Warrior's *Roman Religion. A Sourcebook* (Focus Publishing, 2002), which provides a more focused look at a specific part of Roman life through sources, and David C. Braund's *Augustus to Nero: A Sourcebook on Roman History 31* BC–AD 68 (Croom Helm, London, 1985, and Routledge 2014) and Robert K. Sherk's *The Roman Empire: Augustus to Hadrian* (Cambridge University Press 1988) are useful for some of the more obscure sources but are little concerned with ordinary individuals. Alison E. Cooley and M.G.L. Cooley's *Pompeii. A Sourcebook* (Routledge, 2004) is an outstanding collection of inscriptions, graffiti and other texts from Pompeii but is entirely in translation though the references make it possible to go back to online catalogues of the original texts. L. Bouke van der Meer's *Ostia Speaks. Inscriptions, buildings and spaces in Rome's main port* (Peeters, Leuven, 2012) provides the Latin and a translation for dozens of inscriptions and is most unusual in doing so with a commentary that makes it as accessible to the lay reader as it is to the scholar.

The most obvious problem with selected extracts is that they necessarily omit most of the texts, frequently leaving out material that is also of great interest. Anyone with a serious interest must therefore turn to the full text, including preferably the original Latin and Greek. Fortunately, the books cited above are among those that provide comprehensive references and therefore make it possible to chase up those texts and place the extract in context. There are plenty of other books that tackle life in the Roman Empire, but which do not provide those references. While often enjoyable reads, those books have little practical value as reference works.

In the late 1960s and early 1970s it was still common to find that one's local library had a comprehensive collection of the Loeb Classical Library volumes. These small books contain the full texts of ancient authors in Latin (red) or Greek (green) on the left-hand page and a translation on the right. Today such facilities are a thing of the past, as the sales of library copies of these books prove. The author, for example, owns several used volumes which once belonged to the City and East London College Library and the South Shields Public Library (among others). These books are still available new, but at almost £20 ($25) each, a set of the five volumes for Tacitus will cost almost £100 (US$125) which compares badly with the trivial cost of a paperback translation. They are, however, indispensable for anyone engaged in serious long-term study.

All is not lost, though. The internet has transformed access to these texts, the translations of many of which are long out of copyright. Thanks to sterling efforts by Bill Thayer, a large selection of these texts, now out of copyright, is available online on his magnificent website at https://penelope.uchicago.edu/Thayer/e/roman/texts/. The Perseus Digital Library (https://www.perseus.tufts.edu/hopper/) is another marvellous online resource. Focused searching will throw up other websites dedicated to the works of specific authors. Seneca's *Moral Letters to Lucilius* can, for example, be found here: https://en.wikisource.org/wiki/Moral_letters_to_Lucilius, Martial's *Epigrams* here: https://topos-text.org/work/677, and Pliny the Younger's *Letters* here: http://www.attalus.org/old/pliny1.html. Sometimes, though, these sites depend on archaic Victorian or older translations which can seem impenetrable to a modern reader.

There are, of course, numerous other translations available, many in print in affordable editions. The English translations in the Penguin Classics and Oxford World's Classics series are among the most widely available, but they necessarily involve the most popular texts, or selections. Valerius Maximus and Aulus Gellius, for example, are only available in printed form in the Loeb series. Moreover, these other translations do not always bother with the standard numerical sub-divisions of these texts, a universal system designed to enable the reader to identify a specific passage in any edition.

Translations can never be regarded as definitive. There is no such thing, and nor can they always cope with colloquialisms without resorting to substitutes. Latin and Greek, however well understood, can be translated in different ways because the form of expression is usually different from English, though in varying degrees. A phrase

435

in Latin might, for example, require only a handful of words where English might take ten or more to say the same thing. Even so, it can sometimes be a struggle to unravel the exact meaning of the Latin, which may remain opaque.

2. EPIGRAPHIC SOURCES

The position with inscriptions is more challenging for the modern reader. The originals are invariably abbreviated in some way. While contraction tends to follow established patterns, some abbreviations remain obscure to this day. This is far more likely to affect personalized texts, for example on tombstones, or those referring to special or unique circumstances. Although online catalogues of Roman inscriptions are now available, these do not normally feature translations and often not illustrations, being restricted to the original transcribed text. These are of relatively little use to the modern reader because the texts require specialist interpretation and knowledge. For this book I have mainly used the Clauss-Slaby online epigraphic site https://db.edcs.eu/epigr/epi.php?s_sprache=en which allows inscriptions to be searched for in a variety of different ways (including by key words) and which provides references to all the traditional catalogues. It is these references that I have used in the notes to this book. Entering these in the search boxes in the following ways will bring up an inscription's text. For Dessau's *ILS* (*Inscriptiones Latinae Selectae*), the format is D xxxxx, where the xs represent a five-digit number: thus *ILS* 610 must be entered as D 00610. For *CIL* (*Corpus Inscriptionum Latinarum*), which is divided into volumes, the format is CIL xx, xxxxx. Thus *CIL* 4.2178 must be entered as CIL 04, 02178.

CIL is also available here: https://cil.bbaw.de/en/ though the site cannot be described as currently easy to use.

Very few works are available which attempt to explain Roman inscriptions to a wider audience, which is a shame. The best modern guide is Alison Cooley's *The Cambridge Manual of Latin Epigraphy* (Cambridge University Press, 2012).

3. GENERAL HISTORIES OF THE ROMAN WORLD

For those interested in exploring Roman history further there are numerous titles to choose from. Every year sees more books targeted at this perennially popular subject. The most recent include Tom Holland's *Dynasty: The Rise and Fall of the House of Caesar* (Little, Brown, 2015) and its sequel *Pax: War and Peace in Rome's Golden Age* (Abacus, 2023). Mary Beard's *Emperor of Rome: Ruling the Roman World* (Profile, 2023) follows on from her *SPQR* (see below) by looking at the experience of being a Roman emperor. Dexter Hoyos's *Rome Victorious: The Irresistible Rise of the Roman Empire* (Bloomsbury, 2023) is a concise thematic overview of Roman history within a chronological structure, focusing on how the Romans managed to pull off what on the face of it seemed an unlikely outcome for a once small and insignificant Italian settlement.

There are also plenty of reliable older titles which can still be found. Cary and Scullard's *A History of Rome* (3rd edn, Macmillan, 1975) is no longer in print but remains a detailed and solid traditional account. More recently, Philip Matyszak's *Chronicle of the Roman Republic. The Rulers of Ancient Rome from Romulus to Augustus* (Thames & Hudson, 2003) is a well-illustrated and easily digestible history of Rome's early kings and the Republic. Its companion volume, Chris Scarre's *Chronicle of the Roman Emperors* (Thames & Hudson, 2012) completes the story. Colin Wells's *The Roman Empire* (Fontana, 1992) has been around for a long time, but is an excellent introduction to the time of the emperors from 44 BC to AD 235 as well as being still readily available. H.H. Scullard's *From the Gracchi to Nero: A History of Rome 133 BC to AD 68* (Routledge, 2010), and which first appeared more than sixty years ago, has yet to be surpassed as an introduction to the collapse of the Republic and the Julio-Claudian dynasty. To these can be added other modern works, such as Martin Goodman's *The Roman World 44 BC–AD 180* (2nd edn, Routledge, 2011), and Brian Campbell's *The Romans and Their World: A Short Introduction* (Yale University Press, 2015).

All the titles so far mentioned are, of course, primarily concerned with the ruling class and major events, reflecting our principal sources.

There are many books on everyday life in Rome. Gregory S. Aldrete's *Daily Life in the Roman City* (University of Oklahoma Press, Norman, 2004) is a useful thematic study with chapters concerned with entertainment, threats, death, religion, the economy and others, primarily in Rome, Pompeii and Ostia. Lionel Casson's *Everyday Life in Ancient Rome* (Johns Hopkins University Press, 1999), is another option. Mary Beard's widely acclaimed *SPQR* (Profile Books, 2015) is a personal and very readable survey of life across the whole Roman world. Jocelyn Toynbee's *Death and Burial in the Roman World* (Johns Hopkins University Press, 1971) is a classic work that ought always to have a place in a personal library of books about the Roman world. Roy and Lesley Adkins have provided two useful reference works: *Dictionary of Roman Religion* and *Handbook to Life in Ancient Rome* (Oxford University Press, 1996 and 1998 respectively).

Some of these books conscientiously supply full references to the ancient sources cited. An unfortunate development in recent years has been increasingly to dispense with these. This practice is a pity because it separates the modern reader from the ancient world and is an obstacle to further research.

Any serious bookshop with a history section will offer a variety of titles on general Roman history, periods within that era, biographies of individual emperors and books concerned with Roman military history, women either within the imperial dynasties or more generally. Online searches show up countless opportunities.

Modern works relevant to specific points will be found within the endnotes.

ACKNOWLEDGEMENTS

First must come my wife Rosemary who has lived with my obsession with the Roman world for more than forty-five years since we met at the University of Durham. She has endured numerous long 'shifts' accompanying me around Rome, Ostia, Pompeii and Herculaneum, and patiently tolerated listening to my thoughts about this book and others. I'd like to thank Richard Beswick of Little, Brown for welcoming the prospect of a companion volume to *Gladius* and playing an important role in the original gestation of the idea and approach as well as later when it came to sharpening the text and focus. Norah Cooper of the Roman Archaeology Group in Perth, Western Australia, has been an extraordinarily helpful and willing editor, laboriously reading the text as it was written and patiently pointing out numerous infelicities from mistakes to repetitions and confusion. Her impact on the text has been immeasurable, her own experience of Rome and the other locations being invaluable. Professor David Kennedy of the University of Western Australia has been kind enough to let me speak on many occasions to the Roman Archaeology Group and thereby try out my ideas. The probing questions from members have also been very helpful. I'd also like to thank at Little, Brown the following: Zoe Gullen, Richard Collins, and Marie Hrynczak, for their professionalism and assistance with seeing the text through to publication.

LIST OF ILLUSTRATIONS

COLOUR PLATES

All photographs are by the author

Section One

Tile from Ostia, bearing the pawprint of a dog and the footprint from a sandal with characteristic nails. The circular tile was probably destined to serve as a segment in a composite column used extensively in Roman domestic architecture but captures a moment in the hustle and bustle of a tilery in the city when a new tile was trodden on before being fired. The business was probably owned by a freedman, and the footprint was probably made by a slave.

Tomb of the baker Eurysaces, Porta Maggiore, Rome. A freedman who became wealthy in the mid-first century BC supplying bread for the dole. His tomb was made in the form of a bread oven. It survived by being built into a city gate (now demolished) 300 years later. c. 30–20 BC.

A selection of Roman coins. Top row: brass sestertii of Nero, Vespasian, Trajan, and Marcus Aurelius. Note that Nero's face has been cut in as a casual gesture of *damnatio memoriae*. Middle row: Republican silver *denarius* (110–109 BC), copper *quadrans* of Caligula, gold aureus of Nero, copper *as* of Domitian, brass *dupondius* of Domitian, silver denarius of Trajan. Bottom row: double-denarii (antoninianii) of Caracalla, Gordian III, and Probus showing gradual debasement, silvered bronze follis of Maximianus I, gold solidus of Constantius II. All struck at Rome except the last two (Cyzicus and Antioch respectively). To the left and right: US quarter dollar and UK 10p for scale.

The Thermopolium of Asellina, Pompeii. A painting of the *Lares* (household gods) overlooks the tavern's food-serving bar with the tops of large ceramic jars which contained the food. Pompeii had around ninety or more known such establishments in the excavated area. First century AD before 79.

Herculaneum, the entrance hall (*atrium*) to the Suburban Baths, among the best-preserved Roman baths buildings. The herm sculpture doubled as a fountain for patrons. Probably built by a member of the senatorial family, the Nonii, c. AD 40. The structure provides an unmatched experience of wandering around the dark vaulted chambers of a small urban bathing establishment.

Herculaneum, so-called House in Opus Craticium. As the population rose, one response to demand for accommodation was to replace the traditional atrium house with cheaper buildings made of a timber frame with rubble walls. These made it possible to create self-contained apartments upstairs and downstairs, expanding the space by building out over the sidewalk. The design was flimsy and susceptible to fire.

This example was built c. 62–79. By the late first century the design was giving way to better built apartment blocks.

Pompeii, House of the Menander. Skilful use of lines of sight, adjusted column spacing and placement of rooms allowed the creation of visual axes to maximize the effect on a visitor. This is the view from the entrance corridor through the public spaces of the atrium hall and across the peristyle garden to decorated exedrae beyond. Examination of the plan (see text, Chapter 3) shows how this was achieved.

Ostia, the House of Diana. Ostia preserves parts of many brick and concrete four- to five-storey apartment buildings of the type that proliferated throughout Rome from the late first century AD on, designed to reduce the risk of fire. Accommodation was basic, but walls were usually plastered and painted. The ground-floor street frontages were occupied by shops. The street leads to the Capitol temple, visible at the end and dedicated to the Capitoline Triad of Jupiter, Juno, and Minerva. Built c. 150.

Pons Aemilius, Rome. Several bridges joined the main part of Rome on the east bank of the Tiber to the western region, now known as Trastevere, and were filled with foot and wheeled traffic constantly. The Pons Aemilius dated back to the third century BC but was rebuilt in travertine by Augustus. It was damaged several times in antiquity and the Middle Ages. Now only a small section survives.

Ostia, entrance to the warehouse and commercial headquarters of the freedmen Epagathus and Epaphroditus whose names suggest they were of Greek origin. Businessmen like them were the bedrock of Rome's commercial activities throughout the imperial period, some doing extremely well out of the opportunities afforded by supplying and feeding cities across the Empire but none more so than Rome. Built c. 150.

Tombstone of the freedmen Demetrius and Philonicus, from Tusculum, near Rome. Their former master, one Publius Licinius, would have set them up in businesses and in return expected their loyal service. The stone carries depictions of the tools of their trades. Demetrius appears to have been a carpenter (right-hand side), while Philonicus seems to have worked in the mint striking coins (top). It is unclear why they were buried together, unless it was a simple matter of friendship, economy and convenience though it is likely they died at different times. c. 30–10 BC.

In the traditional Roman *atrium* house rainwater that fell through the *compluvium* roof opening collected in the *impluvium* pool beneath. From here it drained into a subterranean tank. Next to the *impluvium* was usually a stone cylinder through which buckets were lowered by rope to draw up water for the household's use. The wear from countless such operations caused the prominent grooves visible here, and bear witness to the endless drudgery household slaves were forced to endure. House of the Black Salon, Herculaneum, destroyed in 79.

Ostia, Piazza of the Corporations. Around a large open piazza shipping companies had offices where merchants and customers could negotiate contracts. Outside each one, mosaic panels indicated the individual companies' businesses. This company displayed an image of a lighthouse, probably Ostia's (but modelled on the Pharos at Alexandria). It was likely involved in shipping grain from Egypt and Sicily. Once offloaded, the grain was transported up the Tiber on barges to be stored in massive warehouses for sale or distribution as part of the grain dole.

Pompeii, an electoral slogan. Pompeii's street walls were liberally painted with inscriptions (programmata) from the annual election campaigns. This one is in support of Lollius, a candidate for the aedileship. In highly abbreviated Latin (*Lollium d(ignum) v(iis) a(edibus) s(acris) p(ublicis) o(ro) v(os) f(aciatis)*), it read, '*I beg you to elect Lollius, suitable for roads and public and sacred buildings*'.

Ostia, tombstone of Petronia Stolida, the most dutiful daughter, by her parents Caius Petronius Andronicus and his wife Petronia Maritima. Petronia Stolida had lived twenty years, twenty-two days and four hours during the second century AD. *Stolida* means 'dull-witted' or 'stupid'. Their daughter's condition had clearly not affected her parents' love for her. They had paid for a well-carved, but small, marble memorial stone which had been carefully affixed to Petronia's brick and tile tomb.

Ostia, tomb of Gaius Annaeus Atticus in the form of a diminutive brick pyramid to hold his cremated remains in the cemetery on the Isola Sacra between Ostia and Portus. The tomb's inscription says he came from Aquitania in Gaul and that he was a painter. He died aged thirty-seven but there is no mention of a wife or family. The monument was probably inspired by the pyramid of Cestius, a member of the senatorial order, whose impressive tomb still stands, now incorporated into the Aurelian Walls of Rome by the Ostian Gate.

Section Two

Trajan's Markets, flanking the Via Biberatica, built into the Quirinal Hill on the eastern side of Trajan's vast new forum built from the spoils of his Dacian war. Rows of commercial premises were laid out in a semicircle that respected the eastern exedra of his forum. Although the forum and basilica have largely been lost or remain buried, the market structures remain well preserved. Part has been used for a modern museum. c. 106–117.

Ostia, public latrine at the forum. A rare survival of this essential urban facility. There were no cubicles. Waste dropped into a leat below. Clean water flowed in from an aqueduct around the floor into which patrons dipped sponges to clean themselves. This water flowed into the lower leat along with other water that washed the solid and liquid waste on into the sewers and presumably the Tiber or the sea. Rome would have been replete with numerous similar arrangements. Second century AD.

Coin reverse designs were used for state messaging, often with deities and divine personifications. Top row: Spes (Hope), 41 (Claudius); Roma 64 (Nero); Minerva 80 (Domitian); Salus (Health of the Emperors) 162–3 (Marcus Aurelius and Lucius Verus). Second row: Victory c. 80 (Vespasian, posthumous under Titus); Laetitia (Joy) 219 (Elagabalus); the Faithful Army 238–9 (Gordian III); Mars Propugnator (defender of Rome) 243–4 (Gordian III); Aequitas (Equity) 245–7 (Philip I); Uberitas (Fruitfulness) 250–1 (Trajan Decius). Third row: Fortuna with her rudder and globe 151–2 (Antoninus Pius); the Dioscuri 211–206 BC; Felicitas Publica (Public Happiness) 73 (Titus, as Caesar); the Aqua Marcia (aqueduct) of 144 BC commemorated in 56 BC; Romulus and Remus and the Wolf 142 (commemorating Rome's first millennium under Antoninus Pius). Bottom row: Temple of Jupiter Capitolinus, Rome, 78 BC; Securitas Perpetua (perpetual security) 281–2 (Probus). All struck at Rome except the last, at Ticinum.

Triumphal procession, terracotta relief from Rome. Triumphal processions amounted to spectacular street theatre and reinforced a sense of superiority and entitlement among the population of Rome. Here a pair of barbarian captives, probably Dacians, are displayed chained in a cart pulled by horses as part of a parade of prisoners and spoils.[*] Probably Trajanic, c. 107.

Wall-painting panel from Pompeii depicting a pair of lovers, perhaps just married. The man is by convention shown with darker skin, the woman as pale and thus implying she was chaste and protected within her family household. She entertains him with a lyre. Mid-first century AD.

---

[*] https://www.britishmuseum.org/collection/object/G_1805-0703-342

Antistius Sarculo was a priest who apparently fell for one of his female slaves. His solution was simple: he freed and married her. She became Antistia Plutia. Their funerary monument, which was erected for them by two more of his freedmen, shows the two as an austere and elderly couple. c. 30–10 BC.

The mysterious tomb on the Via Appia of Gaius Rabirius Hermodorus, freedman of Gaius Rabirius Postumus, Rabiria Demaris (possibly his wife and also a freedwoman), and Usia Prima, priestess of Isis. Although the first two can be stylistically dated to the mid-1st century BC and their connection to the minor nobility Rabirii family, Usia appears to be unrelated. The stylistic differences, for example her hair, and the lettering in her name, suggest the third original figure has been re-carved to show her a century or more later. In other words, the tomb had simply been hijacked for Usia by obliterating an earlier occupant. This was a common practice.

Ostia. Tombstone of Titus Flavius Crathis, an imperial freedman, and Flavia Sosuza, his slave and freedwoman (and presumably wife), and their freedmen and freedwomen. By the fourth century the stone had been removed from the tomb, which had probably fallen into ruin, to the city's House of the Porch where it was reused as a drain cover with perforations cut through the text. No effort was even made to conceal the surviving lettering (this displayed stone in situ is a cast of the original).

Gladiators. A painting of a bout in the arena from the tomb of the aedile Marcus Vestorius Priscus, just outside the Vesuvian Gate at Pompeii. Vestorius Priscus had probably laid on gladiatorial events in Pompeii's amphitheatre to encourage voters to support him. This was typical of his class, emulating the emperor's entertainments in Rome and before then those of the senators and imperators of the late Republic. First century AD before 79.

447

Theatre of Marcellus, Rome. Begun by Caesar and completed by Augustus in the name of his deceased nephew and former intended heir Marcellus. The building is the only theatre in Rome with any meaningful extant remains. The stage and seating area, or what remains of them, are still buried. Apartments occupy the upper part. Such venues featured entertainments ranging from tragic and comic plays to musical performances, pantomime, and other diversions.

Temple of Portunus (a harbour god), Forum Boarium, Rome. Apart from the Pantheon, this is one of the most complete ancient structures in Rome. It was converted into a church in the ninth century but restored to its ancient appearance in the Fascist era. In recent years it has been heavily restored, and much stonework replaced. Built c. 80–70 BC, replacing an earlier structure.

Rural shrine in a fantasy setting, Villa San Marco, Castellamare di Stabiae. Romans of all classes loved indulging dreams of rustic bliss. Wall-paintings were a popular way of creating trompe l'oeil scenes of a mythologized depiction of the countryside. Mid-first century AD before 79.

The three surviving columns of the Augustan-date Temple of Castor and Pollux in the Forum. Like all such temples, the building fulfilled several roles. It served as an art gallery and was home to commercial premises. Among the latter was a cobbler's where a raven lived. The bird was a superb mimic and shouted out the names of members of the imperial family during the reign of Tiberius. It was later killed by a rival cobbler who resented the attention the raven attracted.

Frigidarium (cold room) of the Baths of Diocletian, Rome. Although restored and modified (including raising the floor) by Michelangelo in 1563–6 to convert the ruins of the frigidarium into the church of Santa Maria degli Angeli, the building today gives a good idea of the vast enclosed space contained by Roman public baths, and of the natural light creeping in through the attic vault windows. Originally completed and dedicated in 305–6.

Tomb memorial of Pomponius Hylas and his wife Pomponia, made of stucco and a mosaic using glass tesserae. The couple shared their underground burial chamber a few metres from the Via Appia with at least eighteen other burials of unrelated people. All were cremated and deposited in urns. The likelihood is that they were all members of a burial club and paid subscriptions to maintain their right to a place. The association may have been a private concern, a business run by a third party, or operated on behalf of a commercial guild. There would have been a surface monument but that is long lost. Early first century A D.

Mosaic from a house in Pompeii (Region I Insula 5, building 2). On the left are symbols of wealth and on the right, poverty, suspended from a balance. The skull symbolizes how death will come to rich and poor alike.

INDEX

The majority of personal names are not indexed. The priorities here are themes, topics, and places.

465